Russian Embassies to the Georgian Kings, 1589–1605

Volume I

Edited by
W.E.D. ALLEN

Routledge
Taylor & Francis Group

LONDON AND NEW YORK

First published by Ashgate Publishing

Published 2016 by Routledge
2 Park Square, Milton Park, Abingdon, Oxon OX14 4RN
711 Third Avenue, New York, NY 10017, USA

Routledge is an imprint of the Taylor & Francis Group, an informa business

Founded in 1846, the Hakluyt Society seeks to advance knowledge and education by
the publication of scholarly editions of primary records of voyages, travels and other
geographical material. In partnership with Ashgate, and using print-on-demand and e-book
technology, the Society has made re-available all 290 volumes comprised in Series I and
Series II of its publications in both print and digital editions. For information about the
Hakluyt Society visit www.hakluyt.com.

ISBN 13: 978-1-4094-4599-9 (hbk)

WORKS ISSUED BY

THE HAKLUYT SOCIETY

RUSSIAN EMBASSIES TO THE
GEORGIAN KINGS

VOLUME I

SECOND SERIES
No. CXXXVIII

ISSUED FOR 1970

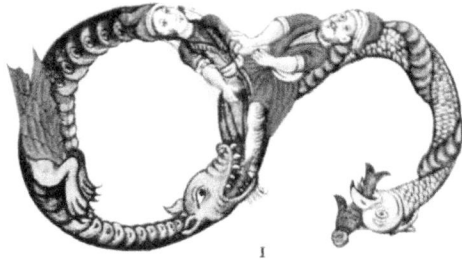

Thani

Mani

Tsani

Jani

Illuminated capital letters from a MS. of Saba Sulkhan Orbeliani's Dictionary of the Georgian Language for Mzedchabuk Orbeliani, the Judge of Atsqviri (Atskhur) in 1724.

RUSSIAN EMBASSIES
TO THE
GEORGIAN KINGS

(1589 - 1605)

VOLUME I

Edited with Introduction, Additional Notes, Commentaries
and Bibliography by

W. E. D. ALLEN

Texts translated by
ANTHONY MANGO

CAMBRIDGE
Published for the Hakluyt Society
AT THE UNIVERSITY PRESS
1970

PUBLISHED BY
THE SYNDICS OF THE CAMBRIDGE UNIVERSITY PRESS
Bentley House, P.O. Box 92, 200 Euston Road, London, N.W.1
American Branch: 32 East 57th Street, New York, N.Y. 10022

Printed in Great Britain
by Robert MacLehose & Company Limited
at the University Press, Glasgow

CONTENTS

VOLUME I

CONTENTS

vi

CONTENTS

VOLUME II

*Notes on Russian relations with Kakheti and Kartli
between 1590 and 1604*   *page* 369

The Texts: Part II

CONTENTS

CONTENTS

LIST OF MAPS AND ILLUSTRATIONS

LIST OF MAPS

VOLUME I

VOLUME II

xi

LIST OF ILLUSTRATIONS

Volume I

FOREWORD

HAKLUYT gave the first account of the English part in the spread of the maritime peoples of the West across the oceans of the world at the turn of the fifteenth century. During the same period events of comparable consequence were taking place on a continental scale in eastern Europe and northern Eurasia. The capture of Constantinople by the Ottoman Turks in 1453 presaged an effort to restore that geographical unity of the Mediterranean and Near Eastern lands which had taken form in earlier state structures: the Byzantine, Roman and Hellenistic empires. Again, the traditional connections of the Ottoman Turks with inner Asia and their identification with the *mystique* of the Islamic world revived the Arabian concept of latitudinal expansion eastward beyond the Caspian to Bukhara and central Asia and westward as far as Morocco and the coast of the Atlantic. In northern Eurasia, the emergence of the Muscovite Grand Dukedom as the successor state to the Mongol Golden Horde on the Volga soon became a challenge to the Ottoman empire all along the northern flank of the sphere of Turkish influence from the Dniepr and the Don, draining to the Black Sea – beyond to the Caspian, to the Ulu-tau *massif* and to the headwaters of the West Siberian rivers, draining to the Arctic Ocean.

The basis of this Russian expansion was 'fluvial' – down the rivers flowing to the Black Sea and the Caspian and, later, along the Siberian rivers. The decisive events in the first phase of expansion were the overthrow of the Tartar khanates of Kazan (1552) and Astrakhan (1554) and the projection of Russian power in a longitudinal direction: on the axis – White Sea – Caspian – Iran. It is notable that this policy was encouraged by Elizabethan England whose merchants were active as advisers, explorers and, even, planners at the court of Ivan IV. Again, the Russian drive south proved welcome enough to the Safavid rulers of Persia who were harassed from the west and from the north-east by pressures from the Otto-man Turks in the west and from the Uzbek Turks in central Asia. A major clash between the Ottoman empire and the Muscovite state became inevitable. The main lines of latitudinal and longitudinal expansion crossed in the region stretching from the Crimea along the north Caucasian steppe to Astrakhan and the Volga basin. The nodal point was indeed, perhaps, Besh-tau, 'the five mountains' (*R. Pyatigorye*), commanding the ways west to the Crimea, north-east to Astrakhan, south-east along the Caspian coast to Shirvan and Persia, and due south through the Terek gorge to the Georgian lands. In the five mountains, the Khans of the Golden Horde had kept camp and court and in that region Tokhtamysh had challenged Tamerlane. During the sixteenth century the Circassian princes of Great Kabarda had become established there. They attracted the alliance of Ivan IV in the years before the first big Russo-Turkish war broke out (1569–70); and it was they who intro-duced the Georgian kings of Kakheti into the ken of the Muscovite Chancery.

South of the main chain of the Caucasus, the Georgians had been the victims of the power politics of the Ottoman and Safavid empires during the three earlier quarters of the sixteenth century. With the approach of the Russians to the northern Caucasus, the struggle for military control and diplomatic influence over the whole of the Caucasian isthmus became triangular – or even quadrangular – since the Khans of the Giray dynasty in the Crimea, although vassals of the Porte, frequently pursued their own policies.

In Southern Caucasia, since the middle of the fifteenth century, the rather loosely knit Kingdom of Georgia (*G. Sakartvelos samepo*) had disintegrated as the result of varied trends and circumstances. The Black Death, the prolonged wars of resistance against Tamerlane at the turn of the fourteenth century and, finally, the fall of Constantinople and the subsequent elimination by the Turks of the 'factories' of the Italian trading cities which sustained the economic life of the Black Sea countries all the way round from the mouths of the Danube to the Crimea and Circassia – all these factors had contributed to the decay of the brilliant monarchy of the Georgian Middle Ages. There had emerged as successor states three small kingdoms: Kartli (central Georgia), Kakheti (eastern Georgia) and Imereti (western Georgia); and four smaller principalities in the west: Samtskhe or Saatabago, Guria, Mingrelia and Abkhazia; Russian interest was naturally drawn to these survivors of the world of Orthodox Christianity round the Black Sea. During the four decades – 1564–1605 – no less than seventeen embassies were exchanged between the Russian tsars and the Georgian kings ruling in Kakheti; the last, in 1604–5, also visited the Kartlian king.

The records of these embassies survived in part in the archives of the Russian state. They were first examined in detail by Marie-Félicité Brosset, the eminent French scholar who became the pioneer of Georgian studies in Russia during the reign of Tsar Nicholas I in the mid-nineteenth century. Brosset published his 'Examen Critique' of the records of the embassies in *Bulletin de la classe des sciences historiques, philologiques et politiques de l'Académie Impériale des Sciences de Saint-Pétersbourg*, tomes I and II, 1844–5. Brosset made valuable comparisons with contemporary Georgian, Armenian, Persian and Turkish sources and this work should be read in conjunction with his other weighty volumes – to which reference is made in the following Introduction and Bibliography.

Forty years later, S. A. Belokurov published the Russian texts covering the period 1578–1613 in *Russian relations with the Caucasus (Snosheniya Rossii s Kavkazom)*, Moscow, 1889. Further details on Belokurov and his work are cited in the Bibliography. Although frequently noted by modern Soviet historians, this volume has become extremely rare in western Europe. The copy catalogued in the Library of the British Museum seems to have been mislaid; the one from which the following translations have been made was found by the editor in a bookshop in Tiflis in 1926.

The texts published by Belokurov are often laborious reading since they are compiled in the 'officialese' of the Russian Chancery of the sixteenth century. The writers are repetitive, unimaginative and preoccupied often with the detail of diplomatic protocol and the *minutiae* of religious controversy within the Orthodox Church. Nevertheless they illumine the Russian mind of the period and, in their matter-of-fact way, reflect the particulars of Russian daily life and administrative practice. Again, they are of value in giving an intimate picture of life and custom among the peoples of the northern and central Caucasus and in Georgia – which is not available for the period in any other source.

The geographical interest of the texts is considerable; they give the first extant accounts of the crossing of the main chain of the Caucasus from north to south and many details of the geography of Kakheti and Kartli.

The documents relating to the embassies of Zvenigorodski and Antonov (1589–90) and of Tatishchev and Ivanov (1604–1605) have been selected for translation as giving the most detailed observations on topography and ethnology, as well as for their patches of dramatic narrative: the murder of the Kakhian king Alexander II; and the secret negotiations for the marriages of the son and daughter of Tsar Boris Godunov with members of the Kartlian Royal House. The account of the embassy of Sovin and Polukhanov (1596–9) duplicates many of the details of the earlier and later embassies; but some extracts which illustrate conditions of life in Caucasia have been included in Volume II.

In the translation an attempt has been made to preserve the flavour and style of the *Prikaznoy yazyk* even where stilted and archaic English had to be used to achieve this purpose. On the other hand, it was decided to omit repetitive passages as well as excessively long accounts of negotiations on matters of very minor importance which merely impeded the flow of the narrative. All omissions are indicated by dots (...); the length of omissions can be judged by reference to the pages of Belokurov's text which are given in the margin.

The documents are written without regard to the rules of *oratio obliqua*, the past and the present tenses being used indiscriminately. The tense of the original has been retained wherever this did not conflict too openly with English usage; a device for this purpose, where possible, has been to place passages in the present tense inside quotation marks.

Belokurov's text required very few emendations: all of them are indicated in the footnotes.

To explain the texts, particularly in their geographical and ethnological detail, it has proved necessary to add footnotes. These have been kept as short as possible. Where it has seemed of interest to expand a theme beyond the scope of the footnote, the material has been relegated to the Commentaries which form a major part of this work. The editor is responsible for the Commentaries which are not initialled. Contributions by the translator are indicated by the initials AM. Where a Commentary is the joint work of the editor and the translator, the fact is indicated by the initials WEDA/AM, or, alternately, AM/WEDA depending upon who did most of the work.

In the footnotes and in the Commentaries, the editor has drawn often on the *Geographical description of Georgia*, prepared in the first decades of the eighteenth century by the great Georgian historian and geographer, Prince Wakhusht

Bagration. While Wakhusht's manuscript maps were the basis of the *Carte générale de la Géorgie et de l'Arménie* published by the French geographer J.-N. Delisle in Paris, 1768, the *Description* remained in manuscript until M.-F. Brosset edited the Georgian text with a French translation for the Russian Imperial Academy of Sciences in 1842. Wakhusht's *Description* is a late example of the oriental school of geographical exposition as exemplified by the Turks Evliya Chelebi and Katib Chelebi in the preceding century, but it is well to recall that the prince lived for many years in Moscow and the influence is evident of the 'Statistical Accounts' of different countries which were current in Europe during the eighteenth century. The *Description* of the learned Georgian forms the link between the crude handbook which is the Book of the Great Map and the sophisticated Caucasian studies of the eighteenth century by soldiers like Gärber and Steder or the adventurer Reineggs, and trained Academicians, like Güldenstädt, Gmelin and Pallas.

Wakhusht is the basic classic for the study of Caucasian historical geography and for this reason the editor has thought fit to reproduce L. I. Maruashvili's comparatively recent appreciation which appeared in *Voprosy Geografii*, Vol. 31, 1953, see below, Vol. II, pp. 573–86.

Volume II contains also Commentaries on the Archival Sources and on the Book of the Great Map (*Kniga glagolemaya Bolshoy Chertezh*), which is frequently cited in the footnotes and Commentaries. The first manuscripts of this work date from the middle of the seventeenth century and no original of the map described has survived. In 1840 a text, itself now rare, was edited by G. I. Spasski for the Society of Russian History and Antiquities. It is apparent that the sections relating to Caucasia were based on the reports of the earlier Russian missions.

Some genealogical tables are given at the end of Volume II in order to clarify the complicated relationship of the Caucasian royal and princely families and their connections with the Russian, Ottoman and Persian ruling houses.

It had been the intention of the editor to add a critical bibliography with biographical notes on some of the earlier travellers in the Caucasus to whom reference is made in the notes and Commentaries; but limitations of time and space have made it necessary to restrict this section.

A wealth of illustration has been available in contemporary maps and miniatures which have not so far been edited in English. It has only been possible to publish a small selection of these. The miniatures of Asafi and the numerous drawings of Castelli – who was a near contemporary of the events described – really merit treatment in separate works.

ACKNOWLEDGMENTS

THE genesis of this book dates back over forty years when, in the month of June 1926, I first acquired from a street bookstall in old Tbilisi (Tiflis) a copy of Belokurov's rare volume on 'The relations of Russia with the Caucasus'. It was in 1955 that Anthony Mango undertook to translate the documents covering the embassies of Zvenigorodski and Tatishchev. My own contribution was to edit the texts in the context of the contemporary scene and to try to elucidate the topographical and social background of the events described. Soon after completing the translation Mango joined the staff of the UN in New York. He continued to provide some items for the Commentaries and footnotes and began the preparation of an index but it was not his fault that the vicissitudes and diversions of my own life delayed completion of the work for twelve years.

This delay was in one respect fortunate since an invitation to attend the 800th Jubilee of the poet Shota Rusthaveli in Tbilisi in September 1966 enabled me to renew contact with Georgian scholars and learned institutions after an interval of forty years. A second invitation in the summer of 1967 allowed me to spend some weeks in the countryside of Kakheti and Kartli and to see many of the places mentioned in the texts.

In 1966 (in company with Sir Harold Bailey who was the guest of learned bodies in the Autonomous SSR of Northern Osetia and in the Autonomous District of Southern Osetia) I was able to make the traverse both ways of the Georgian Military Road under the guidance of the Osetian scholar and lexicographer, Professor Abayev, himself born in Kobi near the headwaters of the Terek.

In 1967 I repeated the journey accompanied by my nephew Robin Allen. On this second journey, it would be difficult to name all the officials and Party Chairmen, town mayors and museum curators who combined kindness with gargantuan hospitality in the country towns of Georgia. But I was particularly indebted for encouragement and help to Academician Irakli Abashidze, the distinguished poet who was then Chairman of the Georgian Writers' Union; to Mr Zhghenti, Secretary of the Georgian Society for Friendship with Foreign Countries; to Academician George Tsereteli, Professor of Semitic Studies at the University of Tbilisi; and to Academician Shalva Amiranashvili, the Director of the State Museum of Art in Tbilisi and brilliant interpreter of the history of Georgian art. Not least, Mr Gela Charkviani, Reader in English at the University of Tbilisi, by his notable efficiency and invariable good humour, made sometimes arduous travelling conditions into an enjoyable adventure.

Versions of a few of my Commentaries were published as papers in *Bedi Kartlisa* and in *Oxford Slavonic Papers*. In this connection I am obliged to Dr K. Salia, editor of *Bedi Kartlisa*, for giving me the opportunity of offering preliminary material for the consideration of Georgian scholars.

Comment and advice on specific problems came generously from the late Professor Vladimir Minorsky; from Professor Emeritus George Vernadsky of Yale; from Professor Cyril Toumanoff of Georgetown; from Dr Laurence Lockhart; and from Professor Charles Beckingham.

During my years in Turkey I learned much about the history of the Crimean Tartars and the Nogays from Professor A. Z. V. Togan of Istanbul University and from Professors Halil Inalcik and A. N. Kurat of Ankara University. I am indebted to Dr V. L. Ménage for his kindness in summarizing Asafi from the original manuscript in Istanbul University Library; and to Mrs Mellaart for procuring for me coloured slides and photographs of the miniatures. Mr Andro Gugushvili, who for almost half a century has tutored the small band of enthusiasts for Georgian studies in England, made some translations from Georgian and read through the Commentaries. Professor D. M. Lang was generous with gifts and loans of books and some sapient advice, though he does not necessarily agree with all my etymologies. Mr Humphrey Higgens read through the completed work and contributed to the preparation of the Bibliography. Major Evan Ralphs gave useful help in summarizing some Russian sources. And Miss Anne Pentland re-drew the maps from my almost illegible drafts.

The Director of the Gosudarstvenny Istoricheski Muzey in Moscow courteously provided the photographs of the miniatures reproduced in Plates 4 and 5; and Hero of the Soviet Union Professor Irakli Tsitsishvili (through Professor Lang) the views reproduced in Plates 8 and 9. The Director of Istanbul University Library kindly gave facilities for the photographing of the miniatures in Asafi's MS. And, nearly forty years ago, the Librarian of the Biblioteca Nationale in Palermo allowed me to photograph a number of drawings by the Theatine Father Cristoforo Castelli – undoubtedly the most vivid surviving record of life in Georgia during the first half of the seventeenth century.

Two successive Honorary Secretaries of the Society, Mr R. A. Skelton and Dr Terence Armstrong, amongst their manifold activities, have shown restraint and patience over the delays in the completion of this work and have given valuable editorial advice.

Lastly, Anthony Mango and I would like to recall the enthusiastic help and encouragement of my late wife, Nathalie Maximovna (Natasha) Allen. Her familiarity with old Muscovite and Cossack lore and her excellent knowledge of the nuances of the English language made her a perfectionist in the interpretation of difficult points. Well do I remember her pertinaceous hunts through the formidable dictionaries of Old Church Slavonic, of Sreznevski and of Dahl. Flaws that remain either in the texts or in the Commentaries must be attributed to the loss of her collaboration and to the flagging abilities of the editor.

Whitechurch House,   W. E. D. ALLEN
Cappagh, Co. Waterford   14 June 1967

NOTE ON TRANSLITERATION AND ON THE SPELLING OF PROPER NAMES

In the transliteration of geographical and personal names, the general principles in the Guide for Editors of the Hakluyt Society's Publications have been followed. These are based on the RGS System II, as revised by the Permanent Committee on Geographical Names for British Official Use (PCGN). But as M. Aurousseau, the editor of the 1942 edition, observed 'there are at least ten systems for the transliteration of Russian in use in Great Britain and the United States' – apart from the systems used by the Russians themselves, the French, Germans, Italians, Turks and others. Further, Russian, Caucasian and continental scholars (including M. Dumézil, the greatest living authority on Caucasian dialects) have worked out complicated special alphabets – sometimes incomprehensible to the layman – for rendering sounds peculiar to the different languages of Caucasia. Again, the latinization of Turkish presents some special problems since the systems evolved in the Turkish Republic and in Azerbaijan and other Turkic-speaking republics of the USSR differ in many details.

In transliterating Russian names we have tried to give the non-specialist reader an approximate rendering of the way in which the word is pronounced in Russian, without the need for diacritical marks or other artificial conventions. The only points that need be noted are as follows:

The letter *g* is to be pronounced as in *get*; the letter *u* corresponds to the sound of *oo* in *boot*; the combination *zh* is pronounced as *s* in *pleasure*. The Russian short *i* (which always follows another vowel) has been rendered as *y* pronounced as in *yes*. Somewhat artificially, *y* has also been used for Russian back *i*, which always follows a consonant and which does not occur in English. In terminations where the short *i* follows an ordinary *i*, the former has not been transliterated (e.g. Zvenigorodski, instead of Zvenigorodskiy); this is a departure from normal non-specialist practice which traditionally employs the letter *y* to render the Russian phoneme. Final *y* has been retained for the combination back *i* followed by short *i*. The English letter *y* (to be pronounced as in *yes*) has also been used in rendering Russian words in which a soft consonant is followed by a vowel or a vowel is followed by the Russian letter *e*; where, however, the Russian *e* is initial or follows a consonant, it has been rendered as *e* (though this is not strictly correct phonetically).

In the transliteration of Georgian names the general principles adopted by the editors of *Georgica* have been followed (see articles by A. Gugushvili, 'The Georgian Alphabet', *Georgica*, Vol. I, No. I, and 'Classification of Georgian Sounds', Vol. I, Nos. 2 and 3). For simplicity, in a work which has no pretensions to being philological, diacritical marks have been omitted (e.g. Kartli for K'art'li, Mtiuleti for Mt'iulet'i). For Georgian place-names the Georgian form has been used in preference to the Russianized form (e.g. Kakheti and not Kakhetia, which should, if anything, be Kakhia; Kartli and not Kartalinia). On the other hand, Mingrelia, so familiar to sixteenth-century Europeans, has been preferred to Georgian Samegrelo.

In the case of Russian versions of Georgian names (e.g. Yuri for Giorgi), the Russian version has been retained in the original text, and the Georgian form has been used in the footnotes and Commentaries.

The refinements of the Georgian alphabet of forty letters themselves present many difficulties. For instance, the river Chorokhi may be transliterated as Dchorokhi, Tchorokhi or (in Turkish form) Çoruh. The word for 'river' can be rendered *tsqali, tskali, dzqali, dskali*. For convenience I have adhered to the spellings used in my *History of the Georgian People* (1932) – which correspond generally to the tables formulated by A. Gugushvili (1937). Briefly, I have ignored the refinements of Georgian ejaculatory and expletive sounds – using *ch* to represent *dch*, *tch*; *tsq* to represent *tsk*, *d*$_z$*q*, etc. *J* has been used to represent *d*$_z$*h* as in Janashvili, but in transliterating the titles of works in Russian I have retained the Russian *d*$_z$*h*, i.e. Dzhanashvili. The differing forms are equated in the index.

In the case of Georgian proper names, the laws of euphony in the Georgian language provide that all proper names terminate in a vowel, thus: King Wakhtang – *Mepe Wakhtangi*, but Wakhtang the King – *Wakhtang Mepe*; King David – *Mepe Daviti*, but David the Second – *Davit Meore*. In transliterating Georgian proper names into English, I have dropped the terminal *i* (e.g. Wakhtang, Wakhusht, Manuchar), but in the case of a few names such as Giorgi and Dmitri I have retained the terminal *i* for obvious reasons of euphony. In the case of certain Georgian names, such as Daviti (David), Aleksandre (Alexander), Swimoni (Simon), Kostantine (Constantine), I have adopted the English forms; on the other hand, I have retained Georgian forms as in Giorgi (George) and Ioanne (John). There is, of course, a precedent to follow in this matter as, for instance, the use in English books of the Russian Ivan for John, Fedor for Theodore, but of Peter and Paul instead of Petr and Pavel. In Russian names, notably those combined with patronymics, I have used the Russian transcription, as in Aleksey Mikhaylovich (not Alexis Michaelovich).

A major difficulty lies in the use of Arabic names in Turkish, Persian and Russian. In the sixteenth century the Turks and Persians used Arabic names written exactly as in Arabic but pronounced differently and usually, though not always, transliterated differently in western writing. Thus, in Turkish the

Arabic name Muhammad is pronounced, and nowadays written, as Mehmet. Some older western writers preferred to write it as Mahomet, or Mohamed. Russian writers use Magomet or Mukhamed. In the present work Muhammad has been preferred for Persians and Central Asians under Persian cultural influence, and Mehmet for Ottoman Turks and Crimean Tartars within the Ottoman sphere. Other spellings occur in the titles of western works under reference and have been retained in their contexts.

Some familiar geographical names have been kept in their anglicized forms (e.g. Tiflis, not *G*. Tbilisi;[1] Trebizond, not *T*. Trabzon). Except in commonly accepted forms (e.g. Iraq), the rendering of the Arabic *qaf* by *q* has been abandoned in favour of the Turkish *k* (e.g. Kars, not Qars, Kazvin, not Qazvin).

The very nature of the problem makes inconsistencies unavoidable, but these are probably preferable to unfamiliar spellings which would result from too close adherence to scientific systems of transliteration devised for special purposes such as library catalogues.

[1] The Georgian form *Tbilisi* has been followed in citing post-1917 names of institutions and books.

ABBREVIATIONS

Akty	*Akty sobranniye Kavkazskoyu Arkheograficheskoyu Kommissiyeyu.*
BK	*Bedi Kartlisa.*
BSE	*Bolshaya Sovetskaya Entsiklopediya.*
BSOAS	*Bulletin of the School of Oriental and African Studies.*
BTTK	*Belleten, Türk Tarih Kurumu.*
BU	*Biographie Universelle.*
CHOID	*Chteniya v Obshchestve Istorii i Drevnostey.*
DNB	*Dictionary of National Biography.*
DRV	*Drevnyaya Rossiyskaya Vivliofika.*
EI	*Encyclopaedia of Islam.*
EVT	*Early Voyages and Travels to Russia and Persia.*
GOPMK	*Gosudarstvennaya Oruzheynaya Palata Moskovskogo Kremlya.*
IA	*Islam Ansiklopedisi.*
IM	*Imago Mundi.*
IZ	*Istoricheskiye Zapiski.*
Iz Gos	*Izvestiya Gosudarstvennoy Akademii Istorii Materialnoy Kultury.*
Iz IMK	*Izvestiya Istorii Materialnoy Kultury.*
Iz Kav	*Izvestiya Kavkazskago Otdela Imperatorskago Geograficheskago Obshchestva.*
Iz RAN	*Izvestiya Rossiyskoy Akademii Nauk.*
JA	*Journal Asiatique*
JAOS	*Journal of the American Oriental Society.*
JRAS	*Journal of the Royal Asiatic Society.*
Kav Kal	*Kavkazski Kalendar.*
Kav Sbor	*Kavkazski Sbornik.*
KBCh	*Kniga glagolemaya Bolshoy Chertezh.*

KRO	*Kabardino-Russkiye Otnosheniya.*
MAK	*Materialy po Arkheologii Kavkaza.*
NED	*New English Dictionary.*
OI	*Ocherki Istorii SSSR.*
OID	*Ocherki Istorii Dagestana.*
OSP	*Oxford Slavonic Papers.*
RBS	*Russki Biograficheski Slovar.*
SMK	*Sbornik Materialov dlya Opisaniya Mestnostey i Plemen Kavkaza.*
SPA	*A Survey of Persian Art.*
SSKG	*Sbornik svedeniy o Kavkazskikh Gortsakh.*
SSTO	*Sbornik svedeniy o Terskoy Oblasti.*
TVOIAO	*Trudy Vostochnago Otdeleniya Imperatorskago Russkago Arkheologicheskago Obshchestva.*
TVP	*Travels of Venetians in Persia.*
VDI	*Vestnik Drevney Istorii.*
ZKO	*Zapiski Kavkazskago Otdeleniya Imperatorskago Russkago Geograficheskago Obshchestva.*
ZKV	*Zapiski Kollegii Vostokovedov.*
ZVO	*Zapiski Vostochnago Otdeleniya Imperatorskago Russkago Arkheologicheskago Obshchestva.*

(For fuller details of these publications see Bibliography at end of Vol. II.

For abbreviations of book titles see under authors' names in Bibliography.)

INTRODUCTION

The capture of Astrakhan by the Russians in 1554 gave them effective control of the whole course of the Volga and potential command of the Caspian Sea (where the Safavid régime in Iran never maintained fighting ships). As George Vernadsky has observed, 'from a geopolitical point of view Ivan IV's dash down the Volga to Astrakhan was an important move since it cut the steppe zone into two sectors, each of which could be taken care of separately'.

Complex causes had led to this latest achievement of the rulers of Muscovy; but political and military events had accelerated the process: not least the divisions within the Hordes – Golden, Blue and Nogay – and the long wars between Tamerlane and Tokhtamysh, the last great ruler of the Golden Horde which had controlled the middle Volga until the end of the fourteenth century and dominated the separate Russian dukedoms. The Muscovites, with an agricultural economy feeding urban centres based on a network of rivers, were beginning to fill the vacuum created by the decline of the pastoral and mercantile life of the Hordes. The new Russian ascendancy on the middle Volga had attracted much of the central Asian trade, through Kazan, to Nizhni-Novgorod and Moscow. Their further establishment in Astrakhan tended to divert along the Volga the trans-Caspian trade which had formerly gone through Tana (Azov) to the Black Sea ports. Again, there were soon complaints to be heard in Bukhara and Istanbul that the Russians were obstructing the pilgrim traffic which passed from central Asia through the Black Sea ports to the Bosporus and thence to the Holy Cities of Arabia. The prestige of the Sultan as Caliph was seriously involved in this issue. In Iran, the Safavid dynasty – sponsors and protectors of the Shi'a heresy in Islam – were also blocking the transit of Sunni pilgrims from central Asia through Meshed; there were many protests about the arrests, pillage and ill-treatment of pilgrims. And beyond the theological and dynastic rivalries of the Ottomans and the Safavids, was the important economic issue of the control of east Caucasian silk production – the distribution of which was centred in Shemakha – and the rich traffic in rugs and other fabrics which was concentrated in the flourishing city of Tabriz. The Russian control of Astrakhan and the development of the Volga route through Muscovy to Poland and the Baltic offered an attractive alternative to the Persians who were otherwise dependent on the Gulf ports controlled by the Portuguese or on the routes to Aleppo or Trebizond which were in Turkish hands. Beginning with Anthony Jenkinson, the English merchants of the Muscovy Company sponsored and encouraged political accord and trade between the Persians and the Muscovites.[1]

The Ottoman empire then just passing the maximum stretch of its power in the last decades of Sulaiman the Magnificent, was not slow to intervene to shore up the remnants of nomad Turkish power which had spread over the great steppelands round the northern shores of the Black Sea and the Caspian. The Tartar dynasty of Giray, descendants of Chingiz Khan established in the Crimea, were their principal allies. On the whole, the military situation of the Ottomans was stronger than that of the Muscovites. As Karl Marx has observed, 'the Ottoman empire was the only truly military power of the

[1] For background of these events and recent literature in Russian and Turkish see W. E. D. Allen, *Problems of Turkish power in the sixteenth century*, London, 1963, pp. 15 ff. (Allen, *PTP*). For Jenkinson and other Englishmen in Russia, see *Early voyages and travels to Russia and Persia by Anthony Jenkinson and other Englishmen*, edited by E. Delmar Morgan and C. H. Coote (*EVT*), Hakluyt Society, London, 1886, in 2 vols., *passim*.

middle ages'.[1] Their artillery was the most advanced in Europe and their corps of trained professional soldiers, the janissaries, had a formidable impact on the still knightly levies of the Polish and Hungarian kingdoms. The Turkish commanders were recruited from these trained professionals and were generally more capable than the amateurish Polish and Hungarian magnates; or the Russian *boyars*, often selected for command according to their seniority in the hierarchy of the Muscovite nobility; or the chieftains of the great Turkoman tribes who commanded Persian armies in the field.[2] The Ottomans controlled the Black Sea and had a complete naval ascendancy which enabled them to deny the Russians access to the mouths of the steppeland rivers: Bug, Dniestr, Dniepr, Don. (Only the Cossacks, in their light *chaykas*, had the enterprise from time to time to challenge single Ottoman war vessels and to harass Turkish merchant shipping.)[3] Through the Crimean

[1] Marx cited from *Arkhiv Marksa i Engelsa*, Vol. VI, Moskva, 1939, p. 189.

[2] It was only in 1550 that Ivan IV formed his first trained and regularly paid regiments of *streltsy* (lit., 'archers' who later became musketeers); and it was not until the end of the century that Shah Abbas I established his corps of *tufanjis* ('musketeers'). Even after the disastrous wars of the middle of the seventeenth century, the Polish magnates refused to allow their kings to maintain regular troops. When war broke out, the kings remained dependent on the goodwill of the magnates in bringing their own levies into the field and on German mercenaries – hastily hired.

[3] The best near-contemporary description of the Cossacks is to be found in the rare work of Le Sieur de Beauplan, *Description d'Ukrainie, qui sont plusieurs Provinces du Royaume de Pologne. Contenuës depuis les confins de la Muscovie iusques aux limites de la Transilvanie. Ensemble leurs moeurs, façons de vivre & de faire la guerre*, Rouen, 1660 – together with a folding map which is the first good detailed delineation of the Ukrainian lands. For curious particulars of Cossack attacks on Sinope and Trebizond early in the seventeenth century, of their presence in Mingrelia and of their despatch of an envoy to Shah Abbas, see *Voyages de Pietro Della Valle, gentilhomme romain, Dans la Turquie . . . la Perse*, etc., Rouen edition of 1745, Vol. 3, pp. 264–9, 363–4, 429. The word *chayka* means 'gull' in Russian: Dahl, *Tolkovy slovar*. It has been identified, doubtfully, with Osmanli Turkish, *shaika*, 'boat', Vasmer, *Russisches Etymologisches Wörterbuch*, 3 vols., Heidelberg, 1953–8, Vol. 3 (Vasmer, *REW*).

khans, the Ottomans could dispose of thousands of irregular cavalry: during campaigns these hardy bandits were accustomed to live off the country they were pillaging; their staple diet was *shashlyk*, gobbets of meat roasted over the cinders on the points of their *kinzhals*,[1] and *kumys* (mare's milk). During the sixteenth and seventeenth centuries, in some of their big raids, the Crim Tartars reached the suburbs of Moscow (1570), Cracow (1648) and Vienna (last in 1683). On their retreats, they would drive before them tens of thousands of prisoners, peasantry and townsfolk (and nobles when they could catch them) for sale in the slave markets of the Crimea. (Khürrem Sultan, the favourite wife of Sulaiman the Magnificent and the mother of Sultan Selim II, the daughter of a Ukrainian priest, was a captive of one of these raids). To the east of the Black Sea, the Tartar cavalry of the Giray khans could be brought into action against the Russians in the steppes between the Don and the Volga. They harassed, and sometimes allied with, the Circassian tribes of the western Caucasus and the valley of the Kuban. During the long Ottoman wars against the Safavid monarchy in Persia, the Turks brought the Crim Tartars into action in Daghestan and Shirvan where they proved equal to the Turkoman cavalry of the Shahs. In the northern Caucasus the diagonal of the marches of the Crim Tartars from the Taman peninsula to the Koysu and the Shevkal's capital at Tarku crossed the line of Russian communications from Astrakhan to the Terek and the Daryal Pass into Georgia; and their goings and comings were a subject of recur-

---

[1] *kinzhal*: the long straight double edged dirk, grooved and tapering to a fine point, carried by a variety of peoples of the Eurasian steppes and the mountain zone of the Middle East. The *kinzhal* was worn on a thin leather strap across the left groin and was used for a stabbing thrust with an upward movement of the right hand. These weapons, still carried in the Caucasus, do not differ at all from specimens found in Luristan graves and dated to the beginning of the first millennium B.C. The origin of the word is obscure, as there are many varieties (*hanzhar*, etc.) among Turkic-speaking peoples and among the tribes of the Caucasus, cf. Vasmer, *REW*.

rent conflict and dispute between the Muscovite Chancery and the Ottoman Porte during the three decades between 1570 and 1605.[1] (The Muscovites and the Ottomans, equally, repudiated responsibility for the warlike activities of the Don and Terek Cossacks and the Crim Tartars.)

The struggle between the Russians and the Turks for control of the Pontic and Caspian basins was long and of epic proportions. Until the middle of the eighteenth century the Volga remained the only great southward flowing river over which the Russians had the mastery. Two centuries were to pass before the Russians really established themselves in the Crimea and secured permanent possession of the great fortresses commanding the outlets to the Black Sea – Akkerman, Kinburn, Ochakov and Azov (T. Azak.)

During the five decades which followed the Russian capture of Astrakhan in 1554, the policy of the Ottoman sultans and the Crimean khans was directed to reconstituting the belt of Turkish states along the Volga and setting a check to Russian penetration south round the shore of the Caspian and southwestward along the line of the Terek into Georgia. This was the explanation of the Don–Volga canal project, inspired by the Circassian Kasim Pasha, and sponsored by Mehmet Sokollu, perhaps the greatest of Ottoman Grand Viziers. In the autumn of 1569, Kasim Pasha laid siege to Astrakhan, when Banister and Duckett of the English Muscovy Company were held up there for some weeks. In 1570 Devlet Giray made his great cavalry drive against Moscow and burned much of the timber-built capital of Ivan IV.[2] Notwithstanding the failure of Mehmet Sokollu's 'grand design', the hold of the Muscovites

---

[1] Good near-contemporary descriptions of the way of life of the Tartars and their military tactics are given by Beauplan and by the Turkish travellers Asafi and Evliya Chelebi who actually campaigned with them.

[2] For summary of these campaigns, citing contemporary sources, see Allen, *PTP*, pp. 22–9.

on the Volga estuary remained in doubt for two decades, and convoys down the river were always subject to attack by the Nogays and wild bands of Circassian and Cossack outlaws. Nevertheless, the situation gradually became more stable; in 1582 the Russians built a stone wall round their new settlement at Astrakhan; and in 1589, the year when Prince Semen Zvenigorodski passed through on his embassy to King Alexander of Kakheti, the construction of a fortress was finished. The majority in the new city were Russians, but there grew up large Armenian and Tartar suburbs; and many Persian and Indian – and some few Georgian and even Chinese – merchants settled there.[1]

Yet for a century and a half, until the campaign of Peter the Great in 1722, Russian progress in the Caspian basin was remarkably slow. In the northern Caucasus, at first, they enjoyed the support of the princes of Greater Kabarda; and south of the main range, the kings of Kakheti – notably Alexander II and, later, Taymuraz I – were pressing for a policy of consistent support against the Shevkal, and against the Turks and Persians. Until Peter the Great embarked on his ambitious enterprises in naval construction which ultimately enabled him to concentrate a formidable and disciplined armament in the Volga estuary – the logistics of the sixteenth and seventeenth centuries remained a serious handicap to a Russian forward policy in the Caucasus. The technical problems of transport over long distances, of the concentration and conservation of supplies at Astrakhan, and of the forwarding of equipment and materials to the forts along the Terek and the Sunzha, epidemics and defective financial administration – all these factors presented persisting practical difficulties which are recorded in official documents.[2] The same difficulties are to be perceived in

---

[1] For Astrakhan, see further Commentary 7: 'The towns along the Volga route'.

[2] See further Supplementary Documents, 3: 'Logistics on the Terek'.

the records of the protracted Ottoman attempt to establish a permanent régime in Shirvan and Daghestan during the two decades which followed the victories of Lala Mustafa Pasha and Özdemiroghlu Osman Pasha in 1578. Troops were often short of supplies; sometimes starving and mutinous. In the winter of 1578–9, in the first year of victory, there were some ten thousand deserters, according to Asafi, the biographer of Özdemiroghlu Osman. 'The troops were very fearful of the winter. Some abandoned their horses and walked. Many of the army died.' Leading personalities proved recalcitrant and insisted on returning to their domains in more agreeable parts of the empire. When replacements arrived, they were found to be often old or sick men.[1]

Regional political units, based on local supplies and popular recruitment, were sometimes able to withstand the armies of distant imperial powers. Alexander, ruler of the small but flourishing Kingdom of Kakheti, could assemble a host of some 10,000 men, and a detachment of 500 trained musketeers, to impress the Russian ambassador Zvenigorodski. Simon of Kartli, in brilliant guerrilla operations, expelled the Ottoman armies from his hereditary territories. The Shevkal could rally some fifteen thousand horsemen from among the Kumyks and Avars and inflicted two disastrous defeats on the Russians.[2]

In the conditions of the sixteenth and seventeenth centuries the tribal elements in Daghestan, reinforced on occasion by trained contingents from Turkey or Persia, proved capable of opposing any Russian progress by the traditional route of invasion along the Caspian foreshore. In the eighteenth century

[1] For Ottoman difficulties in the Caucasus, see Asafi, *Sheja 'atname*, MS. TY 6043 of Istanbul University Library, f. 22 v., ff. (The editor is indebted to Dr. V. L. Ménage for a summary of this work.)

[2] For Alexander's military review, see below, Chap. 4; for Simon of Kartli's guerrilla operations, Allen, *History of the Georgian People*, London, 1932, pp. 177–9 (Allen, *HGP*); for the Shevkal's victory over I. M. Buturlin, see below, Chap. 15.

the expedition of Peter the Great occupied the Caspian littoral as far as Baku but the Russian invasion petered out in several years to a dreary failure without defeats. The same deficiencies in organization – in supply, transport and, above all, in sanitary measures – which were to cause the dreadful Russian losses at Ochakov and in the Crimea later in the century, ruined the Russian offensive effort in Shirvan, Ghilan and Mazandaran during the years from 1723 to 1732. The effect of these logistic conditions was to freeze the Russian strategic position in Caucasia to the north of the mountains – along the line of the Terek. And the valley of the Terek, forming, as it did, the second, and more difficult, avenue of approach from the Volga basin to southern Caucasia and the Middle East, became the main direction for Russian penetration into Georgia. It is one of the ironies of history that between the sixteenth and eighteenth centuries, the Georgian rulers, preoccupied with the continuous pressure from the Avars and other tribes of Daghestan and with the recurrent offensives of Ottoman and Persian armies, actually urged the Muscovite rulers to open up the routes along the Terek and the Avar-koysu with a view to consolidating communications and giving them consistent support against their Muslim neighbours.

2. GEOGRAPHICAL BACKGROUND

The main chain of the Caucasus Mountains has always been the dominant factor in the economy and in the political and military life of the isthmus which separates the Pontic and Caspian basins: the first so 'European', the second so 'central Asian' in natural and cultural characteristics.

The complex ranges of the Caucasus Mountains, stretching some six hundred miles in a general direction north-west to south-east from the Taman peninsula on the Azov Sea to the Apsheron peninsula on the Caspian, is the natural limit of the mountain zone of the Middle East comprising the Iranian and the Taurus highlands, themselves a westerly extension of the Himalayan system. The Crimean coastal range is the last westerly outlier of this wide world of mountains.

In the north, the slopes of the main chain of the Caucasus descend to the north Caucasian Steppe. In this direction are 'the five hills' called in Turkish Besh-tau, Russian Pyatigorye, which form a watershed between the Kuma and some westerly feeders of the Terek, all flowing eastward to the Caspian. The steppe in its western part is a projection of the grasslands which are fed by the rivers flowing to the Black Sea. The Kuban, like the Don, belongs essentially to the Pontic river system. The low Stavropol ridge running north to the Manych Depression forms the divide between the western and eastern steppes. Eastward, the North Caucasian Steppe disappears in the sandy flats and littoral swamps stretching to the Volga and forming part of the old bed of the Caspian Sea, an extension of the arid zone of the Aralo-Caspian Depression. This steppe is typical of the desiccated lands which edge the 'great heartland' of inner Asia. In the sixteenth century this north-east Caucasian steppe was inhabited by the Little Horde (*Kishi Ordu*) of Nogay Tartars, who were displaced only in the eighteenth century by the Mongol-speaking Kalmucks.[1]

The main chain of the Caucasus Mountains consists of a series of parallel ridges. These ridges are linked by necks or saddles which give access from north to south of the main chain. The connecting ridges form wide upland glens, often at

---

[1] The Kalmucks were deported *en masse* by the Soviets in 1943–4, following the German invasion of the northern Caucasus. For an account of these people, see the article by V. Bartold in *Encyclopaedia of Islam* (*EI*), 1st ed. The best description of them, before they had passed fully under the influence of the Russians, is to be found in the rare work of Xavier Hommaire de Hell, *Les Steppes de la Mer Caspienne, le Caucase, la Crimée et la Russie Méridionale, voyage pittoresque, historique et scientifique,* Paris and Strasbourg, 1843–5, 3 vols, with folio Atlas, including some coloured plates of Kalmuck life.

a great elevation. Typical examples are upper Svaneti and the Tush and Khevsur glens in northern Kakheti. Here communities have lived in almost complete isolation during all the known period of history.

The granitic backbone of the Caucasus chain runs as a single wall right across the Caucasian isthmus from sea to sea and separates the basins of the rivers of the northern slope from those of the southern. It thus represents the transverse water divide of Caucasia. The overlapping parallel ranges are all shorter in length than the main chain, but the principal parallel range, called, in Russian, *Bokovoy* (Flanking) is higher than the main chain and gives rise to some of the most notable peaks of the Caucasian system.

The western Caucasus, under the influence of the moist climate of the Black Sea basin, is heavily forested and the snow-line is lower than in the eastern mountains, which come under the desiccating influence of the Aralo-Caspian Depression.

There are more than seventy tracks and paths across the main chain of the Caucasus, some of which are only suitable for pack-transport and others for men marching in single file. In many cases they are blocked by snow for all but two or three months of the year.

The main chain could be by-passed by the sea route along the Circassian coast; but here cliffs and great forested bluffs come down to the sea. No through road along the coast was completed until after the Second World War. Right down to the First World War, Turkish sea-power effectively blocked movement along this coast. In the sixteenth century, all the way from Poti in Imereti to Taman and the Crimean ports, Turkish blockhouses and warships held the Circassian tribes in a network of control; the western Caucasus was quite inaccessible to the Russians who did not then control even the lower estuary of the Don. Equally, the second coastal route along the foreshore of the Caspian, was controlled at its northern entrant by the rather powerful Shevkal of Tarku. Where the foreshore narrowed to a mile or two, the ancient fortress of Derbent within its famous double walls, blocked all movement south. It fell to Peter the Great in 1723; but otherwise remained, alternately, in Turkish or Persian hands until the beginning of the nineteenth century. In the latter half of the sixteenth century, it was losing its commercial ascendancy as the entrepôt for the trade of the western and southern shores of the Caspian to Shemakha and Baku; but, strategically, it retained importance as the opposing base to Russian Astrakhan. The Shevkal, the Turks and the Persians, were all concerned to control Derbent, in Arabic *Bab-al-Abwab*, the Gate of Gates, with its strong walls, its easy access to reinforcement from the mountain tribes, and its fabulous prestige.

Blocked out from the coastal routes, the Russians were forced to develop the most difficult of all, that by the valley of the Terek whose famous gorge bisected the main granitic ridge of the Caucasus from south to north and divided the great chain into two almost equal halves. Thus, from the latter half of the sixteenth century, Russian penetration into Georgia and the Middle Eastern lands beyond, came to be directed along the axis: Volga–Terek.[1]

[1] For a convenient general description of the Caucasian chain, see Allen and Muratov, *Caucasian battlefields,* Cambridge, 1953, Chap. 1 (Allen/Muratov, *CB*). Baddeley's *Rugged flanks of Caucasus,* Oxford, 1940, 2 vols. (Baddeley, *RFC*), is a mine of information for the central and eastern Caucasus with acute commentaries on the works of earlier travellers. For some incomparable descriptions of scenery and mountaineering conditions, Freshfield, *The exploration of the Caucasus,* London and New York, 1896, 2 vols., is still outstanding; valuable notes on peaks, passes and approaches in Vol. II, Appendix B. (The author makes a bibliographical error, p. 249, in attributing the authorship of *La Souanéthie Libre* to Déchy instead of to R. Bernoville.) For recent Soviet surveys, see N. A. Gvozdetski, *Fizicheskaya geografiya Kavkaza,* vyp. 1, Moskva, 1954, *Obshchaya chast: Bolshoy Kavkaz*; and Maslov (ed.), *Severny Kavkaz,* Academy of Sciences of USSR, Institute of Geography, Moskva, 1957. For the Volga–Terek route, see the article by W. E. D. Allen, 'The Volga–Terek route in Russo-Caucasian relations' in *Bedi-Kartlisa* (*BK*), Vols. xv–xvi (Nos. 43–44), Paris, 1963, pp. 158–66.

3. THE TEREK ROUTE THROUGH THE CAUCASUS

Four hundred miles in length, the Terek river has been since ancient times a significant feature in the political and military geography of Caucasia. Its source is from a glacier on the crest of Zilga-khokh on the southern flank of the main ridge of the Caucasus at a height of 2,700 metres. It flows first in a south-easterly direction and then turns north at the village of Kobi and penetrates the main ridge through the celebrated ravine of Daryal to enter the north Caucasian plain a few miles to the south of Vladikavkaz.[1] In its upper course it is an impetuous mountain stream. After Darg-khokh, it receives several large streams flowing from the north-western slopes of Caucasus: Ardon, Cherek, Chegem, Baksan and Malka. The banks become lower and the river widens. After cutting through the Sunzhenski and Terski ridges, the Terek takes a right-angled turn to the east. In its middle course between the junctions of the Malka and the Sunzha, the stream of the Terek broadens with numerous branches interspersed with islands. After the junction with its right-bank tributary, the Sunzha, the Terek flows in a north-easterly direction, becoming deeper and more easily navigable. But it carries along with it a mass of detritus and the bed of the river tends to form banks. After Kargalin-skaya *stanitsa*, the Terek divides into a number of channels and falls to the Caspian in a broad delta which is said to extend at the rate of 100 metres a year. Fed by glaciers, snow and rains, and by numerous tributaries, the life of the Terek is unstable and there is a constant struggle against summer floods, particularly in the lower reaches.[2]

[1] Vladikavkaz – 'Lord of the Caucasus'. It was renamed Ordzhonikidze in honour of the well-known Georgian Bolshevik who was liquidated by Stalin during the 1930s. The town has now been accorded the Osetian name of Dzaudzhikau.

[2] For the Terek river, cf. article in *Bolshaya Sovetskaya Entsiklopediya*, (*BSE*) 1st ed., Vol. 54, pp. 101-2 (all future references to this work are to the 1st ed.). See also Baddeley, *RFC*, *passim*; Gvozdetski,

From the most ancient times, the Terek valley – like that of the westerly flowing Kuban – seems to have been a focus of human activity. According to Strabo and other classical writers, the gorge at Daryal was fortified in the first century B.C. in the time of the Iberian Kingdom.[1] The rich archaeological finds at Koban, north of the gorge, and indications of early mining activities, witness a high cultural development during the Bronze Age. If, as some historians believe, the difficulties of the terrain exclude the likelihood of the Terek valley having been used as a migration route during the period of the movements of the Cimmerians and the Scythians to the south of the Caucasus, infiltrations by small groups through the Daryal and over the higher *cols* of the central Caucasus were probably not uncommon. Indeed, the Huns appeared in Svaneti in the fourth century A.D.; and in the seventh century the Khazars came south to support Emperor Heraclius in an attack on Tiflis, then held for the Sassanids by the Iberian ruler, Stephanos.[2]

The wealth of the Aorsi, recorded by the classical authors, is evidence of prosperity in the north Caucasian steppe during the first century B.C. It is likely that the Aorsi had their centre in the Besh-tau hills; they were the cultural predecessors of the Alanic kingdom of the early Middle Ages. In each period, the people of the steppe round Besh-tau were famous as breeders of horses and cattle and controlled traffic in goods passing north–south along the valleys of the Terek and the Sunzha. The wealth of the Khazar kingdom on the Volga and round the northern shores of the Caspian was derived, at least in part, from the north Caucasian steppe; and, later, in the thirteenth century, when the Mongols had destroyed the Alanic kingdom

Maslov. S. G. Gmelin, *Reise durch Russland* (Gmelin, *Reise*), 4 Parts. Spb. 1784, Part IV, gives the best early account of the natural history of the Terek valley.

[1] Strabo, *Geography*, Loeb ed., Book XI, iii, paras. 5–6.

[2] cf. Brosset, *Histoire de la Géorgie* (*HG*), Part I, Book 2, pp. 226–7.

(by an attack coming from south of the Caucasus along the Caspian littoral route through Derbent), the region round Besh-tau, between the upper waters of the Kuma and the middle course of the Terek, became a favourite summer camping ground (*yayla*) of the Golden Horde.[1]

Long before the arrival of the Russians in the Volga estuary, the importance of the Terek route was clear to the Italian cartographers of the Caspian in the fourteenth and fifteenth centuries. The Italians, particularly the Genoese in Kaffa and Tana and their stations along the Circassian coast, were active in the trans-isthmian traffic as early as the thirteenth century. The Kabardans, according to Dubois de Montpéreux, retained down to the nineteenth century an oral tradition of

[1] For the wealth of the Aorsi, see Strabo, Book XI, v, 8. Also Ellis Minns, *Scythians and Greeks*, Cambridge, 1913, p. 107 and *passim*. Minns accepts the identification of the Aorsi with the Yen-ts'ai of the Chinese annals and with the later A-lan-a (Alans).

The latest work on the Khazars by M. I. Artamonov, *Istoriya Khazar*, Leningrad, 1962, emphasises the intimate links of the Khazars with the Caucasus.

In the fourth decade of the fourteenth century Ibn Battuta visited Uzbek Khan of the Golden Horde and describes 'the city of al-Māchar, a large town, on a great river (the Kuma), one of the finest of the cities of the Turks, and possessed of gardens and fruit in abundance'. From al-Māchar (Madzhari), he travelled four days to Bish-dagh (Besh-tau) – where 'there is a hot spring (*R. Kislovodsk*, bitter water) in which the Turks bathe and they claim that anyone who bathes in it will not be attacked by any disease'. From Bish-dagh he returned to the neighbourhood of al-Māchar – where the *mahalla* or *urdu* of Uzbek Khan was expected – 'and we saw a vast city on the move with its inhabitants, with mosques and bazaars in it, the smoke of the kitchens rising in the air (for they cook on the march) and horse-drawn wagons transporting the people. On reaching the camping place they took down the tents from the waggons and set them on the ground, for they are light to carry, and so likewise they did with the mosques and shops', cited from Sir Hamilton Gibb, *The travels of Ibn Battuta*, Hakluyt Society, Cambridge, 1962, Vol. II, pp. 479–82. (On his map, showing Māchar on an unnamed river, Gibb seems to confuse the Kuma – to which he gives a multiple estuary – with the Terek.) For views and plans of of Madzhari, see P. S. Pallas, *Travels through the southern provinces of the Russian Empire* (Pallas, *Travels*), London, 1812, 2 vols., Vol. I, pl. XI–XIV.

intercourse with the Genoese who were said to have had a large settlement in the valley of Kislovodsk.[1] Again, the existence of settlements of western traders on the north Caucasian steppe is indicated in the curious story of Josafat Barbaro about the raid of fanatical bands of dervishes from Derbent 'into Tumen' (at the estuary of the Terek) who, 'when they arrived at a river called Tero, which is in the province of Tezechia (Circassia) and about the mountaigne Caspio, where are many Catholic Christians, they slew them all'.[2]

The Fra Mauro Map of the middle of the fifteenth century and the so-called Borgia Map clearly indicate the rivers Kuma and Terek (Terco is named on the Borgia Map) and the valleys of the Aragvi and the Ksani leading into Georgia. The post-station Kobi, south of the gorge of the Terek and at the foot of the Krestovaya *col* which links the upper course of the Terek with the higher valley of the Aragvi, is named on both maps; and on the Borgia Map the Main (*Glavny*) and Flanking (*Boko-voy*) ridges of Caucasus are shown, and even the tribal name *Tusch*. Indeed, this latter pointer seems to hint that the caravans of the Genoese moved south-eastward into Kakheti with its silk-growing districts along approximately the same route which the Russian embassies were to follow over a century later.[3]

---

[1] W. Heyd, *Histoire du commerce du Levant au Moyen Age*, réimpression, 2 vols., Leipzig, 1923, Vol. II, pp. 93 ff., 555 ff.; also an article by F. S. Zevakin and N. A. Panchko in *Istoricheskiye Zapiski (IZ)*, III, 1938, pp. 72–139, 'Ocherki po istorii Genuezskikh koloniy na zapadnom Kavkaze v xiii i xv vv.', particularly pp. 86 ff.

For the tradition recorded by Dubois, see his *Voyage Autour du Caucase*, etc. (Dubois, *Voyage*), Vol. I, p. 80.

[2] *Travels of Venetians in Persia (TVP)*, Hakluyt Society, London, 1873, p. 89. These dervishes were probably the Shi'a followers of Shaikh Haydar of Ardabil, d. 1487, cf. *TVP*, pp. 185 (*bis*) ff.

[3] Cf. *Imago Mundi (IM)*, Vol. XIII, 1956, plates to article by L. Bagrow, 'Italians on the Caspian'; also ibid., x, 1953 article by G. Caraci, 'The Italian Cartographers of the Benicasa and Freducci Families and the so-called Borgiana Map of the Vatican Library', pp. 31 and 38 ff. Also *Iran*, Vol. VI 1968 article by J. Richard 'European Voyages in the Indian Ocean and Caspian Sea (12th to 15th centuries)', pp. 45–7 and 50–1.

For the end of the fifteenth century, the Genoese, Giorgio Interiano, gives an excellent description of the tribes along the Circassian coast. The Russians had little direct contact with the western Caucasus until the embassy of Elchin to the Dadiani of Mingrelia in 1639–40.[1] Apart from the casual details on topography recorded in the reports of Russian ambassadors to Kakheti in the later part of the sixteenth century, the first 'scientific' account of the Terek and northern and eastern Caucasia which has survived from Russian sources is in the Book of the Great Map (*Kniga glagolemaya Bolshoy Chertezh*). No copy of the map itself has been traced in the Russian archives; the Book appears to have been a guide to this document and was from time to time brought up to date. Serbina believes the seventh recension of the section which covers Caucasia to have been edited by Prince Grigori Suncheleyevich Cherkasski, paramount chief of the Pyatigorsk (Besh-tau) Kabardans, who died 1672.[2] G. S. Cherkasski was doing his editorial work nearly three quarters of a century after the embassies of Zvenigorodski, Sovin and Tatishchev, but it is probable that the details of the book which he was bringing up to date derived something from their reports. Another half century later, Wakhusht finished his descriptions and maps of Kartli north of the Kura, Oseti (*G. Ovseti*) and Kakheti. Although not without errors, Wakhusht's work was the first

[1] There is a convenient translation in French of Interiano in Dubois, *Voyage*, Vol. I. The original edition is Giorgio Interiano *Della vita de Zychi, altrimente Circassi*, Venezia, 1502, apud Aldum Manutium.

Elchin's mission to the Dadiani was first summarized by Brosset, *EC/BHP* Vol. III, Nos. 5–7, cols. 102–12, and No. 11, col. 160; documents were published by Belokurov in *ChOID*, 1887, Vol. II; and the text in Lurye and Müller (edd.): *Puteshestviya Russkikh Poslov xvi–xvii vv.*

[2] The text of *Kniga* was edited and published by G. I. Spasski, Moscow, 1840, a copy of which is in the Library of the British Museum. Cf. also the article by Serbina in *Istoricheskiye Zapiski* (*IZ*), Vol. 14, 1945, and further, ibid., Vol. 23, 1947; and an article in *Russki Biograficheski Slovar* (*RBS*) under G. S. Cherkasski, who was the son of the Kabardan *mirza* Suncheley (= 'of the Sunzha').

really comprehensive account of the topography of the central Caucasus and the upper valley of the Terek. Wakhusht was related by marriage to the Kabardan princes and there is evidence that he knew well Oseti and the upper valley of the Terek; it is curious that he makes use of the Ingush name *Lomeki* for the upper course of the Terek (*G.* Tergi). But Wakhusht, unfortunately, limited his famous *Geographical Description* to the countries which he regarded as properly forming part of the ancient kingdom of Georgia. He says little of the country north or east of Oseti and the westerly feeders of the Terek, although he must have followed the classic route along the Sunzha and the lower Terek when he accompanied the numerous suite of his father King Wakhtang VI on their withdrawal, in 1724, from Tiflis to Astrakhan.[1]

The Sunzha is the most important right-bank affluent of the Terek. Its course, with its numerous small tributaries and many crossings, was the short cut from the Cossack settlements on the lower Terek to the upper stream of that river where it emerges from the Daryal gorge. The Sunzha has its source in Mat-khokh, to the north-west of its longer affluent, the Assa. The two streams flow north to cut through the Black Mountains (*R.* Chernye Gory). Some 150 miles in length, the Sunzha only becomes a large river after its junction with the broad and turbulent Argun. Over the last twenty miles the combined streams of the Sunzha, Assa and Argun wind across the steppe to enter the Terek in a series of complex bends which make almost complete circles. The upper valleys of these rivers were, in the sixteenth century, covered with magnificent beech-forests, which in the nineteenth century enabled the 'sly Chechens' to maintain their prolonged resistance to Russian conquest.[2]

[1] For Wakhusht and his work, see Vol. II, Commentary on the Sources, 3.
[2] For detailed description of the valley of the Sunzha, see *Sbornik Svedeniy o Terskoy Oblasti*, Vladikavkaz, Vol. I, 1878, pp. 49 ff; an original

4. 'THE FREE TEREK COSSACKS'

During the sixteenth and seventeenth centuries a rather original mixed culture grew out of the intercourse between the Cossacks settled along the Terek and Sunzha and the neighbouring inhabitants of the mountain zone – Kumyks, Avars, Chechens, Ingushes, Kabardans and Osetians. There were many combinations, and relations between the Cossacks and the tribesmen did not really harden until the eighteenth century. Then the progressively bureaucratic aspects of Russian rule along the Cossack Line (inevitable in the pattern of contemporary administrative techniques) and the attempts at proselytization on the part of the Orthodox Church (which were countered by Islamic propaganda sponsored by the Ottomans) provoked bitter antagonisms and chronic conflict. In the earlier period, the Kabardans welcomed Russian support against the Nogays, while the Chechens were subject to pressures from the Shevkal and the Avar khans; some Ingush clans mistrusted their Chechen neighbours; and both Ingushes and Osetians resented pretensions to overlordship on the part of the Kabardan princes.

The first Free Cossack communities, mostly composed of 'outlaws' from the Don and the Volga, settled round the estuary of the Terek about the middle of the sixteenth century. The relations of these early Cossacks, living independent of the authority of the Muscovite government, with the neighbouring Kumyks, Chechens and Kabardans, were not always unfriendly. They took wives from the neighbouring tribes, and there was some penetration of Russians into the Black Mountains, as witnessed by the remains of fortifications and

and picturesque account in Steder's *Tagebuch*, Spb., 1797, pp. 5–7; also Baddeley, *RFC*, Vol. I, *passim*; A. N. Genko, 'Iz kulturnogo proshlogo Ingushey' in *Zapiski Kollegii Vostokovedov*, Vol. v, ii, 1930, pp. 691 ff. (commenting on Steder). For the Chechen resistance to the Russians during the first half of the nineteenth century, see J. F. Baddeley, *The Russian Conquest of the Caucasus (RCC)*, *passim*, based on the original Russian sources.

place-names such as Urus-Martana (Russian Martin). Some of these Cossacks made their way as far as Georgia and in the third quarter of the sixteenth century several hundreds, drafted on the orders of Tsar Ivan IV, were in the employment of King Levan of Kakheti.[1]

The number of aliens among the Terek Cossacks was very great, whole *stanitsy* being non-Christian; but the Grebentsy (Cossacks of 'the Ridge' running along the south side of the Sunzha, to the south-east of modern Grozny) admitted only Christians or those who consented to become such. (Comparably, the Zaporozhian Cossacks, 'beyond the rapids' of the Dniepr, insisted on the kissing of the cross by new recruits, but were ready to accept fugitives of all nationalities: Poles, Moldavians, Germans, some Italians – and even Turks.) The wives of the Terek Cossacks were often of native birth – probably for the most part Chechens with some mixture of Kumyks; and to this influence it is said that the Cossacks owed their comparatively advanced agriculture and much else. The Cossacks of that day were probably at best the equal in culture of the Chechens and Kumyks and certainly inferior to the Circassians, to whom belonged the Kabardan princes and people. 'Kabarda served as a lawgiver to the Grebentsy in matters of fashion,' and from there they took their light and convenient military equipment and arms, their methods of warfare, *dzhigitovka* (feats of skill on horseback), and the graceful tunic buckled at the waist with a narrow leather belt and swinging down to the knees – known as the *cherkesska*.

As regards dwellings, the typical Russian *izba* was forgotten, and instead appeared the Kabardan *una*, with its open gallery and its internal construction, arrangement and decoration. All that remained of the Russian village was, externally, the street,

---

[1] D. Chubinov, ed., *Kartlis Tskhovreba* ('The Life of Kartli'), Spb., 1854, pl. 107; cf. also V. L. Tatishvili, *Gruziny v Moskve*, Moskva, 1959, p. 23.

and, internally, the stove. (Here again, the Zaporozhian *kurens* may be compared with the communal long-houses of the maritime Circassians; indeed a strong Circassian influence may be suspected among these Cossacks of the Dniepr who, in, contemporary Russian documents are called, simply, 'Cherkasses'.)

Two kinds of culture – both new to the Cossacks – were probably borrowed from the Kumyks: those, namely, of the vine and of the silkworm, which flourish on the banks of the Terek to this day, having doubtless been supported through times of trouble and danger by the Cossack's passion for drink and his wife's delight in finery. Certainly until the Revolution, the Grebentsy women were noted for their good looks and free manners, and both in colouring and features, as well as in their semi-oriental costumes, they showed very strongly the strain of native blood in them and the continuing influence of Kabarda.[1]

5. 'TEREK-TOWN'

At different times this name was applied to no less than three settlements along the Terek. The foundation of the first town

[1] Many details in Section 4 have been cited from Baddeley, *RCC*, Chap 1, cf. also S. G. Gmelin, *Reise*, Vol. IV, Spb., 1774, pp. 27–32, for a good account of the Grebentsy: 'When they first came to the Terek they bought and married many Tartar women, and have become half Tartar in their speech, outlook and conditions ... But now (1774) they only marry among themselves and hardly understand the speech of the Mountain Tartars' (i.e. Kumukhs and Chechens). Gmelin distinguished three strata among the Cossacks of the Terek: (*a*) the old *Grebentsy* who came in the early sixteenth century; (*b*) the *Terski*, literally 'of the Terek', who were originally Cossacks of the Don settled by Peter the Great on the Sulak and moved to the Terek under Empress Anna (1735); (*c*) a third group, two-thirds from the Volga and one-third from the Don, who were brought in between 1720 and 1771. In 1772, Gmelin, p. 23, met the 130-year-old father of the then Ataman of the Grebentsy, who must have been born about 1642 – a curious link with the generation which followed the personalities in our texts. There is a fine description of life among the Grebentsy in Leo Tolstoy's novel, *The Cossacks*, written between 1852 and 1862 (English trans. by Rosemary Edmonds in Penguin Classics, 1960).

1. 'Osman Pasha crossing the ice' (of the Straits of Kerch).
From the *Sheja'atname* of Asafi, MS. TY 6043, fol. 196r. of Istanbul University Library.

dated back to 1563 when, after his marriage to Maria Tem-
ryukova, daughter of the Kabardan prince Temryuk Aydaro-
vich (C. Kemirgoko), Ivan IV sent a mission and troops to
build a town on Temryuk's territory. 'We do not know its
situation nor its fate' but it was probably on the border divid-
ing the lands of Temryuk from the vassals who had revolted
against him.[1] Little more is known of the second town founded
in 1567. It was on the left bank of the Sunzha, on the peninsula
formed by the junction of the Sunzha and the Terek.[2] In 1571
the Russian ambassador at the Ottoman Porte was explaining
that it had been built to protect Temryuk against his enemies.
Its existence became a major issue between the Tsar, the Sultan
and the Crimean Khan. There was an agreement to abolish the
town in 1574, but Smirnov doubts whether the undertaking
was ever carried out.[3] At any rate, between 1578 and 1585 a
new or restored town was established at the junction of
the Terek and Sunzha. It is probable that it was from the older
or newer of these two settlements that the ambush was organized against the column of Özdemiroghlu Osman marching
from Derbent to Kerch in October 1583 – of which Asafi gives
a first-hand account illustrated by miniatures.[4] In different
documents there are references to *Sunzhenski ostrog*, *Ust
Suyunchi*, *Terki*, *Sunzhi*, etc. *Staro-Sunzhenskoye* still appears on
modern maps (Caucasia: 1 in 210,000, Sh. G5).

Between the autumn of 1587 and the spring of 1588, Russian
officials and troops were busy building a fortified town on the

[1] Belokurov, *Snosheniya Rossii s Kavkazom* (Belokurov, *Snosheniya*),
p. lxxxiv and n. 28.
[2] N. A. Smirnov (ed.), *Istoriya Kabardy*, Moskva, 1957, p. 42 (*Ist.
Kabardy*).
[3] N. A. Smirnov, *Politika Rossii na Kavkaze v xvi-xix vekakh*, Moskva,
1958, pp. 29 ff. (Smirnov, *Politika*).
[4] Cf. Asafi, ff. 182–8, MS. TY 6043 of Istanbul University Library,
showing two miniatures, 186 r. and 188 v., of this action: 'The Rus attack
the Ottomans as they cross' and 'Asafi's brother wounded – the Rus in
their stockade'. (The former is reproduced here as plate 6, facing p. 293).

flats north of the southern branch (Tyumenka) of the estuary
of the Terek, which flows into the Caspian opposite the
Agrakhan peninsula. This was on or near the site of the
former Kumyk settlement of Tyumen (where Barbaro had
reported a massacre of Roman Catholic Christians towards the
end of the fifteenth century). In Russian documents there is a
reference to a prince of Tyumen (*Tyumenski knyaz*) for the
years 1555 and 1567.[1] Soon after this date – probably during the
war years 1569–70 – free Terek Cossacks had taken over here.
The new settlement was sometimes called Tyumen-new-town
or Tyumen-fort-on-the-Terek but soon, simply, Terek-town
or Terki. The stronghold was intended to control the Shevkal
of Tarku, a potential ally of the Ottomans and of the Crimean
Tartars, although he had shown himself ready on more than
one occasion to seek the favour of the Tsar. The wooden
stockaded walls of the new Terki were hurriedly thrown up
under pressure of negotiations with the Kabardans and King
Alexander of Kakheti, who continued to urge for some years
a combined Russian and Georgian attack on the Kumyks and
the Avars. Terki soon became the permanent advance base
between Astrakhan and the Cossack 'lines' along the Terek
and the Sunzha. Here, Russian ambassadors of the last quarter
of the sixteenth century – Birkin, Zvenigorodski, Vsevolodski,
Sovin, Nashchokin and Tatishchev travelling between Astrakhan and Kakheti enjoyed the last – or on return the first –
amenities of 'civilised' life. Beyond Terki lay the perils and dis-
comforts of the river journey along the Terek and the Sunzha,
the chancy anxieties of hospitality in the *kabaks* of the Kabardan
princes, the perilous transit of the Daryal gorge, the long ride
under the southern flanks of Caucasus, and the tented life and
tricky negotiations wherever they found the king in the forests
and valleys and country towns of Kakheti.

In 1636, when the Holstein diplomat Olearius passed

[1] Belokurov, *Snosheniya*, pp, li, lxxx.

through, Terki had grown to a place of some importance – with a standing garrison of 2,000 men; it was well fortified and furnished with heavy artillery. The town at that time contained the Old, the New and the Ghilan caravanserais, a bazaar and streets of shops, luxuriant gardens and communal baths, customs houses, courts for the sale of drink and the transaction of business, cathedral and parish churches and a monastery where the mountaineers were baptized. 'A prosperous town', observed the historian of the Terek Cossacks, 'where the Terek army was numerous and lived well'. Beside the Cossacks, and numerous Russian officials and their families and servants, and Armenian, Georgian and Persian merchants, some of the mountain tribes had their own *slobody* or 'free quarters' round the outskirts of Terki: notably the Okok, who may be identified with the Akko group among the Ingushes, and the Michkizy or Minkizy, a branch of the Chechens. Shikh Mirza of the Okok was a good friend of the Russians and his nephew had been received in the Kremlin.[1]

6. THE TRIBES OF THE NORTHERN CAUCASUS: CIRCASSIANS AND KABARDANS

There were many undertones, deriving from old historic conflicts, among the ethnic groups of the northern Caucasus. The long ascendancy of the Alans (Yas, Os) along the northern edge of the Caucasus had been broken by the Mongols in the thirteenth century. Later, in the last decade of the fourteenth century, the Golden Horde, formed by the Mongol conqueror Batu, had been shattered by the victory of Tamerlane over

---

[1] V. I. Larina, *Ocherki istorii gorodov Severnoy Osetii*, p. 16, citing Popko, *Terskiye Kazaki so starodavnikh vremen*, Spb., 1880, p. xii; also Olearius, *Voyages très curieux et très renommez faits en Moscovie et Perse*, Amsterdam ed. of 1727, 2 vols. fol., edited by le Sieur de Wicquefort (Olearius/W.), showing a fine engraving of Terki opposite p. 483 (reproduced here as plate 2, facing p. 32). For some further details, see the article by Allen, 'The Volga-Terek Route', in *BK*, cited on p. 11, n. 1 above.

Tokhtamysh at Tartarup on the Terek. The Os had survived in the mountains and had, indeed, descended into the central districts of upper Georgia. Their clan structure, dominated by noble families, had little in common with the wilder and freer communities of the Chechens and Ingushes who tolerated no first men among equals. In the first half of the sixteenth century, the Kabardans – Circassians whose social structure has been compared to that of a military order – had moved from the Crimea along the line of the Kuban and assumed the ascendancy formerly enjoyed by the Golden Horde. In the third quarter of the century, when Temryuk made his alliance with Ivan IV, the Kabardan princes were still comparative newcomers, threatened by the Nogays and the Crim Tartars – successor states of the Golden Horde – and by the rather powerful Shevkal of Tarku. Hence, perhaps, as Baddeley has observed, is partly explained the readiness of the Kabardan princely families to attach themselves to the Tsar.[1]

The Circassians or Cherkesses (*T.* Çerkesler) represent a stock formerly much more widely distributed round the shores of the Pontic basin. They are the descendants, indeed, of the old pre-Indo-European 'Maeotic' stock of the first millennium B.C., which formed a substantial proportion of the population of the Hellenic city states then flourishing round the shores of the Crimea and the eastern Pontus: and they had been, earlier, constituents of the complex racial background of the Cimmerian and Scythian hordes. Circassian place-names are to be identified in many parts of the Ukraine; and the Circassians formed an important element in the population of the Crimea until the eighteenth century. They survived with gallant tenacity in the mountains of the north-western Caucasus and along the valley of the Kuban until the Russian conquest in the sixties of the nineteenth century. Old Russian documents refer

---

[1] Baddeley, *RFC*, Vol. II, pp. 210 ff. For further on the Kabardans, see below, Commentary 12: 'The princely families of Kabarda'.

24

frequently to the Cossacks as Cherkesses and there was clearly a very substantial substratum of Circassian blood in the very mixed population of the northern Caucasus and the Black Sea coast-lands as far west as the Dniepr. But this is only one aspect of the remarkable dispersion of the Circassians. In the classical world and down to the Middle Ages, the slave market was the normal mechanism for maintaining the labour supply of civilized countries. Hence it was an instrument for imposing a continual process of redistribution of population. As slaves and soldiers the Circassians were celebrated in the Byzantine and Islamic worlds; and they finally rose to fame in the Mamluk corps which dominated Egypt from the later Middle Ages until the generation of Napoleon. The Mamluk corps was, in fact, a sort of foreign legion which was recruited largely from the western Caucasus and the Kipchak steppe. There is evidence, too, that there was a two-way influence and that the military ascendancy of the Kabardans, who were masters of the north Caucasian steppe from the beginning of the sixteenth century, owed something to the discipline and techniques of the Mamluk 'brotherhood'.

There is a certain touch of a rather naive 'colonialism' in the account of the way of life of the Circassians in the sixteenth century in the official Soviet *Ocherki Istorii SSSR*. Circassian culture was, in fact, original and sophisticated in the sense that Polynesian culture may be said to have been. They had a complicated social hierarchy which, though 'slave-owning' (as were contemporary Middle Eastern and European societies) was formal, disciplined and, often, kindly. They were skilled gardeners, boat-builders and fishermen, noted horse-breeders, brilliant in guerrilla tactics on their own terrain; and acute politicians who could quickly adapt themselves to the manners and court life of Istanbul, Bakhchisaray or Moscow. While they remained among their own forests and hills, they led lives which, if bucolic, were agreeable and certainly compared well with contemporary existence in Gaelic Scotland or Ireland – or for that matter in the fuggy and bug-ridden log houses and fever-infested alleys of Russian officials living in Astrakhan.

The political organization of the Circassian tribes of the western Caucasus was loose and haphazard. While the Shapsughs were, perhaps, the most numerous group, there was, west of the Kuban, no paramount prince – as there was in Kabarda. At the same time, in the Russian sources for the middle and second half of the sixteenth century, some 'princes' of the western tribes are mentioned; and in their dealings with Moscow they often worked together and spoke in the name of 'the whole Cherkess land'.[1]

In the north Caucasian plain, between the upper Kuban and the Sunzha, the Kabardans had a more developed social structure. By the latter half of the sixteenth century, Kabarda was divided into several wide domains governed by the members of related 'princely' families who claimed common descent from the chieftain, Inal, who had led them from the Crimea and settled the country to the east of the Kuban with a stronghold and centre in the Besh-tau hills. There were 'greater and lesser princes' according to the Russian sources. In their remote environment, these princes, with their privileged bands of armoured retainers, had something of the ascendancy and the prestige of the Livonian Knights among the Balts. At the same time the rivalries and animosities of the different princes of the house of Inal recall the feuds among

---

[1] For a recent summary of literature on the Circassians, see articles by Quelquejay, Ayalan and Halil Inalcik, under 'Çerkes', in *EI*, 2nd ed.; and a longer study by Mirza Bala under 'Çerkesler' in *Islam Ansiklopedisi* (*IA*), the Turkish version of *EI*. The best descriptions of life among the Circassians, before their dispersion by the Russians in the 1860s are to be found in the poems and stories of Lermontov; in Dubois, Vol. 1; and in James Stanislaus Bell, *Journal of a residence in Circassia during the years 1837, 1838 and 1839*, 2 vols., London, 1840. (Louis Vivien's Paris edition of 1841 with its learned introduction and notes is in many ways to be preferred to the English original.)

the various branches of the MacDonalds in the contemporary western Highlands of Scotland. The Kabardan term for their princes was *pshe* – originally heads of families, elders. As a united and privileged group, the princely families controlled their 'serf' population, themselves owing allegiance to the eldest brother. The estates of the princes consisted of groups of *kabaks* or rural settlements. These were composed of tents and hutments – which were sometimes moved from one area to another, according to the vicissitudes of seasons and local wars. The Kabardan princes had no manors nor castles, unlike the contemporary Polish nobility and Cossack colonels in the Ukraine, but they seem to have taken refuge, on occasion, in strongholds built of stone which could not be captured without 'cannon and arquebuses' and which were probably the ruins of the castles of the earlier Alanic culture in the northern Caucasus. Here, it may be observed that the ruling classes all over the Middle East and round the Pontus spent much of the year in a rather luxurious tented life, taking their dues in kind from the enserfed population and passing their time in great hunting expeditions. This way of life was followed, on a grander scale, by the Turkish Sultans and the Persian Shahs, the Georgian kings and the great Polish magnates in Podolia and the Ukraine. It explains the relative modesty of palaces and private houses of the royal or rich in Istanbul, Tabriz, Isfahan, Kazvin or Tiflis by comparison with the contemporary private architecture of western Europe. Among the Kabardans, as among the Turks, Persians and Georgians, wealth was represented in costly tents and rugs, costumes and fabrics, armour, arms and plate, great herds of thoroughbred horses, slaves, hounds and falcons. It was, in fact, a very mobile world, deriving its wealth from stock-raising, handicrafts and mutual plunder.

On the north Caucasian plains, agriculture had been traditional, back to Scythian times. In Kabarda it was developed to the extent that in years of good harvest the Russian posts along the Terek hastened to lay in supplies of grain from their Kabardan neighbours. The staple crop was millet. Hunting and fishing were also important sources of supply; and fishing rights along the rivers, as in the Gaelic far west with its somewhat comparable culture, were a frequent cause of feud and conflict.

After the *pshe* or princes, the leading class in Kabardan society were the *work* (Circassian) – the *uzdeni* of the Russian sources which use this Tartar term. The better sort among the *work*, the *tlakotlesh* and the *dezhenugo* – the *kozlary* and *duzhnyuki* of the Russian sources – were recruited from the immediate kinsmen of the *pshe*. They constituted the mounted detachments of the leading princes; they wore armour and carried long lances and sabres. They corresponded to the *druzhiny* of the early Russian princes; and may be compared to the 'tacksmen' who formed the 'tail' of the Gaelic chieftains in contemporary Highland society. Some of these 'best men' were masters of their own *kabaks*. The class of *work* as a whole were free to travel from one estate to another and they composed the permanent council of the prince which he was obliged to consult as we note in the negotiations of the Prince of Little Kabarda with Zvenigorodski.

Among the groups dependent on the *pshe* and their *work*, Russian sources mention the 'black people' (*chernye lyudi*), the *tl'fokot'l*: the settled population who had been mastered by the Kabardans at the beginning of the century. They were doubtless a mixture of the autochthonous Circassians (*Adighe*) who were living to the east of the Kuban with some elements of Alans and Tartars. They were also the *yasiry* or captive slaves taken in war.

Like the Circassians of the Black Sea coast, the Kabardans, in the sixteenth century, were by no means united. The internal history of Kabarda is a record of bloody clashes between the different princes. In these affrays they would set fire to each others' settlements, trample down the crops and lead off the captured serfs as prisoners – often for later sale as slaves. However, the notion of 'the whole of the Kabardan land' existed among the Kabardans and attempts were made to unite the country.

One of the Kabardan princes bore the title of 'great', 'the chief prince', interpreted by the Turks as *vali*. This title was not patrilinear. After the death of a 'chief prince', a new prince would be chosen from among the elder members of the princely line according to precedence; he would be 'placed' in his dignity by a council 'of the whole of the Kabardan land'. At these councils other questions might be decided: as, for instance, in 1589, the ratification of the allegiance to the Tsar by the whole Kabardan people. On that occasion, Prince Yansokh 'summoned the council in Kabarda, assembling with the Kabardan princes and with all the *mirz̧y* and *uz̧deni* and with all the land'. A recent Soviet historian supposes that in the sixteenth century such councils still preserved a democratic character to a marked degree and that the participation of the peasants was not restricted, if only for the hearing of the decisions taken by the *work*.

The situation of Kabarda, which controlled the exits from the mountains on to the winter pastures of the north Caucasian plain, enabled the princes to assert a certain ascendancy over the tribes of the central Caucasus who were more backward than the Kabardans in their economic and social development and in their military techniques. The dependence of the Osetians on the Kabardan princes was clearly established in the sixteenth century.[1]

[1] For social conditions and terminology in Sections 6–11, the editor has drawn on *Ocherki Istorii SSSR: Period Feodalizma, konets xv veka – nachalo xvii veka*, Academy of Sciences of USSR, 1955 (*OI/PF/xv–xvii vv.*), pp. 818–873.

Further on the Kabardans see Commentary 12: 'The princely families of Kabarda'.

7. THE CENTRAL CAUCASUS: OSETIANS, CHECHENS AND INGUSHES

Following the Mongol conquest of the north Caucassian steppe in the middle of the thirteenth century, elements of the population of the old Alanic kingdom had taken refuge in the mountains and gorges along the western tributaries of the Terek. The Alans themselves, in their day, had been a master people speaking a language which has been classified as west Iranian; but the ethnic composition of their kingdom was, doubtless, mixed, containing a substantial proportion of Circassian blood, with some elements of Khazar, East Slav and even Gothic origin. Alanic penetration into the central Caucasus and the northern districts of Georgia dated back to centuries before the Mongol invasions. Certainly as early as the eleventh century, Georgian sources indicate that the Georgian kings favoured them as mercenaries. There were marriages between the Alanic princely families and the Georgian royal house: the second husband of the celebrated Georgian Queen Tamar (1184–1212) was the Alan, David Soslan. To the Georgians, the Alans (As or Yasi) were known as *Ows*, plural *Owsni*, and their country as Owseti, hence the Russian hybrid *Osetiny*, and the anglicized Osetians, which latter form is the most convenient for our text. The conditions of life in the mountains, where the economy was based on stock-raising, led to a static way of life. The ingrowing patriarchal clan was characterized by the dominance of the elders of the family, the cult of the hearth, and the blood-feud. Feudal relationships, which are revealed only in the later sources, grew gradually out of the patriarchal-tribal customs. How the process of feudalization was continuing throughout the sixteenth century may be judged from the ancient architectural works which have survived: the *galuani* or stone-built castles of the Osetian feudal lords which were designed for large families. The dependence of the Osetians on the Kabardan overlords who controlled the northern exits from the gorges of the Terek and its affluents is evident from seventeenth-century sources which note the payment of tribute (*yasak*) in cattle, grain and slaves. On the whole the Osetians remained miserably poor and their only sources of living, beyond their meagre stock-raising, lay in porterage over the passes and, alternatively, in hold-ups of passing convoys. In each case, it was customary to pay them off in bales of cloth.[1]

East of the Terek gorge, the country to the north and north-east of the main granitic ridge of the Caucasus was the setting for varied ethnic, social and economic conditions. Over the high pastures and in the deep ravines of the feeders of the Sunzha lived patriarchal communities of very democratic type. Here, according to Baddeley, no man would accept 'princely' rank, even when pressed by his fellows. The people generally called themselves *maarul*, 'mountaineers' – which is reflected in the *Tavlistan* of the Russian maps, from Turko-Tartar *tau*, mountain; and in Daghestan further east, from Turkish *dagh*, mountain. The names *Chechen* and *Ingush*, familiar in the litera-ture of European travellers, are comparatively recent appella-tions of communities identified by the Russians with local place-names.[2] *Chechen* derives from the great *aul* Chechen on

---

[1] For the Osetians, see article by Bartold/Minorsky under 'Alān' in *EI*, 2nd ed.: 'The Alāns were the ancestors of the present-day Ossets whose name (in Georgian: Ows-e'ti) is derived from Ās (very probably the ancient Aorsi: al-Mas'ūdī, II, 10, 12, al-Arsiyya guards in Khazaria) who were apparently a sister tribe of the Alāns. The Armenian Geography calls the westernmost Alāns "Ashtigor" (As-Digor), and the Digor are the western division of the present-day Ossets, while "Asi" in Osset refers to the still more westerly region near mount Elbruz, which the Ossets must have occupied too in early days.' Cf. further Chap. 15, p. 503, n. 1; and see A. Z. V. Togan, article 'Allān' in *IA*.

[2] For the democratic practices of the mountaineers, see Baddeley, *RFC*, Vol. I, p. 218. For *Tauli* or Mountain Turks, see Douglas Freshfield,

the banks of the Argun; the first documentary reference dates from the year 1708. *Ingush* derives from the village of Angusht, first attested by Wakhusht in 1724. The Chechens call themselves *Naktchoi* (Baddeley) with which may be compared the west Circassian *Natukhoi* (Dubois de Montpéreux). The name implies 'family', 'stem', and has Armenian and even, perhaps, western pre-Celtic connotations as in Pictish *necht*.[1] Of the Ingush self-name, *Ghalgha* or *Galgay*, Wakhusht gives the Georgian form *Ghlig(os)* – whence the district of Ghligveti shown on his map of Oseti. *Ghligos* he describes as the mythical grandson of *Durdzukos*. This latter name is found in Georgian sources as early as the tenth century A.D.; and Genko believes that 'for the most ancient epoch *Durdzuk(os)* signifies the whole of the northern Caucasus'. He suggests that the origin of the name may be detected in the word *durdzuq* which survives among the contemporary Osetians with the meaning of 'rock-pit', i.e. ravine. Thus the Durdzuks of the Georgian sources would be the 'people of the ravines'. This may be compared with the tribal name *Okok* in Zvenigorodski's reports, rendered in Steder's *Tagebuch* as *Agi*. Genko gives the Inguish form as

The exploration of the Caucasus (Freshfield, *Exploration*), 2 vols., London, 1896, Vol. I, p. 60 and *passim*. J. G. Gärber, 'Opisaniye stran vdol zapadnogo berega Kaspiyskogo morya, 1728 g.' (Gärber, *Opisaniye*) printed in M. O. Kosven (ed.), *Istoriya, geografiya i etnografiya Dagestana, xvii–xix vv.: Arkhivnye materialy* (Kosven, *IGED*), Moscow, 1958, states that the word *tau* applies to the highest peaks and ridges and *dagh* to mountain regions of medium altitude. Thus, *Tavlintsy* means people living along the high ridges.

[1] Cf. W. E. D. Allen, article 'Ex Ponto', I and II: 'Heni-Veneti and Os-Alans' in *BK*, Nos. 30–1, pp. 41–3, for detailed refs. The same sense is preserved in the Osetic word for 'clan', *mukkagh*, or *m'iggag*, 'rod, plemya, familiya, semya', cf. Kasayev, *Osetinsko-Russki slovar*, 1952, p. 236; also *m'ig*, 'sperma, semya'. These compare rather closely with Irish MS. variants, *meic, mic*. For Celtic elements in the Pontic steppe, as neighbours of the Alans, see Minns, cited above, Rostovtseff, *Iranians and Greeks in South Russia*, Oxford, 1922; Sulimirski, 'The Forgotten Sarmatians' in *Vanished civilizations*, London, 1963, pp. 279–98.

TERKI.
Ville de la Circassie, dans l'Asie.

2. Terki town, c. 1634. From Olearius/W., Vol. 1, pp. 452/3.

aqqij, Chechen *aqquoj,* and he interprets the name of the Ingush and Karabulak settlements along the upper waters of the Sunzha, Akhin-yurt, as Ingush *oekhi T. yurt,* meaning precisely 'villages of the ravine'.[1]

The Arab geographers called the Caucasus 'the Mountain of Languages'; and there has been great differentiation of language among the small and often isolated communities who inhabit the great range. Modern philologists, shying away from the late Professor Marr's 'Japhetic' classification, have defined the languages of the Caucasus as 'Ibero-Caucasic' and, while comparisons remain hazardous, there is found to be some affinity between the western (Circassian) and eastern (Daghestan) groups. The Georgian dialects constitute a southern group which has very distinct characteristics.

Physically there are no very marked differences between the various peoples of Anatolia and the Caucasian isthmus.

That peculiar type which is native to these parts, so called autochthonous – 'out of the ground' – is quite permanent, always resurgent, mastering the bodies of new masters. The strong-boned physique, the broad square head with its thick growth of wavy hair and beard, the wide dark eyes, the sallow skin, are bred to these mountain countries from the Ice Age. This type is called Armenoid, or more appropriately Alpine; it spread to Europe in prehistoric times along the mountain belt as far as the Pyrenees, and over Iran to the Pamirs; and it had filtered down through Palestine to Egypt, surviving as all types, mostly in those parts which were likest to its homeland. The peasantry of western Asia, whether they be called

---

[1] Genko, p. 704 and p. 686, n. 1; also Steder, *Tagebuch,* p. 44. And cf. Baddeley, *RFC,* Vol. II, Map 2, *Kii* commune on an affluent of the Tchanti-Argun. The Galgay (Georgian, *Ghligi*), may be compared with the Gelae of classical writers, cf. Strabo, *Geography,* Book XI, v, 1. They were neighbours of the *Legae,* see p. 39, n. 1. The names seem to survive in Ghilan and Lahijan (*-an* being a plural suffix), districts round the southern shore of the Caspian, cf. Minorsky, *A history of Sharvan and Darband (HSD)* Cambridge, 1958, pp. 14–15 and n. 1.

Georgian, Armenian or Turkish, are of this autochthonous stock – 'out of the ground'.[1]

Some variations from this autochthonous 'Alpine' stock may be noted in the blond 'Nordic' types to be found among the Kurds and in a minority of the Osetians, Georgians and Kabardans. And along the Pontic coast, extending eastward to Mingrelia (ancient Colchis) and Circassia, the 'Atlanto-Mediterraneans' of Deniker's classification, remained a persistent element from prehistoric times. From the curiously contradictory accounts of the Colchians in Herodotus and Hippocrates, it would seem that a 'Nordic' group was settled at one time in western Georgia but failed to survive. In the fifth century B.C., two centuries after the Cimmerian and Scythian invasions of Caucasia, Herodotus could compare the Colchians to the Egyptians in their 'black' colour and their woolly hair. But Hippocrates' description would seem to apply to a blond 'Nordic' group in process of degeneration – probably the remnants of a ruling horde descended from Cimmerian or Scythian invaders of two centuries earlier. On the other hand, in Wakhusht's description of the Mingrelians and Imeretians, it is possible to conceive the epanastasis of the older brunet people described by Herodotus (the Heniochi or people of pre-Colchian Aea).[2] Indeed, Wakhusht's description applies well enough to the brunet 'Mediterranean' or 'Atlanto-Mediterranean' strain which survives in western Caucasia and

---

[1] Cited from Allen, *HGP*, p. 21. For the anthropology of Caucasia see article by A. Javakhishvili, 'The Caucasian race' in *Georgica*, Vol. 1 Nos. 2–3, London, 1936, pp. 92–108, reproduced from *Tbilisis Universitetis Moambe*, Vol. III, 1923. For later views on the anthropology of Anatolia, see articles in *Belleten* of Turkish Historical Association; and Bayan Afet Inan, *L'Anatolie, le pays de la 'race' turque: recherches sur les caractères anthropologiques de la Turquie*, Geneva, 1941.

[2] Cf. Herodotus, Book II, 104–5; Chadwick and Mann, *The medical works of Hippocrates*, Oxford, 1950, pp. 104 ff. Wakhusht (Prince Wakhusht Bagrationi): *Description géographique de la Géorgie par le*

along the Pontic coast, as also in the Balkans and the Ukraine and which 'the Russian anthropologists now call the Cherkess or Pontic type when found elsewhere in Russia'.[1]

The high granitic spine of Caucasus was a barrier to the mass movement of peoples in a meridional direction. But there was infiltration over the high passes by raiders, and by groups seeking pasturage in lower valleys or service as mercenaries. That invading armies in large numbers could penetrate the Terek gorge is questioned by some writers (Baddeley). But in later periods, at least, there is evidence in the campaigns of Timur and Shah Abbas against the Georgians of successful operations up the valleys of the Aragvi and the Ksani as far as the Daryal gorge. In early historic times, it is possible that the Cimmerians, in their flight before the Scythians, used the Terek route – although they could hardly have brought their wagons through. Evidence survives in place-names of penetration by the peoples of the north Pontic steppe into the Central Caucasus and Daghestan. The variations of the root K-m-r are notable in the eastern mountains: Ghimri, Gremi, Gümürü (later Aleksandropol – the commanding strategic position facing Kars across the Arpa-chay). For Scythic elements see n. 1 below. The names of pre-Aryan 'Maeotic' peoples may be detected in the Batsi (G. Batsebi), the ancient Bessoi, known to the writers of the Hellenistic world in several enclaves

---

Tsarévitch Wakhoucht publiée d'après l'original autographe par M. Brosset, Spb., 1842 (Wak./Brosset) p. 343. Cf. also 'Tsarevich Vakhushti, *Geografiya Gruzii:* vvedeniye, perevod i primechaniya M. G. Dzhanash-vili', Tiflis, 1904 (Wak./Jan.). This work was published as *Knizhka* XXIV, *vypusk* 5 of *Zapiski Kavkazskago Otdela Imperatorskago Russkago Geograficheskago Obshchestva,* (*ZKO*). (The editions of both Brosset and Janashvili are bibliographical rarities.)

[1] C. S. Coon, *The Races of Europe,* New York, 1948, p. 633. In *Traditio,* Vol. xv, pp. 17–18, Toumanoff observes that 'there were, also, in Caucasia, a number of Scythian and Cimmerian enclaves'. See also, W. E. D. Allen, 'Ex Ponto', V, 'Heniochi – Aea – Hayasa', in *BK*, Nos. 34–5, p. 80.

between the Balkans and Taman. These people crossed the main ridge to pasture in the upper valleys of Kakheti only in the seventeenth century by leave of the Kakhian kings.[1]

Tinen, the mythical father of Durdzukos and 'the most distinguished of the sons of Kavkasos' (Wak./Brosset, p. 427), has been equated by Genko, following Golovinski, with the name of the Tindy 'a very ancient people who lived in the land of the Galayevtsy (Ingushes) and moved thereafter – it is not known whither or when'. It is tempting to hazard that the Tindy represented the Thyni of Herodotus, 1, 28, who were associated with the Mysians (= Mushki = G. Meskheni) and Phrygians in the eastward movement of Thracian peoples into Anatolia during the period of the decline of the Hittite empire.[2]

8. DAGHESTAN: KUMUKHS AND KUMYKS, KAYTAKHS AND AVARS[3]

The mountains north and north-east of the main spine of Caucasus descend in steep ridges to the Caspian. Over a stretch of less than a hundred miles altitudes vary from twelve thousand

[1] For the Batsi, see Commentary 15: 'Metsk, Batsk'; also Allen, *BK*, Nos. 30–1, pp. 43, 47.

[2] Tinen/Tiret: cf. Genko, p. 704; the name is first attested in Georgian sources by Leontius of Ruissi in the eleventh century A.D.

[3] For the history of Daghestan, with bibliographical indications, see articles by Bartold/Bennigsen, 'Dāghistān' in *EI*, 2nd ed.; by Mirza Bala, 'Daǧistan' in *IA*; and 'Dagestanskaya ASSR' in *Bolshaya Sovetskaya Entsiklopediya*, 1st ed. (*BSE*, 1st ed.). M. O. Kosven (ed.) usefully covers the political and social history at the turn of the sixteenth century in *Ocherki istorii Dagestana*, Moskva, 1957, Vol. I, pp. 90–141.

Still basic and often used as a source in modern Soviet books, is the solid work of E. I. Kozubski, *Pamyatnaya Knizhka Dagestanskoy Oblasti*, Temir-Khan-Shura, 1895; it concludes with a valuable bibliography of some 273 pp. For physical geography, with numerous maps and illustrations, see A. F. Viktorov and others, *Dagestanskaya ASSR*, Makhachkala, 1958; for recent tribal survey, A. D. Daniyalov (ed.), *Narody Dagestana*, Moskva, 1955; for art and handicrafts, E. V. Kilchevskaya and A. S. Ivanov, *Khudozhestvenniye promysly Dagestana*, Moskva, 1959, with 91 excellent plates.

feet to below sea-level. These ridges are penetrated by the precipitous ravines of several rivers: the principal are the northward flowing Argun which falls to the Sunzha; and the Andi and Avar *koysus* which run in a north-easterly direction and eventually unite to form the Sulak. The lower course of the latter river flows across the plain into a marshy estuary some sixty miles to the south of the mouths of the Terek. South of the Sulak, along the coast of the Caspian as far as the Samur, numerous smaller streams find their way direct from the eastern slopes of the maritime ridges into the inland sea. The foreshore of the Caspian formed the main route of access between the north Caucasian steppe and the Persian provinces of Shirvan and Azerbaijan. Marshy or sandy in alternate patches, this low-lying strip was as wide as ten miles between Makhachkala and Manaskent and narrowed to a mile at Derbent – which at least since Sasanian times was regarded as the strategic and commercial key to South Caucasia.

A series of princely domains had long since taken form in the mountains which overlooked this route and extended northward to the Sulak. In the period of the wars between the Khazars and the Arab Caliphate, in the ninth and tenth centuries, there are many references by the Persian and Arab geographers.[1]

In the sixteenth century, the most important of the princes of Daghestan was the Shevkal or Shamkhal of Tarku. The Shevkal was the ruler of the Kumukhs – who are frequently referred to in our texts as the Kumyks. As Baddeley, Bartold and Minorsky have all observed these two peoples are distinct and should not be confused. The Kumukhs speak an east Caucasian language. During the sixteenth century, the Shevkals extended their territory from their old capital in the mountain

---

[1] For the history of this period, see V. Minorsky, *Hudūd al-ʿĀlam: The regions of the world*, Oxford, 1937; idem, *HSD.*; Artamonov, *Istoriya Khaẓar.*

village of Kumukh, on a high ridge to the north-east of the
great peak of Djulti-dagh (4131 m.), towards the Caspian
coastland. They were accustomed to winter in the coastal plain
round the *yurt* of Buinak, returning in the summer to the highlands round Kumukh. The Shevkals extended their rule northward to the Sulak and made their principal seat at Tarku. They
thus became masters of the Kumyks – pastoralists speaking a
Turkish dialect. Minorsky believes these Kumyks to have
been a remnant of the Kipchaks who may have contained a
nucleus of Khazars reinforced and assimilated by later arrivals
from the Kipchak steppes.[1] He finds that 'it is indeed possible
that *Qumiq* is only a Turkish pronunciation of Ghumiq/
Qumukh, because the rulers of these (originally Qipchaq)
Turks, who bore the name of Shamkhāl came from Ghazi-
Qumūkh'. Bartold observes that the Kumyks speak an archaic
dialect connected with Komanic and quite different from the
language of their northern neighbours, the Nogays – which
became a literary language in the second half of the nineteenth
century.[2]

Like *Chechen* and *Ingush*, the name *Kumukh* in mediaeval
times seems to have been derived from the toponym.[3] The
Kumukhs called themselves *Lak* or *Lakẓ*. According to
Minorsky (*HSD*, p. 80, n. 1) this name consists of *lak/lag*
(a 'man' in local languages) plus the Iranian suffix of origin – *ẓ*.
In Russian (with metathesis) *Leẓg-in* was used somewhat
indiscriminately for all the inhabitants of Daghestan, but in

[1] Minorsky, *HSD*, p. 96, n. 1; and ibid., p. 107, n. 2.

[2] Bartold under 'Daghestan' in *EI*, 1st ed.; this article is still worth
reading in conjunction with Bartold/Bennigsen's article under 'Dāghistān'
in *EI*, 2nd ed.

[3] The word *kumukh* seems originally to have had the significance of
gorge or defile; later to be identified with the people living in its vicinity,
see p. 32 above for *durdẓuq* in the sense of rock-pit or ravine. In the view
of Garstang/Gurney, *The geography of the Hittite empire*, London, 1958,
p. 38, the fortress of Kumaha in Hayasa 'equates fairly easily' with Kemakh
at the head of the great gorge of the western Euphrates.

local use and in the Arab geographers the term applies *only* to the tribes of southern Daghestan.[1]

South-eastward of Kumukh lay the domains of the *Utsmi* of Kara-Kaytakh, and of the Mas'um of Tabassaran and the Khan of Kiurin.[2] These territories touched the river Samur – beyond

[1] The name forms *Lak – Lek – Lik – Luk* are very old in the prehistoric onomastics of the Middle East and Eurasia. For *Lakku-Lukku*, cf. Garstang/Gurney, pp. 45–6, 76–81 and *passim*. In Georgian, the old name for the Suram range is *Likhis-mta* – 'the mountains of Likh'. In Osetian, the form occurs as *laeg*, man, cf. Dumézil, *Journal Asiatique* (*JA*), Vol. CCXLVI, *fasc.* i, 1958, pp. 81–8; it can be a pre-Indo-European fossil in Osetian, like *durdzuq*, see above, p. 32. The *Lugi* appear in the Ponto-Baltic world where they are associated with the Veneti – who are generally identified (or confused) with early Slavs. In this connection Aytek Namitok, *Origines des Circassiens, Ière partie* (all published) (Namitok, *Origines*), Paris, 1939, p. 141, n. 4, observes that the Circassians call the Lesghians of Daghestan by the name of *Hanovatché* (= Heniokhes = Heneti/Veneti). The 'pair' recurs in the Vindelici round Lake Constance (Lacus Venetus), cf. Strabo, Book I, i, 5, and Book IV, vi, 8, for their savagery in war. Pliny and the Peutinger Map name the northern *Lugi – Lugi-Sarmati*; the name probably survives in the Turkish name for the Poles – *Lyakh*.

[2] *Shevkal/Shamkhal of Tarku, Utsmi of Kara-Kaytakh, Mas'um of Tabassaran; Nutsal of the Avars*: According to Minorsky, *HSD*, p. 104, these titles do not occur either in the *Ta'rīkh al-Bāb* or other Arabic sources. 'These later – and still mysterious – titles, have nothing to do with the Sasanian honorifics which were still remembered in early Islamic times.' In *EI*, 2nd ed., under 'Dāghistān', Bartold/Bennigsen state: 'The title of Ma'ṣūm, borne by the prince of Tabassarān, was identified with the Arabic word *ma'ṣūm*. Likewise, Arabic etymologies were invented for the Kaytāk title of *ūsmī* ('renowned', from *ism* = name) and for the Kāzī-Kūmūk's *shāmkhāl*. The word *shāmkhāl* was alleged to derive from *Shām* – Syria. Another root was also found for this word, namely *shāh-ba'l*. It is not impossible that such etymologies also had some influence on the pronunciation of the titles in question. It is obviously not by chance that the title of the prince of the Kāzī-Kūmūk appeared in the oldest Russian documents in the same form (*shewkal* or *shawkal*) as in Sharaf al-Dīn Yazdī. Clearly the Persians and the Russians could not have corrupted *shāmkhāl* into *shawkal* independently of each other.'

According to Reineggs/W., Vol. I, p. 92, 'the prince of Kaidek still bears the name of *Hemse*, which is corrupted into *Utzme* or *Utzumm* (for the latter cf. Turkish *Pasha-m*, 'my Pasha')'. See further pp. 97–8, for the author's discussion of the name Shamkhal. For the origin of the even more

which lay the Khanate of Kuba on the north-eastern border of Shirvan.

South-westwards of Kumukh was the country of the Avars: bounded on the south-west by the great ridge of Bogos with its peak at 4151 m; on the north-east by the Andi, and on the south-east by the Nukatl ranges. From the flanks of Bogos, the deep ravines of the Andi-koysu and the Avar-koysu led eventually towards the Sulak; and over the shoulders of the great ridge difficult paths gave access into the valleys of Kakheti.

Towards the end of the sixteenth century, the Avars were the allies and rivals of the Shevkal; during the seventeenth and eighteenth centuries with the weakening of the power of the rulers of Tarku, they assumed an ascendancy in the politics of Daghestan and proved formidable enemies of the Georgian kings.

According to the eighteenth century traveller, Reineggs, *'Awar, Oar, Uoar, Uar,* is the name they give themselves in their own dialect . . . The prince is called Uar-Khan, Leski-Khan, and, according to the Mongol dialect, *Hiung-Zag-Khan,* "Great Ruler of the People".[1] Baddeley, for the end of the nineteenth century, states that 'Avar is said to be a Turkish word meaning restless, vagabond, etc. and was borrowed by the Russians from the Koumuiks. The Avars, who ignore it, call themselves individually by the name of the aoul or community to which they belong, but all agree in saying that they are Maaroulal (mountaineers) and their language Maaroul Mats

obscure *nutsal*, cf. Brosset, *Rapports sur un Voyage Archéologique dans la Géorgie et dans l'Arménie exécuté en 1847–1848, 1ier livr.*, with Atlas, Spb., 1849, *2ième livr.*, 1850 (Brosset, *VA*), *1ier rapport*, p. 77, when the author, travelling in Kakheti is accommodated for the night by the village *natzwal*. Prof. D. M. Lang has pointed out that *natzwal* comes from *natsvaleba* 'to deputise', *natsvali* 'deputy', 'lieut. governor'. Thus the Avar title would seem to derive from Georgian.

For the title *Shevkal/Shamkhal*, we have adhered to the form *Shevkal* which occurs in the Russian documents.

[1] Reineggs/W., Vol. 1, p. 229.

(mountain language); though the northern Avars call their southern brethren Bagoualal, meaning poor, rude people, and this division corresponds pretty exactly to the linguistic one of the two main dialects, the line of demarcation being just south of Khounzakh. A Russian writer says . . . that they once spread farther north, and were probably nomads on the Koumuik plain. There is even some indication that they dwelt north of the Caspian and, if so they were, doubtless, driven into the mountains by stronger tribes from the north.'[1] *Avare* in Turkish seems to have had the same general sense as *kaẓak*: wanderer, vagrant, and, in a pejorative sense, idler. *Avary* survived in Russian folk memory in the form *Obry* and the expression 'perished like Obry'; and Vernadsky recalls that the Czech *Obr*, giant, derives from the name Avar.[2]

Erckert did not exclude a connection between the Avar invaders of Europe in the early Middle Ages and the group of the same name surviving in Daghestan. On the basis of anthropological data, he stated that the Avars were the most mixed race in Daghestan, a phenomenon which he found especially noticeable in the neighbourhood of Khunzakh. He admits the probability of the Avars having received additions, at least, from the Ural-Altaic peoples and adds that 'in measuring heads at Khounzakh we were struck involuntarily by the occurrence of Finnish types'. He then cautiously enough suggests a connection between Khunzakh and Hun, observing that in any case Hunnish peoples dwelt to the north of the Caucasus from the fourth to the sixth century as Uigur and Kutugur, and when they disappeared were replaced in turn as lords of the steppe by Bulgarians, Sabirs, Avars and Khazars.[3]

[1] Baddeley, *RCC*, p. xxx.
[2] Vernadsky, 'The Spali of Jordanes and the Spori of Procopius' in *Byẓantion*, Vol. XIII/i, p. 266, n. 2.
[3] Cited from Baddeley, *RCC*, p. xxxi.

The best and latest discussion of the background of the Avars of Daghestan is to be found in Minorsky's *History of Sharvān and Darband*, pp. 97 ff. In writing of the *Sarir* of the Arab geographers – 'the people of the Master of the Throne (*ṣāḥib al-Sarir*)', Minorsky remarks: 'Like in many similar cases, the dynasty of the Sarīr may have been of foreign origin and *Avar* presents a striking analogy with the name of the well-known Altaic conquerors of the fifth century A.D. In this direction one might quote an additional title, *khāqān al-jabal*, which, according to Balādhurī, 196, Anūshirvān granted to the ruler of the Sarīr. Among the officers of the ruler our source mentions *tarkhāns and baṭriqs*,[1] of which the first category is Altaic by name. Such argument is not peremptory, for the penetration into Daghestan of Turkish titles and ranks might have taken place under the influence of the *neighbouring* Khazar kingdom ... Theoretically, it is quite possible that there were some Altaic infiltrations into the basin of the Qoy-su, or that the ancient dynasty ruling over the mountaineers was of Altaic origin.'

Minorsky found evidence also of an Alanic element among the Avars: 'We see the Saririans allied now to the Alans and the Khazars (in 902), now to the Alans alone (during the formidable raid on Shirvan in 1032), and now "to various Turks" (in 1064).' He notes further traces of the Alans in the district of Masqat lying north of the Samur. Observing that this Arab name is nothing but a popular etymology, he finds that the original name of the district was *Maskut* or *Mashkut*, from the Massagetai who were settled there. 'One can remember here that, according to Ammianus Marcellinus, xxxi, 22, 12, the Alans were the ancient Massagets (*Halanos ... veteres Massagetas*); therefore the old settlers in *Masqat* may have been Alans. The river flowing south of Darband is called *Rubas*,

[1] *Baṭriq* would appear to be Greek *Patrikios* – infiltrated, perhaps, through the Georgians.

which in Osset would mean "a fox" (cf. the name of the more southerly Samur "a marten").[1]

The position of *Shevkal* was not patrilinear but was accorded at a council 'of the best men of the Kumyk Land', meeting originally in the mountain *aul* of Kumukh, to one of the elder of the late Shevkal's kin. The Krym-Shevkal mentioned in the reports of the Russian ambassadors seems to have been a sort of heir apparent, like the *Nur-al-din* among the Crimean Tartars. There is some confusion as to this personality and his status. He was certainly not 'the Crimean Shevkal' as indicated by a recent Soviet historian; it would seem rather that he was the Shevkal of Ghimri, a large and powerful *aul*, some twenty miles to the west of Buinak and overlooking the junction of the Andi-koysu with the Kara-koysu. This *aul* was strategically well placed for the seat of the heir-apparent. During the period of our embassies Krym-Shevkal was at feud with the ruling Shevkal of Tarku and had taken refuge with King Alexander of Kakheti who had granted him a fief at Elisu in the extreme south-east of Kakheti – hence he is sometimes described as Elisu-Sultan. The feud was an element in the weakening and

[1] Minorsky, *HSD*, p. 78 and n. 13. His views have been confirmed by recent archaeological excavations: see article by B. A. Kuznetsov, 'Alany i rannesrednevekovy Dagestan' in *Materialy po Arkheologii Dagestana*, *tom* II, Makhachkala, 1961, pp. 265–70. In the context of Alanic penetration into Daghestan, it is worth recalling the observation in Reineggs/W., Vol. I, p. 108–9, 'For a long period of time the Ghazi-Kumuk bore the name of *Kesch* from an Alanic tribe that lived there. Some of the inhabitants of Kumuk really remember it with pride; and trace their origins from the Alans . . . Yet according to the opinion of other learned Kumuks, Kesch was the old proper name of the Lesghaes, and Alan nothing more than the plural of *Ell, All or Ill*, a tribe, people or horde, according to the Lesghae idiom.' The name *Kesch* could imply a Circassian rather than an Alanic connotation, cf. *Kashak*, as in Mas'udi; but this author (eleventh century A.D.) indicates a close friendship between the Ghumiq, who were then Christian, and the Alans. During the same period there were matrimonial links between the rulers of the Alans and of al-Sarir (the Avar country – which remained Christian under Georgian influences) until the fourteenth/fifteenth century, cf. Minorsky, *HSD*, pp. 155–6 and 99.

gradual disintegration of the Shevkalate at the turn of the sixteenth century.[1]

The Shevkal and his numerous kin – the Khans, and their children, the Mirzas and Beks or Beys – were the privileged class among the Kumukhs. The so-called 'Adat of the Beys', which was written down at a later period, sharply differentiated between this class and the mass of the people. The mounted detachments of the Khans and Beys were made up of *uzdens* – free 'cavaliers' comparable to the same category in Kabarda; there are references to 'the best propertied *uzdens*' (*sala uzdeny*).

There is only fragmentary information about the working population. Russian sources refer to 'the black people' (*chernye lyudi*), 'the ploughland people', and the *yasyry*, who seem to have been prisoners taken in war – as in Kabarda. The term 'ploughland people' doubtless refers to the native enserfed peasantry – *chagars* or *rayyat*. The Kumukh *yasyry* included Russians, Michkizy (Chechens), Georgians, Cherkesses, and even people from Bukhara and Urgench in central Asia. Raids through the mountain defiles leading into Kakheti provided many captives who were employed as farm servants and shepherds and there must have been a marked strain of Georgian blood in many of the *auls* of Daghestan; but the mass remained the autochthonous 'black people', united in communities (*dzhamaaty*) which had conserved their tribal characteristics and *tukhum* (family) organization.[2]

In the lowlands round the mouth of the Sulak, the Shevkal

---

[1] Elisu (G. *Eliseni*) was the country bounded on the west by the lower Alazani, and on the north and south by its affluents, the Belokani and the Gishi – a country full of orchards and game, where silk, rice and cotton could be grown, Wak./Brosset, p. 309. It was a borderland between the Georgians and the Lesgians of Jari – 'a motley race', according to Reineggs/W., Vol. I, p. 201; and the Kakhian King doubtless found the exiled Krym Shevkal useful in restraining his countrymen.

[2] See *OI/PF/xv–xvii vv.*, pp. 824 ff.; and p. 824, n. 1, for refs. to nineteenth-century and current literature on political and social conditions in Daghestan; also *OID*, Vol. I, pp. 90–120.

was master of 'the best arable lands and hay-fields and of the fisheries'. A list of his receipts in kind gives a good picture of a relatively prosperous economy: cattle, sheep, bulls, rams, horses, buffaloes. Corn, butter, rice, honey and fish are also mentioned. Manufactures occur twice: felts and woollens, and fire-arms and gun-powder. (Some villages, like Kubachi, specialized in metal-work).

Conditions in Kaytakh were similar to those existing in the Shevkalate. Again, the succession to the position of *utsmi* lay among the elders of his kin and was subject to election. Powerful *beys* had their mounted 'tails' of *uẓdens*. But outlying communities in the higher mountains showed more independence than in Kumukh; and the 'Resolutions' of the Utsmi, written at the beginning of the seventeenth century reflect an undertone of resistance in the tribal communities against the 'feudal' pretensions of the *beys*. For the end of the sixteenth century, it is recorded that in the *magal* (community) of Urszhemil the inhabitants insulted the son of an Utsmi who 'had come to collect dues'.

In Avaria, the tradition of the patriarchal-tribal structure remained strong and the more remote districts villages were organized in free communities, often allied to neighbours, where the power of the Khans was virtually ignored.[1]

Apart from Derbent and the extreme south of Daghestan, there was little industrial or commercial activity. Even Derbent which, in the thirteenth and fourteenth centuries, had been a thriving port and centre for trade, was losing its lead to

[1] According to Reineggs/W., Vol. II, p. 230, many Avars served as mercenaries to neighbouring princes – as far south as Karabagh. In the eighteenth century, Omar Khan of the Avars lived very well in the only house in Daghestan with glazed windows. He ate off gold and silver plate and kept open house to all and sundry. While the common people paid no obeisance to the Beks or *Tschenk-ah* (members of the Khan's house born of mothers not of princely blood), they prostrated themselves before the prince, kissing the ground with head uncovered and, then, the sole of his foot, *ibid.*, p. 232.

Shemakha, Baku and Genzha. Although frequently interrupted by the Turko-Persian wars, an important trade-route traversed coastal Daghestan but its influence on local life was limited to the needs of the transit traffic. The production of small groups of artisans – who had flourished for centuries in some of the mountain villages – had attained a high degree of excellence, notably in rugs and arms, but output was inconsiderable in size and was consumed in local barter.[1]

Thus, throughout the mountain regions of Caucasia, a low level of production, the absence of towns, and sparse and difficult means of communication, tended to limit the formation of any effective political units. Various local 'semi-states' and tribes waged war from time to time with their neighbours and were ready to seek passing and uneasy alliances with the powerful empires to the north and south of the great range.

In the last quarter of the sixteenth century, as a recent Soviet historian has put it, the Russian state was following 'a firm and lively policy' in the northern Caucasus. This policy was intended to bar the Turks and Crimean Tartars from penetrating into Transcaucasia and Iran by the Caspian coastal route and, at the same time, to prevent the consolidation of any Turko-Crimean hegemony over the Circassians and Kabardans and the extension of the Sultan's influence over the Shevkal and the other Sunni communities of Daghestan. 'This policy of the Russian Government led to serious complications in Russo-Turkish and Russo-Crimean relations, and provoked those attacks, menacing to the Russian state, which were undertaken by the Crimean Khans against Moscow in 1571, 1572 and 1591.'[2] At the same time the development of political relations between the Caucasian peoples and the Russians contributed to the success of the eastern policy of

[1] For Derbent, see Commentary 9: 'Derbent and Baku'. For a recent survey of the handicrafts of Daghestan, see Kilchevskaya/Ivanov, *Khudozhestvennye promysly Dagestana*, Moskva, 1959, with numerous plates, also *OID*, Vol. i, pp. 74–89, 116–20.

[2] *OI/PF/xv–xvii vv.*, p. 835.

the Muscovite Tsars. In the 1550's this process accelerated the Russian assimilation of the Khanate of Astrakhan. It had a marked influence on the course of the long wars between the Turks and the Persians south of the main chain – an influence which, on the whole, favoured the Persians and made possible the restoration of the Safavid control of Shirvan and Georgia in the first decades of the seventeenth century. Again, by blocking out the Turks from Daghestan and the western littoral of the Caspian, Russians and Persians ensured the continuity of the trade route from the mouth of the Volga to the great textile centres in Shemakha and Tabriz.

9. THE GEORGIAN KINGDOMS

South of the main chain, the Little Caucasus (Suram or Meskhian Mountains, G. Likhis-mta) forms a ridge, 1500 to 1800 metres in height, thrown off at a right angle and linking the Great Caucasus with the Armenian Highlands. To the west of the Suram Mountains, the wide basin of the Rioni (ancient Phasis) is an emerged part of the bed of the Black Sea and belongs to the climatic and natural world of the Pontus. It is heavily forested even today, and marshy and unhealthy along the shoreline. Wakhusht, himself a native of Kartli, is lyrical on the beauty of this fabled land of Aea.[1] East of the Suram Mountains, the rivers Kura and Aras (Araks), flowing through the mountains of central Georgia and eastern Armenia, reach the arid steppe of Azerbaijan which forms as does the Kalmuck steppe to the north of the main chain, a part of the Aralo-Caspian Depression. From the southern slopes of Caucasus, the Kura (G. Mtkvari) is fed by numerous affluents – Ksani, Aragvi, Yori, Alazani – which from early times nourished a thriving pastoral and agricultural life. Great mineral riches – copper, silver, lead, iron and gold and lapis-lazuli – stimulated

[1] Wak./Brosset, pp. 341 ff.

trade and urban life; and from the first millennium B.C. varied cultures had flourished in the sunny valleys sheltered by the great chain. In the Middle Ages, the Kingdom of Georgia (*Sakartvelos samepo*) had been a famous state. Weakened by the Mongol conquest in the thirteenth century and further enfeebled by the campaigns of Tamerlane at the turn of the fourteenth century, the united kingdom had, during the fifteenth century, gradually dissolved into a congeries of contending principalities. There were three kingdoms now: Kartli, the core of the former united Kingdom in central and northern Georgia with the old capital at Tiflis (*G.* Tbilisi); Kakheti, north of the Kura and comprising the valleys of the Iori and the Alazani – with a rather rustic capital at Gremi; and, west of the Suram Mountains, Imereti – where kings maintained a court in the antique and partly ruinous cathedral town of Kutais (*G.* Kutaissi) – which even in Strabo's time had flourished as Kotatissium. Further to the north-west, were the sovereign principalities (*G. samtavro*) of Mingrelia (*G.* Samegrelo) with a centre at Zugdidi; and Abkhazia (*G.* Abkhazeti) – where the princes had no fixed urban abode. In the south-west, over the uplands between the river Chorokh and the sources of the Kura, lay the famed 'Meskhian land' of the Georgian poets, Samtskhe, called also Sa-atabag-o, 'the land of the Atabeg'. The small principality of Guria occupied the coastal hills and the marshy foreshore of the Black Sea between the borders of Samtskhe and Imereti.[1]

Deterioration in social conditions had been taking place during the political disintegration of the centralized monarchy. The new and weak principalities were shared out in seignories (*G. satavado*) where ungoverned lords had increased their

[1] For history of Georgia, see Brosset, *HG, passim,* more recently Allen, *HGP*; Berdzenishvili, Dzhavakhishvili, Dzhanashia, *Istoriya Gruzii, Chast* I, Tbilisi, 1946 (all published); Manvelishvili, *Histoire de Géorgie,* Paris, 1951; D. M. Lang, *The Georgians,* London, 1966.

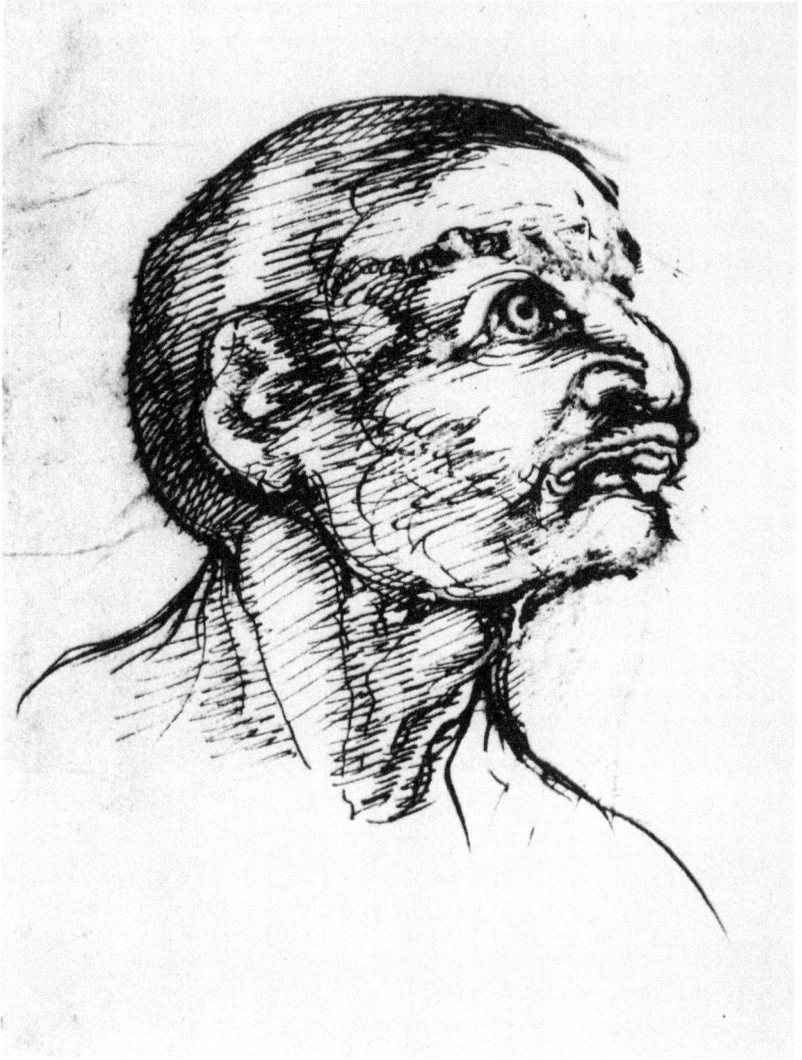

3. A Georgian (?Mingrelian) peasant type. After Castelli.

feudal rights over other classes. During the fifteenth and sixteenth centuries the class of individual free farmers disappeared.
The term *glekhi* which originally meant a farmer, whether free
or not, became synonymous with *qma*, serf. In documents of
the period, serfs are designated by various names according to
the nature of their obligations. There were *medzhinibi*, stable-
men; *medzhogore*, kennel-men; *moinale*, literally, serving men;
mezutkhe (from the word *zutkhe*, a sturgeon) who caught stur-
geons for the lord; and *moagape*, who were dedicated to the
preparations for funerals and other chores connected with the
service of the church.

The obligations of the peasantry tended to increase with the
passing of the years; different forms of forced labour became
customary and the payment of quit-rent was enforced. Forced
labour, which once had taken up only a small number of days
during the serf's year, had, by the fifteenth century become
'continual work'; and the measures of weight and capacity
which served for the assessment of quit-rent in kind increased
from ten to twelve times between the fourteenth and eighteenth
centuries.

A valuable historical document which reflects the social and
economic conditions of the working people is preserved in the
form of 'The Great Register' (*Davtar*) of peasants belonging to
the Abkhazian (West Georgian) Patriarchate in the sixteenth
century. From this document the weight and diversity of the
taxes and obligations borne by the peasantry become clear. The
Register enumerated these obligations village by village and
by taxed areas. In the composition of quit-rent in kind there
were *saklave* – i.e. 'cattle to be slaughtered', fowls, fish, piglets,
eggs, butter, cheese, curds, salt, garlic, wine, wood and hay.
Some of these offerings were required seasonally for some
special feast-day. Thence derived the various names for the
offerings: *samachrobo saklave*, cattle to be slaughtered for the
estate owner at the time of the grape-harvest; *sakuliero*, dues

for 'butter week'; *sakachobo*, dues to be collected at the time when small horned cattle were calving; *sapurobo*, a collection made on occasions when the lord was intending to give a feast. The *sastumro* or entertainment of the estate administrators and provision of accommodation for them was an additional and disliked burden on the peasantry. The heaviest part of the forced labour is described as *mushaoba* and *tvirti*, literally, the burden, the load, the weight. This seems to imply the porterage of heavy materials, stone, timber, etc., at the behest of the lord. Under *mushaoba* was included, also, harvesting, hay-making, etc. The carters' and waggoners' forced labour was well known during the period of the Mongol hegemony under the name of *saiame*. Other obligations mentioned in the Register are *lashkroba*, military service; and *mgzavroba*, literally journey, implying the obligation of the peasant to accompany his lord when he was travelling around.

Under the conditions of a restricted feudal economy, with its low level in the production of commodities, the receipts of the feudal lords of Georgia were largely made up of payments in kind, as well as by forced labour – all of which dues were covered by the term *begara*.

The different categories of peasants in Kakheti are indicated in a decree issued by King Alexander II at the end of the sixteenth century in which regulations of a traditional type are laid down for the maintenance of the so-called *ulupa* in favour of the *mo'uravni*, who were provincial prefects directly responsible to the crown. As the document shows, the occasion for the issue of the decree was a collective complaint 'of all, every single one', of the inhabitants of the village of Chiauri against the mo'uravi Goshpar on account of his 'endless violence and lawlessness'. It was stressed that the weight of the *ulupa* ('the *ulupa* business') was the most important subject of the complaint. In his decree the King laid down that the assessment of the tax-payers was to be made in accordance with their circumstances. The document distinguishes four kinds of tax-payer. The first were those most easily able to pay – 'powerful people' – who should pay their full share of the *ulupa*. The last category covers indigent, beggarly people, *beʒmiskini*, 'very poor men' (a word also current in Tabriz).

In the towns of mediaeval Georgia, the citizens (*mokalake*) had attained a certain status. In Shota Rusthaveli's thirteenth-century poem, *The man in the panther's skin*, there is evidence that merchants had no little influence and social standing at court. Organized in guilds, the merchants and artisans were of very mixed origins: indeed, Georgians were outnumbered by Armenians, Jews and Persians. The perennial Turkish and Persian invasions of the sixteenth century completed the ruin of the older towns of central Georgia – Tiflis, Mtskheta, Gori, Ali and Suram – which had already suffered severely during Tamerlane's campaigns at the turn of the fourteenth century. Merchants and tradesmen tended to quit the older towns and to move to districts which were less exposed to the recurrent movements of armies. Other towns gained in standing, such as Khopi, Anaklia and Rukhi in western Georgia, and Akhaltsikhe and Akhalkalaki in Samtskhe. All these were in the zone of Ottoman political influence and of Pontic commerce. In the east, in Kakheti, Zagem, Gremi, Areshi (Bazar) and Telavi began to touch prosperity: they were centres of the silk and wine and dye producing districts which fed Shemakha and Tabriz and the Iranian economy.[1]

[1] Georgian social conditions in the Middle and later Middle Ages, with references to Georgian terminology, have been treated in Allen, *HGP*, pp. 221–90, where extensive use is made of the work of I. Javakhishvili, *Kartveli Eris Istoria* (several vols. in various editions), Kakabadze, Takaishvili and other Georgian scholars – in the interpretation of whom the author was indebted to A. Gugushvili. A basic work, with many curious details, is Wakhusht's *Geographical description of Georgia*, particularly the Introduction (see the editions of both Brosset and Janashvili). A recent summary, with useful refs. to Georgian technical terms is to be

A recent Soviet historian has tried to detect the elements of a 'class struggle' developing in the towns and villages of sixteenth-century Georgia; and certainly the social and economic undertones of Georgian history have been rather overlooked by earlier generations of historians. It was natural that landowners should try to compensate themselves for the losses which external enemies and their own political dissensions had brought upon Georgian life by intensifying their exploitation of the lower orders. But the measures introduced by the feudal lords only exacerbated social contradictions. There was an increase in the number of runaway peasants (which was, equally, a phenomenon of contemporary life in the Muscovite dominions – there tending to recruit the numbers of the 'free' Cossack communities along the Dniepr, the Don and the Yaik rivers). These fugitive Georgian peasants were called *akrili*, from the word *akra*, to flee, to run away. The result, in the long run, was a number of deserted, run-down or escheated estates (in Georgian, *naokhari, partakhti,* etc.) which passed out of cultivation and, often, were grazed by groups of Turkoman nomads or gypsies.[1] The periods of desolation and economic decline became protracted. The royal finances dwindled. Towns and markets fell into decay. Capacity for defence, particularly in Kartli and Imereti, became weak; and the authority of the central power – which under the mediaeval Bagratid kings had been quite complex and extensive – was undermined.

In 1555, the Ottoman Sultan and the Persian Shah came to an agreement under which their respective zones of influence and exploitation in Georgia were clearly defined. *Likhtimereti* (i.e. 'the country on *that* side of the Mountains of Likhi' – or

found in *OI/PF/xv–xvii vv.*, pp. 836–9. For economic conditions in Georgia in the later Middle Ages, see Allen, *HGP*, pp. 321–58.

[1] For the Caucasian gypsies, see K. P. Patkanov, *Tsygane: neskolko slov o narechiyakh zakavkazskikh tsygan: Bosha i Karachi*, Spb., 1887; also Karst, *Origines Mediterraneae (OM)*, pp. 381–4, 533 ff.

Suram), together with western Samtskhe rested with the Turks. *Likhtamereti* ('the country on *this* side of the Mountains of Likhi'), with eastern Samtskhe, was recognized as the Persian sphere of influence. The old latitudinal unity of Georgia 'from Pitsunda to Derbent', out of which had grown the united kingdom of the Middle Ages, thus disappeared; and the new political agreement affirmed, in economic terms, the 'Pontic' orientation of western Georgia, looking towards Istanbul and the Crimea and subject to the maritime supremacy of the Turks on the Black Sea; and the Caspian orientation of the eastern provinces, dependent on the 'silk routes' to Shemakha and Tabriz.

Following the successful Turkish campaigns begun in 1578 and the period of civil and dynastic strife throughout Iran, the whole of Georgia passed to the Turks under the Ottoman-Safavid treaty of 1590. However, the peace of 1612 restored the zones of influence agreed under the Turko-Persian treaty of 1555.

During the last half of the sixteenth century, following the treaty of 1555, conditions developed in diverse ways in the separated kingdoms and principalities of the old kingdom. Throughout the sixteenth century, Kartli, the core of the old kingdom, was passing through a period of severe economic and political decline. The continuous invasions of the Turks and Persians, and the painful circumstances of growing social oppression led to progressive depopulation. There was nothing to parallel the massive deportations of tens of thousands of the Kakhian peasantry to Persia by Shah Abbas I in the first decades of the seventeenth century; but in Kartli, in the sixteenth century, the sale of serfs to the Turks and Persians was rampant. Despite the protests of the monarchs and the Church, the nobility did not hesitate to participate in this profitable traffic. Akhaltsikhe, seat of the Georgian atabegs of Samtskhe who were often in close relation with the Turks, was the principal mart. Anarchic conditions, and the dread of slavery, encouraged great numbers of the population to take flight to the northern mountainous and forested districts of Kartli and into Kakheti. In the 1540s only a third of the former population remained in south-eastern Kartli; and in the 1560s the eastern part – the rich mining district along the valley of the Debeda along which also ran the route to Tiflis – was utterly deserted.[1] Tiflis, the historic capital and commercial centre for all Trans-caucasia, had already as early as the end of the fifteenth century become, according to the statements of the Venetian ambassadors to Uzun Hasan, a miserable little town although its merchants still managed to sustain a lively trade.

Kartli, in the sixteenth century, was divided into a number of seigniories (*sa-tavad-o*), some of which were ecclesiastical and others secular. The first were under the control of the patriarch and the bishops; the latter were ruled by the heads (*tavad-n-i*) of the great feudal clans (*gwari*). Junior members of the family of the ruling *tavadi* – brothers, uncles and cousins – all had their own properties where they fortified themselves in castles and towers. There was a distinction between their personal possessions (*sakutari, sataviso*) and property which was regarded as inherent in the clan (*sakhaso*), such as ploughlands with dependent peasants, pastures, herds, forests, orchards and vineyards. In time of war these junior members of the ruling family had to bring into the field an agreed number of fighting men who were rallied under the direct command of the *tavadi*.

Bloody strife frequently broke out among neighbouring *tavadni*; as a result the clan lands were sometimes broken up or reduced in size. The murder or exile of the feudal lords and the slaughter or deportation of the peasants dependent on them

---

[1] Cf. Allen, *HGP*, p. 59 for references to mineral riches in copper, lead, gold, lapis-lazuli and porphyry in this region. See also A. A. Yessen and B. E. Degen-Kovalevski, 'Iz istorii drevney metallurgii Kavkaza', *Izv. Gos. Akademii Istorii Mat. Kultury*, vyp. 120.

were commonplace events. The stronger the *tavadi*, the more contemptuous was he inclined to be of royal authority. The entry of a daughter or a sister into the *harim* of the Shah or the Sultan (as in the case of the Shalikashvilis and the Jaquelis in Samtskhe) would encourage their insolence and their opportunities for political manoeuvre. On the other hand, the lesser seigniories, or junior rivals of ruling *tavadni*, would be inclined to seek justice or protection from the King.

The upper strata of the feudal lords (the *didebul-n-i* – a word which may perhaps be rendered literally as 'grandees') were divided into several grades which are cited in detail by Wakhusht.[1] Pride of place was given to antiquity of origin but wealth and political influence counted for much and the rise of some of the more powerful families was relatively recent. For instance, at the turn of the sixteenth century, the Eristavis of the Aragvi were 'new men'; Giorgi Saakadze, the most significant figure in Georgian politics in the first decades of the seventeenth century, was a petty noble of obscure origin. In Kakheti, the Andronikashvilis claimed descent from the Byzantine emperor, Andronicos II Komnenos; and the Cholokashvilis, closely allied with the blood of the Kakhian Bagratids, upheld a family ascendancy through nearly four centuries; on the other hand the Chavchavadzes seem to have emerged from the ranks of the lesser gentry only in the eighteenth century.

The stronger the seigniory of a *tavadi*, the greater the number of his small-holding vassals (*aznaur-n-i*). But the largest number of *aznaurni* were in direct allegiance to the crown. The king's *aznaurni* carried out the same duties, whether for Church or prince, but they were in a comparatively privileged position and could attract the personal favour of the king – as in the case of Giorgi Saakadze. All the positions at court, except the highest which were hereditary, were open to the king's *aznaurni*.

---

[1] Wak./Brosset, pp. xxix ff. Frequently the words *mtavar-n-i* or *tavad-n-i*, heads, chieftains, lords, are used instead of *didebul-n-i*.

The *aznaurni* of the feudal lords had not the same opportunities.

Up to the 1570s, the Kartlians had carried on a desperate and pertinacious struggle to maintain their independence. David VIII (1505–15), Luarsab I (1531–58), and Simon I (1558–69) were real national leaders and did credit to the ancient House of Bagrationi. But the long wars exhausted the strength of Kartli and, following the Turko-Persian partition of 1555, many of the *tavadni* came to favour submission to the Safavids. In 1569 Simon had been taken prisoner by the Persians and his brother David who had become a Muslim was installed as ruler in Tiflis under the style of Da'ud Khan. Weak and unpopular, David had never been able to consolidate his position as a Persian viceroy; and in 1578, when the Turks invaded the Persian zone of Transcaucasia, the harassed Shah, Muhammad Khudabanda, released Simon from internment in Shiraz and sent him into Kartli to wage war against the Turks. During the following three years, in guerrilla operations, Simon was able to clear most of the country of the invaders who had difficulty in maintaining communications with their remaining strongpoints at Dmanisi, Lori, Tiflis and Gori. Although an opium addict, ailing and neurotic, Simon was skilful in the field, of an acute political intelligence and a soaring ambition. He aimed at the reconstitution of the old united kingdom. Between 1582 and 1588, he was intervening in Samtskhe where he was able to establish his son-in-law, Manuchar, as Atabeg. But his attempt to conquer Western Georgia ended in disaster when he was defeated in a forest battle by the Dadiani of Mingrelia. His last and costly triumph was the capture of the Turkish fortress at Gori after a long siege (1599). In the following year he was taken prisoner by the Turks in an insignificant skirmish and ended his days as a prisoner in the Seven Towers in Istanbul. Although the Russian ambassadors never encountered King Simon, his formidable but erratic personality casts its shadow over their negotiations in Kakheti and Kartli at the turn of the century.

During the sixteenth century, both situation and events favoured the more easterly Kingdom of Kakheti, which between the eleventh and the fifteenth centuries had been no more than a province of the old united kingdom of Georgia.[1] Kakheti was off the main route of Turkish military expansion; and the kings (of a collateral line of the Bagratids), more prudent and less gallant than their kinsmen in Kartli, pursued a policy of temporizing between Turks and Persians.

Again, Kakheti had the advantage over other parts of Georgia of flanking the great Ghilan–Shemakha–Astrakhan 'silk route'. The Kakhian kings, together with their nobles, were able to participate in this trade which had attained an international character. Jewish colonies in Kakheti were of very ancient origin and the activities of their skilful and industrious merchants were seconded by the considerable number of Armenians and Persians who were settled in the market towns. There was a substantial export trade in raw silk, vegetable dyes, wines, horses, sheep, and also rugs to Shirvan and Azerbaijan. This local prosperity encouraged the movement of population from the harassed lands of Kartli.

Moreover, the royal power in Kakheti was stronger than in other parts of Georgia during the sixteenth century. Originally rebels themselves against the monarchy in Tiflis, the earlier kings of the Kakhian line proved shrewd and ruthless in their dealings with their own *tavadni*. The third king, Giorgi II (1511–13), after his village coronation at Bodbe, had massacred his leading nobles whom he suspected of intriguing with the Kartlian king for a reunion of the old kingdom. He

---

[1] For the earlier history of Kakheti up to the end of the eleventh century, see Minorsky, *HSD*, *passim*. The kingly name, Akhsartān, common in the local dynasty, was of Alan origin, *ibid*, p. 67, n. 1. The kings bore the title of *koriskus* ('chorepiskopus'); ibid., p. 162. This may indicate dual monarchic and priestly functions.

proceeded to abolish the system of hereditary eristavates and named from among his own lesser men provincial governors (*mo'urav-n-i*) whose tenure of office was dependent on the royal will. In the Kakhian army, the traditional four 'banners' (*sadrosho*) of the old kingdom were organized but they were placed under the command of bishops instead of the great territorial lords (*eristav-n-i*). To the authority of these episcopal commanders both the *mo'uravni* and the *tavadni* had to submit. Wakhusht states that by these means the Kakhian kings 'won over to themselves a number of true men' – in other words they aimed at securing the attachment of the lesser gentry (*aznaurni*).

Other measures introduced by the Kakhian kings imply a strengthening of the royal power and, at the same time, an intensification of the conditions of serfdom. These measures aimed at the regulation of the obligations of the peasantry to the royal power and its representatives. The peasants were divided into four categories: (i) those who paid the full tax to the *mo'uravi*; (ii) those who paid half the tax; (iii) those who paid a quarter; and (iv) the *bezmiskini*, the indigent who paid no tax.[1] Under the conditions of a firm and subtle administration and a temporizing external policy which avoided the devastating incursions of the Muslim powers which were ruining contemporary Kartli, life in Kakheti attained a certain stability during the sixteenth century. Only the internal feuds within the royal family and the raids of the mountaineers from Daghestan which broke out after the death of the cunning old

---

[1] '*Bezmiskini*': It is interesting to recall the word 'mesquin' in English and French, in the sense of 'mean, sordid, shabby'. One is tempted to associate the word in its present context with the ancient Mesks (*G.* plur. *Meskhni*). Cf. also mediaeval Italian, *Mongrello* (Mingrelian) for 'fool', Allen, *HGP*, p. 342, citing Josafat Barbaro. The name of a former tribe or people which has sunk into the ethnic underworld is often used in a pejorative sense; cf. 'Welsher' for a man who absconds; Ickeny (dial. 'donkey') – from (?) ancient Iceni; and in Russian, *kholop* or *smerd* for a serf – both originally ethnic terms. Also *Dago*, supposed to be a corruption from Diego, the Spanish equivalent of James.

King Levan (1520–74) provoked some recurrent strife. Wakhusht could write that:

'Kakheti was so thickly peopled that a wild animal was scarcely to be found, so that Alexander who had a passion for the chase would say "Would to God that Kakheti were devastated in my time. I should then have game in plenty." '

'That was what happened', comments Wakhusht, 'under his grandson, Taymurazi, who had never, poor devil, the time to hunt.'[1]

Despite the reputation for toughness of the men of some particular districts, the Kakhians proved softer and less resolute in war than their Kartlian neighbours who followed the brilliant Simon in his guerrilla operations and, in the 1580s, rose in mass against the Turkish occupation. 'As a result of mixing with the Persians', comments Wakhusht, himself a Kartlian, 'the Kakhians had taken them for a model in eating and drinking and in giving themselves to a soft life and an improper affectation in dressing after the Persian manner. In this way they gradually abandoned their Georgian customs and introduced those of the Persians.'[2]

10. EARLY RELATIONS OF KAKHETI WITH RUSSIA

After the capture of Astrakhan, Levan had had some intercourse with the Muscovite court in 1558; and the Russians were not slow to interest themselves in the Christian Orthodox kingdoms beyond the great chain of the Caucasus.[3] It was about this time that *The Tale of Queen Dinara* – a mythical interpretation of the great Georgian Queen Tamar – spread in Russia. Harassed by his feud with the Shevkal, who had been an ally of his father, and stimulated by the civil strife in Persia

---

[1] Wakhusht's *Histoire de Kakheth* in Brosset, *HG*, Vol. ii/i, pp. 154-5.
[2] Ibid., p. 153.
[3] Tatishvili, *Gruziny v Moskve*, p. 23.

after 1576, Alexander II (1574–1604) began to favour more intimate links with Moscow. As Brosset has observed, relations of which no record survives probably developed between the Kakhian kings and Moscow during the three decades which intervened between Levan's gesture in 1558 and the first record of a Russian reconnaissance in Kakheti made by I. D. Rusin in 1586. On his return to Moscow, Rusin brought with him as ambassadors from Alexander, the Greek monk Kiril Xanthopoulos and the Circassian Khurshit. There can be little doubt that these two men had been selected for their knowledge of the Greek and Russian languages and, perhaps, they had earlier been in Moscow. On 11 April of the following year (1587), the Georgian ambassadors left Moscow, accompanied by a Russian mission led by Rodion Petrovich Birkin. It was only on 3 July that they reached Astrakhan. After a difficult journey along the Terek and the Sunzha and over the mountains they finally came into Kakheti and were received by King Alexander on 26 August. Between 3 and 28 September, Birkin had no less than nine audiences of the King who proved reluctant to kiss the cross in token of vassalage to the Tsar except on conditions which were not acceptable to the Russian mission.[1]

In Persia, during the preceding two years, the situation had been deteriorating. Co-operating with the Ottomans, the Uzbek Khan Abdullah had taken Merv and Herat in 1585 and had overrun Khurasan. In the following year Özdemiroghlu Osman Pasha had taken Tabriz. The Russian *voyvodes* in Siberia were able to relieve the pressure from the east by supporting the Kazakhs against Abdullah; and in the west, over against the Crimea, in 1587, the Russians sent a Crimean pretender, Murat Giray, accompanied by two *voyvodes*, to Astrakhan where he began recruiting an army of Don Cossacks,

[1] For these early missions, see Brosset, *EC/BHP/*II, Nos. 14–15, cols. 211–28; Belokurov, pp. 10–45.

Cherkesses and Nogays of the Great Horde with the intention of pursuing his designs on the Crimean khanate. The Sultan's *divan* in Istanbul had taken seriously these moves for indirect Russian intervention and, during September 1587, while Birkin was negotiating with Alexander, it was decided to launch an attack against Astrakhan for the coming spring.[1] The Shevkal, Kara-Musal, a Sunni, was known to favour the Ottoman Sultan against the Safavids, his former Shi'a overlords, and the presence of Turkish troops in Derbent strengthened his resolution. Alexander was anxious lest he be trapped between the Turkish forces in Kartli and Shirvan and the Kumukhs and Avars descending over the high passes of the main ridge of Caucasus. He was insisting that the Russians should attack the Shevkal and build a permanent fortress on the Andi-koysu which should relieve pressure from the north-east against his own dominion. Birkin pointed out that such an establishment would require a standing garrison of 2,500 men and call for an annual provision of 25,000 *chetverts* of grain; he wanted to know whether Alexander was prepared to cover the costs. Alexander offered an annual supply of stallions and silk but pleaded poverty and protested that he could not supply rugs and woven fabrics, since these were made not in Kakheti but in Persia. Finally the King agreed to a formula for kissing the cross; at the same time stressing his need for urgent help against the Shevkal.

It was now so late in the year that Birkin found that a return over the mountains would be impracticable and decided to spend the winter in Kakheti.

On 15 October 1587, a Persian envoy, Hoja Mahmud, arrived at Zagem to announce the deposition of Muhammad Khudabanda and the accession of the young Shah Abbas I. On 20 December, a Lithuanian from Kiev, Evetz Filipko Andreyev, a prisoner of the Turks who had escaped to the

[1] See Allen, *PTP*, p. 36.

Persians in Kazvin, presented himself to Birkin in Zagem. He gave interesting details of the struggle between the Spanish and Turkish missions in Kazvin to influence the policy of the new Shah. The Shah, with that saturnine humour which was to develop with the years, received the Spanish and Ottoman ambassadors at the same time and their suites came to blows. In the end, the Shah resumed hostilities against the Turks. Alexander continued in an awkward situation. On 25 February 1588, a Persian ambassador, Jamshid Khan, visited Alexander and took the opportunity to have conversations with the Birkin mission. Two months later, a Turkish *chaush* arrived at Zagem to demand free passage for Turkish troops through Kakheti to Derbent and Baku and provisions sufficient for a regiment. Relying on the potential support of Persians and Russians, Alexander refused. In the early summer, Birkin seems to have left Kakheti, for he reached Astrakhan on 9 July 1588 and Moscow on 16 October. His mission had taken just over eighteen months.

Three Kakhian ambassadors accompanied Birkin on his return to Moscow: the Greek Kiril Xanthopoulos, the Cherkess Khurshit, and the Kakhian royal *aznauri*, Kaplan Vachnadze, who was in the close confidence of the King. With them were the envoys of Prince Alkas of Little Kabarda and of Shikh Mirza of the Okok (Chechens). On 31 October 1588, the party was received in audience by Tsar Fedor Ivanovich. In attendance was his brother-in-law, the powerful boyar, Boris Godunov, Lord Lieutenant of Kazan, who, both before and after his own accession to the throne, was to show an intense interest in Russian policy in the Caucasus and Siberia. Two Tartar interpreters were present – an indication, as Brosset suggests, that Turkish was the most convenient language in which the Caucasians could communicate their views to the Russians.

On 27 February 1589, the ambassadors were received by the

Treasurer of the Empire who informed them that the Tsar was ready to take the Kakhian King under his protection; that he would send priests, master craftsmen and artisans of all sorts, falcons and falconers – for the King particularly favoured the noble sport – and an ambassador, Prince Semen Zvenigorodski, accompanied by the dyak Torkh Antonov.[1] Questioned as to the best route to follow, the Georgian ambassadors replied that the way through Circassia was long and difficult and that it would be shorter to cross the lands of the Shevkal but that a strong escort would be necessary. They seem to have implied that the escort should be sufficiently numerous for garrisons to be left at certain strong points in the Shevkal's country but they were told that the principal intention would be to intimidate the Shevkal and compel him to give a son or brother as hostage – a normal Russian practice among the Circassian princelings. To this Kaplan answered that any such guarantee from the Shevkal would be illusory since he had as many sons as dogs and that to make sure of him it would be as well to plant a garrison in his capital: that with 20,000 men the Russians could finish off the 12,000 men whom the Shevkal could bring into the field. (The events of 1594, when the Russians were roughly handled by the Shevkal were to prove the frivolous optimism of the Georgian view.)

Asked for particulars as to the best route through Daghestan, Kaplan gave details which remain rather obscure:

From Terek-town to Tyumen . . . 1 day on horseback, 2 days on foot.
From Tyumen to Tarku . . . 2 days on horseback, 4 days on foot.
From Tarku to Kafyr-Kumukh . . . 1 day on horseback, 2 days on foot.
From Kafyr-Kumukh to Kozanich . . . 1 day on horseback, 2 days on foot.

[1] For the Georgian mission to Moscow of 1588–9, see Brosset, *EC/BHP* Vol. II, Nos. 14–15, cols. 229–33; Belokurov, pp. 53–61.

From Kozanich to Kazi-Kumukh Safurski – a place already held
by Alexander, 4 good days on horseback.
From Safurski into Kakheti, 2 days on horseback.[1]

In all, 11 days on horseback or 22 days on foot: this calcula-
tion, which made no allowance for delays or for the slowness of
a convoy loaded with baggage, was presumably based on the
time made by couriers exchanged between Alexander and the
Shevkal. Brosset finds difficulty in identifying the places mentioned on this route. It would seem to have followed the valley
of the Andi-koysu. In the high alps north-west of the Andi-
koysu, Reineggs places the Gaifur (*Kafir*, pagan, as distinguished by the Arabs from the Muslim *Gazi*, victorious)
Kumukh. This district is more than a day's ride from Tarku;
but within that span, Bronevski, on his early nineteenth-century
map, places a village of Kafyr-Kumukh which may well have
been Kaplan's first stage from Tarku. The difference can be
explained by a winter *kishlak* of some part of the Kafyr-
Kumukh on the slope towards the Caspian. Kozanich has not
been identified, but Brosset recalls the name of Khozanos, the
mythical son of Lekos, eponymous progenitor of the Laks, who
gave his name to the district of Khozaniketi. Reineggs (the
transcriptions of whose place-names by his editor were very
faulty) shows on his map as south of the Kafyr-Kumukh a tribe
called *Zaetaehaer*, otherwise unknown under this name. They
'reckon about a thousand families' and 'speak a peculiar
language'. It is possible that these people may be identified with
the 'Safurski Kumukh' of the Russian sources. At any rate,
tracks over the main ridge of Caucasus, west of the massif of
Bogos, lead down into Kakheti to the north-east of Alaverdi
and Gremi.[2]

---

[1] Brosset, *EC/BHP* Vol. II, Nos. 14–15, col. 230; Belokurov, pp. 58–9.

[2] Reineggs/W. does not show Kozanich on his map, but refers to
Kasanisch as being the residence of the brother of Dish-siz Muhammad
('toothless Muhammad'), the governor of Kazi-Kumukh in the latter part

Kaplan also proposed an alternative route – from the Sunzha, through the lands of the Okok and the 'Black Prince' and across 'Avaria'. The Avar-koysu, indeed, runs south-west of the Andi-koysu and would have been even more dangerous and impracticable than the first alternative. It is probable that the route by the Argun affluent of the Sunzha was intended. This, by difficult tracks west of Tebulos-mta, gives access to Pshaveti and the upper valley of the Aragvi. Eventually the new mission stuck to the route along the Terek and the Sunzha which Rusin and Birkin had used before them.

After a farewell audience of the Tsar on 22 March 1589, Kaplan Vachnadze left Moscow on 18 April. On the 23rd of the same month, Prince Semen Zvenigorodski, with a numerous staff, took the road to Georgia: his adventures are the subject of our first text.

11. SHIRVAN AND AZERBAIJAN: THE PERSIAN PRESENCE IN CAUCASIA[1]

Already in 1587, following the victories of Abdullah Khan in Khurasan and of Özdemiroghlu Osman at Tabriz, Shah

of the eighteenth century (Vol. 1, pp. 109–10). For Khozaniketi, see Wak./Brosset, p. 425. It is worth noting that there is a Kochanis near Çölemerik in Hakâri where, at the end of the last century, the Nestorian inhabitants had fair complexions with blue eyes but raven hair (cf. D. C. Hills, *My travels in Turkey*, London, 1964, p. 235, citing Lord Warkworth, *Notes from a diary in Asiatic Turkey*, London, 1898, pp. 148–9). Cf. also the homonyms mount Shat (a shoulder of mount Kazbeк) and mount Şat in Hakâri, (Hills, pp. 160–5); Galiate (Hills's map, pp. 146–7) and Georgian Gvileti (Genko, p. 697); Medi (Hills's map) and Chechen Mida (Genko, p. 707); Ingush *mat* for shoulder or ridge, Mate Merza in Hakâri, and Albanian (Illyrian) Matija.

[1] For early history of Shirvan and Azerbaijan, see Minorsky, *HSD* and his *Studies in Caucasian history*, London, 1953; also his article in *EI*, 2nd ed., under 'Ādharbaydjān'. In *IA*, A. Z. V. Togan's article under 'Azerbaycan' and M. Fuat Köprülü's under 'Azeri' are long and original contributions. In *BSE*, under 'Azerbaydzhanskaya SSR', B. Gurko-Kryazhin's treatment of the historical section is superficial; but some useful Soviet works have recently appeared: Efendiyev, *Obrazovaniye*

Muhammad Khudabanda, in the last months of his harassed reign, had sent a certain Andi Beg to Moscow with the offer to cede the towns of Derbent, Shemakha and Baku to the Russians in return for aid against the Turks. The boyar I. V. Godunov had taken advantage of this situation to break to the Persian envoy that the Kakhian King Alexander had placed himself under the protection of the Tsar. He had added that the Shevkal had asked the Turks to prevent the Russians from building a fortress on the Terek and had imprisoned his own son, Alkas Mirza, for giving convoy to the embassies of Rodion Birkin and the monk Kiril. Andi Beg had replied that one could rely on the word and the honesty of King Alexander but not on the Shevkal – even when he offered hostages from among his numerous sons. Late in 1587 Andi Beg returned to Persia in the company of a Russian ambassador, Grigori Vasilchikov, who had instructions to ask the Shah to force the Shevkal and the Kakhian king to stand firm against the Turks. At Astrakhan they got the news of the accession of Shah Abbas I; and in Kazvin Vasilchikov communicated his instructions to Ferhat Khan, the Georgian favourite of the new monarch. 'The Shah confirmed from his mouth rather than from the depth of his heart' the engagements into which his father had entered.

On taking leave of Vasilchikov, who was accompanied on his return to Moscow by another Persian embassy which included Andi Beg, the Shah gave assurances of his friendly disposition towards the Tsar and stated that he himself was leaving for Shirvan. The Russians informed the Shah that the Tsar, at that very time, was sending troops to the Terek with orders to

Aʒerbaydʒhanskogo Gosudarstva Sefevidov v nachale xvi veka, Baku, 1961; Shakhmaliyeva (ed.), *Puteshestvenniki ob Aʒerbaydʒhane,* Baku, 1961, Vol. I – covering travellers' accounts from the sixteenth to the eighteenth centuries; Guliev, *Bibliografiya Etnografii Aʒerbaydʒhana, Chast* I, Baku, 1962. A new work of original research is Kütükoğlu's *Osmanli-Iran Siyasi Münâsebetleri* ('Ottoman-Iranian Political Relations') Vol. I, 1578–90, Istanbul, 1962.

prevent any expedition from the Crimea penetrating into the Persian provinces from the north. 'The Shah was not, in fact, very pleased with all this, but as the arrangements had been agreed with his father the ambassadors declared that their master would welcome the establishment on the Terek of a friendly power.'[1]

An understanding of the conditions of the Safavid state and of the nature of the Persian presence in the Caucasus is necessary to an appreciation of the events further described.

The Safavid state, which represented in political form the essential geographical unity of the Iranian plateau enclosed within its peripheral ranges, was markedly different in character from the Ottoman and Muscovite empires. These two latter organisms were military bureaucracies which had inherited many of the political and administrative traditions of the Byzantine empire: each had been influenced in varying degrees by the ideas and techniques of the Mediterranean and west European world. But the centres of these two empires were a long way from the Ponto-Caspian isthmus. A thousand miles of river communications – only newly opened up – separated Moscow from the garrisons along the Terek. A comparable distance lay between the great barracks and shipyards round the Bosporus and the remote and unpopular commands in Erzurum, Tiflis, Azov (Azak) and Derbent – whither only ambitious soldiers were willing to go to try their luck with a view to later promotions to the more lucrative and agreeable governorships in the western provinces of the Ottoman empire.

By contrast with its neighbours the Safavid empire remained, in essence, an agglomeration of great tribal units. They were knit together into a common geographical background by the prestige and allure of the age-old culture of Persia which dated back before the time of the Achaemenids. Persian was the

[1] Brosset, *EC/BHP* Vol. ii, Nos. 14–15, col. 216.

language of this culture of the Iranian plateau; Persian art and literature and manners cast their charm alike over the Kurdish mountain lords, Turkoman nomad chieftains, over the Armenian mercantile communities with their own hard Christian puritanism, and, to an appreciable extent, over the Georgian nobility who were able, at the same time, to maintain an ambivalent loyalty to the romantic traditions of the mediaeval kingdom and the Georgian Orthodox Church.

For several centuries the Persians had been ruled by dynasties originally nomadic in origin. The Mongols had overthrown the Seljuks; and Turkoman 'successor states' had struggled for hegemony after the disintegration of the Timurid empire during the fifteenth century. Strength had come from the north-west, from Azerbaijan, where the great Turkoman confederations who struggled for power – the Black Sheep (*Kara-Koyunlu*) and the White Sheep (*Ak-Koyunlu*) – contested for ascendancy. These people spoke Turkish dialects. Tabriz was a Turkish-speaking city, and remains so today. The majority of the inhabitants of Azerbaijan and of the Caucasian provinces of Aran and Shirvan adhered to the orthodox Sunni creed. It was only at the end of the fifteenth century that the family of Shaikh Safi of Ardabil emerged as the revivalists of the Shi'a schism, which for a long time had remained an undertone in the religious life of Iranian Islam. The Shaikhs of Ardabil, themselves of Turkish origin, destroyed the Ak-Koyunlu hegemony in a decade of fighting at the turn of the fifteenth century and the new Safavid dynasty was established. In essence it was north-west Iranian; indeed, near-Caucasian. Ardabil remained the holy city of the Safavids. Tabriz was their capital until the Ottoman wars forced their move to Kazvin. It was only at the end of the sixteenth century that Shah Abbas I, intent on freeing himself from the insolence and political domination of the great Turkoman tribal chieftains, finally chose Isfahan as his capital and gave emphasis to the Persian rather than the Turkoman character of his empire. He preferred the merchant class over the tribal chieftains and took a keen interest in the details of industry and commerce. He built new towns – particularly favouring the truly Persian regions of Ghilan and Mazandaran; and to develop them he transported tens of thousands of Georgians and Armenians from Caucasia. To new Julfa, the Armenian quarter outside Isfahan, were sent the inhabitants of (old) Julfa on the Aras river. As Balkan Slavs were recruited into the Ottoman Janissary Corps, so Shah Abbas drafted into his *tufanji* (musketeer) battalions – formed perhaps on the advice of the English adventurer Anthony Sherley – and also into his regular artillery and cavalry units, large numbers of Georgians, forcibly (and sometimes not very reluctantly) converted to the Shi'a sect of Islam. In this he desired to make himself independent of the military support of the truculent Turkoman and Daghestani chieftains who had exploited the anarchic conditions in the country after the death of Shah Tahmasp; at the same time his curious love-hate relationship with the Georgians can be explained by the Georgian strains in the Safavid royal house and by his own numerous Georgian friendships.[1] At the turn of the sixteenth century, the Safavid monarchy remained near-Caucasian but now with a Perso-Georgian rather than a Turkoman emphasis; and the great centres of its influence in Tabriz, Ardabil, Shemakha and the Caspian provinces gave it a proximity to the Caucasus and an intimacy with Caucasian conditions which neither the Ottomans nor the Muscovites enjoyed. The upshot of the quarter of a century's struggle for hegemony, between 1578 and 1605 was that Shah Abbas – a dominating personality and a monarch in a field where his antagonists were represented only by military commanders and diplomats – ousted the Ottomans from their earlier conquests and set a check to Russian political penetration until a century

[1] See further Commentary 8: 'Shah Abbas and his Georgian connections'.

later when Peter the Great, a ruler of comparable stature, appeared on the scene.

Many West European and Soviet historians have been in the habit of describing social conditions in Caucasia as 'feudal', the latter often using the term in a pejorative sense. It is, however, not really scientific to compare conditions in Caucasia – even in Georgia – with the system of polity which prevailed in Europe during the Middle Ages, and which was based on the relation of superior and vassal arising out of the holding of lands in feud. Characteristics of the feudal system had developed in Georgia but even here social conditions reflected many of the aspects of the tribal-patriarchal (clan) organization which survived in the Scottish Highlands until the middle of the eighteenth century. In Georgia, we find 'clans' (*G. gwari*) like the Baratashvilis in Kartli or the Tseretelis in Imereti. The chief would be a great *tavadi*, numbered among the exclusive few of the aristocrats who were named *didebulni*; but their condition was comparable to that of the chieftains of the Scottish Highlands rather than to that of the territorial magnates, the fruit of primogeniture, in England, France or Spain. Similarly, in the Karabagh *massif*, to the north of the Aras, where five families of Armenian *meliks* (literally, kings) survived through the eighteenth century, the ruler's status was that of clan chieftain rather than of hereditary territorial magnate. Conditions were comparable over the great Kurdish areas bordering on Caucasia and extending down along the chain of the Zagros; and among the Turkoman tribes (*oymaks*) in Azerbaijan, eastern Anatolia and Khurasan. Particularly among the mountain tribes, agriculture and some horticulture were secondary means of livelihood; nomadism had been abandoned but vast herds of horses and cattle and flocks of sheep continued to sustain an economy which in every detail of life was based on the consumption of animal products – hides and wool, meat, milk and butter. As contrasted with the old nomadism of the

Turkomans, transhumance – the seasonal movement from highland to lowland pastures (from *yayla* to *kishlak*) – was the order of the year. Opportunities for war and loot were welcomed, but the long distance movements of the nomad age had been abandoned in the Middle East after the death of Tamerlane.

In Shirvan, bordering on Kakheti, and in the more settled parts of Azerbaijan, the early Safavid monarchs had driven out the greater part of the old Turkish nobility who were attached to the Shirvan-shahs and other local rulers like the Khans of Sheki and Nukha. In Shirvan and Azerbaijan much of the land was apportioned either to the crown (*divani*), to the Shah's family (*khass*) or to religious and charitable institutions (*vakf*). Lands still in private hands were on long lease-hold (*mulk*). Revenue from the *divani* went to the maintenance of the army and of state functionaries; the *khass* sustained the expenditure of the royal court. The lands retained by private families were held on a 99 years tenure during which time heads of family could dispose of them as they pleased; but at the end of this period they had to pay a 'fine' to procure renewal of their rights from the Shah.[1]

During the sixteenth century the chiefs of the great Turkoman tribes acquired increased strength and prestige. These *Kizilbash* ('red heads' from the red caps which they wore originally as a mark of their adherence to the Shaikhs of Ardabil) tribes were all of Ghuzz (Turkoman) origin; their names and number vary according to different authorities. Outstanding among them were the Afshar, Bayat, Zulghadir, Ustajlu, Kajar, Rumlu, Shamlu and Takallu. As the names of some of them indicate, they had originally migrated from

[1] See *OI/PF/xv–xvii vv.*, pp. 859–60. For the best analysis of the workings of the Safavid state, see Minorsky, *Tadhkirat al-Mulūk: a manual of Safavid administration* (*TAM*), Cambridge, 1943; for contemporary accounts, Iskander Munshi, Pietro della Valle, and (later) Chardin.

Anatolia and northern Syria during the period of the protracted wars at the beginning of the century between Shah Ismail and the Ottoman Sultan Selim I. The chiefs of the Kizilbash tribes gradually transformed themselves into more or less hereditary Khans who shared out a part of the tribal lands among their closer kinsmen. From them were recruited, more often than not, the governors of provinces (*beglerbegleri*, literally 'lords of lords'), such as Tabriz, Erevan and Genzha. Since the time of Shah Tahmasp I, the government of Genzha and Karabagh had been vested in the family of Ziyad-oghlu Kajar, and Kakheti, lying on the northern affluents of the Kura, at a considerable distance to the north-east of Genzha, was somehow linked up with Karabagh.[1] At the same time Kakhian influences in the Khanate of Sheki, most northerly district of Shirvan, were, from time to time, quite strong. In fact the population of all this borderland was very mixed and there were fluctuations in the emphasis of political influences.

The peasantry of Azerbaijan, like their Georgian neighbours, were subject to a network of taxes and obligations. In Azerbaijan, the more direct control of the Shah's officials imposed many duties in the construction of buildings and roads and in the cleaning of irrigation canals; on the other hand forced labour for the land-owners was on a lesser scale than in Georgia – not exceeding three to six days a year. The condition of the Muslim peasants, free always of the threat of transportation and slavery, was certainly better than that of the Georgian *glekhni*, and Chardin found that 'ils vivent assez à leur aise.'[2]

The whole Shi'a revival covered many undertones of social

[1] Minorsky, *TAM*, p. 166.
[2] Ibid., pp. 22–3, citing Chardin, *Voyages*, ed. Langlès, 10 vols. and Atlas, Paris, 1811, Vol. v, pp. 387–90. 'Chardin was greatly impressed by cunning wiles which the peasants used in order to obtain a diminution of their liabilities under the pretext of bad crops . . . Chardin concludes with the rather unexpected statement, which he himself finds singular, that "le seigneur est celui qui a toujours (*sic*) du pire et qui est lésé".'

and economic discontent expressed often in a mystical fanaticism which was scarcely distinguishable from mass hysteria. These discontents had extended as far as western Anatolia where the Dervish orders were the leaders of revolt against Sunni orthodoxy, which expressed the spiritual discipline inherent in the pattern of the Ottoman state. When the Safavid house, leaders of the Shi'a revival, themselves became the lords of Iran and Azerbaijan, discontents took form in loyalist movements in favour of the deposed Shirvan-shahs. In 1537, there had been a widespread popular revolt in support of a certain dervish who gave himself out to be the son of a Shirvan-shah. In the towns of Azerbaijan, great trading and manufacturing centres like Tabriz and Shemakha, a sturdy and often violent radicalism was endemic among the citizens. In modern Tabriz, indeed, it is not difficult to scent the natural air of turbulence and anarchic individualism which characterizes a tough, hard-living people. In these towns, in the sixteenth century, the tradesmen were united in guilds (*asnaf*) but there were many day labourers and poor folk who lived by casual labour on the edge of starvation.

In the middle of the sixteenth century, the prosperity of Kakheti, Sheki and Shirvan was centred on the city of Shemakha; raw silk, with wool, dyes and hazel-nuts was the bulk of business. Anthony Jenkinson had sponsored the foundation of an English 'factory' there in 1562 and he had the backing of the Beglerbeg, Abdullah Khan Ustajlu. Russian merchants from Astrakhan were already active and, when Jenkinson left Persia for Astrakhan, Abdullah Khan sent, under his protection, an envoy to the court of Ivan IV. In northern Shirvan, on the border of Sheki and Kakheti, just south of the Gishi affluent of the Alazani, the town of Areshi (? ancient Georgian, *Hereti*) was the local collecting centre for the silk trade; it was famous for its green dye. In the 1570s Julfa, on the northern bank of the Aras, at the junction of roads leading from Karabagh to

Tabriz and Khoy, was growing in importance. Its population did not exceed 20,000 but it was the favoured centre of the richest Armenian merchants who carried on business with the far west – with Venice, Marseilles, Lisbon and Amsterdam. In the 1570s the annual figures for the export of silk through Aleppo to the Mediterranean attained 500 *kharvars* or 30,000 *batmans*. In return Aleppo sent through Julfa 18,000 pieces of Venetian stuffs. Other Azerbaijan towns, like Turkish Ordubad and Armenian Akulis, shared in this prosperity. These towns received important privileges from the Safavid Shahs. They were placed in the 'free' category of the Shah's personal possessions; they paid their taxes direct to the treasury and were thus immune from the arbitrariness and greed of the local beglerbegs and khans. Julfa, indeed, enjoyed the right of self-government through an elected officer (in Persian, *kalantar*, Armenian, *kagakapet*), who was directly responsible to the Shah.[1]

Tabriz, until 1548 the capital of the Safavid dynasty, was one of the most powerful cities in the Middle East, with no less than 300,000 inhabitants. Here were manufactured silk and woollen fabrics, carpets, shawls, shagreen leather, gold, silver and iron work. One of the disciplines of both Ottoman Sultans and

[1] See *OI/PF/xv–xvii vv.*, pp. 862–3, citing sources. Shemakha was badly ravaged during the Turko-Persian campaigns of 1578–90. Evliya Chelebi (von Hammer's English ed., Vol. II, pp. 159–62), gives a good near-contemporary description of 'old' Shemakha. For earlier history, see Bartold's article under 'Shīrwān' in *EI*, 1st ed., and Minorsky, *HSD*, *passim*. For 'new' Shemakha, built in the eighteenth century, under the orders of Nadir Shah, see Reineggs/W., Vol. I, pp. 186–9. For Sheki, see article under 'Shekki' by Minorsky in *EI*, 1st ed. In 1578, Alexander of Kakheti, then an ally of the Turks, occupied Sheki and it became an Ottoman *sanjak*. After the Safavid recovery in 1606, Georgian influences continued and Evliya Chelebi, as late as 1647 (Hammer ed., pp. 286–93), considered it to belong to Georgia 'because the Georgians had founded it'. For Sheki in the eighteenth century, when it was ruled by a dynasty founded by an Armenian priest converted to Islam, see Reineggs/W., Vol. I, pp. 190 ff. For the office of *Kalantar*, see Minorsky, *TAM*, p. 81.

Safavid Shahs was to make themselves proficient in at least one handicraft and it is said that Shah Tahmasp I, before he degenerated in his middle age, was a skilled weaver. The working people of Tabriz were, however, ill disposed towards the Safavids; the Venetian envoy, Alessandri, reported that Shah Tahmasp was detested on account of his greed and his heavy claims for taxes. Indeed, it is probable that it was this circumstance, and not only the recurrent threat of Ottoman invasion, which induced the Shah, in 1548, to remove his seat of government from Tabriz to smaller and more tame Kazvin.

Little is known of the internal life of the towns of Azerbaijan in the latter half of the sixteenth century. However, a clear manifestation of the undertones of class struggle is to be noted in the rising of the *serbedars* or 'gallows birds' in Tabriz which has been curtly described by Hasan Beg Rumlu, one of the local nobility. According to this source, the ranks of the rebels were recruited from 'common people', 'rabble', 'tramps' and 'riff-raff'. These town poor were, however, reinforced by small traders and artisans. The leaders of the rising were called *pehlevans*, which was the name given to members of the corporation of champion wrestlers, the exponents of one of the traditional popular sports of the Middle East. The rising was directed against the notables at the head of the administration, the rich merchants and the *seyyids* who were very much involved in the wholesale trade of the city. As stewards of the industrial workshops and shops belonging to the *vakf*, these descendants of the Prophet and leaders of the Shi'a faith extracted extortionate dues from the artisans and small traders.

The rising took place in 1571–2. The details are worth recalling because they give a picture of the underworld of the great Persian city which is not found elsewhere. The occasion was the oppression of the unpopular governor (*hakim*), the Turkoman Allah-Kuli Beg Ustajlu. The mob beat up one of his military servants (*mulazim*), and the ring-leader was executed.

Ferment increased when the *hakim* showed his intention of preventing the public funeral of the executed man. Allah-Kuli Beg himself, with his guard, was routed by the mob who then besieged him in his palace. Attacks on the houses of nobles, *seyyids, kadis* and rich people throughout the city became general. Their houses were wrecked and their families beaten up.

'And in every street', writes Hasan Beg Rumlu, 'someone from among these common people would raise the standard of authority: the *pehlevan* Yari in the quarter of the Shield-Makers (*sanjaran*); Nashmi in the quarter of Derdjuye; Sherif, the son of the lame Mustafa at the Cypress Gates (*serv*); the son of the Shawl-Maker in the quarter of Mikhad-Makhan; Aga Muhammad at the Naubar Gates; the *pehlevan* Avaz on the Maydan; Aslan at the Alalya Gates; Mirza-i Melikani and Gekcha in the quarter of the Camel-Drivers; and Alya-i Hasan-Jan in the quarter of Shesh-Kilyan'.[1]

With the flight of the governor, authority passed into the hands of these ring-leaders who seem to have carried on some sort of government for about two years. Strife among the Kizilbash tribes and a movement against the landowners in Ghilan prevented the ageing Shah from sending a punitive expedition. He preferred to negotiate through another member of the Ustajlu clan, the discreet and diplomatic Yusuf Beg, who was able to persuade the *kedkhudas* or syndics of the guilds to bring the people to peace and the acceptance of a new governor.

---

[1] *OI/PF/xv–xvii vv.*, pp. 863–5, citing original sources including Iskander Munshi, *Tārīkh-i-'ālem-ārā-yi 'Abbāsī* (*TA*) lithographed ed. of A.H. 1314; Hasan Beg Rumlu, *Ahsanu't-Tawārīkh*, Gaekwad Oriental Series, Baroda, 1931; *Sheref-name*, ed., Velyaminov Zernov, Spb., 1862, Vol. 11, pp. 241–3; I. I. Petrushevski, 'Vosstaniye remeslennikov i gorodskoy bednoty v Tebrize v 1571–1573 gg' in *Sbornik Statey po Istorii Azerbaydzhana, vyp.* 1, Baku, 1949, pp. 220–4.

For Shah Tahmasp, 'buying and selling with the cunning of a small merchant', see *Travels of Venetians in Persia* (*TVP*), Hakluyt Society, London, 1873, p. 219 (twice); and for the social ferment in Tabriz, ibid., pp. 223–4; 'Certainly one may say that the chiefs of districts are more masters of the city than the king.'

But this compromise did not satisfy the poorer classes and a fresh revolt soon broke out under the *pehlevan* Yari. This time the Shah procured the intervention of Sohrab Beg, son of the Khan of Karadagh, the great ridge to the north-east of Tabriz. The Turkomans surrounded the rebel quarters and after a tough fight the rebels capitulated and their leaders were executed.

The Ottoman campaigns of 1578–90 brought serious devastation and temporary economic decline to Azerbaijan. Özdemiroghlu Osman's capture of Tabriz in 1585 was followed by a popular outbreak which provoked a massacre of some 15,000 of the inhabitants by the Turkish troops. In spite of the fact that the *Shariat* forbids Muslims to be sold into slavery, Iskander Munshi states that the Turks deported large numbers of Shi'a *seyyids* to Istanbul where they were sold to 'Frankish' merchants.[1]

It is clear from contemporary Ottoman historians that the Porte regarded the occupation of Kartli and Azerbaijan as permanent and, despite the parlous economic condition of the empire, it invested considerable resources in manpower and materials in an attempt to stabilize its military and civil administration. Much time and effort was spent on fortifying and supplying a network of fortresses to hold down the conquered provinces. Akhaltsikhe and Kars were linked through Dmanisi and Lori, and, also by way of Gori, with Tiflis. In Azerbaijan – in Genzha, Shemakha, Areshi, Baku, Derbent, Nakhichevan and, lastly, in Tabriz, fortifications were renovated and strengthened. Large garrisons, increased by the adherence of some local Sunni elements, were maintained; the field forces were augmented by the introduction of hordes of Tartar cavalry from the Crimea. The conquered territories were divided into *vilayets* and these were partitioned into *sanjaks* – some of which were allocated to local notables

[1] Iskander Munshi, *TA*, p. 375.

from among the Azerbaijanis, Shirvanis and Kurds. Thus, under the name of *sanjaks,* some of the former semi-feudal domains were preserved or, in cases, revived. The chieftain of the Kurdish tribe of the Mahmutlu retained, as a *sanjak-bey* in the service of the Sultan, the district of Maku as his hereditary fief. In other areas, needy Turkish military men were given holdings (*timarlar*) as a reward for their services and to strengthen the vested Ottoman interest in country districts. The arrival of new masters, the need of supplies for the army in garrison and in the field, for materials and forced labour on the new fortifications, and the movements of the Crimean cavalry led to the pitiless pillage of the occupied provinces. The Ottoman conquest was not popular, even among the Sunnis whom it was the practice, now, to favour. The Armenian historian, Arakel of Tabriz, complained that the inflated taxes and the requisitions and embezzlements of the Sultan's officials, oppressed Armenians, Georgians and Muslims alike. The people sought relief in flight and whole districts were deserted. During the 1590s a reaction in opinion was taking place in favour of the Safavids. In Azerbaijan many of the tribal chieftains and rich merchants were in contact with the court of the new young Shah Abbas I: notably the Kurdish ruler of Salmas, Gazi Beg, and Khaybat Beg Ulama-oghlu of the powerful Takalu Turkomans (originally migrants from Tekke in south-western Anatolia during the reign of Sultan Selim I). Even the Armenian Patriarch of Echmiadzin, David, was in secret negotiation with the Shah.[1]

During the first decade of his reign Shah Abbas was playing for time to restore the shattered authority of his house and the ruined economy of Iran.

Persian relations with Russia were at first reserved and gradually hardened with the increasing confidence of the Shah.

---

[1] Cf. *OI/PF/xv–xvii vv.,* pp. 871–2; also Asafi and Iskander Munshi, *passim.*

In 1591 a Persian herald (*R. gonets*) named in the Russian sources as *Kaya* (from P. *Kâhya,* a steward) reached Moscow by way of the Kumukh lands where he was robbed of his belongings. It was the year following the conclusion of peace between Shah Abbas and Sultan Murat III, but the herald brought an oral message, repeating the old proposal of Shah Muhammad Khudabanda, that the Russians should themselves take Derbent and Baku; he complained also that no Russian ambassador had accompanied Andi Beg on his return from Moscow. The Russian explanation was that the Tsar had received news that the Shah and the Sultan had made peace without informing him. A formal treaty was offered to the Persians. No reference seems to have been made to Derbent, Baku, 'the Iberian Land' or Kabarda.[1] Indeed, at this juncture, the Russians were themselves contemplating a *détente* with the Ottomans. They were, in fact, convinced of the weakness of Persia and alarmed by the Perso-Turkish treaty of 1590. (In the course of the following year (1593), G. A. Nashchokin arrived in Istanbul to negotiate with Sinan Pasha.)[2]

In 1592, another Persian ambassador, Hajji Khusrau (Azi-Khosrov) came to Moscow with a message of friendship which made no reference to 'the Iberian Land', the Shevkal or to Kabarda. The ambassador was informed by Boris Godunov that Alexander of Kakheti had sought the Tsar's protection and that an army under Boyar Khvorostinin had been sent against the Shevkal.

Azi-Khosrov travelled back in 1593, accompanied by a

[1] Brosset, *EC/BHP* Vol. II, Nos. 14–15, cols. 263–4. See also N. I. Veselovski, *Pamyatniki diplomaticheskikh i torgovykh snosheniy Moskovskoy Rusi s Persiyey* (Veselovski, *PDTS*), Vol. I, *Tsarstvovaniye Fedora Ivanovicha,* Spb., 1890, published as Vol. xx of *Trudy Vostochnago Otdeleniya Imp. Russkago Arkheologicheskago Obshchestva:* for the mission of the *gonets* 'Kaya', see pp. 170–3; for the next mission of Andi Bek, see pp. 3–4; for Azi-Khosrov (text below), see pp. 176–83.

[2] Cf. Allen, *PTP,* p. 37 and n. 113.

Russian ambassador, A. D. Zvenigorodski. He was instructed to inform the Shah that the Tsar had taken Alexander of Kakheti under his protection at the latter's request and for the sake of the Christian faith; the Shevkal's misdeeds were listed. Zvenigorodski was to tell the Shah that in the past the Kabardan Cherkesses had lived in the neighbourhood of Ryazan and had been the Sovereign's servants but that 'having seceded (from the Russian sovereigns) they fled from Ryazan and went to live in the mountains'; they had returned to the fold under Tsar Ivan.[1]

Zvenigorodski was also instructed to ask the Shah for the return of the Kakhian prince Constantine, a son of Alexander II. The Shah already felt confident enough to raise the Georgian question with Zvenigorodski. He recalled that the Georgian princes had been tributaries of Persia; and he asked the Tsar not to press the war against the Shevkal since the latter had also been the Shah's vassal. With regard to Constantine, the Shah said that the prince was free to go if he desired, but

[1] Brosset, *EC/BHP* Vol. II, Nos. 14–15, cols. 264–5. For the story that the Kabardan Cherkesses had been vassals (*kholopy*) of the Tsar who had fled from Ryazan, see Belokurov, p. 569. As we know the Kabardan Cherkesses had migrated comparatively recently from the Crimea, see Commentary 12: 'On the Princely Families of Kabarda'. But the fact that there were Circassian elements settled in the region between the rivers Oka and Tsna as late as the beginning of the sixteenth century is repeated in contemporary Russian sources and is scarcely open to doubt. They may have been an indigenous *enclave* whose settlement dated from remote times, or they may have been descended from the bands of Circassians and Alans whom the rulers of the Khazars and, later, of the Golden Horde, were accustomed to employ as frontier guards, cf. W. E. D. Allen, *The Ukraine: A History* (Allen, *Ukraine*), Cambridge, 1941, p. 70. In the mid-sixteenth century, these Ryazan Cherkesses changed sides (as did many of the Tartar *begs* of the declining Horde – including Kasim to whom was allotted the Kasimov *tsarstvo*) and participated in the later Russian campaigns against Kazan and Astrakhan. A probable explanation of the official Russian claim is that some of the Ryazan Cherkesses may have moved off to join their compatriots already settled in Kabarda.

For Knyaz Andrey Dmitriyevich Zvenigorodski, see *RBS* under name; for his mission to Persia, Veselovski, *PDTS*, Vol. I, pp. 221–326.

4. Arrival of the Kabardan envoy in Moscow in 1566 with a request for the construction of a fort at the estuary of the river Sunzha. From a miniature in the Collection of the Holy Synod, Gosudarstvenny Istoricheski Muzey, No. 962, p. 605 (ref. *KRO*, Vol. 1, opposite p. 12).

Constantine himself declined to go to Russia, declaring that he was a Muslim. The Shah also told the Russian ambassador that Alexander had been paying tribute to the Sultan and had killed one Persian ambassador and imprisoned another.[1] These discussions did not prevent the Russians from pursuing their operations against the Shevkal – which had been agreed with Alexander. However, in 1597, Khvorostinin met with a serious setback, incurring losses of some three thousand men.[2]

In the years 1596–7 the Shah began to show that he was already conscious of the growing strength of his position. According to Sovin, the Russian ambassador then in attendance on Alexander of Kakheti, Abbas under threat of war demanded in marriage the king's daughter – already promised to the Dadiani. (A niece of the queen, a lady, of the Amilakhori family, was sent instead.) Sovin also reported that Abbas was asking for a sister of Sultan Murat III in marriage – with a dowry to consist of Derbent, Shemakha and other towns occupied by the Turks.[3]

These years Abbas was heavily involved against the Uzbeks. His recovery of Meshhed and Herat in 1597–8 was followed by the loss of Balkh in 1600–1 and heavy fighting in which large numbers of men died through sickness and he had to abandon the bulk of his new artillery.[4] It was during the year 1600 that an embassy from Boris Godunov arrived in

[1] Brosset, *EC/BHP* Vol. II, Nos. 14–15, cols. 263–6.
[2] Recent Soviet historians tend to slur over this first Russian reverse in Daghestan. Khvorostinin captured Tarku and the Shevkal was wounded; but the failure of Alexander of Kakheti and the Krym-Shevkal to support the Russian incursion, compelled the Russian commander to withdraw to the Terek (see *RBS* under 'Khvorostinin, Knyaz Andrey Ivanovich).
[3] Brosset, *EC/BHP* Vol. II, Nos. 14–15, cols. 265–6 and n. 121. According to the Russian Ambassador, V. V. Tyufyakin, Abbas celebrated his marriage with 'the daughter of the Georgian tsar' in Isfahan in November 1589, cf. Veselovski, *PDTS*, I, p. 447.
[4] See article 'Shah Abbas I' by R. M. Savory in *EI*, 2nd ed.

Kazvin led by the Boyar A. F. Zhirov-Zasekin. Again, the ambassador had to assert that Alexander had placed himself under the protection of the Tsar. There were also further explanations about the Shevkal who, the Russians claimed, had detached himself from the Shah and had made approaches successively to the Crimean Khan and the Sultan.[1] It was only in the years 1603–4 that the Shah was able to concentrate definitely on affairs in Azerbaijan, Shirvan and Georgia. The international situation was propitious since the Ottoman empire, weakened by the 'Long War' on the Danube, was in a state of chronic disorder; moreover their military position in Georgia had been shaken by the guerrilla campaigns of King Simon of Kartli and the strength of their garrisons had been reduced to meet commitments in other parts of the empire. In Russia, after two years of serious famine, the regime of Boris Godunov was approaching dynastic and social crisis. (From the numerous Persian and Armenian merchants in Astrakhan, Kazan and Nizhni-Novgorod, Shah Abbas cannot have been without news of these trends.) The period of the rapid victories of Shah Abbas in Azerbaijan and Shirvan, and his ruthless intervention in the Kakhian kingdom, is covered in the account of the embassy of Tatishchev to the Kings of Kakheti and Kartli – which forms Part II of the texts printed in these volumes. The victories of Shah Abbas brought in a further period of Persian hegemony in Kakheti and Kartli which endured for a century until the fall of the Safavid dynasty and the intervention of Peter the Great in Caucasia in the third decade of the eighteenth century.

An ironic tail-piece to all this first Russian effort to penetrate Caucasia is to be found in the story of the two Russian em-

[1] Brosset, *EC/BHP* Vol. II, Nos. 11–15, cols. 293–4 and n. 11, stating that four folios are missing from Zasekin's report in the Central Archives. For Aleksandr Fedorovich Zasekin, see *RBS* under name. For his mission to Persia, Veselovski, *PDTS*, Vol. II, 1892, pp. 28–143.

bassies which were sent to Shah Abbas during the 'Time of Troubles' (*Smutnoye Vremya*). During the brief reign of Tsar Vasili IV Shuyski (1606–10), Prince Ivan Romodanovski was sent to Persia to remind the Shah that Alexander of Kakheti had been 'under the Tsar's hand' and to complain about the murder of the King and his son Yuri by Prince Constantine at the Shah's command; the Shah was to be asked to keep out of Georgia which had been a Christian state from old times. Romodanovski was killed in Saratov by outlaws on his way down the Volga to Astrakhan (1606).[1] Relations between Moscow and the Shah were only renewed in the year 1613, shortly after the election of Tsar Mikhail Romanov, when Mikhail Tikhanov and the under-dyak Aleksey Bukharov (probably, by his name, of Uzbek origin) were sent to Persia overland from Samara through Urgench with the Persian ambassador Amir Ali Beg. The Volga route to the Caspian was not under control – since the Cossack *ataman* Zarutski was holding Astrakhan on behalf of Marina Mniszek and her infant son by the second False Dmitri. The Russian ambassadors carried no instructions about 'the Iberian Land'; but they were to ask the Shah not to give aid to Zarutski.[2] Such was the reversal of fortunes in the Caspian basin since a quarter of a century earlier when Shah Muhammad Khudabanda had been inviting the Russians to take Derbent and Baku for themselves. Shah Abbas did not give aid to Zarutski but from

[1] Brosset, *EC/BHP* Vol. II, Nos. 14–15, cols. 334–6; Veselovski *PDTS*, Vol. II, pp. 144–50; cf. also *RBS*, under name 'Romodanovski, Knyaz Ivan Petrovich', which states that he was killed on his return journey up the Volga. Romodanovski came of the ancient Starodubski branch of the family; the name – like that of Bukharov, see text below – may have been of Muslim origin.

[2] See Belokurov, *Snosheniya*, pp. 576–7, and for many curious details Veselovski, *PDTS*, Vol. II, pp. 277–312. The Shah was campaigning in Georgia in 1614, where, according to Tikhanov, he received an ambassador from Emperor Matthias, asking him not to make peace with the Turks, cf. Veselovski, ibid., p. 299.

1614–16 onward proceeded to the methodical conquest of the Kingdoms of Kartli and Kakheti.[1]

[1] In July 1614, Ivan Brekhov followed Tikhanov to Persia to inform the Shah of the collapse of Zarutski. Zarutski's envoy, Ivan Khokhlov, had met Tikhanov in Kazvin, and returned with him to Russia by way of Shirvan and Tarku, cf. Veselovski, *PDTS*, Vol. II, p. 293 ff.

PART I

THE EMBASSY OF ZVENIGORODSKI
AND ANTONOV
(1589–90)

CHAPTER I

INSTRUCTIONS FOR THE ROAD

O N the 23rd of April 7097,[1] the Sovereign Tsar and (84)
great Prince Fedor Ivanovich of all Russia sent off as
ambassadors to the Georgian land, to the Iberian
king Alexander, Prince Semen Zvenigorodski and dyak Torkh
Antonov, and along with them the cathedral monk and former
treasurer Zakhkhey and the black priest Iosaf,[2] both from the
Troitsko-Sergiyevski monastery, and deacon Feodosi from
the Chudov monastery, as well as the cathedral priests Bogdan
from the Prechistenski Cathedral and Dmitri from the
Arkhanilski Cathedral and deacon Fedor, and icon-painters.[3]

And such is the instruction given to Prince Semen and to (94)
dyak Torkh on how they are to carry out the Sovereign's
affairs:

[1] The year 7097, from the creation of the world. According to the
Byzantine chronology, which was in use in sixteenth-century Russia,
the world was created in 5509 B.C. but year 1 came to be reckoned from 1st
September, 5508 B.C. 7097 minus 5508 therefore equals A.D. 1589. All
dates given in the text follow the Julian calendear; in the sixteenth century
the difference between the Julian and Gregorian calendars (the latter in use
in the west) was ten days – thus Julian 23 April= Gregorian 3 May.

[2] Brosset, *EC/BHP* Vol. II, Nos. 14–15, col. 233, gives the family name
of Zakhkhey as Souroftsov (= Surovtsov). Iosaf was a regular priest, called
'black' from the colour of the garb and hood worn by clerics who took
monastic vows. Most parishes were served by 'white' secular priests who
were sometimes only semi-literate. In this respect a parallel can be drawn
with late mediaeval England, cf. A. R. Myers, *England in the late Middle
Ages*, Harmondsworth, Middlesex, 1953, p. 67. In the seventeenth century,
Chardin, perhaps with a pinch of Huguenot malice, remarked the semi-
literacy of priests in Georgia, *Travels*, 1686 ed., pp. 209–10. For costumes
of ecclesiastics see Olearius/W., Vol. I, 366.

[3] For these monasteries and cathedrals see Commentary 1, (a), (b), (c),
and (d): 'Monasteries and cathedrals in and around Moscow'.

The Sovereign Tsar orders them to go as ambassadors to the Georgian land, for his own affairs and for those of the country, and along with them he has sent off the ambassadors of Alexander, king of Georgia, Prince Kaplan[1] with three of his assistants, and also Batay, nephew of Shikh murza of the Okok, and Bikan and Aslanbek with their assistants, ambassadors of the Kabardan princes Solokh and Alkas, nine men in all.[2] And, at the supplication of the Georgian ambassadors, the cathedral monk Zakhkhey and the monk priest Iosaf and the monk deacon Feodosi, from Sergey's Monastery of the Life-giving Trinity; and two priests from the Cathedral of the Dormition of the Immaculate Mother of God, Bogdan and Dmitri, and deacon Fedor and three icon-painters have been sent with them to the Georgian land for the correction of the Christian faith; and the falconer Ivan Sychov has been sent with them with the Sovereign's falcons . . .

Orders have been given for the issue of the sovereign's horses at Astarakhan . . . Ten horses under church vessels and under books and under vestments and under various church ornaments, and under paints and under the Sovereign's treasure of all kinds and under falcons and under five bales of provisions . . . From Terek-town they are to proceed to the site of the abandoned settlement on the Sunzha, where captains from Terek-town are stationed in a blockhouse[3] . . . And when Prince Semen and his companions arrive in the new town on the Terek, Prince Semen and dyak Torkh Antonov should

---

[1] Prince Kaplan: identified by Brosset, *EC/BHP* Vol. ii, p. 233, as Qaplan Watchnadzes (= Vachnadze); cf. also Wak./Brosset, p. 47, for Watchnadze, a family of *mtavarni* of ancient lineage in Kakheti.

[2] For Shikh murza of the Okok, see Commentary 14: 'Shikh murza of the Okok and "the Little Mountain Lands" '. For the Kabardan princes Alkas and Solokh, see Commentary 12: 'The princely families of Kabarda'; and Commentary 17: 'The personality of Solokh'. Aslanbek was an *uzden* or 'squire' of Alkas.

[3] For *gorodishche* and other Russian military terms, see Commentary 2.

tell the commanders, Prince Andrey Ivanovich Khvorostinin[1] and his comrades that they should *send off*[2] *the Cherkess envoys ahead of the Sovereign's ambassadors and should send word with the former that Solokh and Alkas and Shikh and the Avar prince*[3] *should escort the Sovereign's ambassadors as far as Georgia and should send their brothers or children and nephews as hostages to Terek-town. They are instructed to send a sotnik with five or six Cossacks,* good and enterprising, who had been there previously, *to the Avar prince with similar instructions. The escort should consist of 300 mounted streltsy*[4]*; and if there is bad news they are ordered to take with them a further 150 foot and 50 horse* . . . They should proceed to the Georgian land without delay through the Cherkess land either through the territories of Shikh murza of the Okok and of the Avar prince and of the Black Prince, or through the lands of the Kabardan prince Alkas, whichever places and whichever road prove suitable in accordance with the news and after questioning local inhabitants and guides; wherever it is better and straighter and less dangerous – by that road they should proceed . . . And when Prince Semen and his comrades will arrive among the Cherkesses at Shikh murza's *kabak,*[5] they should send messengers

[1] A. I. Khvorostinin was born in Moscow in the 1520s. In 1566 he defended Volkhov against the Crim Tartars and, later, Pskov against Stephen Batory. Recalled from Pskov in 1582, he held successive commands at Kolomna, Nizhni Novgorod, Alatyr, Shatsk and Ryazan. In 1588–90 he was the first Russian general at Terek-town. He returned to the Caucasus in 1595-7 when he led an expedition against the Shevkal but was surrounded at Tarku; he fought his way out and retreated to the Terek with the loss of 3,000 men. In 1598 he was transferred to the Ukraine where he held command at Tsarev-Borisov in 1600-2. Round eighty when he died (1604), he had commanded in the field for nearly forty years. (For details, see *RBS.*)

[2] Belokurov summarized some passages in his edition of the documents. We follow him in italicizing such passages.

[3] For the Avar prince (*nutsal*) see Introduction, Section 8; also Chap. 2, p. 105, n. 2.

[4] *Streltsy:* originally bowmen, later musketeers, see Commentary 2(b).

[5] For the several meanings of the word *kabak*, see Commentary 2(c).

to him asking that he should come to their camp, for there is the Sovereign's bounty and letter addressed to him. And when Shikh murza comes to them, the ambassadors . . . should salute him on behalf of the Tsar, *present the letter and the Sovereign's gracious presents and speak of the escort.* If Shevkal's son Alkas murza now lives together with Shikh murza and serves the Sovereign – *the ambassadors are ordered to behave likewise towards him. The same in the case of the Kabardan princes Solokh and Alkas. If the latter do not agree to come to the ambassadors* and it proves impossible to persuade them – Prince Semen and dyak Torkh should send word to Prince Solokh and to Alkas that they should meet them on horseback on the way,

(95) having indicated the spot. *They should salute the princes, present the letter and the Sovereign's gracious presents and speak of the escort. The same for the Avar prince* . . . And they should say most firmly that the Avar prince should send guides with them as far as the Georgian lands; while the escorting *streltsy* should be sent back from the Avar prince's lands . . . And should news reach them on the Terek about the Avar prince that it would be dangerous to proceed to his land, and should the Avar prince not send his son or nephew as a hostage to Terek-town – then Prince Semen should perforce travel to the lands of Alkas along the former route, and he should tell Alkas and Solokh to escort them to the Georgian lands; and the ambassadors should send back the escorting *streltsy* from the mountains, from whichever spot is fitting, so that they should on no account be led into the mountains; only the fifty horsemen with a *sotnik* who are to accompany them into the Georgian land should be taken along.[1]

And when – if God grants – they reach the Georgian land

---

[1] For Russian relations with the Cherkesses, the Kabardans and with the Shevkal (Shamkhal of Tarku), see Introduction, Sections 6 and 8; for the Avar prince, see p. 89, n. 3 above; for Alkas and Solokh, see p. 88, n. 2 above.

and King Alexander orders them to attend on him – *the ambassadors should say that no other ambassadors should be present at the same time* ... And if there are no ambassadors or envoys from other lands with King Alexander, Prince Semen and dyak Torkh, having come to King Alexander, should salute him in the name of the Sovereign Tsar and great Prince Fedor Ivanovich of all Russia, and they should deliver the speech and present the letter as it is written down, in accordance with the instructions of the Sovereign Tsar and great Prince, and they should present the Sovereign's gracious gifts according to the treasury list. And they should say to King Alexander during the audience that the Sovereign Tsar and great Prince Fedor Ivanovich of all Russia, at the supplication of King Alexander's ambassadors, has sent learned men with them for the correction of the Christian faith[1] ... They are bearers of speeches and a (96) letter on spiritual matters from the Holiest great Patriarch Job[2] of the reigning city of Moscow and of all Russia and from the whole Consecrated Council of the great Russian kingdom to Metropolitan Nicholas[3] and to the whole [Georgian] council; and Metropolitan Nicholas with all the council should instruct them to attend on him. And when the Metropolitan instructs them to attend on him, the monk Zakhkhey with the brethren

---

[1] For religious contacts between Russia and Georgia, see Commentary 3.

[2] For the career and vicissitudes of the Patriarch Job, see Commentary 3.

[3] Tamarati, *L'Église Géorgienne*, p. 365, mentions Nicholas V (1562–97) in a list of Catholicoses 'of whom we know little'. But cf. Brosset, 'Histoire de Kakheth', in *HG*, Vol. II/i, p. 153, n. 3, for death of Catholicos Nicolaos, son of King Levan in 1591. See also text, p. 216 *infra*, for King Alexander's reference to his 'third brother who is now Metropolitan'. This prelate was already ailing at the time of Zvenigorodski's visit. He was, in fact, a half-brother of the king, born to Levan by the daughter of the Shevkal Kara-Musal. See also *BK*, Nos. 41–2, article by N. Salia, 'Les chefs de l'église Géorgienne', pp. 14–16, where Nicolaoz V, son of King Levan of Kakheti, is numbered 114th Catholicos of Georgia (1584–91).

and the priests and the deacon, having come to the Metropolitan, should present Patriarch Job's salutation and benediction, and they should deliver the speech and should present the letter according to the instruction that has been given to them; and Prince Semen and dyak Torkh should not accompany them to the Metropolitan . . .

(97)   And Prince Semen with his comrades should find out in the Georgian land all information about the Kizilbash[1] and the Iberian[2] and the Turk and the Shevkal – the situation in which each one is . . . And if Prince Semen is obliged to winter [in Georgia], Prince Semen with his comrades should send three or four mounted *streltsy* and five or six Georgians with an exact report to the Sovereign, and should address it to the commanders on the Terek, Prince Andrey and his comrades; and from the Terek a couple of *streltsy* should be allowed to proceed with the letter to the Sovereign in Moscow.

And a memorandum to Prince Semen Grigoryevich and to dyak Torkh. If King Alexander or his retinue start asking them why the Sovereign has sent his envoys to the Kizilbash Shah, Prince Semen and dyak Torkh should say that the Kizilbash Shah sent his envoy to our Sovereign asking to be accepted into brotherhood and friendship, and wanting to stand together

---

[1] Kizilbash: 'Red-Head', a pejorative nickname in common use among the Turks to describe the red-turbaned followers of the Safavid rulers of Persia, see Commentary 4: 'The Kizilbashes'.

[2] Here, 'the Iberian' stands for King Simon of Kartli. Iberia was in narrow definition the classical name for central Georgia (cf. Strabo, Pliny, etc.). Under Greek influence the name came into use among the Georgians themselves (*Kartvelni*, country: *Sa-kartvel-o*) in correspondence with foreign kings. In the present text it will be seen that the kings of both Kartli and Kakheti represented themselves to be 'the Iberian king' (the former with more reason as the legitimate heir of the united Georgian monarchy of the fifteenth century). The Muscovite rulers later assumed among their titles that of 'Tsar of the Iberian Land'.

Forms of the name *Iber* are of great antiquity in Caucasia (for refs. see Allen, *BK*, No. 30, 1959, p. 7; also Kuftin, *Arkheologicheskiye raskopki v Trialeti*, Tbilisi, 1941, pp. 163 ff. and n. 91).

with our Sovereign against the Turk. And our Sovereign has acceded to his prayer and wants to stand together with him against the Turk and, to confirm this, our Sovereign has sent to the Shah his envoy Grigori Vasilchikov.[1] And the ambassadors should find out how the Kizilbash Shah received Grigori and whether he wants to be in friendship and brotherhood with the Sovereign and is sending his ambassadors. They should act in accordance with the news.

And if they are asked what the present relations are between the Sovereign Tsar and the Lithuanian king, Prince Semen Grigoryevich and dyak Torkh Antonov should say that the Lithuanian state, the Polish Crown and the Lithuanian Grand Duchy, have no sovereign now, and they intend to supplicate our Sovereign to take them under his royal hand, so that both their states should stand together with our Sovereign against the infidel Moslems.

And if they are asked what the present relations are between the Sovereign Tsar and the Roman Caesar, Prince Semen and dyak Torkh should say that the Roman Caesar has sent his grandees as ambassadors to our Sovereign asking that he should confirm finally the alliance and should join with him and stand together against their mutual enemies. And all Christian sovereigns, the Roman Pope and the Spanish king and all Italy

---

[1] Grigori Vasilchikov was a member of the gentry class who may have owed his rise to a connection with Anna Vasilchikova, one of the mistresses of Ivan IV. He was sent to Persia in the latter part of 1588 and returned to Moscow in the summer of the following year. The purpose of the embassy was to explore the possibilities of an alliance between Russia and Persia with the object of checking the aggrandizement of the Ottoman Empire (see Introduction, Section 11 and Commentary 60). The mission was inconclusive and several years were to elapse before negotiations were resumed.

In 1592 Vasilchikov was sent to the Kola peninsula to delineate the frontier between Russian and Danish Lappland, Norway then being under the Danish crown (cf. Veselovski, *PDTS*, Vol. I, *Tsarstvovaniye Fedora Ioannovicha* = Vol. xx of *TVOIAO*, 1890, pp. 1–112, for embassy of Vasilchikov).

and the Venetian prince have sent their envoys to our
Sovereign; and they are asking him to join with them against
the Turk who rules over Christian states; and all Christian
sovereigns, having joined together, should all as one stand
against these unbelieving Hagarenes.[1] And our Sovereign, the
great Sovereign Tsar and great Prince, has sent his envoys
to all these Christian sovereigns and he wants to join with them
against the Turk and all the Moslems.[2]

(98)   And if they are asked about Bukhara and about Urgench,
Prince Semen Grigoryevich and dyak Torkh should say that
Bukhara and Urgench and Izyur and Khiva send their ambassadors to our Sovereign; and even now Bukhara and Izyur
have sent their ambassadors to our Sovereign asking that he
should extend his grace to them and keep them under his royal
hand.[3]

And if they are asked about Siberia, they should say that the
Siberian kingdom has from the first been an eternal patrimony
of our Sovereigns. And Siberia was taken by the great
Sovereign Tsar and great Prince Ivan Vasilyevich of all Russia,
great-grandfather of our present Sovereign, nearly a hundred
years ago, and he imposed tribute of sables and black foxes.
And in recent years they tried to secede and began not to pay
tribute; and our Sovereign's father, the great Sovereign Tsar
and great Prince Ivan Vasilyevich of all Russia, of blessed
memory, sent his commanders and Volga Cossacks against
Siberia. And the commanders and the Cossacks went and beat
the Siberian king Kuchum and drove him from Siberia and

[1] Hagarenes: the descendants of Hagar and her son Ishmael 'who
dwelt in the wilderness of Paran' (*Gen.* xxi. 21). The Byzantines and
Georgians had applied this name to the Arabs but in Russia the term came
to cover Muslims in general and Turks in particular.

[2] For contemporary Russian relations with Poland and the west and
for the proposed 'Grand Alliance' against the Turks, see Allen, *PTP*,
p. 34 and nn. 98, 99, giving summary and detailed refs.

[3] For contemporary Russian relations with the central Asian khanates,
see Commentary 5.

took Siberia; and they captured alive Prince Magmetkul, the brother of King Kuchum, and they brought him to the Sovereign, and he is at present in the Sovereign's service. And now, under our Sovereign, the great Sovereign Tsar and great Prince Fedor Ivanovich of all Russia, the Sovereign's commanders and many men live in Siberia, and many towns have been built there along the river Tura and the great river Ob and along the Irtysh, and churches have been erected and much tribute comes to our Sovereign from the Siberian land, sables and black foxes and all other animals.[1]

And a memorandum to Prince Semen Grigoryevich and dyak Torkh Antonov. Whilst in the Georgian land they should secretly find out what the present relations are between the Georgian King Alexander and the Turk and the Kizilbash Shah. Had ambassadors or envoys or messengers from the Turk and from the Kizilbash Shah been there recently before them? And if they had been there, with what purpose did they come and on what business? And did the Georgian King Alexander send ambassadors to the Turk and to the Kizilbash Shah and on what business? And if he did so, whom by name had he sent and on what business? Having found this out in secret they should make a note of it in writing. And while they are there they should also try to find this out: what are the present relations of the Turkish Sultan with the Kizilbash Shah? Have Turkish ambassadors and envoys visited the Kizilbash and for what purpose? And did the Kizilbash Shah send his ambasadors and envoys to the Turk and on what business? And was there war this summer between the Turk and the new Kizilbash Shah?[2] And what pashas came and how many Turks were there with them and what did they do to the Kizilbash land? And the (99)

---

[1] For details on these personalities and places, see Commentary 6: 'The Russian conquest of Sibir'.

[2] For 'the new Kizilbash Shah', Abbas I, see Commentary 8: 'Shah Abbas and his Georgian connections'.

towns which the Turk has taken from the Kizilbash, Derbent and Baku and other towns, are they all still in the hands of the Turk?[1] And are there many Turks garrisoned in these towns? And did the present Kizilbash Shah send his army against Turkish towns? And has the Kizilbash Shah now taken back any towns from the Turk and, if so, which? And is the present Kizilbash Shah beloved in his land, by the Kizilbash people? And has the Kizilbash army increased under him? And in the future what do they expect of the Kizilbash Shah and the Turk: do they want war or do they want to be at peace? And on what conditions do they want to be at peace? And except for the Turk, is the Kizilbash Shah at war with anyone and, if so, with whom? And with what sovereigns is the Shah at peace? They should also enquire about this. Has the Kizilbash Shah received a message from the Caesar or from Spain or from France and about what? Having found all this out in secret, they should write it down in their register.

And while they are in the Georgian land, they should attend to all the Sovereign's affairs and should seek all news in accordance with these instructions from the Sovereign and God's enlightenment.

And a memorandum to the ambassadors Prince Semen Grigoryevich and his companions. When, if God grants, they come as ambassadors to King Alexander, and he asks them to kiss his hand, Prince Semen should kiss the hand first, and after him the monk Zakhkhey, and after the monk Zakhkhey dyak Torkh Antonov, and after Torkh the priests, first the monk and the two lay priests and then the monk deacon and the lay deacon and the *sotnik* from Astarakhan and the falconer and the interpreters.[2] And if King Alexander asks them to sup with

---

[1] See Commentary 9: Derbent and Baku.

[2] Interpreter, Russ. *tolmach*: Kotoshikhin reports that there were about seventy interpreters on the staff of the *Posolski Prikaz* in the early seventeenth century, but Belokurov, *PK*, states that there were only twenty-

5. Despatch from Moscow down the Volga of a Russian squadron with artillery for the construction of a fort at the estuary of the Sunzha. From a miniature in the Collection of the Holy Synod, Gosudarstvenny Istoricheski Muzey, No. 962, p. 613.

him – Prince Semen should sit at the important place at table and the monk Zakhkhey should sit below him, and dyak Torkh Antonov should sit opposite the monk Zakhkhey – these three should be served from the same dish. And beside the monk Zakhkhey should sit the monk priest and the monk deacon and the falconer Ivan Sychov; and beside Torkh should sit the priests Bogdan and Dmitri and deacon Fedor and the *strelets sotnik*, and next to them should sit the interpreters, and opposite them the icon-painters.

And a memorandum to the ambassadors Prince Semen and dyak Torkh. When they will travel from Nizhni towards Kazan and they and the Georgian ambassadors start meeting messengers from Kazan and from Astarakhan, Prince Semen and dyak Torkh should say – and persuade the Georgian ambassadors in conversation – that messengers are on their way to the Sovereign from Astarakhan bearing letters to the effect that the Shevkaly prince has sent to the Sovereign's commanders on the Terek asking that the Sovereign should extend his grace to him, and saying that he will make amends in everything to the sovereign and will be under his royal hand . . . And if the (100) Iberian ambassadors start saying that the Shevkaly prince only sends his messengers to the Sovereign so that the Sovereign should not send his army against him . . . Prince Semen and Torkh should say to the ambassadors: 'We are telling you the news we have heard about Shevkal. The army is marching to the Terek and when Shevkal hears this his supplication will be

two interpreters in 1622. (Possibly the decline in numbers was due to the Time of Troubles). The interpreters – whose work was oral – got an annual salary between 15 and 40 rubles and a living allowance. There were also fifty translators, who dealt with documents and books; their pay was higher: 50 to 100 rubles p.a. and a bigger living allowance. The *Prikaz* had staff who could interpret and translate from Latin, Swedish, German, Greek, Polish and Tartar (Kotoshikhin, pp. 86, 87). Belokurov, *PK*, who says that the *Prikaz* had a staff of six translators in 1617, reports that in the sixteenth century young men were being sent to Constantinople to learn Greek and to north Germany for German.

all the greater. The Terek will not be left without an army and without large reinforcements in the future ... The foremost task of the Sovereign's commanders will be to ensure that Shevkal submits to the Sovereign and makes firm peace with King Alexander and opens the road and sends hostages to our Sovereign. And we shall tell you all the news which comes from the Terek and what instructions the Sovereign sends after us as a result of this news; you yourselves are seeing the army which marches to the Terek.' And as for those men from the escort who will stay behind on the Volga at the Portage and at Uvek, Prince Semen and dyak Torkh should say that they have been left behind to gather the Volga and the Don Cossacks ...[1]

(108) And the following gracious gifts have been sent by the Sovereign to the Iberian king Alexander and to the Cherkess princes and murzas.

To King Alexander:

Forty sables, worth 100 rubles,
One thousand ermines, worth 30 rubles,
Fifteen fish teeth, five pud in weight, worth 70 rubles,
A cuirass for 20 rubles,
A helmet for 20 rubles,
And three falcons. In all to the value of 240 rubles, not counting the
  falcons.[2]

To Prince Shikh:

A topcoat of velvet and gold, lined with sables, worth 50 rubles,[3]
A *kaftan* of silk with gold, worth 15 rubles,[4]

[1] See Commentary 7 for the Volga route and the towns along it mentioned in the text.
[2] For furs, fish teeth and cuirasses, see Commentary 10; for royal falcons and falconry in Russia and Georgia, Commentary 26.
[3] A topcoat (*R. shuba*): possibly from German *Schube, Schaube*; through Italian *giubba*, from Arabic *jubba*; but the word may have reached Russia direct from the Arab world (cf. Vasmer, *REW*, Vol. III, p. 433).
[4] A *kaftan* of silk with gold: *kaftan kamchat*: *kaftan* is the Turkish form

A black hat for 7 rubles,
A cuirass, worth 5 rubles.

And to Prince Alkas:

A topcoat of velvet and gold, lined with marten, worth 30 rubles.

And to Shevkal's son Alkas murza, who lives with Shikh:

A topcoat of velvet and gold, lined with marten, worth 30 rubles.

To the Avar prince:

A velvet and gold topcoat, lined with sables, worth 60 rubles,
A black fox hat, worth 10 rubles,
A cuirass, worth 10 rubles.

To his brother the Black Prince:

A velvet and gold topcoat, lined with sables, worth 40 rubles,
A black fox hat, worth 7 rubles,

To the Kabardan prince Solokh:

A velvet and gold topcoat, lined with sables, worth 50 rubles,   (109)
A *kaftan* of silk with gold, worth 15 rubles,
A black fox hat, worth 7 rubles,
A cuirass, worth 10 rubles.

To his son Alkas murza and to his nephew Ibak, a velvet topcoat each, lined with marten, each worth 25 rubles.

of the Persian *khaftan* which occurs already in the *Shahnama*. It was a kind of long tunic with sleeves which in time of war was worn over the mailshirt. Among the Ottoman Turks, *kaftan* was originally a name for a robe of honour which – less important than the sable-skin – was granted on the occasion of appointment to an office (cf. Cl. Huart in *EI*, 1st ed.). This explains the significance of the gift to Shikh Murza. *Kamchat= Kamka*: a loanword from Kazan Turkish, possibly of Chinese origin (cf. Vasmer, *REW*, Vol. 1, p. 514, citing Radlov). It was a closely woven and fairly heavy fabric with an identical pattern on each side; it could be plain or multi-coloured, silver and gold threads being sometimes woven in. Various types of *kamka* were imported into Russia from Turkey and Persia (cf. Fekhner *TRG*, p. 68 and pl. between pp. 64–5; Victoria and Albert Museum *Brief guide to Turkish woven fabrics*, HMSO, 1950).

And such is the Sovereign's letter sent to the commanders on the Terek regarding the departure of the Sovereign's ambassadors and of the Iberian ambassadors and their escort:

From the Tsar and great Prince Fedor Ivanovich of all Russia to our commanders Prince Andrey Ivanovich Khvorostinin and his assistants in the new town on the Terek. We have sent to the Georgian land to King Alexander our ambassadors Semen Grigoryevich Zvenigorodski and dyak Torkh Antonov ... And we have ordered Prince Semen and his comrades and the Georgian ambassadors to travel from the Terek to the lands of Shikh murza of the Okok and then to the lands of the Avar prince and of the Black Prince or to whichever places it is deemed suitable. And we have ordered that horses be issued to the Georgian ambassadors and to the Cherkesses at Astarakhan – 23 horses to the Georgian ambassadors and under their chattels, and 13 horses to the Cherkesses; and our ambassadors Prince Semen and his comrades have been instructed themselves to buy horses at Astarakhan and in your town on the Terek for the monks and the priests and the interpreters and the falconer, at the right price at which horses are bought in Astarakhan and in your parts. When you receive this letter and Prince Semen with his companions and the Georgian and Cherkess ambassadors arrive among you on the Terek, you should – after speaking to Prince Semen – immediately give leave to the Cherkess ambassadors, Shikh's nephew Batay and Solokh's ambassadors Bikan and Aslanbek with their companions, to proceed on the horses which they had been given at Astarakhan to Shikh and to Solokh and to Alkas ahead of the ambassadors Prince Semen and his companions and of the Georgian ambassadors. And you should send word by them to Shikh and to Solokh and to Alkas that we have sent our ambassadors Prince Semen Grigoryevich Zvenigorodski and his companions to the Iberian King Alexander, and that they are to travel to the lands of Shikh and then of the Avar prince.

And if it proves impossible to travel to the Avar's lands, you should instruct the ambassadors to proceed to the land of Prince Alkas. You should cause this to be done in accordance (110) with local conditions and news. And our bounty for them has been sent with our ambassadors. And Solokh and Alkas and Shikh should show their service to us by conducting our ambassadors to whichever places are suitable, together with our men who will be escorting them; they should conduct our ambassadors as far as the Georgian land and they should allow the escort to return home. And should it happen that you do not hold as hostages in Terek-town any of the brothers, children or nephews of Solokh, Alkas or Shikh, you should send word to them about hostages, asking that they should send their brothers and nephews and children as hostages to you at Terek-town ... And after consultation with Prince Semen you should also send to the Avar prince Natsal a *sotnik* and five or six reliable and skilful Cossacks who have visited these parts before; and Shikh murza should send his nephew along with them ... And if the Avar gives a son or a nephew of his as hostage, the *sotnik* should ride with this hostage to you on the Terek to meet the ambassadors; and he should send a messenger about this ahead of him.

And you should send off the ambassadors, Prince Semen and his companions, and the Georgian ambassadors, towards the lands of the Avar prince by whichever route is more convenient and less exposed to attacks by Shevkal and other mountaineers who are disobedient to us; and you should send guides with them as far as the lands of Shikh murza of the Okok or of Prince Alkas, to wherever it is convenient according to the local situation, so that the ambassadors should reach the Georgian land safely. About the escort, a letter has been written to you (111) from the Kazan palace[1]; you are ordered to send up to fifty

---

[1] *iz Kazanskogo Dvortsa*: The Kazan Palace housed the government services concerned with the administration of the former kingdoms of

mounted Terek Cossacks under a *sotnik* and up to 300 foot under a *golova* from the two Astarakhan detachments of 800 men which will come to you from Astarakhan with the ambassadors; or more, according to what the news will be, so that our own and the Iberian ambassadors may proceed in safety from attacks by Shevkal. And you should carefully keep in Terek-town the hostages sent by the Avar prince and the Kabardans Solokh and Prince Alkas and Shikh murza of the Okok, and keep them supplied with food so that they should suffer no want during the time our ambassadors are on their way to or from the Iberian land. And if our ambassadors will spend the winter in the Iberian land, you should release the *murzas* held as hostages and should not keep them with you in the winter. And when you will be expecting our ambassadors back from the Iberian land, you should again take hostages from the princes, so that the ambassadors may travel in safety.

And as regards our bounty which has been sent with our ambassadors for the Cherkess princes, you should talk the matter over with Prince Semen, and he should distribute these gifts in your presence if they come to you at Terek-town. And Prince Semen has been ordered himself to distribute on the way the gifts intended for those through whose lands he will be proceeding, be it the Avar and Black princes or Alkas; and Prince Semen has been ordered to leave with you the bounty for those through whose lands he will not be riding; you should have it sent to such princes or distribute it yourselves as soon as they come to your town. We have left it to you and to Prince Semen to act as would suit and benefit our affairs best; and you should attend to our affairs in accordance with this, in consultation with Prince Semen and his comrades.

Kazan and Astrakhan, of Siberia and the lower Volga. This must be one of the earliest – if not the earliest – documentary reference to the Palace: cf. *Brockhaus and Efron* where the first notice is said to date from 1599. It was originally a wooden building near the *Posolskaya Palata* (cf. *Istoria Moskvy*, Vol. 1, p. 220 and map opposite p. 104, point 30).

You should send us a detailed report in writing about all this: who will be sent as hostages by the Cherkess princes, and how you will send off our own and the Georgian ambassadors, and through what lands they will travel – so that we know all this. And if the Avar prince Natsal does not give a hostage and if it is dangerous for the ambassadors to travel through his land without hostages, our ambassadors Prince Semen and his companions should travel through the lands of Alkas by whichever route is suitable . . .

And having sent off our ambassadors to the Georgian land, you should immediately detail and send off to Prince Shevkal a body of Cossacks or *streltsy*, having selected two or three able men who have been at Shevkaly, know the road and speak Tartar; or it might be suitable to send some of Shikh's Terek Cherkesses; and with them, Prince Andrey, you should send to Prince Shevkal a letter in your name. And a copy has been sent to you as a specimen of the letter which you should send in your name to Shevkal. You should instruct the translator Semen to make a copy in Tartar writing and, having sealed it with your seal, you should, Prince Andrey, send it to Prince (112) Shevkal to whichever place is nearest. And you should also send an oral message from yourself to Shevkal saying that we now wished to send our large army against him because he did not seek our grace towards himself and has not so far sent anyone to us although, earlier on, he had himself wished to send his ambassadors to us with the supplication to be taken into our grace. At the intercession of Prince Murat Kireyev,[1] we have not yet sent our army against him, in our expectation that he would right his conduct towards us . . . And should the Shevkaly prince mend his ways in the future – he should without fail send his son or his nephew and his men to you as hostages . . . Following his supplication and the improvement in his conduct,

[1] For Murat Giray (= Kireyev), a son of the Crimean Khan, see Commentary 11.

we have ordered you to live quietly with Shevkal and (have ordered you) not to start a war against him, but to stand by him against his enemies; and we have commanded you to give him our men with firearms on taking hostages from him . . . And, thereupon, Shevkal should himself march together with you against Aslanbek and his comrades who disobey us and are his enemies, and we shall command you to send our army with firearms to conquer Aslanbek and bring him under our royal hand, and separate him from the Turk and Crimea. And, first of all, Shevkal should show his service and his good faith towards us by not molesting the Iberians in any way and by not making war on them; and as for our ambassadors who have gone to the Iberian land and who will be coming back from the Iberian land, and those who will be travelling to our realm from the Iberian land in the future, and any merchants who will be travelling to you on the Terek from the Iberian land, the Shevkaly prince should not molest any Iberians in any way, and he should open the road from the Iberian land to our realm, and should allow free travel . . . And if it not be suitable to send a message to Shevkal at that time, you should send the message to him after having sent off our ambassadors to King Alexander. And you should act in this as will be suitable according to local conditions. You should read the copy which has been sent to you as specimen of the letter that you should send to Prince Shevkal; and you should translate the passages which are proper to local conditions and should insert them in your message in the way most likely to profit our affairs, in accordance with local conditions . . . And you should send reports to us at the *Posolski Prikaz* so that we are acquainted with the matter . . . Written in Moscow on the 14th day of May in the year 7097 [1589].

(113)
ad fin.

CHAPTER 2

JOURNEY THROUGH KABARDA

To the Sovereign Tsar and Great Prince Fedor Ivanovich (117) of all Russia, thy bondsmen Ondreyets Khvorostinin and his assistants do homage.[1] Sire, in a letter from Astarakhan received on June 24th, your Majesty's ambassador Prince Semen Zvenigorodski and dyak Torkh Antonov wrote to us, your bondsmen, asking that before their arrival we should send messengers to the Avar prince and to the Black Prince[2] and to the Kabardan Cherkesses for your Majesty's ambassadorial affairs. And we, your bondsmen, on the same day sent the *strelets sotnik* Nikita Zinovyev, and with him three *streltsy*, Boriska Fedorov and his comrades, with letters to the Avar prince and to the Black Prince in accordance with your Majesty's instructions; and we also wrote to Shikh murza for the same purpose, that he should come to us at Terek-town on your Majesty's affairs. And, Sire, in a letter received on July 24th, the *strelets sotnik* Nikita Zinovyev wrote to us from the Okok that the Georgian prince Alexander's men, Kazan's son Baygram and Mokholey's son Kelyay,[3] had come

---

[1] *Kholopy tvoi*: 'thy bondsmen'. For discussion, see Commentary 13: The term *kholopy*.

[2] The Black Prince: brother of the Avar Khan (*Nutsal*). His son refers to him by name as 'Karakusha', *T.* eagle, black or handsome bird (p. 118 below). There was a celebrated Turkish Mamluk of the same name in the service of Saladin (cf. *EI*, 1st ed. sub *Karakush*). When Thomas Sackville, himself a veteran of the Turkish campaign of 1595, received G. I. Mikulin, the ambassador of Boris Godunov, in London on 6 January 1601, the latter mentioned among his master's feudatories, 'The Black Prince of the Ovar Land' (cf. D. S. Likhachev, *Puteshestviya*, p. 174 and n. 32).

[3] Mokholey seems to correspond to the well-known Georgian family Maghala-shvili or Maghala-dze, lords of Kavtis-khevi in Upper Kartli

to Shikh murza[1] to enquire about your Majesty's ambassadors and about their own Georgian ambassadors. And on their arrival they said that the Avar prince Natsal is no more and that, Sire, no-one has yet assumed principality among the Avars; and Shikh murza instructed the *strelets sotnik* Nikita Zinovyev not to ride to the Avar. And we, your bondsmen, wrote to Shikh murza that he should send his nephew or some of his leading *uzdens*[2] to find out who will be prince among the Avars, and to convey to the Black Prince our letters which were sent with the *sotnik* ... And Shikh murza and the *strelets sotnik* wrote to us, your servants, that Shikh had sent messages by his *uzdens* to the Avars and to the Black Prince. And, Sire, as soon as the message reached him, Shikh murza came to us, your servants, at Terek-town; he said on arrival that he had sent off our letters to the Avars and to the Black Prince and has found out who was to be prince among the Avars. Kanbuluk, the son of the Avar prince, is to be prince. And this son of the Avar sent word to Shikh that he has not hastened to Terek-town because his position is not yet firm; but he will come very soon together with the Black Prince's son ...

And, Sovereign, on August 6th your Majesty's ambassador Prince Semen Zvenigorodski and dyak Torkh Antonov and

(cf. Wak./Brosset, p. 196, n. 3). Normally subjects of the Kartlian king, their overlords the Amilakhoris (Wak./Brosset, p. 488), were in relations with the Kakhian court and it might well be that one of the Maghalashvilis was in the service of Alexander. For reproduction of fresco of Maghaladze family in the church of Tsinarekhi, see Berdzenishvili, *IG*, p. 376. *Kelyay*= Kolya, a diminutive of Kostantine (Constantine).

[1] For Shikh murza (properly *mirza*), see Commentary 14: Shikh murza of the Okok and 'the little mountain lands'.

[2] *Uzden*: According to Vasmer (*REW*, Vol. III, p. 177), 'Edelmann d. Kaukasischer Bergwohner'. A loanword from Turko-Tartar, cf. Kuman (Coman) *özden* 'frei, adlig'. Equivalent to the Kabardan *work* or *vork*, petty nobles, generally kinsmen, who formed 'the tail' of the *pshe* or prince (cf. Introduction, Section 6 and Commentary 12). These *uzdens* may well be compared to the contemporary 'tacksmen' of the Scottish Highlands.

the monk Zakhkhey of the Trinity arrived at Terek-town and told us that before their own departure we should send off the ambassadors of Alkas and Solokh who had been sent on an embassy to you, Sovereign. And we, your servants, gave instructions that these ambassadors should not be sent off, because we had written many times to Solokh and to Alkas asking that they should come to us, but they have not come to us at Terek-town and have not sent their men; but, Sire, we have instructed that one man each from Solokh's and Alkas's embassies should be sent to them so that they should know that your royal bounty had arrived at Terek-town for them and that their ambassadors are also at Terek-town . . .

And having discussed the matter, we sent off Prince Semen on August 23rd having resolved, Sovereign, that he was to (119) travel to the lands of Alkas; and the Georgian ambassadors also said that there is no better road to Georgia than that. And, Sire, we sent an escort with your Majesty's ambassadors of 50 mounted free Terek Cossacks, your Majesty's men; and we sent free Cossacks for the reason that not one man has enrolled in the mounted *streltsy* on the Terek. We sent the Cossack *sotnik* Ivan Petrov to Astarakhan to enrol mounted *streltsy* but, Sovereign, no mounted *streltsy* were enrolled at Astarakhan either.[1] And we also sent with the ambassadors 50 mounted *streltsy* who had come from Astarakhan and 200 foot *streltsy* and Cossacks from Astarakhan, and 50 foot from the Terek Cossack settlers of Grigori Poltev's regiment.[2] And, Sire, we sent the Cossack captain Vasili Onuchin with 200 *streltsy* and Cossacks to the Sunzha ahead of your Majesty's ambassadors; and we ordered them to hold and fortify all the crossings so as not to let through any men after your Majesty's ambassadors

[1] For Astarakhan = Astrakhan at the end of the sixteenth century, see Commentary 7(g).

[2] For the Terek, see Introduction, Section 3, 'The Terek route through the Caucasus'; and 4, 'The free Terek Cossacks'.

until they reach the Georgian land.[1] And, Sire, we also sent 100 free Terek Cossacks to the crossings . . .[2] Since they were to travel through the lands of Alkas, Prince Semen and dyak Torkh left with us, your bondsmen, your Majesty's bounty for the Avar prince – a golden velvet topcoat lined with sables and with seven silver buttons, a hat made of the necks of black foxes and a cuirass; and for the Black Prince – a topcoat of Bursa velvet with gold, lined with sables, with seven silver buttons, and a hat made of the necks of black foxes . . .[3]

(120)   When Prince Semen camped on the Sunzha, there rode up to the Sunzha Mamstryuk[4] and Kanbulat's nephew Buzuruk murza, and Solokh and Alkas, and the Black Prince's son Geleya and two *uzdens* of the Avar prince Kanbuluk; they were on their way to Terek-town in answer to our letter. And Prince Semen said to them that they should first escort him and, having

---

[1] For the Sunzha river, see final paragraph of Introduction, Section 8. The Sunzha is the main right bank affluent of the Terek.

[2] For the free Terek Cossacks, see Introduction, Section 4.

[3] Barkhat Burski: The Turkish town of Bursa (Brusa) was a major centre for the production of silk and other woven fabrics. Velvet made there was very popular in Russia, where it was used for clothing, room hangings, coverlets, etc. The material often contained gold and silver thread (cf. Fekhner, p. 70). For description of designs of Turkish velvets, see *VA/TWF*, pp. 13–15, plates 15–20.

[4] Mamstryuk or Mastryuk, son of Temryuk (Kemirgoko) was the second of the three brothers of Maria Temryukovna, the Kabardan wife of Ivan IV. After his father's death, about 1573, he was made Prince of Kabarda by the Russians to whom he had proved a staunch ally. Together with his elder brother, Domanuk, he was later killed by his cousin Kazy who had invited them to drink mead and then kept them in chains for three days. 'The genealogy of the Kabardan and Cherkess murzas and princes', printed in Belokurov, *Snosheniya*, p. 3 ff., ascribed the murder to envy because Mamstryuk, a man of fine and noble presence, was feared in Kabarda. A third brother, Saltanuk, baptized as Michael, lived at the court of Ivan IV and was for some years a favourite of the dread Tsar. He was executed in 1571 (see *RBS*, under 'Cherkasski, knyaz Mikhail'). Of turbulent temper, Saltanuk, too, was a strikingly handsome man (see portrait medallion reproduced in *Istoriya Kabardy*, p. 41). Further, see Commentary 12, 'The princely families of Kabarda', p. 270.

done so, should go to Terek-town. And, Sire, these princes and murzas who came to the Sunzha were willing to accompany Prince Semen and they swore to him that they would accompany your Majesty's ambassadors as far as the Georgian land; Alkas gave four *uzdens* as hostages because, Sire, he did not have a son or a nephew with him on the Sunzha . . .

Your Majesty's ambassadors left the Sunzha on September 13th.

Broadcloth had been sent here, Sovereign, for distribution to foreigners who would want to serve you, Sire; and all this broadcloth has been distributed to the Kabardan princes and *murzas* and *uzdens* and to those who took the oath[1] and are now serving you, Sovereign; we, your bondsmen, wrote to you about this before now. And, Sire, there is nothing left to give as your royal bounty to the *murzas* or *uzdens* or Cherkesses who will come to Terek-town in the future and would want to serve you, Sovereign. It is better to give them your Majesty's (121) bounty straight away, even though it be not much. And most of all your Majesty's bounty is needed for Khotov[2] because his service to you, Sovereign, is great. Send your Majesty's command about this to us, your bondsmen.

With these letters we, your servants, have sent to you the Cossack settlers, *sotnik* Ivan Petrov and Nikita Zinovyev; and we have sent Nikita Zinovyev for the reason that he spent the whole winter and spring in Kabarda on your Majesty's affairs

---

[1] *shert dali*: Russian documents distinguished between an oath by a Christian, who was said to have 'kissed the cross' and that sworn by a Moslem: the latter were said to 'give *shert*' (= *T. shart*, condition, agreement, contract, from Arabic) 'according to their faith'. For an engraving of Russians taking an oath by kissing an icon, see Olearius, Vol. I, p. 322.

[2] Khotov: son of Avzaruka (or Aznover) a staunch friend of the Russians. In a letter received in Moscow in September 1589, Andrey Khvorostinin wrote to the Tsar from the Terek: 'Khotov is a prominent man in Kabarda. All the Kabardan princes and *murzas* and *uzdens* heed his advice in everything and no-one can be appointed great prince among them unless he agrees' (Belokurov, *Snosheniya*, p. 75).

109

and gathered information for you, Sire, and was sent to Shikh, to the Okok and to all the Cherkesses. He will relate everything to you, Sovereign, for he knows which Cherkesses serve you, and what their customs are. And, Sovereign, together with them we sent to you Vasili Terentyev who will petition you on behalf of the Cossack settlers about their needs . . . [End of document]

(127)
ad fin.

The Sovereign's ambassadors Prince Semen Zvenigorodski and dyak Torkh Antonov reached Moscow on November 15th [1590]. And they presented a report to the Sovereign on how they had attended to the Sovereign's affairs in the Iberian land . . . And this is the report . . . :

(128)

[When they reached Terek-town] the commanders Prince Andrey and his assistants told the ambassadors Prince Semen and dyak Torkh that they did not hold any brothers, children or nephews of the Cherkess princes Solokh and Alkas as hostages in Terek-town; these Cherkess princes did not come to the new town on the Terek, nor did they send anybody. The commanders received the news that Solokh and Prince Alkas are the allies and friends of the Shevkal prince and that they had sworn fealty to the Turk and to the Crimea. On the other hand, Shikh murza visits Terek-town and serves the Sovereign.[1]

The commanders also said that they had sent the *strelets sotnik* Nikita Zinovyev along with three Cossacks to the Avar and to the Black Prince with a request for hostages; they bade him ride by way of Shikh's settlement . . . And to Kabarda, to the Cherkess princes Solokh and Alkas they sent the *strelets* Grishka Ivanov and the Cossacks Demka Ivanov and Nikiforka Semenov; and they sent word by them that Solokh and Alkas should come . . . to Terek-town to receive the Sovereign's bounty, and should bring trustworthy hostages with them.

[1] For *Terski-gorodok* and *gorodishche*: see Introduction, Section 5 and Commentary 2(a).

This *sotnik* Nikita Zinovyev wrote to them, the commanders Prince Andrey and his assistants, that when he arrived at Shikh's, two of King Alexander's men – Baygram the son of Kazan and Kelyay the son of Mokholey also came to Shikh. They said to him that King Alexander had sent them to Shikh murza to enquire about the Sovereign's and his own ambassadors and find out how soon they would reach Terek-town, and to study the roads: which route would be preferable. And they investigated the route: the ambassadors would be safe to travel to the Metsk mountain ranges, to Shikh's people, to the lands of Burnash and of Amaley, and to the Batsk mountain ranges; and this land of Batsk is ruled by their sovereign Alexander...[1]

And they gave two letters to him, the *sotnik*, from King Alexander... and *sotnik* Nikita sent both these letters to Prince Andrey and his assistants. And the ambassadors Prince Semen and dyak Torkh took these letters from the commanders and gave orders that they should be translated and copied out twice; they sent one set of copies to the Sovereign and the other they kept themselves. And as for the originals, they gave Prince Andrey and his assistants the letter which was addressed to the commander, and they gave Prince Kaplan and his assistants the one that was written to the Georgian ambassadors... And as regards what King Alexander wrote in his letter to his ambassadors about the Sovereign's army, the Georgian ambassadors said to Prince Semen and dyak Torkh that the Sovereign had extended his grace to their sovereign King Alexander at his supplication, and ordered that a numerous army be lent to him against Shevkal. But they now see that the army which came with them to Terek-town is not big...

And the ambassadors Prince Semen and dyak Torkh said: (129) *ad fin.* 'One thousand two hundred of the Sovereign's men with fire-arms have come to Terek-town with us from Astarakhan

[1] For Metsk, Batsk: see Commentary 15.

to reinforce the troops ready on the Terek, and another big army on horses and in boats will be sent against Shevkal after us, for we have been ordered by the Sovereign to travel in (130) haste, since our journey is long . . . If Shevkal so much as dares not to mend his ways towards the Sovereign and not be at peace with King Alexander, where could Shevkal hide from the Sovereign?'

On August 21st Shikh murza arrived at Terek-town. And the ambassadors Prince Semen and dyak Torkh, having consulted the Terek commanders, Prince Andrey and his assistants, issued orders to give him quarters in the courtyard. And on the same day, the ambassadors sent the *strelets sotnik* Grigori Kutarinov and the interpreter Ivanis Dragichev to fetch Shikh; and they bade them tell Shikh that he should ride to their camp for there was the Sovereign's bounty and letter to him.

And Shikh murza rode up to the camp; the ambassadors bade him come to their tent – and Shikh came to the tent. And the ambassadors Prince Semen and dyak Torkh saluted him on behalf of the Sovereign and handed him the letter and made the speech according to the Sovereign's instructions; and they gave him the Sovereign's bounty according to the list; and Shikh murza did homage on the Sovereign's bounty. He said that he intends to serve the Sovereign till his death, as he and his father had served the Sovereign and the latter's father, the Sovereign Tsar and great Prince Ivan Vasilyevich . . . And he brought as a hostage his nephew Batay, whom he had sent on an embassy to the Sovereign. And Prince Semen and dyak Torkh sent Batay to the commanders, Prince Andrey and his assistants.

Answering the ambassadors' questions, Shikh murza said the following about the Cherkess princes Solokh and Alkas, and about Shevkal's son Alkas murza and about the Avar prince and the Black Prince, and about Shevkal and the

Kumukh and the Georgian news, and about the best route for the ambassadors to follow:

Solokh and Prince Alkas are at present the allies of Prince Shevkal and they all side with the Turk and with Crimea. A Crimean prince visited Prince Aslanbek this spring with bounty (131) from the Turk, so that they should serve the Turk and Crimea together with Shevkal; and these princes, Solokh and Alkas, visited the [Crimean] prince and accepted the bounty. And Prince Alkas at present lives two days' ride away from his former settlement to which Rodion Birkin and Petr Pivov had made their way when they were travelling through Kabarda; the spot where Alkas's settlement [*kabak*] used to stand is at present empty. Alkas was chased out in war by Aslanbek's kin – by Yansokh and his brothers and by Aslanbek's man Yansokhchisy, because Alkas had killed Katmas and Karbek, the sons of Kalabaty, his brother; and Kalabaty's sons are their kinsmen. Aslanbek himself, the great prince of Kabarda, died about six weeks previously; and it is reported that the whole Kabardan land intends to give his throne to his brother Yansokh. He, Shikh, sent his nephew to the Avar prince and the Black Prince, but he still does not know who has firmly assumed principality among the Avars. Shevkal's son Alkas murza used to live near his, Shikh's settlement, but he now lives in the Shevkal land, in the settlement of his brother Sarkh; he was chased out of his own settlement by the Kumyk princes Kolprov and Budachey, the sons of Smail [Ismail]. Shevkal's son Alkas murza now lives in captivity, and he, Shikh, sent his man to him, but his man did not reach him, and he does not know whether Alkas murza is still alive or not. And about the route, Shikh said that he knows all the roads; it is preferable to travel by the old road followed by Rodion Birkin rather than by one of the two roads to the lands of the Avar prince and the Black Prince investigated by King Alexander's men; the journey by those routes lies through the mountains and is long and hard for men and packhorses.[1]

And the Georgian ambassadors Prince Kaplan and his assistants also said that it is better to take the road followed by Rodion Birkin . . .

(132)   The ambassadors Prince Semen and dyak Torkh left Terektown in boats for the Sunzha on the 23rd day of August; and Shikh murza travelled with them. In addition to their former escort of 50 mounted *streltsy* who had been given to them at Astarakhan instead of mounted Terek *streltsy* − since no mounted *streltsy* had enrolled on the Terek[2] − and in addition to the *sotnik* and the forty Astarakhan *streltsy* who were to go with them to the Georgian land, the commanders Prince Andrey and his assistants gave them an escort of 250 Cossack foot from Astarakhan and the Terek under three *sotniks* and forty-three free mounted Terek Cossacks under three atamans. The *sotnik* with the mounted *streltsy* and the atamans with the free Cossack horse and the twenty *yurt* Tartars [who had received the Sovereign's command to escort the ambassadors as far as the Sunzha] were sent off from Terek-town by the ambassadors Prince Semen and dyak Torkh along with their own horses to the Sunzha overland.[3] The *streltsy* and Cossack foot travelled in boats with the ambassadors . . .

[1] A route through 'the lands of the Avar and the Black Princes' must have led from the Sunzha up the valley of the Khulkhulau to Botlikh and the Andi-koysu and thence to Khunzakh and the valley of the Avar-koysu. From here, there was access through the Dido country into Kakheti. It was a difficult and dangerous way (cf. Commentary 41: The Didos). Although the Georgians had no military control over the tracks through Didoeti (see text below, p. 211), there is evidence for considerable Georgian influence in Avaria as far east as Antsukh and Khunzakh − where a Georgian inscription has been recovered; see Genko, pp. 727 ff. and *Novy Vostok*, Vol. 5, 1924, p. 244.

[2] Emending the Russian text to read: *chto na Terke konnye streltsy ne pribralis* (by adding *ne*).

[3] Yurt Tartars was the term applied to those living in Astrakhan and nearby villages. They claimed descent from the Tartars of the Golden Horde and were related to the Nogays. The term *yurt* means (a) a moveable hut; and, (b) a family plot, or land belonging to a tribe of nomads who

Prince Semen and dyak Torkh reached the Sunzha on the 8th day of September. And the Cossack captain Vasili Onuchin (133) came to them and said that Chapolov, son of Aslanbek the great prince of the Kabardan Cherkesses, and Kanbulat's son Kudenek, and Kudenek's cousin Buzuruk murza, and two of Khotov's nephews, Azlov and Shumunuk – who is a brother-in-law of the Shevkal prince – had come to the Sunzha on September 4th; and some 60 of their *uʒdens* and ordinary Cherkesses came with them. They encamped some two versts from the blockhouse. He asked them why they had come, and these princes replied that they were waiting for the Sovereign's ambassadors who were on their way to the Georgian land . . .

Aslanbek's son Prince Chapolov, with Kudenek and Buzuruk and two of Khotov's nephews and some forty of their (134) *uʒdens* and Cherkesses rode up on September 9th to the camp of the ambassadors Prince Semen and dyak Torkh, who bade them come to their tent . . .

Prince Chapolov swore fealty to the Sovereign and took the oath on behalf of his uncle Yansokh and his brothers and $\substack{(135) \\ ad\,fin.}$ Yansokh's children and nephews and all his kin and the whole of his land . . . Kudenek's cousin Buzuruk murza and Khotov's nephews also took the oath on the same charter which had been sent to the ambassadors from Moscow by Busurman Bely . . .[1]

Chapolov and Kudenek said about Solokh that Prince Auzachek-saltan, brother of the king of the Crimea, spent the winter with Solokh whom he asked for his daughter in marriage for the king of the Crimea; the prince took the daughter from Solokh this spring and rode off to the king of the Crimea. And the king took this daughter of Solokh.[2]

had settled in permanent homesteads (Brockhaus and Efron). For good illustration of (a) above, see Le Brun, Vol. I, opposite p. 96.

[1] For these Cherkess personalities, see Commentary 12: 'The princely families of Kabarda'.

[2] Auzachek-saltan (= Saadet Giray), see Commentary 11: 'Murat Giray'.

(136)
ad fin.

The Cossacks Grisha Ivanov and Nikiforka Ivanov, who had been sent by the Terek commanders to fetch Solokh and Alkas, also came to the ambassadors Prince Semen and dyak Torkh on the Sunzha. And they said that Mamstryuk, having taken them with him, had journeyed to Solokh in order to bring him under the Sovereign's hand. Having heard the commanders' letter, Solokh gave them no answer ... He ordered that they, the Cossacks, be robbed of their horses and saddles and bridles. Mamstryuk mounted them on horses which he had obtained from friendly *uzdens*. And when another letter about escorting the ambassadors came for Solokh, they again took it to him. Mamstryuk and Kudenek and Khotov camped some five versts from his settlement but did not visit him, fearing him since he is a strong man in Kabarda; he does not love them because he says that they had brought the Sovereign's men to the Terek and because the Sovereign had ordered the building of a town on the Terek for their benefit. Having heard the letter, Solokh said that he would not ride to escort the Sovereign's ambassadors until Prince Murat Kirey bade him do so.[1] 'I act', he said, 'according to Prince Murat Kirey's letter; and I am not going to the commanders at Terek-town.' They, the Cossacks, heard in his settlement that all his *uzdens* want to serve the Sovereign and are bringing him round to it, saying to him: 'The whole of Kabarda has now held council to serve the Sovereign, and you want to oppose such a great Sovereign and the whole of Kabarda.' And the brother of Bikan, whom Solokh had sent on an embassy to the Sovereign, also supplicated Solokh and said: 'How can you not serve the Sovereign, and forsake my brother? I shall leave you for another prince.' But Solokh refused them all, saying 'How

(137) can I leave the Crimea, and Shevkal and the Kumyks? Two of my daughters and many kinsmen and clansmen are in

---

[1] For Murat Giray (= Kireyev), see Commentary 11.

the Crimea and in the land of Shevkal and the Kumyks.[1]'

The same Cossacks and the Terek ataman Sholokh[2] said to the ambassadors prince Semen and dyak Torkh ... that a *chaush*[3] of the Turkish sultan, who was on his way to the Turk's town of Derbent with some 90 men, stayed at Mamstryuk's settlement. He was being conducted by Aslanbek's and by Solokh's men who took him across the Terek at Solokh's settlement and conducted him towards Michkizy,[4] keeping behind the mountains. Mamstryuk did not send this information to the Sovereign's captains in the blockhouse nor did he let them, the Cossacks, leave with the news. They asked him for permission to ride to the blockhouse with the news, and even wrote a letter, wanting to send it to the blockhouse by an Okok Cherkess; and he, Mamstryuk, took the letter away from them and tore it up, and he beat up that Cherkess. And he told them that there was no such custom among Cherkesses as to do evil to a guest in the settlement, and that the *chaush* had come as a guest to him. When he had seen the *chaush* on his way, he sent his own men after him to rob him; and his men stole 10 horses from the *chaush* and brought them to him, while the *chaush's* men killed one of his *uzdens*.[5]

[1] For the complex relations between the Circassian princes and the Crimean Khans, see Commentary 16.

[2] The Terek ataman Sholokh: the name is Caucasian; cf. Kabardan Solokh and Georgian Cholok; it also occurs in Serbian in the form Cholok. That the Terek *ataman* should bear this name underlines the mixture of Russian and Caucasian elements in the make up of the Terek Cossacks, emphasized by Baddeley, *RFC*, Vol. II, p. 210.

[3] *chaush*: In the Ottoman period the term was used for a court official, often employed by the Sultan as an ambassador or envoy to convey or carry out orders; only in the nineteenth century did the term become the equivalent of 'sergeant' in the army (cf. article by R. Mantran in *EI*, 2nd ed. and longer study by M. Fuad Köprülü in *IA*).

[4] Michkizy: cf. Commentary 14, where *Minkizy*, *Michkizy* is identified with canton of Michik. The route would bring the party 'behind the mountains' represented by the Karkalikovski ridge of Felitsyn's map.

[5] An incident characteristic of the rules of hospitality among mountain peoples – including the Gaels of the Scottish Highlands. A visitor was a

And the Black Prince's son Geleya[1] with the Avar prince's
uᵹdens ... arrived on the Sunzha on September 8th. And on
September 9th the ambassadors Prince Semen and dyak Torkh
sent the interpreter Ivan Nikolayev to fetch Geleya ... And
he rode to the ambassadors' camp with the *uᵹdens* and entered
the tent ... The Black Prince's son Geleya and the Avar
prince's *uᵹdens* did homage on the Sovereign's bounty, and
Geleya said:

(139) 'My father Karakusha and my uncle, the Avar prince Natsal,
have long wanted to be in the Sovereign's grace ... but they
have so far had no opportunity to do homage to the Sovereign.
But I have now been sent by my father the Black Prince and by
my cousin Kanbuluk, son of the Avar prince Natsal ... They
want to serve the Sovereign ...'

And the Black Prince's son Geleya swore fealty and took the
oath to the Sovereign on behalf of his father and of his cousin,
Natsal's son Kanbuluk, and of all his kin and of the Avar and
the Black lands ...

Prince Mamstryuk arrived on the Sunzha on September 11th.
And the ambassadors Prince Semen and dyak Torkh sent the
Cossack *sotnik* Nikita Karachurin and the interpreter Ivanis
(139) *ad fin.* Dragichev, bidding them tell him to come to their camp. And
Mamstryuk rode to their camp and came to their tent ...

(140) And Mamstryuk said: 'I now serve the Sovereign as much
as and even more than I had hitherto served the great

kunak or guest so long as he remained under his host's roof or on his host's
lands but might be attacked after passing the bounds. According to
Baddeley (*RFC*, Vol. 1, p. 250), the limit of free and unquestioned
hospitality in Osetia was three days. In Ireland, under the old Brehon
Law (Vol. IV, p. 237), the chieftain grades were bound to entertain a guest
without asking any questions. 'Once a guest had partaken of food in a
house, his host was bound to abstain from offering him any violence or
disrespect under any circumstances.' Here again, the formal limit was three
days (Joyce, *SHAI*, pp. 168, 171). For Mamstryuk see p. 108, n. 4 above;
for obligations of hospitality among Cherkesses, see Nogmov, pp. 31 ff.
[1] For the Black Prince, see p. 105, n. 2 above.

Sovereign's father . . . Ivan Vasilyevich of all Russia and him, the [present] Sovereign. I neither eat nor drink, but I all the time attend to the Sovereign's affairs, day and night, so as to bring all the mountain princes under his royal hand. And among the Kabardan princes, only one is not loyal to the Sovereign – Prince Solokh. All the other Kabardan princes have been brought under the Sovereign's hand. I have been to see Alkas – and Alkas wants to serve the Sovereign and wanted to meet you, the Sovereign's ambassadors. The Sovereign should order his commanders to march with an army against those princes who do not want to be under his royal hand, such as Shevkal and the Kumyks and Prince Solokh and some other mountain princes; and we, the Kabardan princes who are under his royal hand, are all of us ready to march with the Sovereign's commanders with all our men. War should be waged on them urgently, this winter; if the Sovereign's army is not sent against them this winter it will be impossible to conquer them in the summer because they would flee into the mountains. And it is necessary to wage war on them without delay so long as these princes are not all united; once they unite, a numerous army will be needed against them, and it will be impossible to conquer them with a small army. Now they have heard that Aslanbek's settlement with all the princes have come under the Sovereign's hand . . . and therefore they will soon unite.' And he said about the Turkish *chaush* that he was a guest in his settlement. 'It is laid down in our Cherkess customs: when somebody is a guest in a settlement, no evil should be done to him . . . I did not escort this *chaush*; he was escorted by Solokh's men. I sent the free Terek Cossack Sholokh with news to the blockhouse, but Sholokh would not go, saying that he would not be in time, travelling on foot.'[1]   (141)

[1] For the 'free Terek Cossack Sholokh' see p. 117, n. 2 above. He should be distinguished, of course, from the Kabardan prince Solokh, for whom see p. 122, n. 1 below.

And the ambassadors Prince Semen and dyak Torkh said: 'A numerous force with firearms has come with us from Astarakhan to the Sovereign's commanders on the Terek, and another force will reach Terek-town after us; the Sovereign's commanders on the Terek have orders to campaign together with you, princes, against those who disobey our Sovereign and refuse to come under his royal hand. Having escorted us, you should all visit the commanders at Terek-town and come to an agreement with them on how to conquer those who disobey our Sovereign, and how to bring them under his hand; and your troops should be ready by that time . . .'

On September 12th Prince Alkas and some 30 of his *uzdens* came to Prince Semen and dyak Torkh on the Sunzha. And the ambassadors sent the *strelets sotnik* Grigori Kutarinov and the interpreter Ivanis Dragichev to Alkas . . . And Prince Alkas rode up to their camp and entered their tent . . .[1]

(142)
ad fin.
Prince Alkas did homage to the Sovereign on the Sovereign's letter and said: 'I have not visited the commanders as I feared to undertake the journey because of my enemies among the Kabardan princes; but I want to be in the Sovereign's grace under his royal hand, together with my brothers and my children and my nephews and all my kinsfolk and the whole land, and I want to serve him till my death. I myself shall ride to escort you to King Alexander in Georgia . . . Is it not a security and an oath for you that I am going myself with you to Georgia?'

And the ambassadors said: 'You should serve the Sovereign

[1] Alkas was the Prince of Little Kabarda, for whom a gift had been reserved less valuable than that presented to Shikh murza (see p. 99 above and Commentary 12: 'The princely families of Kabarda'). He is to be distinguished from Alkas murza, a son of the Shevkal, who was living under the protection of Shikh murza, and from Alkas murza, son of Solokh (see Commentary 17).

Birkin and Pivov had stopped at the *kabak* of Alkas at the end of July, 1587 (Belokurov, *Snosheniya*, pp. 33–4).

loyally. Take the oath and give hostages, like the other Cherkess princes . . .'

Prince Alkas said: 'Should you not believe me without the (143) oath and without hostages, take me with you bound up, if you want, without letting me out of your sight. And myself I shall not ride away from you. But I cannot take the oath and give hostages.'

And the ambassadors Prince Semen and dyak Torkh said: 'Why can you not take the oath and give hostages?'

Prince Alkas replied: 'I have reached old age, and hitherto people believed my word in everything, and I have never given hostages or taken the oath to anyone.'

The ambassadors said: 'What we know is that there is a Cherkess custom among you princes: you confirm everything by oath and hostages among yourselves; and things do not happen without this, according to your custom. So how can you refuse to take the oath to the great Sovereign and give no hostages?'

And Prince Alkas said: 'I shall take the oath. I shall send my *uzdens* to escort you, but shall not go myself and shall not send my son to the Sovereign and shall not give hostages.'

Prince Semen and dyak Torkh said: 'You can, Alkas, either go to escort us yourself, or not, as you wish. You can see for yourself that we have got many of the Sovereign's men with us, and all the Kabardan princes are also escorting us. So take the oath to the Sovereign and give hostages: for this royal affair cannot be concluded without hostages.'

And Prince Alkas said: 'If the Kabardan princes want to escort you, let them escort you. I am returning home and shall not give you hostages, and your road lies through my land.'

The ambassadors replied: 'If you do not mend your ways towards the great Sovereign, it will be impossible for you, Alkas, to live in your settlement, not only because the Sovereign's commanders on the Terek will send the Sovereign's army against you, but also because of the Kabardan princes who are under the great Sovereign's hand.'

⁽¹⁴³⁾
^{ad fin.} And Prince Alkas said: 'Give me time to talk to my *uzdens*.' He left the tent and talked with his *uzdens*, then went back to the tent and said: 'Put me honestly in the Sovereign's grace, (144) like the other Kabardan princes who are under the Sovereign's hand and who make free use of the fisheries and the chase and all resources along the Terek and the Sunzha and other rivers, and whom the Sovereign's *streltsy* and free Cossacks ferry across the Terek and the Sunzha and other rivers at the crossings, themselves and their men; and when they find it necessary to march against some of their enemies, the Sovereign's commanders give them men. You should treat me in the same way as these princes; and I shall take the oath to the Sovereign and shall give hostages. I am willing to escort you, the ambassadors, and shall send my son with you to the Sovereign.'

The ambassadors Prince Semen and dyak Torkh said: 'The commanders on the Terek have the Sovereign's order for when you mend your ways towards the Sovereign and start serving him loyally. And we shall also write to the Sovereign's commanders about this.'

Alkas did homage to the Sovereign, took the oath on behalf of his children and nephews and all his kinsfolk and his clan and the whole of his land ... And the ambassadors gave Prince Alkas the Sovereign's bounty according to the list, and he did homage to the Sovereign on the bounty.

Prince Semen and dyak Torkh asked Alkas about Solokh: 'Where is Prince Solokh and why does he not come to us? And we have heard that Prince Solokh is your friend, Prince Alkas.'[1]

And Prince Alkas said: 'Solokh is my friend, and in our

---

[1] For the personality and difficulties of Solokh see Commentary 17.

thoughts we are as one man; and Solokh will now come to you.'

Prince Solokh came to the Sunzha on the same day; and with him came some thirty of his *uzdens*, or more. And the ambassadors sent the *strelets sotnik* Grigori Kutarinov and the interpreter Ivanis Dragichev to Solokh . . . and he rode up to the ambassadors' camp within the hour and came to the tent.

(144)
ad fin.

And the ambassadors Prince Semen and dyak Torkh made a speech to Prince Solokh in the Sovereign's name, and they saluted him and handed him the letter according to the Sovereign's instructions. They then told him how he had sent supplicants to the Sovereign asking to be accepted under his royal hand, and how he did not mend his ways towards the Sovereign, and how he should now mend his ways and give hostages, and escort them, the ambassadors, and send his son to the Sovereign – the same things as they had told Prince (145) Alkas.

Prince Solokh did homage to the Sovereign on his bounty and said: 'I have not visited the Sovereign's commanders because of ill health. And now the Kabardan princes, my enemies, are assembled by you; should they tell you, the Sovereign's ambassadors, lies about me out of enmity – you should not believe these princes. Till my death I want to be in the Sovereign's grace under the Sovereign's hand, and serve him together with my children and my nephews and all my kinsfolk and the whole of the land. I shall escort you to the Georgian land and back to Terek-town and I am taking the oath to the Sovereign. And the fact that I shall go to escort you is a security.'

And the ambassadors Prince Semen and dyak Torkh said: 'You must serve the Sovereign loyally. So give as a hostage a son or a brother or a nephew, who can be trusted, so that the Sovereign may be secure in holding you in his Majesty's grace under his royal hand, and that you may be secure in the Sovereign's grace.'

And Prince Solokh replied: 'Prince Alkas has given his *uʒden* Aslanbek as a hostage to the Sovereign, and Prince Alkas is my great friend. You should have faith in the same security, and I shall be under his royal hand secured by this same hostage given by Alkas.'

Prince Semen and dyak Torkh said that it would be insufficient for them, the two princes, to be secured by one hostage.

And Prince Solokh said: 'Let me talk to my *uʒdens*.' Leaving the tent he talked to them and when he came back he said: 'I need not argue about hostages, so long as I enjoy the Sovereign's grace. If I need men against some enemy, the Sovereign should show his grace to me by ordering the commanders on the Terek to give me men, and he should give me the freedom of fisheries and of the chase and of all other resources along the Terek and other rivers, in the places where I enjoyed them hitherto. He should instruct his men not to raid me and my men at the crossings and favourable places along the rivers.'[1]

The ambassadors Prince Semen and dyak Torkh said: 'As soon as you mend your ways towards the Sovereign, take the oath, give hostages and begin serving the Sovereign loyally – the Sovereign's commanders have his order about you, princes; and we shall write to the Sovereign's commanders about you.'

(146) And Prince Solokh swore fealty to the sovereign on behalf of his brothers and of his children and nephews and all his kinsfolk and the whole of his land, and himself and his best *uʒdens*

---

[1] It is interesting to note the formality of the chief taking counsel with his *uʒdens* before committing himself. The cattle fords and fishing rights along the rivers were of great importance to tribal economies throughout the Caucasian area as they were in the contemporary Gaelic world of Ireland and the Scottish Highlands.

took the oath... And the ambassadors gave him the Sovereign's bounty according to the list.[1]

Prince Solokh did homage to the Sovereign on his bounty and said: 'I have been receiving the Turkish Sultan's and the Crimean king's bounty for many years; but from now on, forgetting all this bounty of theirs, I shall bow under the Sovereign's hand. I myself and my children with all my kinsfolk and the whole of the land want to serve only him, the Sovereign, until my death. When you will be on your way back from Georgia, I shall send my son to the Sovereign with you.'

And after that the ambassadors said to Solokh and to Prince Alkas that the whole of Kabarda and the Avar and the Black lands had bowed under the Sovereign's hand, and that the Iberian King Alexander also served the Sovereign, while the Kizilbash Shah had also sent his ambassadors with a petition to the Sovereign. The Shevkal prince had not till now done homage to the Sovereign, and a big army with firearms had come to Terek-town from Astarakhan for operations against him. The commanders on the Terek had the Sovereign's order to send his army and all Kabarda and the Black lands and the Avar lands against Shevkal, and the Sovereign had ordered the Georgian King Alexander to march with all his land against Shevkal. And where could he escape from the great Sovereign?

On the following day Solokh and Prince Alkas rode to the ambassadors' camp and sent word asking to be received on the Sovereign's affairs. And the ambassadors Prince Semen and dyak Torkh bade them come to their tent.

Solokh and Alkas came to the tent and said: 'We have heard from you that the Sovereign has sent a numerous army to

[1] Solokh received exactly the same gifts as Shikh murza of the Okok, except that his cuirass was of twice the value (see p. 99 above). In value they compare with those sent to the Avar prince, but then Solokh was 'a strong man in Kabarda' (p. 116 above).

Terek-town for operations against Shevkal, and has ordered the commanders on the Terek to wage war on him; we supplicate the Sovereign on Shevkal's behalf not to order the dispatch of his army against Shevkal. He will send his ambassadors to petition the Sovereign.'[1]

Prince Semen and dyak Torkh replied: 'Our great Sovereign, the Tsar and great Prince, will not want to shed blood – if Shevkal sends his ambassadors to do homage to the Sovereign without delay. Should Shevkal want to send his ambassadors... he should do so this autumn. And you, Solokh and Alkas, should vouch for this to us. We shall then write to the Sovereign's commanders on the Terek bidding them not to wage war on him before they get the Sovereign's order.'

(147) And Solokh and Prince Alkas said: 'We shall send a message to Shevkal about this or shall ourselves ride to settle with him that he should not delay in sending his ambassadors to do homage to the Sovereign this autumn.'

The ambassadors Prince Semen and dyak Torkh told the Georgian ambassadors that Solokh and Alkas should do homage to the Sovereign on Shevkal's behalf.

Prince Semen and dyak Torkh set out from the Sunzha for the Georgian land on September 14th.[2] And the Cherkess princes Chapolov son of Aslanbek, and Mamstryuk son of Temryuk, and Kanbulat's son Kudenek, and the Black Prince's son, and Shikh murza of the Okok, rode to escort them and the Sovereign's men. Solokh and Prince Alkas told the ambassadors that they would ride ahead and wait for them at the Hot Well on Osman's road...[3] And as for the princes and murzas and *uzdens* for whom no bounty had been sent by the Sovereign, Prince Semen and dyak Torkh distributed to them

---

[1] For Solokh's friendly relations with Shevkal see pp. 116–17 above.

[2] See Commentary 18: 'Itinerary of the ambassadors from Sunzha fort to Daryal.

[3] For 'the Hot Well on Osman's Road' see Commentary 18(a).

squirrel coats and broadcloth and hats and silks of their own. The Sovereign's bounty, the fur coats for Solokh's son Alkas murza and his nephew Ibak, who had not come to the ambassadors and about whom Solokh said that they were away, was taken along by Prince Semen and dyak Torkh in case they should encounter them on the way . . .

On that date the ambassadors Prince Semen and dyak Torkh camped at the Hot Well. And in the night the Terek Cossack Ivashko Gilyanets[1] brought news to the ambassadors, and he said that twenty Cossacks under the *pyatidesyatnik* Maslo stood at Osman's crossing on the river Sunzha; and unknown Cherkesses, about fifteen in number, had come to the crossing an hour before sunset that evening. They raided these Cherkesses and took four men alive, while the others escaped across the river to the Kumyks.

Prince Semen and dyak Torkh sent the Cossack headman (148) Vasili Onuchin, who was escorting them with his men, with the message to find out and enquire who had been attacked and how many people were taken alive. And Vasili Onuchin sent the Cossack *sotnik* Fedor Vladimirov to the ambassadors with the news that the raid was at the Sunzha crossing against Cherkesses who were on their way across the river; Prince Alkas, his *uzden* Smail [Ismail] and two of Prince Solokh's *uzdens* were seized alive in the raid.

The ambassadors ordered Vasili Onuchin to bring Prince Alkas to their camp, and they said to Alkas: 'You swore fealty to the great Sovereign and gave hostages that you would serve him and would escort us, the ambassadors, as far as King

---

[1] *Gilyanets* can indicate a man of Ghilan origin or one so named because he had been in Ghilan. As indicated in Introduction, Section 4, the Terek Cossacks were of very mixed origin. For this name cf. Petros di Sargis Gilanentz, an Armenian adventurer active in Persia in 1723 – on whom see Laurence Lockhart, *The fall of the Safavi dynasty*, pp. 506–9; and C. Minasian, *The Chronicle of Petros di Sarkis Gilanentz* (Lisbon, 1959).

Alexander in the Georgian land. Where did you now try to ride, Alkas? The road to the Shevkal lies that way.'

And Prince Alkas said: 'Prince Solokh asked me to escort his guests, Kumyks who had come to visit him. Prince Solokh has told you about those guests of his.'

And the ambassadors Prince Semen and dyak Torkh said: 'Prince Solokh spoke to us about his guests and asked that we should give orders for them to be escorted to the crossing where you have been captured. We instructed him not to send his guests to that crossing, and we bade Vasili Onuchin escort them across near the blockhouse.'

And Prince Alkas replied: 'I have sinned. I am guilty before God and before the Sovereign, because I have escorted Solokh's guests to that crossing; but I only escorted them to the river, and having escorted them as far as the river, I rode to meet you, the ambassadors. The Sovereign's men assailed me and seized me and two of Solokh's *uzdens*.' And the Cossacks also told the ambassadors that Alkas was taken at Osman's crossing on the side of the river nearest the ambassadorial camp.

Prince Semen and dyak Torkh said to Prince Alkas: 'We have no faith in your hostage now. Give us your son as hostage.'

And Prince Alkas said: 'My son is not with me now. Should you need my son I shall send for him.'

So in addition to his former pledge Prince Semen and dyak Torkh took three of his best *uzdens* . . . and sent them off with the *strelets sotnik* Grigori Kutarinov to Vasili Onuchin at the blockhouse until such time as Alkas should send his son; and they gave him five days to produce his son Aslanbek and send him to the blockhouse. They ordered Vasili Onuchin to release the *uzden* who was captured at the same time as Alkas . . .

(149)   The ambassadors Prince Semen and dyak Torkh left the Hot Well on the 17th day of September; and on that date they

128

camped on the river Sunzha at its lower bend. And on the 18th they camped at the Kholopenski site which had been the town of Temireksak. On the 19th they camped in a meadow where the river Sunzha forms a bend. And on the 20th they camped on the Bystraya stream. On the 21st they camped on the river Terek to the left of Alkas's old settlement. On the 22nd, having twice crossed the Terek, they camped in the Black Mountains.[1]

And on the 23rd Prince Alkas sent two of his *uzdens* to the ambassadors; he did not come himself but encamped some ten versts away. And his *uzdens* said that Alkas brought his son as a hostage. Prince Semen and dyak Torkh sent the *strelets* Orzhenik to fetch Prince Alkas and ask that he should bring his son with him. Prince Alkas sent word with Orzhenik and with his *uzdens* asking that the ambassadors send him a letter authorizing the release of his *uzdens* on the Sunzha, and adding that he would send his son to King Alexander with Alexander's ambassadors.

The ambassadors sent word to Alkas that he should send his son to Vasili Onuchin on the Sunzha; Vasili would take his son and release his *uzdens*.

On the same day Prince Semen and dyak Torkh sent back the escorting *strelets sotnik* Vasili Gnedishchev and his comrades with the *streltsy* and the Cossacks; they entrusted to them the Sovereign's bounty, the fur coats which had been sent for Solokh's son and nephew; they instructed the *sotniks* to hand them over to the commanders Prince Andrey and his assistants, at Tyumen-town, for the reason that Solokh's son and nephew had not met them on the road to receive the Sovereign's bounty. Prince Semen and dyak Torkh themselves set out on September 24th. And on that day and on the 25th they camped beneath Mount Shat about one verst

[1] For the details of the route between 17th and 22nd September see Commentary 18, (b) to (g).

beyond Saltan murza's settlement at Lars, on the river Terek.[1]

Saltan murza came out on foot to meet the ambassadors, and some ten of his men came with him. And he said: 'Before now the Sovereign's envoys Rodion Birkin and Petr Pivov journeyed through my land, this settlement of mine, on their way to the Georgian land, to King Alexander. And on their way (150) back from the Georgian land they again journeyed through my settlement – and I served the Sovereign, escorted his envoys Rodion and Petr through my land . . . And as for the sick men and horses who were with the Sovereign's envoys, Rodion and Petr left such men and horses with me when they were on their way to Georgia. I fed and treated these men and these horses and I sent them off in good health with Rodion and Petr. When they were on their way back from Georgia, Rodion and Petr said that they would notify my service to the Sovereign.'

(150)
ad fin.
The ambassadors Prince Semen and dyak Torkh said: 'You acted well, and that was service towards our great Sovereign . . . And now show your service to the Sovereign again: indicate to us which is the best road to the Georgian land, and yourself escort us as far as the Georgian land . . .'

(151) The ambassadors administered the oath to Saltan murza in accordance with the charter which they used for the Kabardan princes and murzas. And they added to it that whenever the Sovereign's ambassadors, envoys or messengers and various of the Sovereign's men, as well as Georgian ambassadors, envoys or messengers and various men were on their way to or from the Georgian land, he, Saltan murza, should escort them through his land, and perpetrate no wiles against any of the Sovereign's or any of the Georgian men . . .

(152) Prince Semen and dyak Torkh also questioned Saltan murza about the routes. 'Which road did the Sovereign's envoys take on past occasions from your settlement to the Georgian land?

[1] For Mount Shat and 'Saltan murza's settlement at Lars' see Commentary 18, (h) and (i).

130

Should we now follow the same route or is it better to go another way? And in how many days can one reach the Georgian land?'

Saltan murza replied: 'The Sovereign's envoys have hitherto gone from my settlement to Mount Shat, because they happened to be travelling in the summer when there was no snow on the mountains. They took three and a half days by that route to get to Soni-land, which belongs to Prince Aristov; and that Aristov and his land serve King Alexander. But now you cannot cross that mountain because great snows live in these mountains in the autumn. You should now travel along the defile between the mountains, up the river Terek, because little water lives in the Terek now in the autumn, and it is possible to bridge it. Three bridges will be needed across the Terek; and a fourth bridge should be built near Cherebash's settlement.[1] And this Cherebash's settlement belongs to Prince Aristov of Soni-land.[2] It is possible to ride to that settlement in one day.'

And the ambassadors built those bridges. As for the bridge which would be needed below Cherebash's settlement, they told the Georgian ambassadors about it, asking that they should themselves send a message to Cherebash bidding him build the bridge, because his settlement is in Soni-land, and this land of Soni belongs to King Alexander.   (152)

[1] For this part of the route see Commentary 18, (i), (j) and (k). Bridges, in the mountains, according to Baddeley, even at the beginning of the twentieth century, were numerous and unsafe. Along the valley of the Assa he counted no less than twenty-seven over a distance of ten miles and, 'as they consisted mostly of small fir-trees laid across the stream and loosely covered with earth and branches, we were bound to dismount at nearly every one, for the horses' sake' (*RFC*, Vol I, p. 245.) For cantilever construction in Avaria, ibid., Vol. II, p. 35.

For 'the defile between the mountains', see Commentary 19: The Daryal Gorge: its history and topography.

[2] Belokurov, *Snosheniya*, p. 152: 'A tot Cherebashov kabak Aristova knyazya Sonskiye zemli'. The reference is to the Eristav Nugsar of the Aragvi. For discussion of the name 'Soni-land' and its identity with the eristavate of the Aragvi, see Commentary 20(b).

CHAPTER 3

THE ROAD TO GREMI

(152) THE ambassadors Prince Semen and dyak Torkh set off from those parts on the 26th day of September. On that night and on the 27th they camped below Cherebash's settlement; and Saltan murza escorted them that far. But none of King Alexander's officers came to meet them with provisions and carts.

(153) And Prince Semen and dyak Torkh said to the Georgian ambassadors, Prince Kaplan and his assistants: 'When our Sovereign sends his ambassadors to other states, it is customary for them to be held in honour everywhere because of the Sovereign's great name; eminent attending officers chosen from among grandees are sent to meet them at the frontier, and provisions and carts are kept in readiness; and not only ambassadors, but the Sovereign's envoys, too, are received with great honour. We have told you more than once that you should write to your sovereign King Alexander asking him to send men and horses, so that we can proceed on fresh horses. You have seen for yourselves that many of our horses were killed falling down the mountains and that others died.'

And the Georgian ambassadors replied: 'When you told us about this in Terek-town we sent our men from there with a message to our sovereign. We do not know why he has not sent anyone to meet you up to now.'

Prince Semen and dyak Torkh spent a day below Cherebash's settlement because of building the bridge. And on September 28th they camped in Soni-land, having ridden some three versts beyond the great settlement of Soni and the monastery of the Immaculate Mother of God.[1] And when they were some two versts distant from this camp, two *aznaurs* of Aristov prince of Soni[2] came to meet them. They dismounted, removed their hats and said: 'We have been sent by Prince Aristov who bade us provide the Sovereign's ambassadors with all provisions for the men and fodder for horses. Aristov himself will call on you tomorrow, for he is at present away in some distant villages of his.'

On the following day, September 29th, Prince Aristov rode up to the ambassadors' camp about an hour before sunset, and some fifteen of his *aznaurs* were with him.[3]

The ambassadors invited him to their tent. And they bade the interpreters Ivan Nikolayev and Ivanis Dragichev meet him in the camp, and *sotnik* Grigori Kutarinov and the falconer Ivan Sychov were ordered to meet him in front of the tent.

Having come to the ambassadors' tent, Prince Aristov said to them: 'The Georgian king Alexander has sent a letter to me, his vassal prince, bidding me meet you, the Sovereign's ambassadors, in my land, and ride with you as far as his Georgian land; and he commanded me to supply you with a sufficient

[1] For 'the great settlement of Soni and the monastery of the Immaculate Mother of God', see Commentary 20(a).

[2] For 'Aristop (Aristov) prince of Soni', see Commentary 20(b): 'Note on the Eristavs of the Ksani and the Aragvi', and for 'Soni-land', ibid., (c): 'Note on the ethnology of the eristavate of the Aragvi'.

[3] *Aznaur (-i)* – plur., *Aznaurni*: a word signifying 'noble' in the text; cf. Introduction, Section 8, for the special status of the king's *aznaurni*. The word has been derived from the Irano-Armenian root *azn*, formed with the suffix *-ur = ver*, son. According to N. Y. Marr, *azn* denotes birth, origin, descent, and *aznauri* thus means 'son of illustrious birth or origin'. A more homely Georgian equivalent is *gwarishvili* = 'son of *gwari*' (= clan), clansman. (By contrast, the word *uazno* conveyed the idea of low birth). Again, *aznauri* may be compared with the Russian *syn boyarski* – 'boyar's son'; but Janashvili, in his edition of Wakhusht, p. 5, n. 21, gives the equivalent as *dvoryanin. Stolbovoy dvoryanin*, is, perhaps, more accurate (information N.M.A.). For discussion and refs. on *aznaurni*, see Allen, *HGP*, pp. 224 ff.; and more recent and detailed, Toumanoff, *SCCH*, index.

quantity of provisions. Having heard that you had arrived, I sent my *aznaurs* to you, and have now ridden to you myself. You should now proceed to King Alexander.'

And the ambassadors said to Prince Aristov: 'You have told (154) us that King Alexander had commanded you to meet us as soon as we got to your land. It was proper for you to meet us when we reached Cherebash's settlement at the frontier of your land.'

Prince Aristov replied: 'Do not be angry with me because I was not in good time to meet you at Cherebash's settlement. I was away, visiting some of my distant villages.'

On September 30th, having crossed the Terek near its source, the ambassadors camped between the sources of the Terek and of the Araguy;[1] and Prince Aristov rode along with the ambassadors. On the 1st, 2nd, 3rd and 4th of October, they remained encamped on the Araguy below Aristov's settlement, because the river Araguy had been swollen by rain and it was impossible to ford it. On October 5th they camped on the same river Araguy in King Alexander's land, having ridden past the mill and the frontier of Aristov's land.[2]

On October 7th the Georgian monk Kiril came to the ambassadors in their camp and said: 'Our sovereign King Alexander

[1] 30 Sept: 'The Terek near its source': In this context, its affluent the Atchkhoti. The camp must have been in the neighbourhood of Busarchili (Caucasia, 1:210,000, Sh. F 6:42°30 E by 62°25 N); cf. also Déchy's map, Vol. II, *Östlicher Kaukasus*, where he gives an altitude of 2877 m. at the pass and incorrectly marks the Atchkhoti as 'schwarze Aragwa'; also Merzbacher, Vol. I, pp. 69, 84; Vol. II, pp. 43, 705. In the neighbouring, more easterly, Arkhotis Pass, at a somewhat lower altitude, 2793 m., Baddeley (*RFC*, Vol. I, p. 118, n. 1) was turned back by snow in October 1901; hence the ambassadors seem to have been fortunate to have been able to cross the watershed as late as the end of September. For *Araguy* – Aragvi, see Commentary 21: 'The rivers of Kakheti'.

[2] 5 Oct: The exact location of this camp is obscure. The travellers were now in Pshaveti (the country of the Pshav tribe – Old Georgian *P'khov*, the ancient name for both the Pshavs and the Khevsurs). The easterly or Pshavi-Aragvi seems to have been the boundary between Aristov's territory and the Kingdom of Kakheti proper.

has sent his equerry Uman to meet you, and Uman has sent me to you to announce him.'[1]

And the ambassadors bade Uman come to their camp.

Uman came to their camp on foot, and Prince Aristov and the Georgian ambassadors Prince Kaplan and Khurshit, and about a hundred – if not more – of King Alexander's gentlemen and *aznaurs* came with him. Prince Semen and dyak Torkh ordered the interpreters Ivan Nikolayev and Ivanis Dragichev to meet Uman in the camp, and the *strelets sotnik* Grigori Kutarinov and the falconer Ivan Sychov to meet him outside the tent.

And having entered the tent, Uman said: 'My sovereign, King Alexander, has sent me, Uman, his equerry, and his gentlemen to you, Prince Semen and dyak Torkh, the great Sovereign's ambassadors. The King has commanded me to meet you and ride together with you to his court, and he has given orders for sufficient provisions and carts to be supplied to you. And as for the fact that he has sent me so late to meet you, the great Sovereign's ambassadors, my sovereign King Alexander has commanded me to say to you that it was the fault of his

---

[1] Uman: The Georgian form is Oman (-i). Oman was a personal name of the *Kherkheulidze* family who seem to have played a role as *noblesse de robe* at the Kakhian court between the sixteenth and eighteenth centuries: cf. Oman Kherkheulidze, a judge during the later part of the eighteenth century and biographer of King Irakli II (Brosset, *HG*, Vol. II/ii, p. 203); and another Oman Kherkheulidze ibid. (pp. 532 and 546), a royal secretary. *Kherkhe-uli-dze* = 'son of the man of Kherkhe'; and Wak./Brosset (p. 285) mentions *Kherk* obscurely as a former name for the district of Thedzmis-khevi – which he groups with Tianeti and Saguramo, cantons which lie south of Pshaveti and west of the Aragvi (see Wak./Brosset, p. 297). Further south again, the Omanis-khevi (= 'valley of Omani') falls to the Kura.

According to Wak./Brosset, the Kherkheulidzes claimed to be of Os origin; they had migrated from Samtskhe to Kakheti at the end of the fifteenth century 'after the division of the Kingdom'.

For Oman as a folk hero and the epic *Omaniani*, see Janashvili, in *SMK*, Vol. XXVI/i, p. 101; for Kaikhosro Omanishvili (*c.* 1612), see Janashvili, ibid., Vol. XXII/i, p. 57.

ambassadors, Prince Kaplan and his assistants, for being late in writing to him about you; they only did so some four days ago, when you reached Aristov's land. You should not be angered by this.' . . .

(155) On that day the ambassadors camped on the same river Araguy, near the ruined fort of Alexander's son, Prince Yuri[1]; Uman travelled with the ambassadors, whereas Aristov turned back. On October 7th they camped in King Alexander's villages in the meadows by the stream. On October 8th the ambassadors camped by the river Lozan. On the 9th they camped near Uman's village.[2]

The ambassadors Prince Semen and dyak Torkh conversed with Uman while they rode along. And Uman said: 'Our sovereign King Alexander entertains friendship with the Kizil-bash Shah; and the Shah's ambassadors are now at the court of

---

[1] 7 Oct: 'The ruined fort of Alexander's son Prince Yuri'. Probably Lashis-Juari on the watershed between the sources of the Pshavis-tsqali and the Alazani (Wak./Brosset, p. 297 and map 4). The building of a church here was attributed to King Giorgi IV Lasha (1212–23), the son and successor of Queen Tamar. *Lasha* means in Abkhaz 'Light of the World' (cf. Allen, *HGP*, p. 110). Among the Pshavs and Khevsurs the site was an ancient centre of the cult of St George and may well have been a sanctuary in pagan times. For curious details of the cult of St George at 'Lasha's Cross', see Wak./Brosset, pp. 295–7; also Brosset, *VA*, *1er rapport*, p. 89. In our text there seems to be a confusion by the Russians of the names of King Giorgi IV Lasha and the later and insignificant Giorgi (= Yuri), son of Alexander of Kakheti. For this later Yuri, see Chap. 4, p. 161, n. 2.

[2] 8 Oct: 'By the river Lozan' = Alazan (-i), see Commentary 21: The rivers of Kakheti. In the balmy autumn weather, the ambassadors were now descending into the most beautiful and fertile part of Kakheti, over country sloping south and protected from the north by the great ridges of the central Caucasus.

9 Oct: 'Uman's village'. Omali, a village of Pankisis-khevi in Khevsureti (cf. Wak./Brosset, p. 482, col. 1), is a tentative suggestion. It lies on the upper Alazani and is on the line of march from Lashis-Juari to Alaverdi. Pankisi was a centre of tracks converging from different parts of northern Kakheti (cf. Wak./Brosset, p. 323). Wakhusht describes Pankisi as a very fine country, fertile in fruits and grain, and abounding in game – notably wild boars.

my sovereign. I do not know whether I shall encounter them; I believe that my sovereign King Alexander will send them off before our arrival. The ambassador has come from the Kizilbash Shah to our sovereign so that he should stand together with the Shah against the Turk; he, the Shah, is willing to cede some lands to our sovereign to add to his own land in whatever parts our sovereign desires. But I do not know what stage has been reached between the Kizilbash and King Alexander.'

And Prince Semen and dyak Torkh said to Uman: 'How long ago did the Kizilbash Shah's ambassador come to your sovereign, and what road did he take? Was not your sovereign's ambassador to the Shah unable to get back because of the Turks, for which reason our Sovereign's envoy Grigori Vasilchikov[1] took him along from the Kizilbash land to our Sovereign's patrimony, Astarakhan? Our Sovereign's boyars and commanders wrote to us from Astarakhan saying that they would send off your sovereign's ambassador and provide him with an escort.'

And Uman said: 'It was after the departure of your Sovereign's envoy from the Kizilbash land that the Shah's ambassadors came to King Alexander, our sovereign.'

When they reached Krym,[2] the ambassadors Prince Semen and dyak Torkh made enquiries about this, and found out that Uman had been lying, because no ambassadors had come to King Alexander from the Kizilbash.

And in answer to questions Uman also said: 'Kumyk princes attacked my sovereign's borderlands this year. My sovereign King Alexander sent his commanders with an army against them, and they routed the Kumyks and killed more than 400 of them. And Prince Shevkal entertains greater enmity towards our sovereign than any other enemy; secretly coming down

---

[1] For Grigori Vasilchikov, see Chap. 1, p. 93, n. 1.
[2] For Krym (= Gremi), Alexander's capital: see Commentary 25.

from the mountains by day and at night he causes great injury to the borderland of Alexander, our sovereign.'

Answering questions about Alexander's son Araklin, Uman (156) said that he had fled to the Turks, having lost his mind because he had been eating opium. 'He fled accompanied by one man and this man of his later came over to our sovereign King Alexander and said that Araklin had been begging the Turkish king for favours, but nothing has been granted him.'[1]

On the following day, October 10th, Prince Kaplan and Khurshit came to the ambassadors' camp and said: 'King Alexander, our sovereign, has sent his cup-bearer Dmitri and his butler Sheverdyay – who is his, Khurshit's, son – with his bounty: with *argamaks*[2] on which you are to ride to King Alexander, and with fruit. The ambassadors Prince Semen and dyak Torkh should therefore bid them attend.'

The ambassadors bade them come to their camp; and they ordered that they be met by Ivan Nikolayev in the camp and by the *strelets sotnik* Grigori Kutarinov outside their tent.

Dmitri and Sheverdyay entered the tent and said: 'King Alexander, our sovereign, has received news from his equerry Uman that you, the great Sovereign's ambassadors, have safely arrived this far. Our sovereign is very pleased with this, and he has sent you four *argamaks* and a horse on which you are to ride to him. And he has also sent you fruit: half a bale of melons and water-melons, and half a bale of pears, and three bales of apples.'

Prince Semen and dyak Torkh said: 'By the bounty of our great Sovereign, we have safely reached this land; and we do homage for the bounty of King Alexander, your sovereign.'

On the same day, which was a Friday, the ambassadors

[1] Araklin = Irakli, at the time a refugee in Istanbul, who died during this year (cf. Brosset, *EC/BHP*, Vol. 11, Nos. 14–15, col. 235, n. 56).
[2] For *argamaks*, see Commentary 22: 'The horses called *argamaks*'.

Prince Semen and dyak Torkh camped near a monastery, and they reached that monastery at one o'clock at night. Uman said that that was the monastery of St George of Alaverdy,[1] a big place, where Archbishop Gavril and monks and lay priests and deacons live.

On the following day, the 11th of October, Prince Semen and dyak Torkh asked Uman: 'Will the Archbishop have mass in the monastery today, so that we can pray there?'

Uman replied: 'There will be no mass today; but should you want to visit the monastery, go over there.'

And the ambassadors went to the monastery. And half-way in, they were met by Uman with King Alexander's gentlemen and *aznaurs* and the Archbishop's steward with the Archbishop's men, some thirty of them, if not more, who had come down from the porch; and in the porch they were met by a monk in black garb in accordance with the Greek custom, who came out of the church; behind him there were some thirty men if not more, dressed in all kinds of clothes which were indis- (157) tinguishable from lay Georgian dress, some of them wearing hats and others *kalpaks*,[2] and others dressed in *kaftans*.[3]

And the ambassadors asked Uman: 'Is the Archbishop in the church, and what is the rank of the monk and the men who have come out of the church and met us?'

[1] St George of Alaverdy (=Alaverdi). 'The greatest Church in Georgia' according to Shah Abbas' biographer, Iskander Munshi. For details see further Commentary 23.

[2] *Kalpak*: a word of Turkish origin. 'In its original form the kalpak is a cone-shaped sheepskin cap, flattened on top, covering the head down to the eyes and ears, for the manufacture of which skins of darker colour, in people of rank particularly a dark astrakhan, were used and then trimmed with softer fur of a brighter colour' (Babinger in *EI*, 1st ed., *s.v.*). The writer adds that 'neither this dress nor the word kalpak can be proved to have existed before the middle of the XVIIth century', so that it would appear that Zvenigorodski's is the first literary reference to this headgear.

[3] *Kaftan*: see Chap. 1, p. 98, n. 4.

139

And Uman said: 'The Archbishop is not in the church but lies ill because he is very old; and that monk is the Archimandrite and, behind him, you have been met by the priests and the deacons of this monastery.'

The ambassadors entered the church. And in size the church is only a little smaller than the Archangel which stands in the square in Moscow; like it, it has four pillars and a single dome. It is an old building, which had been painted all over; and the painting is visible in some places and invisible in others. The royal gate, with the Annunciation of the Immaculate Mother of God painted on the two halves, was open; there was no canopy over the royal gate. Priests and deacons go up to God's altar through the royal gate, and they walk between the royal gate and the altar without wearing vestments or skull caps. And the priests Bogdan and his brethren went into the sanctuary through the north gate, and said that God's altar was circular and covered with a shirt; there were no fastenings, nor *endyton* nor *antimension* nor cross on it. They said that there was only the Gospels lying on the altar, a small book, not adorned with figures of the evangelists. And on the small altar stood a chalice in silver gilt, and three saucers and a small lance, without any sacred writing on them; while the shroud and the winding sheets were in accordance with the canon. The priests' vestments are without *amice* or crosses. The image of the *deesis* over the royal gate in the church is very old. And in the place of the customary icons there are icons – likewise old – of the festivals on panels, a large hand in size. To the right of these icons is a *deesis* of fine Greek work, including the festivals and prophets, curved and painted on small panels; and in front of it there is a candle in a candelabrum. And to the left, beyond the icons of the festivals, towards the north gate, there are five or six icons a hand across; the icon-painters said that they were of Korsun work. And, still in the church, on the left-hand side, there is a large icon of the Saviour, encased in gold and silver, inset in a stone frame.[1] Near that icon, on a similar panel, there is an icon of George, martyr for Christ, encased and embellished with stones and pearls and pendants; and there is a sabre leaning against it, the sheath encased in gold and silver with stones and pearls.[2] And near this image, on a similar panel, there is an icon – 'All creation rejoices in Thee'[3] – embossed on silver, and gilt; and nearby, on a similar panel, there are the Lord's festivals embossed on silver and gilt. There is a large iron candelabrum in front of these three icons, with lighted candles.

The ambassadors Prince Semen and dyak Torkh asked the (158) Archimandrite to sing a Te Deum and say the Hours for the health of our great Sovereign the Tsar and great Prince Fedor Ivanovich of all Russia and his tsaritsa and great Princess Irina.[4] And the Archimandrite instructed that the Hours be read,

[1] For the sacred decorations of a Georgian church, see Commentary 24, (a), (b), (c).

[2] Sabre leaning against the icon of St George: probably a survival of the sword cult, occurring among the Scyths, Sarmato-Alans and Slavs from very ancient times. Cf. Vernadsky, *Origins*, p. 5: 'In front of the idol (of the god Svantovit in Arkona) was placed a huge sword.' Ibid., p. 37, citing Ammianus Marcellinus, Book XXXI, ii. p. 23, among the Alans 'a naked sword is fixed in the ground and they reverently worship it as their god of war'. Ibid., p. 137, the sword was identified with the cult of St George. At the beginning of the present century, Baddeley (*RFC*, Vol. I, p. 238), came across surviving practices of the sword cult at Akhieti in Khevsureti.

[3] 'All creation rejoiceth in thee.' The title of this icon is taken from a hymn of praise to the Virgin, who is represented holding the Child and enthroned in glory, being adored by angels, saints, the laity and, sometimes, animals. An icon of this type was shown (under No. 14) in the Russian Art exhibition at the Royal Academy in 1959. For an illustration see also plate (following p. 148) in *Kreml Moskvy* (Moskva, 1957). Judging by the subject, the icon seen by the ambassadors might have been of Russian work.

[4] Tsaritsa Irina – wife of Tsar Fedor Ivanovich and sister of Boris Godunov. The Godunovs, together with the Velyaminov-Zernovs and the Saburovs, were descended from Cheta Mirza, a fugitive from the Golden Horde who sought the protection of Tsar Ivan Kalita and was converted to Christianity about the year 1330. He is remembered as the founder of the Ipatyev Monastery at Kostroma. In 1580 the marriage of

but added about the Te Deum that there is no such custom among them.

After hearing the Hours the ambassadors rode to their camp, and Uman with the same people saw them off as far as the place where he welcomed them. Uman said to the ambassadors: 'King Alexander has written to me bidding you remain in this camp until you get his instructions.'

In October 12th Uman came to their camp and said to the ambassadors: 'I have been asked by the Archbishop to beg of you, the great Sovereign's ambassadors, and of the monk Zakhkhey with his brethren and priests, to attend mass at the monastery now, to call on him, the Archbishop, and partake of his bread. The Archimandrite has instructed me to leave it to you to decide who are to celebrate mass – the Sovereign's or the monastery priests.'

And the ambassadors said: 'Our great Sovereign's priests and deacons should officiate in the Te Deum for the health of our Sovereign the Tsar and his Tsaritsa Irina, and should read the Hours; while the Archbishop's priests should celebrate mass. And it would be unseemly for us to partake of the Archbishop's bread without having first been received by your sovereign, King Alexander.'

And Uman also said to the ambassadors: 'My sovereign King Alexander has written to me to the effect that he had sent his ambassadors Kaplan and his assistants to petition your great Sovereign about cannon-smiths ... King Alexander has instructed me to ask you: Have you any cannon-smiths with you?'

Prince Semen and dyak Torkh replied: 'If Prince Kaplan petitioned the Sovereign Tsar about cannon-smiths ... why

Irina Godunova to the devout and weakly Fedor enabled her brother to accumulate power and influence which eventually led to his election to the throne on the death of Fedor in 1598. Irina retired to a convent (ref. RBS).

should the Sovereign refuse? The Sovereign has not refused King Alexander's petition in matters more weighty than cannon-smiths; he has accepted him under his royal hand and has ordered that a castle be built on the Terek for his benefit, and he has stationed men and artillery there. And what you have told us is a minor matter.'

And that day the ambassadors attended a Te Deum and the (159) Hours and mass in the monastery; the Te Deum and the Hours were sung by all the Sovereign's priests and deacons; and mass was celebrated by the Archimandrite with three priests and two deacons from the monastery, in accordance with their customs. Their way of officiating was examined by the Sovereign's priests and deacons, who said that their church service is of the Greek rite, like that of the Patriarch of Constantinople; but they differ in that they enter the royal gate without consecrated vestments, simply, without reverence.

After mass Uman asked the monk Zakhkhey and the priests and deacons on behalf of the Archbishop to call on him and visit him.

The monk Zakhkhey with the priests and deacons visited the Archbishop. On his return the monk Zakhkhey told the ambassadors that when they entered the Archbishop's cell they found him lying down; there were no icons on the walls, but the [Georgian monks] held in their hands an icon of the Saviour in a case. Having got up, the Archbishop gave them his benediction in Greek and said: 'I have lived to a very old age, and God has now willed it that I should see you, men of monkish and priestly status, who pray God for the great Sovereign Tsar and great Prince Fedor Ivanovich of all Russia, a sovereign of the true Orthodox Christian faith. You should not be surprised that I have not received and honoured you, for I am old and ill.' And he invited them to partake of his bread and he, Zakhkhey, begged to be excused, but the priests and deacons stayed to sup at the Archbishop's.

When they came back they told the ambassadors that the Archbishop had instructed his major-domo to treat them honestly in the hall; and the major-domo treated them honestly. And Uman supped with them in the same hall . . .

On October 13th the ambassadors set out from that camp towards Krym . . . and they encamped some two versts from Krym an hour before sunset . . . On October 14th they arrived at Krym.[1] And Uman and the monk Kiril presently came to the ambassadors . . . And Uman said to them: 'King Alexander wants to see the falcon which the Sovereign has graciously sent him; you should therefore send the falconer with the falcon to King Alexander; and when he has looked at it, he will send it back to you immediately.' And the ambassadors sent the falcon with the falconer Ivan Sychov and an interpreter to King Alexander, after Uman had left. Ivan Sychov brought the falcon back to the ambassadors within the hour and said that King Alexander inspected the falcon and placed it on his hand and took off the hood, and is most pleased with the Sovereign's bounty. The King asked him what the falcon's quarry was, and he replied that it was swans.[2]

(160) *On October 15th Uman and the monk Kiril visited the ambassadors and said:* 'King Alexander bids you to attend on him in audience tomorrow . . . He bids you not to present at the audience *the gifts sent by the Tsar to his sons,* but he has commanded that this bounty should be brought to him.' And the ambassadors said to Uman and to the monk Kiril: 'There is God's mercy and benediction from the holiest Patriarch Job of the reigning city of Moscow and of all the Russian kingdom for the sons of King Alexander: icons which have been sent with the monk Zakhkhey. What will now be King Alexander's

[1] For Krym (= Gremi), see Commentary 25.
[2] For King Alexander's passion for the chase, see Allen, *HGP*, p. 150, citing Wakhusht's 'History of Kakheti' in Brosset, *HG*, Vol. II/i, p. 153; and Introduction, Section 9 above. On royal falcons and falconry in Russia and Georgia see further Commentary 26.

pleasure about them?' [*The ambassadors received instructions not to present the icons sent to King Alexander's son, at the audience.*][1]

Prince Semen and dyak Torkh, having entered the chamber, saluted King Alexander in the name of the Tsar; they made the speech and presented the Sovereign's letter of credence and letters patent. They also presented the teachers and icon-painters in accordance with the Sovereign's instructions, and they produced the Sovereign's bounty according to the treasury list. About the gerfalcon they said: 'Our great Sovereign, in extending his bounty to you, King Alexander, has sent you a gerfalcon and a reddish falcon and a speckled falcon from his own royal sport; but two of the falcons, the reddish and the speckled, died in the mountains. You should command that they and their gear be brought in for inspection, King Alexander.'

After the ambassadors, the monk Zakhkhey saluted the King on behalf of the holiest Patriarch Job; he made the speech and presented the letter and handed over the icons with the Patriarch's benediction, in accordance with his instructions. Together with his brethren and the priests he asked King Alexander's permission to visit Metropolitan Nicholas.

And when the ambassadors began reciting the Sovereign's title,[2] King Alexander got up and stepped forward, and on hearing of the Sovereign's grace he bowed in his royal hat down

[1] Belokurov's italics, to indicate that he has summarized the passages in question.

[2] The Tsar's full title, as it appeared in a letter to Shah Abbas, was as follows: 'By the grace of God great Sovereign Tsar and great Prince Fedor Ivanovich, autocrat of all Russia, of Vladimir, Moscow, Novgorod, King of Kazan, King of Astrakhan, Lord of Pskov and great Prince of Smolensk, Tver, of Yugria, Perm, Vyatka, the Bolgars and others, Sovereign and great Prince of Nizhni Novgorod, Chernigov, Ryazan, Polotsk, Rostov, Yaroslavl, Belo-ozero, Liefland, Udoria, Obdoria, Kondia, the Lord of all the Siberian and the Northern lands and the Sovereign and Possessor of many other realms' (Veselovski, I, p. 346).

The title was not static but depended on the politics of the moment;

to the ground; and as for the Sovereign's letters, he took them, lifted them to his face and kissed them, then placed them beside him. And he prayed to the icons and kissed them, and he ordered that the icons which had been sent to him and those which had been sent to his sons as well as the Sovereign's presents be received in front of him; and he commanded that the dead falcons be brought to him in their hoods with all their gear, and he inspected them . . .

When the audience was over King Alexander said: 'Everything belongs to God and to my great Sovereign, the Tsar and great Prince Fedor Ivanovich of all Russia. I am their slave, and my wife and my children and all my realm are God's and his, the great Sovereign's.' About the Metropolitan Nicholas he said that he was not present there at Krym, but that he would send to fetch him and would command him to come. And having said this, King Alexander sat down and invited the ambassadors to kiss his hand; and when they had kissed his (161) hand he bade them sit on his right. And after sitting for a short while the ambassadors rode back to their camp . . . And having escorted the ambassadors Prince Kaplan and Khurshit said: 'You are now all to sup with King Alexander, and a messenger will come from the King to fetch you.'

A messenger having come for them, the ambassadors rode to the King's palace . . . *During the meal* King Alexander said: 'Of what royal descent is our great Sovereign, the Tsar and great Prince Fedor Ivanovich of all Russia?' And the ambassadors replied: 'The royal extraction of our great Sovereign comes from Augustus, Caesar of Rome, who owned the whole universe.'[1] And King Alexander said: 'Our writings likewise

thus, in writing to Shah Abbas, Fedor did not add to the enumeration of his realms the Caucasian and Transcaucasian lands which he mentioned in his letters to West European rulers (Kotoshikhin, p. 3).

[1] The claim by the reigning house of Moscow to royal descent from Augustus was part of the campaign designed to prove that the Tsars were entitled to royal dignity and to confound those in the West, particularly

hold that the extraction of our Sovereign the Tsar comes from Augustus, Caesar of Rome...' And whenever drink was brought to King Alexander in a goblet he looked at Prince Semen and dyak Torkh and ordered the interpreter to say that he was drinking that goblet to them; having drunk, he commanded that a similar goblet be brought to Prince Semen and dyak Torkh... And he ordered his son Prince Yuri and his general Edishey to get up from the table and call a toast to Prince Semen; and he ordered this same Edishey and the generals Zhechinaley and Aslan to call a toast to dyak Torkh; he did this three and four times.[1] After the meal, King Alexander bade the Sovereign's priests sing the Sovereign's health over a goblet. And the priests and the deacons sang a prayer for the health and long life of the Sovereign and of his Tsaritsa, the great Princess Irina. King Alexander drank the first goblet himself, and he offered a goblet each to the ambassadors; and when they had drunk this goblet he let them go.

the Poles, who were contesting that claim. The legend was incorporated in the genealogical tree of the Tsars drawn up in the sixteenth century, and Ivan IV often referred to his royal descent from Augustus. The sixteenth-century compilation known as the *Stepennaya Kniga* reported that the royal rule of the Tsars began with 'Ryurik ... who was descended from Prussus who gave his name to the Prussian land; and Prussus was a brother of the sole ruler of the Earth, the Roman Caesar Augustus.' Ryurik was said to come fourteenth in the line of descent after Prussus (Dyakonov, *Vlast moskovskikh gosudarey*, St Petersburg, 1889). Cf. also Allen, *UH*, p. 63, n. 11, for claim of the Lithuanian nobles to Roman descent.

[1] The personal names of the Kakhian courtiers are obscure. The third king of Kakheti, *Av* Giorgi (= George the Bad), 1511–13, had done his best to suppress the powerful hereditary families of *eristavni* and to replace them in the administration of the country by *mo'uravni* (prefects) removable at the royal will. But the great families, like the Andronikashvilis and Cholokashvilis, often allied by marriage with the royal blood, regained their influence under the successors of Giorgi I. Edisher (= Edishey) is a characteristic personal name of the Cholokashvilis. In the context this Edisher seems to have occupied the post of commander-in-chief (*amir-spasalari*), corresponding to the Grand Constable of mediaeval European states (cf. Allen, *HGP*, p. 258 and *passim*).

On October 16th Prince Kaplan and Khurshit came to the ambassadors and said: 'King Alexander bids you to attend on him.'

And Prince Semen and dyak Torkh rode to King Alexander, and Uman met them in the middle of the courtyard and accompanied them as far as the hall. After a short while King Alexander's confessor Archimandrite Philip and Uman and the monk Kiril came to the hall and said: 'Our sovereign, King Alexander, has ordered that the great Sovereign Tsar's letter patent be translated; he has read it and he does homage for the great Sovereign's grace, the strong protection of his God-assisted royal power.' And King Alexander's confessor and his comrades bowed to the ground in front of the ambassadors. And they also said on behalf of King Alexander: 'Until now I have been in darkness, but by the grace of the great Sovereign I have now come into the light. And it is also written in the Sovereign's letter: he bids me believe whatever you, the (162) Sovereign's ambassadors Prince Semen and dyak Torkh, say; and you say that you are bearers of the Sovereign's command on how he intends to show his grace to me and defend me from my enemies.'

Prince Semen and dyak Torkh said: 'At the supplication of your master, King Alexander, our Sovereign has extended his grace to him and to all his Iberian land; he has accepted them under his royal hand, and he intends to keep them protected from all his enemies. The Sovereign has commanded that a fort be erected on the Terek for his sake and for the protection of his land. At King Alexander's petition, our Sovereign intends to send his army against the King's enemy, prince Shevkal, who disobeys the Sovereign, so that henceforth King Alexander and his land should suffer no injury or damage from Shevkal, and in order to clear the road from the King's land to our Sovereign's patrimony, to Terek-town. King Alexander, your master, should therefore swear fealty to our Sovereign, kiss the cross on the charter and, in accordance with it, he should be loyal in his dealings with our Sovereign, nor should he and all his Iberian land secede from the Sovereign's grace. There is no need to speak much about Shevkal: he will be brought under our great Sovereign's hand.' . . .

Archimandrite Philip with Uman and Kiril went to King (163) Alexander; and having come back they said: 'Our sovereign, King Alexander, has listened to your message which you sent by us, and he bade us say to you: "In the past, there was Christian faith in many realms in these parts; but now, because of our sins, the Turkish king has captured many Christian realms and these realms were so oppressed that they went over to the Moslem faith; only my puny realm has remained and is still of the Christian faith; and I, having heard about the great Sovereign Tsar, who practises the Orthodox Christian faith, sent my men to him with the petition to extend his grace to me, accept me under his royal hand and not abandon me to the infidels, to be brought into the Moslem faith, so that the Christian faith should not be overthrown in my puny realm. And the great Sovereign has extended his grace to me, his slave, and has accepted me under his royal hand into protection. And on that I have sworn fealty to my great Sovereign and have kissed the cross, on that I intend to remain loyal to my Sovereign, myself and my sons, and all my land, until my death. And even should the great Sovereign fling me away from his Majesty's grace, I shall not secede from my Sovereign, even though I were to suffer death for it. Let the Sovereign extend his grace to me and to my land, and command that I be defended from prince Shevkal – for Shevkal is my great enemy. Whenever I happen to wage war on the Turk's borderlands or some other lands, Shevkal wages war on my borderland, and sometimes he raids it by night, killing people and driving others to his country into the Moslem faith; so that he becomes worse than the Turk for me. For the Turkish king sometimes

wages war on me and sometimes I wage war on him,
and there matters rest. The Turk is not too strong for me in
these parts. Let the Sovereign command that the road from
Terek-town to my Iberian land be cleared through Shevkal's
land." '

Prince Semen and dyak Torkh said: 'Our Sovereign intends
to defend King Alexander and his land in the same way as he
defends his own royal patrimony – Astarakhan and Terek-
town and other towns of his. Should Shevkal not be at peace
with your sovereign, where could Shevkal hide from our
Sovereign? And the road through Shevkal's land to your
sovereign's Iberian realm will be cleared.'

Archimandrite Philip and Uman and the monk Kiril went off
to King Alexander. And having come back from him they
said: 'Our Sovereign, King Alexander, bade us ask you, the
(164) ambassadors of the great Sovereign: "Patriarch Job has sent
to me the monk Zakhkhey with his brethren and priests. With
what instructions have they come?" '

Prince Semen and dyak Torkh said: 'His royal majesty our
Sovereign has accepted King Alexander and his land under his
royal hand for the sake of the Christian faith; and your
sovereign's ambassadors Prince Kaplan and you, Kiril, and
Khurshit, supplicated our great Sovereign on King Alexander's
behalf, to extend his grace to him and send learned men and
icon-painters with his ambassadors for the rectification of the
Christian faith. Our great Sovereign has extended his grace to
King Alexander and has sent these learned men to him for the
rectification of the Christian faith, and with them the holiest
Patriarch Job of the reigning city of Moscow and of all the
Russian kingdom has sent, at our great Sovereign's com-
mand, icons with Divine mercy and his benediction to King
Alexander and to his queen and to Nicholas, Metropolitan of the
Iberian land; and he has also sent by them a letter of instruction
to your sovereign King Alexander and to Metropolitan

Nicholas. We presented these learned men and icon-painters to your sovereign at the audience.' . . .

Archimandrite Philip and Uman and the monk Kiril went off to King Alexander. And having come back they said: 'King Alexander our sovereign greatly rejoices at the bounty of the great Sovereign who has sent learned men to him for the rectification of the Christian faith. But Metropolitan Nicholas is at present in our sovereign's displeasure, and they therefore cannot call on the Metropolitan.'

And the ambassadors said: 'If your sovereign is for some reason displeased with the Metropolitan, that is something in which King Alexander is free to do as he sees fit. But this affair is in no way connected with the King's wrath, for it is a spiritual matter. So why should they not call on the Metropolitan?'

Archimandrite Philip and Uman and the monk Kiril replied: 'It is still not known whether our sovereign will command him to remain Metropolitan or whether he will depose him. And for this reason they cannot call on the Metropolitan.'

The ambassadors said: 'The holiest Patriarch Job of the (165) reigning city of Moscow and of all the Russian realm has sent these learned men with his letter of instruction to Metropolitan Nicholas and to the archbishops and bishops and to all the consecrated council, and not to Metropolitan Nicholas alone. Your sovereign King Alexander should therefore bid them call on the archbishops and the bishops and all the consecrated council.'

Archimandrite Philip and Uman and the monk Kiril went to King Alexander. And having come back they said: 'King Alexander has sent orders to the archbishops and the bishops and all the consecrated council; when they will assemble, he will bid the monk Zakhkhey with his brethren and the priests to call on them.'

Prince Semen and dyak Torkh said: 'Inform King Alexander

that he should command the archbishops and the bishops and all the consecrated council to assemble quickly so that we shall not have to spend the winter in King Alexander's land for that purpose, and so that King Alexander can let us return the sooner to our Sovereign.'

Archimandrite Philip and Uman and the monk Kiril went to King Alexander. When they were back they said: 'You cannot now get back to the Tsar, for there has been a big fall of snow in the mountains. You will have to winter in the land of our sovereign King Alexander.'

And the ambassadors asked for King Alexander's permission to send off two or three of their men with letters to the Sovereign, and for his command for the issue of fresh horses for them to ride on and for an escort of the King's men to accompany them to whatever place was deemed suitable.

Archimandrite Philip and Uman and the monk Kiril went to King Alexander. And having come back they said: 'King Alexander bids you send your men off to the Sovereign, and he has issued orders to mount them on his own horses; his men will escort them to wherever proves suitable. And King Alexander also bids us tell you that you should write to your Sovereign to give orders to his majesty's commanders to defend our sovereign King Alexander from Shevkal, and wage war on the latter. Our sovereign King Alexander wants to send a letter to the same effect to your Sovereign by your men. And King Alexander has also instructed us to say to you: "I have heard that the Sovereign has let his great displeasure fall on Rodion Birkin and Petr Pivov who had come to me as his envoys. And I have a custom that whosoever comes to me on an embassy shall not be sorrowful. And these envoys of the Sovereign, Rodion and Petr, came to me and they acted in everything according to the Sovereign's instructions, nor did (166) they do anything evil or disobedient. The Sovereign should show his mercy to them in response to my supplication, and should remove his displeasure from them. I have heard about my own ambassadors that they behaved worse than that, yet the Sovereign was merciful to them for my sake and he covered their guilt." '[1]

And the ambassadors said: 'What is there for us to write to our Sovereign about Shevkal? The Sovereign's boyars and commanders at Astarakhan and on the Terek have got his instructions about Shevkal: they have been commanded to bring Shevkal under the Sovereign's hand. But we shall write to the great Sovereign of King Alexander's supplication about the envoys Rodion and Petr.'

Archimandrite Philip and Uman and the monk Kiril went to King Alexander. And having come back they said: 'Our sovereign King Alexander bids you ride back to your camp.'

The ambassadors rode off to their camp, and Uman accompanied them to the place where he had met them, while Prince Kaplan and Khurshit rode with them as far as their camp.

[1] The documents relating to Birkin and Pivov's embassy to King Alexander in 1587/8 refer to no misdeeds by the Russian ambassadors, and their disgrace was presumably unconnected with their mission to Georgia (cf. short notice on Birkin in *RBS*). Similarly there is no documentary evidence of misbehaviour by King Alexander's ambassadors in Moscow in 1588/9 where, in any case, their movements were severely circumscribed. The Russian official attached to them had received instructions not to allow 'any foreigners, Greeks, Turks, Armenians or others, to visit them in their lodgings or to talk to any of their men, or to allow any of the latter to leave the yard without express instructions' (Belokurov, *Snosheniya*, p. 54; cf. also Brosset, *EC/BHP*, Vol. II, Nos. 14–15, col. 240).

CHAPTER 4

NEGOTIATIONS WITH
KING ALEXANDER

(166) ON October 19th Prince Alkas arrived at Krym to visit King Alexander; and on the same day he sent his *uʒden* Lepsukh to Prince Semen and dyak Torkh to enquire after their health.

The ambassadors asked him why Alkas came to King Alexander and he replied that Prince Alkas was a kinsman, an uncle of King Alexander, and had now come to pay his respects to the King and to bring him a gift of prisoners and fish.[1]

Prince Alkas called on King Alexander on October 20th. The King sent to Prince Semen and dyak Torkh Uman and the monk Kiril who said: 'Prince Alkas begs King Alexander to take his son as a hostage, and he asks, you, the ambassadors, to order the release of his four *uʒdens*, Yanuk and his comrades, who are kept as hostages on the Terek as security for his son.'

And the ambassadors said: . . . 'Prince Alkas swore fealty to our Sovereign, took the oath in accordance with his faith, and gave hostages; but he afterwards proved false and escorted Kumyks, although these Kumyks do not obey the Sovereign.

(167) And the Sovereign's men defeated these Kumyks at the Sunzha crossing and took Alkas alive in that encounter. Having lost faith in Alkas, we bade him add his son to his former

---

[1] Prince Alkas: (Brosset, *EC/BHP*, Vol. II, Nos. 16–18, col. 240, n. 72) described as an uncle of King Alexander, seems to have been a brother of the Shevkal Kara Musal, whose daughter had become the second wife of King Levan.

hostage; and he, Alkas, gave us these *uzdens* of his, Yanuk and his comrades, in place of his son. We have written to the great Sovereign about this; and now it depends on the will of God and the Sovereign what royal orders he will issue in this matter. Furthermore, it befits your sovereign King Alexander to attach Prince Alkas more strongly to the great Sovereign, because Prince Alkas's loyalty is not firm.'

Uman and Kiril said: 'Neither does our sovereign, King Alexander, have faith in Alkas. He does not want to let him go without hostages, so he intends to take his son; and you should yourselves write to the commanders on the Terek not to set free those *uzdens* of his until such time as he brings his son to them.'

Prince Semen and dyak Torkh said: 'We have written to the commanders at Terek-town about this before now.' And they added: 'In the past Prince Alkas levied tribute from King Alexander, but since our Sovereign had extended his grace to King Alexander, it is Prince Alkas who has come with presents for your King . . . It is not for the sake of tribute, for the fifty lengths of golden Kizilbash damask or the ten golden carpets, that our Sovereign has extended his grace to King Alexander.[1] Our Sovereign does not need any of this. There is no such thing as does not exist in our Sovereign's realm. Our great Sovereign has extended his grace to King Alexander and has taken him under his royal hand for the sake of the Christian faith and because such is his royal custom.'

Uman and Kiril said: 'King Alexander, our master, was to have given these silks and carpets as tribute to the great Sovereign. But wars have occurred in the lands where such things are to be found, and it is impossible to obtain such a number of these fine things in King Alexander's realm. Our

---

[1] 'Golden Kizilbash damask and golden carpets': i.e. Persian fabrics and carpets sewn with gold thread. See further Chap. 7, p. 222, and Commentary 43.

sovereign has sent a plea about this to your great Sovereign, asking that instead of the tribute which cannot be found in his realm, the Sovereign should accept fine things as are to be got here.' . . .

The ambassadors replied: 'Our Sovereign has not named the tribute in his letter patent, because he was bountiful to King Alexander . . . That is why our Sovereign has written that King Alexander may send each year to the great Sovereign whatever he has in the way of fine things in his land, *argamaks* or fine horses or whatever else he happens to have: that he (168) should send. And by the grace of our great Sovereign, all the mountain princes and not only Alkas will begin to honour King Alexander.' . . .

And on the same day a Cherkess, a cousin of Khotov, by the name of Abzhuk-Korak, who was Shevkal's brother-in-law, came to Prince Semen and dyak Torkh. On being questioned he said that he had come on an embassy from Khotov to King Alexander to ask the King for the return of Khotov's daughter, the wife of Alexander's son Araklin who had fled to the Turk.[1] He said that he travelled together with Alkas, and he asked the ambassadors: 'Is the Crimean prince, who is Shevkal's son-in-law, now in Moscow?' And the ambassadors replied that he was in Moscow.

Abzhuk-Korak said: 'I have heard at Shevkal's that the Sovereign is very gracious to his son-in-law, the Crimean prince: whatever he asks the Sovereign, the latter gives him. Shevkal is holding counsel with Alkas and Solokh intending to send a message to the Crimean prince (Murat) to ask your Sovereign for men with whose aid to wage war on us – the Cherkesses who are under our Sovereign's hand.'[2]

[1] For Khotov, see Chap. 2 p. 109, n. 2; for Alexander's son, Araklin, see Chap. 3, p. 138, n. 1.
[2] For the Crimean prince, Murat Giray, see Chap. 1, p. 103, n. 1 and Commentary 11.

And the ambassadors said: 'Our Sovereign would not give his men to be used against you . . .'

Abzhuk-Korak then said: 'Your Sovereign should have no faith in the Crimean prince and should not send him to Astarakhan; for there is a Moslem understanding between him and Shevkal and Solokh and Prince Alkas: when the prince arrives at Astarakhan they will get together and bring the Turks to Astarakhan; while the prince will betray the Sovereign and surrender the city.'

And the ambassadors said: 'The Turk's men have been under the walls of Astarakhan before now – and it was not with many men that the Turkish pashas retreated; the Sovereign's men, sallying forth from Astarakhan, killed them all. And now the Sovereign has a more numerous army at Astarakhan than in the past, and a stone fortress has been built. The Turks will be unable to do anything to Astarakhan; even if the Turk himself joins with the other Moslems and brings them to Astarakhan – he will not do anything to it.'[1]

On October 22nd King Alexander sent Uman to the ambassadors Prince Semen and dyak Torkh bidding them attend on him. And the ambassadors rode up to King Alexander's court. They were met at the gates by the monk Kiril; and when they entered the courtyard they were met by the equerry Yuri, and by Uman in front of the hall. And when they were inside the hall King Alexander bade them sit at his right hand, and said: 'We have been autocrats in the Iberian realm for as long as we have been kings, for more than a thousand years. But God has now willed it that the Sovereign Tsar has accepted me under his royal hand for the sake of the Christian faith, and has raised me from the earth to heaven by the mercy which he showed to me in his royal letter patent. . . I rely on his grace not to deliver (169)

---

[1] This is a reference to the Turkish campaign against the Russians in Astrakhan in 1569, for which see Introduction, Section 1; also Allen, *PTP*, pp. 22–9.

me to the infidels. For only my land remains in the Christian faith; and near me all the lands are Moslem. The Turkish king is at present angry with me for doing homage to the great Sovereign; he writes to me that he intends to send his army against me in the summer.' . . .

And King Alexander also said: 'In the old days the Iberian realm was under one king, but our great-grandfather divided this kingdom into three parts. And in recent times one third of the Iberian realm was under my brother-in-law Semen. But he has lost nearly the whole of his kingdom for he eats (170) opium, and always quarrels with Turkish men; Turkish men have built fortresses in his land and have occupied nearly the whole of it. And it is not known what will happen in the future.'[1]

And the ambassadors said: 'Your brother-in-law Semen has lost his land through his own fault, because he did not do homage to the great Sovereign.' . . .

On October 24th the monk Kiril brought two letters to the ambassadors from King Alexander – one for the Sovereign and the other for the commanders on the Terek. And on the same day the ambassadors sent off the *streltsy* Ivashko Bely and Yakush Yasnovski to the Sovereign with the account of their embassy and the two letters sent by King Alexander.

The attendant Lom came to the ambassadors that same day with the message from King Alexander that they were to ride to the village of Chornour,[2] an estate of the monastery of St George of Alaverdy. 'You will not have to stay long in that village. King Alexander will send men to fetch you presently and will ask you to attend on him at the place where you are to spend the winter; and there he will also hold the council about

[1] For King Simon I of Kartli, see Commentary 27.
[2] Chornour = Dchiaouri of Wak./Brosset, p. 313 and Map 4; cf. also Chubinashvili, *AK*, p. 194 for Chiauri.

the Christian faith.' And the ambassadors set out from Krym the same day.

On October 28th the attendant Lom told the ambassadors on behalf of King Alexander to send the Sovereign's icon-painters, Posnik Dermin and his comrades, to the King in the village of Tog, where they were to paint murals in the church; and the ambassadors sent them off on the same (171) day.[1]

On the 14th of November King Alexander sent the attendant Ivan to fetch the ambassadors, instructing them to come to him at the village of Tog; and the ambassadors reached the village on the same day. There were soldiers encamped in tents to a distance of at least two versts, if not more, all round the village; and the tents were at least four hundred in number, perhaps more. The equerry Uman presently came to the ambassadors and said: 'King Alexander did not send for you straight away because he was attending to his private affairs.' And the ambassadors asked Uman to enquire of King Alexander as to when he would command the monk Zakhkhey with the priests and the deacons to attend on the Metropolitan. And Uman said: 'The archbishop and the bishops are with King Alexander, and the King has sent for Metropolitan Nicholas, bidding him come to him.'

On November 15th the tents near the village of Tog were struck and troops lined up on the ground, divided into five regiments, horse and foot, with banners; and there were crosses on the flagpoles.[2] There were approximately ten thousand horsemen in these regiments, if not more, armed with bows and arrows and sabres, with shields and spears. And there were some five hundred janissaries with hand-guns; and in front of the regiments stood some three thousand foot with sabres, bows and shields. This army moved towards King Alexander's court.

---

[1] For the village of Tog or Torga, see Commentary 28.
[2] For the organization of the Kakhian army, see Commentary 29.

The King rode out of the courtyard and began reviewing the regiments. And he sent Khurshit to the ambassadors bidding them and the monk Zakhkhey and the priests and the deacons and all the Sovereign's men to join him among his troops.

Prince Semen and dyak Torkh replied: 'King Alexander desires to show us his army, but we are accustomed to armies; we now see his army and that there are plenty of troops in his land. Your sovereign King Alexander is busy with his own affairs now, and it is not fitting for us to be present. The monk Zakhkhey and the priests and the deacons pray to God for our great Sovereign and are not warriors; so why should they come?'

Khurshit rode off to King Alexander. Presently he came back and said on behalf of the King that the ambassadors and the monk Zakhkhey with his brethren and all the Sovereign's men should ride to the King who was waiting for them; and should they not ride, King Alexander would come to them himself. Khurshit had hardly delivered the message when King Alexander left his regiments and turned towards the ambassadorial tent. The ambassadors rode to meet the King, and the monk Zakhkhey with his brethren rode together with them; and when they came together, they saluted the King without getting off (172) their horses. And Prince Semen and dyak Torkh rode forth at King Alexander's right hand, and Prince Alkas rode on his left. The sceptre was carried in front of King Alexander by his priest Yakim who had been to Moscow on an embassy to the Sovereign; and a banner was borne behind the King. King Alexander was accompanied by his brother-in-law Baygram[1]

---

[1] 'his brother-in-law Baygram'. Brosset (*EC/BHP*, Vol. II, Nos. 16–18, col. 243) suggests Bagrat, son of David (Da'ud Khan) a brother of Simon I. David was named by the Shah King of Kartli, 1569–78. Bagrat (VI) reigned as King of Kartli, 1616–19. He was son-in-law, not brother-in-law, to Alexander, having married his daughter Anna.

and his nobleman Yason and his cup-bearer Korzha[1] and by his courtiers and entourage, some one hundred in all, bearing his insignia, weapons, shields, cuirasses, club and mace; and behind them rode trumpeters and drummers. And the King rode back towards the regiments. He rode up to the banner of the first regiment, and with that regiment was his son Prince Yuri[2]; and Alexander said that that was his own, Alexander's, regiment. And they rode up to the second regiment, and General Edishey[3] and the monk Kiril were there; King Alexander said that that was the right flank. He rode up to the third regiment, and under the banner was his son Prince David[4] and bishop Zakhari of Kisik[5]; and the King said that that was the main

[1] *'cup-bearer'*: This seems to correspond to one of the posts at the mediaeval Georgian court: *Meghvinet-ukhutsesi* – 'Chief of the Wine Servers'; or *Piris-Meghvine* – personal wine-server to the King (cf. Allen, *HGP*, p. 259).

[2] Prince Yuri = G. Giorgi = George: third son of the king, after David and Irakli; married (i), before 1590, a daughter of the Sultan of Elisu Krym-Shevkal who was a brother or cousin of the Shevkal; (ii), a daughter of Kai-Khosro, Pasha of Genzha, about 1602. Was killed, together with his father, in 1605, and was buried at Alaverdi. His son, Yese (Isa Khan), commanded in Kakheti in 1615 for Shah Abbas and was killed in the same year. According to Wakhusht, Giorgi was good-looking, generous, inclined to peace, and gentle to his inferiors (Brosset, *HG*, Vol. II/ii, p. 156).
For the marriage of Giorgi with the daughter of the Sultan of Elisu (= Krym-Shevkal) see also Brosset, *EC/BHP*, Vol. II, Nos. 16–18, col. 250, n. 87; and further, Commentary 35.

[3] Edishey (= G. Edisher), see Chap. 3, p. 147, n. 1.

[4] Prince David (*G. Daviti*), eldest son of King Alexander. Married, c. 1581, Ketevan, daughter of Ashotan, Prince of Mukhrani (a cadet branch of the Kartlian line of Bagratids). She was the mother of King Taymuraz I of Kakheti; in 1624 she was tortured and executed by order of Shah Abbas on account of her refusal to abandon the Christian faith and is a saint and martyr of the Georgian Church. David himself was a bad character, as will be seen from the subsequent text. Wakhusht wrote that he was detested by the Kakhians for his insolence, swaggering ways and irascible character (cf. Brosset, *HG*, Vol. II/i, p. 156). He had, at the same time, a certain gift for poetical composition: see *BK*, 1965, article by K. Salia, 'La littérature géorgienne', p. 74.

[5] For the banner of Kisik (*G. Kisiqi*) see Commentaries 29 and 30.

regiment. And he then pointed to two regiments and said that they, too, were regiments, but he did not name their commanders or say what regiments they were. And having ridden a short distance away from the troops, he left the ambassadors Prince Semen and dyak Torkh and Prince Alkas with his men; and he himself rode alone towards the tent of his queen and his daughters, who left the tent and received him outside the tent-ropes, where they bowed to him. After remaining some time with them without dismounting, King Alexander came riding back. And he ordered all the five regiments to cross the river to the village of Tog, and he himself rode downstream from Tog; having crossed the river he rode up and down the field until all the regiments formed up behind the river, when he began reviewing them again.

And the ambassadors said to King Alexander: 'Your land is full of your army, and when the great Sovereign graciously lends you men with firearms to add to your army – you will be capable of withstanding those who disobey the Sovereign and are your enemies.' And King Alexander said: 'God grant that the Sovereign be in good health for many years. These men are not mine, they are all God's and the Sovereign's men.' And he rode off to his court, bidding the ambassadors return to their camp. When dismissing them he said: 'I shall be holding the council on the Christian faith presently.' Having kept his army for three days, King Alexander disbanded it. And it is a custom with him every year to assemble his army in that village of Tog in the autumn; having inspected it and made its muster, he sends it home with orders to be ready if need be.

The attendant Lom came to the ambassadors on November (173) 20th with a message from King Alexander that the monk Zakhkhey with his brethren should go to church to attend vespers, and that they were to sing at vespers; the King would attend vespers on the eve of the feast of the Presentation of the

Virgin.[1] The priests and the deacons went to the church having taken church music with them; but the monk Zakhkhey did not ride to church, saying that he was unwell. When they were back after vespers, the priests and the deacons said that King Alexander bade them sing vespers and that they did so. And the King bade them be present at matins and at mass, so as to sing matins and celebrate mass. And they, the priests and the deacons, replied that they would be present at matins and at mass and they would sing matins, but that it would be impossible for them to celebrate mass without having been received by Metropolitan Nicholas and by the whole consecrated council and without their benediction; they refused King Alexander's request because there were no altar adornments and it is not known whether the church has been consecrated or not. And on the following day the Sovereign's priests and deacons sang matins, and mass was celebrated by Athanasius from Mount Athos, abbot of the Iberian Monastery;[2] vespers on Sunday were again sung by the Sovereign's priests and deacons. At vespers the king was accompanied by the queen.

On the 20th, again, the equerry Uman rode to the ambassadors with King Alexander's message to send him [the inventory of] the gold and the paints which the Sovereign had graciously sent so that he might be acquainted with the Sovereign's bounty and know for what he should do homage to the Sovereign. And the ambassadors sent off to King Alexander

[1] Celebrated on 21 November.
[2] The Iberian Monastery on Mount Athos, founded by Georgians at the end of the tenth century, had great cultural and religious significance in the relations of Georgia with Byzantium and the Mediterranean world. There is considerable literature on the subject; cf. Tamarati, *EG, passim*; A. Natroyev, *Iverski monastyr na Afone* (Tiflis, 1909). See also, for a genial account of Athos and some reference to *Iviron*, Robert Byron, *The station: Athos – treasures and men* (London, 1949 ed.), with introduction by Christopher Sykes; F. W. Hasluck, *Athos and its monasteries* (London, 1912).

the gold and the paints together with the inventory on the same day.[1]

On November 24th the equerry Uman and King Alexander's confessor Archimandrite Philip and Athanasius, abbot of the Iberian monastery, came to Prince Semen and dyak Torkh and said on behalf of the King: 'Before now the Iberian realm was allied to the Kizilbash state and they stood together against the Turkish king and against other states; but nowadays, for our sins, the Turk is strong in these parts, he has taken many towns from the Kizilbash Shah and from my brother-in-law Semen, and he has imposed tribute on my realm. And the Kizilbash now keeps sending his ambassadors to me asking me to stand together with him against the Turk; while the Turk sends his *chaushes* to me with dire threats, saying that he intends to send his army against me this summer and to build fortresses in my land, because I seceded from him and have supplicated the great Sovereign to be taken under his royal hand. And the Turk's *chaushes* are even now living with me and asking for this year's tribute. And I have been putting them off from day to day in expectation that the great Sovereign's commanders will announce that the Sovereign's army is marching against Shevkal. Will it happen this winter? I sent a Cherkess of mine, (174) Yansha by name, to the Sovereign's commanders at Terek-town to get news when you sent off the *streltsy* with letters to the Sovereign; and I am now waiting for this man to come back at any moment. Shevkal also threatens me now and intends to wage war on my land next summer from his own side. Now I do not know what to do. Four years have passed since the great Sovereign extended his grace to me and took me under his hand; yet the Sovereign's army has not come to

[1] The case endings of the words *zolotu* and *kraskam* indicate that the sentence, as transcribed by Belokurov, is incomplete. The text has been emended by the insertion of the word *rospis* (inventory). The gold was gold leaf or gold paint used in the composition of icons.

defend me. The great Sovereign has now extended his great grace to me and has sent you as his ambassadors to me with his royal letter patent; what he wrote to me in this royal letter has brought me out of darkness into the light: it is as if this letter had fallen to me from the sky and the learned men, the monks and the priests, had come to my land like angels. I rejoice at the great Sovereign's bounty. But the Sovereign, who is a pillar and an edifier of the Christian faith, should carry out his promise, as he wrote in his letter, should protect me from the Moslem Turk and from Shevkal, and should not abandon this last remaining poor Christian state to be pillaged by the Moslems. You can see for yourselves that my puny Christian realm alone holds the Christian faith in these parts and, apart from it, it is all Moslem dominion.'

And the ambassadors Prince Semen and dyak Torkh said: 'Our Sovereign has accepted your master and all his Iberian land under his royal hand . . . has ordered forts to be built on the Terek for his protection, and has installed his commanders and his men and artillery therein; and he has extended his grace to all the mountain Kabardan princes for the sake of King Alexander, so that they should all stand together with him. He has sent his great army against prince Shevkal who disobeys him and is Alexander's enemy; this numerous army has reached the forts on the Terek while the remaining troops will arrive from Astarakhan on horseback and by boat . . . Our great Sovereign's army has not marched against Shevkal so far because his son-in-law, the Crimean Prince Murat Kirey, petitioned our great Sovereign on his behalf . . . Our great (175) Sovereign has extended his grace to the Kizilbash Shah and intends to accept him under his royal hand and protect him from the Turk; and in confirmation of this he sent his envoy Grigori Vasilchikov to the Shah; by now you yourselves know that the Kizilbash Shah received Grigori Vasilchikov with great honours and then sent him back to our Sovereign, and that along with him he sent his grandees on an embassy to do homage to our great Sovereign. And the Kizilbash Shah is not alone in this, for all the Christian sovereigns, the Christian Caesar and the Roman Pope and the Spanish king, and the whole of Italy and the Venetian prince have sent ambassadors and envoys to our Sovereign. They all ask our Sovereign Tsar and great Prince to ally himself with them against the Turk, who is lord over Christian states, and for all Christian sovereigns to unite and all together oppose these infidel Hagarenes. And our Sovereign Tsar and the great Prince has sent his envoys to all these Christian sovereigns, and he intends to join with them in opposing the Turk and all the Moslems. Prince Kaplan and his assistants, your sovereign's ambassadors, saw the Christian Caesar's ambassadors[1] when they were visiting our great Sovereign in Moscow; it looks as though they have not told King Alexander about this. King Alexander should fear no-one, since he is in our great Sovereign's grace and under his royal hand . . .'

(177)   On November 26th the attendant Lom came to the ambassadors Prince Semen and dyak Torkh and said: 'King Alexander bids you sup with him now; so ride you forth.' And the ambassadors rode to King Alexander; they were told that the king was having his meal in the dining pavilion in front of his court. They were met by the monk Kiril and by Khurshit some ten *sazhen*[2] from the pavilion; they dismounted, and were met in the doorway by the equerry Yuri. When they were inside the pavilion, King Alexander bade them sit at his right hand and said: 'How long ago did the Christian faith originate, and under what king?' And the ambassadors replied: 'The Christian faith originated under the great King Constantine

---

[1] This refers to the embassy of Emperor Rudolph II to the Tsar – Nicholas Varkach, Lucas Magnus and their train, who reached Moscow on 20 March 1589.

[2] One *sazhen* = approximately seven feet.

1,300 years ago; and in the Russian kingdom – under the faithful Grand Duke Vladimir some five hundred years ago.' And King Alexander said: 'Prince Alkas came to me, and I have extended my grace to him and have sent him off; he had insulted me in the past; but I have not held it against him because of our kinship, and because he came to me of his own free will. He has sworn to me on his soul that he is to stand with me in the great Sovereign's grace, united against all those who disobey the Sovereign and are my enemies, such as Prince Shevkal and others. He is to send his son as security for this; and I have sent an *aznaur* with him to fetch his son.'

And Prince Semen and dyak Torkh said: 'Prince Alkas (178) may be your kinsman, yet he was your enemy, and levied tribute from Prince Aristov of your land of Soni. Ere now he did not come to visit you; but now, by the grace of the great Sovereign, Prince Alkas has come to you himself; nor will he refuse to hand over his son – all because of our great Sovereign. And not only Prince Alkas, but also Prince Yansokh, to whom our great Sovereign has extended his grace and whom he has made great prince of Kabarda in his brother Aslanbek's place, with all his kin, and all the Kabardan princes and murzas, and the Avar prince and the Black Prince, will be your friends because of the great Sovereign's grace; and they will stand together with you against those who disobey the Sovereign and are your enemies. And Prince Alkas is not a great man in Kabarda.'

King Alexander said: 'Let the great Sovereign only defend me from Shevkal. He will then hear what I shall do and how I shall serve him, the Sovereign.' And the King also said that the Sovereign's priests should sing verses, or he would bid his own priests do so.

And the ambassadors said: 'In our great Sovereign's establishment verses are sung by deacon choristers, but priests of church rank who pray to God for the Sovereign recite the

Lord's Prayer at our great Sovereign's court before the meal, and the prayer "It is indeed fit" afterwards, and they sing to the Sovereign's long life and the long life of his Tsaritsa and great princess, over a health cup.'

And King Alexander said: 'I also have deacon choristers.' And he bade his deacons sing, saying that they were singing a hymn to the Immaculate Mother of God. He bade his attendants bring a full goblet of drink which he held in his hands, standing up. He then bade the Sovereign's priests sing, and they sang 'Rejoice, O Queen'. And King Alexander said: 'I drink this cup to the health of the great Sovereign Tsar and great Prince Fedor Ivanovich of all Russia'. And having drunk this cup, he offered a similar cup to the ambassadors Prince Semen and dyak Torkh. And after the meal the Sovereign's priests recited the prayer 'It is indeed fit', at King Alexander's bidding; and then the Georgian priests did likewise. After the prayer he dismissed the ambassadors . . .[1]

And on November 30th the attendant Lom came to Prince Semen and dyak Torkh and said: 'King Alexander bids you and the monk Zakhkhey with his brethren attend on him. Archbishop Gavril of the monastery of St George of Alaverdy and archimandrites and abbots are at present with the King; but Metropolitan Nicholas is not with them.' . . .

(179)   The ambassadors and the monk Zakhkhey with his brethren rode off to King Alexander. And some ten *sazhen* from the dining pavilion they were met by Khurshit and the monk Kiril, and in front of the dining pavilion they were met by King Alexander's dyak Zhurat and by Abbot Athanasius. Having entered the pavilion the monk Zakhkhey, in the name of the holiest Patriarch Job, recited the speech and delivered the benediction and salutation and presented the icon and handed

---

[1] 'Rejoice, O Queen' and 'It is indeed fit': two canticles in praise of the Virgin, the second of which exalts her above the Cherubim and Seraphim.

the letter to Archbishop Gavril, in place of Metropolitan Nicholas. King Alexander, who remained standing at that time, then said: 'The great Sovereign Tsar and great Prince Fedor Ivanovich of all Russia has extended his grace to me, his slave, and has sent his ambassadors to me, while his father, the holiest Patriarch Job, who prays to God for him, has extended his grace to those who pray for me, and has sent learned men, the great monk and the priests. And I rejoice that the Orthodox Christian faith will shine forth.' Archbishop Gavril, having received the icon and the letter of instruction, bowed to the ground and, after kissing the icon, he presented it to King Alexander; and the King kissed it and passed it on to Bishop Zakhari of the Kisik monastery. And in addition to them there were about ten archimandrites and abbots at the council. After he had spoken King Alexander sat down and bade the ambassadors and the monk Zakhkhey with his brethren sit down likewise. Having remained seated for some time, the ambassadors went away ...

The monk Zakhkhey with his brethren stayed behind and enquired of King Alexander as to when he was to attend on Archbishop Gavril and all the consecrated synod for a spiritual council. And the King said: 'I have not yet made my peace with the Metropolitan; and when I make my peace with him I shall bid you attend on him. I shall hold the great council (180) on Easter Day; I have postponed this matter until Easter Day. I shall now issue orders to give you a church; and you should command the priests to officiate.'

And rumour has it that King Alexander's quarrel with the Metropolitan is because of this: In the year [70]97, Patriarch Theolipt[1] came from Constantinople to Georgia, to King

---

[1] Theoleptus II, Metropolitan of Philippopolis, ascended the Oecumenical Throne on 20 February 1585. Several incumbents followed each other in quick succession between 1585 and 1589 while Patriarch Jeremiah was in exile (*Dictionnaire de Théologie Catholique*). It is not clear how long Theoleptus remained on the Patriarchal Throne; he may have been

Alexander, to collect alms, and he brought with him an episcopal rochet; and the King commanded that this rochet be given to Archbishop Gavril of the monastery of St George of Alaverdy and that he should be blessed to officiate in it. And Metropolitan Nicholas insisted that from the earliest times the Metropolitan, alone in all the Iberian land, had worn the episcopal rochet, and there had never been another rochet worn by anyone other than the Metropolitan.

On December 16th the attendant Lom came to the ambassadors Prince Semen and dyak Torkh and said: 'King Alexander will presently be riding past your tent on his way hawking; so be in your tent.'

And presently King Alexander rode out of his courtyard and took the direction of the ambassadorial tent; and he was followed by some one hundred of his *aznaurs*, on horseback and on foot, in festive dress. When he was near the tent ropes Prince Semen and dyak Torkh left the tent and went to the ropes, where they saluted the King; they also did homage to him for his gracious bounty, in sending them each an *argamak*.

King Alexander enquired after their health and said: 'How could I not be bountiful to you? Everything belongs to God and to the great Sovereign. Now I am letting you go to Zaem,[1] so go and spend some time there. Come back to me before Christmas, so that we may break the fast together.'

And the ambassadors said: 'You are free to command where we shall go.'

And King Alexander rode back to his court; and there were no hawks or hunt servants with him.

The ambassadors proceeded to Zaem on the same day,

---

deposed in 1586, in which case he would have been an ex-Patriarch in the year 7097 (1588/9).
[1] For Zaem, see Commentary 31: 'The town of Zaem, Zagem, Zegan, Zakam'.

and the attendants Ivan and Lom rode with them. And on the 27th of December the monk Kiril came to them, bringing four letters – two letters addressed to King Alexander, one (181) from the commander Prince Andrey Khvorostinin and the other from the Cossack captain Grigori Poltev, and two letters for the ambassadors – one from Prince Andrey and the other again from Grigori Poltev – all of them with the seals broken. The ambassadors ordered that copies be made of the letters sent to King Alexander; and they gave the originals to the monk Kiril. . .

Copy of letter: To the Christian King Alexander, by the grace of God sovereign of the Georgian land, I, Grigori Poltev, servant of the Orthodox Tsar, do homage. I came to Kabarda at the Sovereign's command on the 21st of November, against those who disobey the Sovereign and did not want to come under his hand, but who entertained friendship with the Turks and the Crimean king and with Shevkal and with the Kumyks. I brought with me the Sovereign's men with fire-arms and a Cherkess army, and I waged war and burned their settlements, and have brought the whole of Kabarda under (182) the Sovereign's hand. I have cleared the road to you and have sent your ambassadors from Kabarda back to you. Your envoy Yansha witnessed this war, as he accompanied me on the expedition; he will tell you everything in detail, and your ambassador Usein, who had been to the Kizilbash, will do likewise. I lost many horses in this campaign and, Sovereign, you should show your grace to me and send me mounts for use against your enemies. And you should present a sabre to me in your bounty. This affair, and my service, are altogether yours. We are now thinking of marching against the Kumyks . . .

And such is the letter from the commanders on the Terek to the ambassadors: (121)

To the lord Prince Semen Grigoryevich and to dyak Torkh Antonov, Andrey Khvorostinin and his comrades do homage.

You sent to us the *streltsy* Ivashka Bely and Yakush Sosnovski with a letter for the Sovereign and a narrative of your embassy. But, my lord, you have not written to us why you have to winter in Georgia. Shevkal continues to do homage to the Sovereign; he frequently sends ambassadors and himself wants to visit us. When he visits us, we shall make a great pact with him so that the Sovereign's men shall travel from us to Georgia and the Georgians to us through his land. Whatever news you will have about Shevkal – you should not keep us in ignorance. Without fail you should tell Alexander that he should not allow Alkas to leave . . . And if he lets him go, he should take hostages from him, his son or his nephew, and we shall take a son or a nephew as a hostage here.

[Grigori Poltev's letter ran:]

To the lord Prince Semen Grigoryevich I, Grisha Poltev, beg your favour and do homage. God preserve you, my lord, with all under your command. And should you favour me with enquiring after me – I am still alive and in Kabarda on the 2nd day of December. I have been sent to Kabarda because of (122) those who disobey the Sovereign; I have with me 750 men with firearms and the Kabardan prince Yansokh and his nephews – Kazy murza with his brothers, the children of Aslanbek and of Bulat and many murzas are also with me. By the mercy of God and the good fortune of our sovereign the Orthodox Tsar we have brought the entire Kabardan land under the Sovereign's hand and . . . we have burnt out the settlements and destroyed their belongings . . . You should give this letter to Torkh Antonovich to read. I do homage to you, my lord, and to Torkh Antonov . . . great homage; and (? will he favour me) with good silk for a *kaftan*.[1]

(182)   Prince Semen and dyak Torkh said to the monk Kiril about the opening of the letters: 'There is no such custom anywhere

---

[1] For these Kabardan personalities, see Commentary 12: The princely families of Kabarda.

to break the seals on somebody else's letters; this dishonours us, and so King Alexander should command that he who broke the seals on these letters be found. And should it be that King Alexander himself broke the seals on these letters of ours, he is free to do so; but even this should not have happened.'

And the monk Kiril said: 'King Alexander himself broke the seals on these letters; and having heard these letters read, he has sent them to you and bade me tell you that the seals had been broken by him in person.'

And the Cherkess Yansha said in answer to questions: 'King Alexander sent me to escort the Sovereign's *streltsy* as far as Tyumen-town. The commander Prince Andrey Khvorostinin kept me at Terek-town for two days, and he then sent me back to King Alexander; he gave me these letters and gave orders that I should be escorted as far as the Sovereign's army which is stationed under Grigori Poltev among the Kabardan Cherkesses. And it so happened that Grigori Poltev and many Kabardan princes and murzas were conducting a campaign at that time against the settlements of the Kabardan prince Solokh; and in my presence they burnt down and conquered some thirty of his settlements and perhaps more. And when the Sovereign's army neared Solokh's own settlement – he came out on foot to Grigori Poltev, with his children and *uzdens* and he brought with him Andey's son, (183) Shevkal's grandson, whom Shevkal had sent him as a hostage; Solokh supplicated Poltev not to wage war on him and declared that he is willing to serve the Sovereign. He told Poltev to take as hostage from him whomsoever he wished; and Grigori Poltev took from him his son and Shevkal's grandson, Andey's son, and twenty of his best *uzdens*. And Grigori let me go with these letters and he ordered the Cherkesses to escort me.'[1]

[1] 'Andey's son': presumably a son of Shevkal Andi, who succeeded Sarkhai about 1589 and who was the eldest son of Shevkal Choban, see p. 592 below for genealogy of the Shevkals; also Kosven, *OID*, p. 94, n.5.

The monk Kiril also said to the ambassadors on behalf of King Alexander: 'This same Cherkess Yansha has given news to our Sovereign; and you should secretly question him about this news.'

And the ambassadors questioned Yansha who said: 'I have heard from King Alexander's ambassador Useinbek, who had been to the Kizilbash land to see the Shah, and who was taken to Astarakhan by Grigori Vasilchikov, from where he was sent to Terek-town by the Sovereign's commanders, and whom the commanders on the Terek sent off to King Alexander along with me, Yansha – that the Crimean prince [Murat Kirey] begged the Sovereign to allow him to go to Astarakhan and to give him an army, and to order the Great and the Lesser Nogays[1] and the Cherkesses to march with him. He would start operations against Shevkal and the Turk's towns and would clear these towns, Derbent and Shirvan and Shemakha, and all the towns which the Turk captured from the Kizilbash Shah; and he would bring Shevkal under the Sovereign's hand and would recover his wife from Shevkal. But things will not happen this way, for Prince Murat Kirey intends to betray the Sovereign. As soon as the Sovereign sends him off

---

[1] According to Bartold (*EI*, 1st ed. under Mangit), the people called Nogay by the Russians are called Mangit by Abu'l Ghazi and other oriental sources. A tribe (*oymak*) of the Golden Horde, they nomadized over the steppe from the Yaik as far as the Crimea. They were divided into the Greater (*ulu*) and Lesser (*kichi*) Hordes. In the latter part of the sixteenth century, they were harassed by the Yaik (Ural) Cossacks and decimated by famine, pestilence and civil war. Jenkinson has left a pitiful account of them (Hakluyt, *PN*, Vol. 1, p. 363). In 1604 the boyar Semen Godunov was sent to Astrakhan with full powers to settle the differences among the Nogays. Some groups were settled in the steppe between Astrakhan and the Terek. See Howorth, *HM*, Vol. II, pp. 1036–41; Baddeley, *RCC*, pp. 44 ff.; cf. also Togan, *TT*, pp. 137 ff. For the seventeenth century, Melchizedek Thevenot printed the Dominican Luca's account of them; Aubry de la Mottraye gives interesting details for the early years of the eighteenth century. For records of Russian relations with the Nogays, see *DRV*, *Prodolzheniye*, *chasti* vii–xi.

to Astarakhan and gives him an army, he and the Nogay murzas and Shevkal and the Cherkess princes who are not under the Sovereign's hand will establish intelligence with the Turk and will start designs on Astarakhan and on Terek-town and on Alexander's realm, for they all hold the same Moslem faith. Yet the Sovereign has let the prince go to Astar-akhan, and he is expected at Astarakhan at any moment. Useinbek was given this news at Astarakhan by a yurt Tartar, but he did not tell me his name.'

Thereupon the monk Kiril said: 'The ambassadors should report this news to Terek-town and to Astarakhan, so that the Sovereign should not put faith in Prince Murat Kirey and should not permit him to remain at Astarakhan. Even if Murat is at Astarakhan, the Sovereign should not allow many Nogays to come to him, so that he should not perpetrate some evil on Astarakhan. "And if anything befalls Astarakhan [King Alexander said] I shall abandon my poor realm and shall run where my eyes take me."

Kiril went on: 'This same Cherkess Yansha also informed King Alexander that Shevkal's grandson, the son of Andey, (184) who lived as a hostage with Prince Solokh, and whom Grigori Poltev has now taken, had told him: "King Alexander your sovereign used to be under the Turkish king's hand together with Shevkal and Solokh and Alkas, but he has since sup-plicated the Muscovite Sovereign to wage war on us and convert us to the Christian faith: but before the Muscovite Sovereign can come to his aid, Shevkal and Solokh and Alkas and the Turk's men will come to Alexander's land and will establish a fortress at Zaem this spring."'

Prince Semen and dyak Torkh said: 'And what of it if Prince Murat Kirey begged our great Sovereign to let him wage war on Shevkal for not sending him his wife who is Shevkal's daughter? Even if our Sovereign lets Prince Murat Kirey go with his army to wage war on Shevkal, the prince

will not be alone in this army. Our great Sovereign has many
kings and princes in his service . . . and he also sends his great
nobles and commanders with his army. The expedition will
not depend on Prince Murat Kirey alone. The Turk sent his
army to Astarakhan before now . . . and what has he done to
Astarakhan? The Sovereign's men sallied forth from Astarakhan and inflicted a crushing defeat. And now there are more
of the Sovereign's troops at Astarakhan than at that time
and the Sovereign ordered the construction of a strong stone
fortress and has installed powerful artillery there. Who could
so much as look at Astarakhan, let alone subject it to some evil?
Your sovereign King Alexander should not even entertain
the thought – for such a thing cannot happen – that the Nogays
could secede from our great Sovereign and join up with the
Turk and with Shevkal and with the Cherkess princes. The
Nogay great princes and all the *murzas* of the two Nogay
[hordes] have always been the servants of our Sovereign; and
the princes Urus and Urmamet have now come under our
Sovereign's royal hand even more firmly than in the past. . . .
What need is there to talk much with you, Kiril, about Astarakhan and the Nogays and Shevkal? You were at Astarakhan
yourself and saw the Sovereign's army and fortress and
artillery, and you heard that the Nogays serve the Sovereign
(185) and come to Astarakhan; and their brothers and children and
nephews and grandchildren are kept as hostages at Astarakhan, and you have seen them there yourself. Even if there
had been no hostages, where could the Nogays escape from
the Sovereign's men? Shevkal will be brought low even by the
Kabardan and other mountain princes and the Avar prince and
the Black Prince who are under our Sovereign's royal hand, as
soon as the Sovereign permits them to wage war on him . . .
And even now the commanders have written to us from
Terek-town in the letter which you have just brought us that
Shevkal is already subjected to great pressure, and that the

Sovereign's men have taken the river Koysu from him and want to build a fortress on the river Koysu ...'[1]

And the monk Kiril said: 'The great Sovereign can do anything; but Shevkal should not be believed even though he is supplicating the great Sovereign, for his great loyalty is to the Turk ... And King Alexander bade me tell you that you should get two men ready for dispatch to Astarakhan and Terek-town with this news, and that you should write to the commanders to wage war on Shevkal this winter. And our sovereign King Alexander intends himself to write to the Cherkess princes in Kabarda and to send them his bounty so that they should march against Shevkal with the Sovereign's commanders.'

And the ambassadors said: 'This information is insufficient and not enough [to justify] sending messengers to Astarakhan and Terek-town. The Sovereign's commanders at Astarakhan and on the Terek already hold the Sovereign's order about Shevkal, whom they are commanded to press and to bring under the Sovereign's hand. But should King Alexander order us to send messengers, we shall not resist — so long as men can get through, because of the snow.'

And the monk Kiril said: 'I shall notify all this to King Alexander; and in the meantime get ready the men whom you may send.'

Prince Semen and dyak Torkh asked the monk Kiril: 'Has King Alexander now made his peace with the Metropolitan and where is he now, and what are the King's instructions about the monk Zakhkhey and his brethren visiting the Metropolitan?' The monk Kiril said: 'King Alexander has made his peace with the Metropolitan who will presently join the King in the village of Tog; and he will arrive with the king at Zaem shortly. King Alexander will then summon

---

[1] 'The River Koysu', later known as the Sulak, see Introduction, Section 8.

the monk Zakhkhey with his brethren to call on the Metropolitan.'

(186) And the monk Kiril rode off from Zaem on the same day to King Alexander.

CHAPTER 5

MATTERS TEMPORAL AND SPIRITUAL

O N the 3rd day of January [1590], Ukron, the lord of (186)
Zaem, and the attendants Ivan and Lom came to the
ambassadors Prince Semen and dyak Torkh and
said: 'King Alexander has written to us that he will arrive at
Zaem from the village of Tog for Epiphany; and he has ordered
horses to be sent for you on the eve of Epiphany. He bids you
ride to the village of Tog – so get ready to start.'

And the ambassadors said: 'Why does not King Alexander
keep us by him? For we have the Sovereign's affairs to impart
to him. And it is dishonouring for us, the great Sovereign's
ambassadors, that King Alexander should come to Zaem
himself and send us away from him. Write this to your
sovereign.'

And Ukron and his comrades said: 'King Alexander bids
you ride to the village of Tog for it is impossible to get food
for you at Zaem during the king's stay there; and we do not
dare write this to our sovereign.' Ukron also said: 'I am riding
to join my sovereign. If you find it necessary to attend on
our sovereign, send your own messenger with me to King
Alexander.'

The ambassadors sent the interpreter Ivan Nikolayev to
King Alexander on the same day; and they instructed him to
ask the King's officials to announce his coming to their
sovereign.

Returning the next day, the interpreter Ivan said that on
reaching the village of Tog he reported to Abbot Athanasius,
and the abbot spoke to King Alexander. The king bade him

come to him and said: 'Give Abbot Athanasius the message which the great Sovereign's ambassadors sent by you.' And he spoke to Abbot Athanasius. The abbot went to King Alexander and when he was back said to him: 'The King bids the great Sovereign's ambassadors remain at Zaem. King Alexander himself will come to Zaem after Epiphany. He intends to keep the great Sovereign's ambassadors by him at Zaem; and he is now sending Ukron, his lord at Zaem, to the ambassadors with this message.' And [Ivan said] that Abbot Athanasius also said to him: 'King Alexander and the queen are dejected, for they got news that his son Prince Araklin had died in Turkey, and his clothes have been brought to King Alexander; and as for the *aznaurs* who fled with him to Turkey, they have sent a message to King Alexander begging for permission to return and asking for letters of immunity that he will not punish them.'

(187)   And on the following day Ukron came to the ambassadors Prince Semen and dyak Torkh and said: 'King Alexander bids you stay at Zaem and has given me instructions for the attendants about provisions.'

On January 26th King Alexander arrived at Zaem and Metropolitan Nicholas with him.

On the 28th dyak Ters[1] came from King Alexander to the ambassadors and said: 'King Alexander bids me ask you whether you are experiencing any inconvenience or shortage of provisions. And he bids you attend on him tomorrow as he intends to deal with you about all the Sovereign's affairs and to let you go back to the Sovereign soon.'

And the ambassadors said: 'We are suffering no inconvenience or shortage of provisions. But we ourselves have told King Alexander before now that our great Sovereign's affairs should be attended to, and that he should give us leave to

---

[1] Dyak Ters. It is possible that the form 'Ters', given as a proper name may be simply a Russian version of the Georgian word, *mdserali*, scribe.

return while it is still possible to travel along the rivers, before the floods begin.'

King Alexander did not send anyone for them on the following day. But on that day he seized the Kizilbash commander Amamut with his wife and children, after having invited them to sup with him, and he had them sent to a prison. This Amamut had been stationed below Genzha but the Turks had defeated him, and he had come to King Alexander with what were left of his men and begged the king to allow him to settle in his land.[1]

On January 30th dyak Ters came to the ambassadors and said: 'You were to come to King Alexander yesterday, but the king was busy with his own affairs. The defeated Kizilbashes, whom the Turks had routed near Genzha, complained to King Alexander against their general Amamut, saying that their defeat was caused by Amamut, who was encamped without precautions and kept them hungry and did not give them provisions although he had large supplies from the Shah; so they obtained provisions by raiding away from the camp. And the Turks came upon them at that time and defeated them and seized their wives and children; and Amamut was the first to flee – and he is not to their liking as a commander. [They therefore asked] the king to permit them to choose another commander from among themselves. And King Alexander ... extended his grace to the Kizilbashes allowing them to settle in his land, and he bade them choose a commander from among the Kizilbash officers. And they chose Alebekh; and he and the Kizilbashes are at present taking the oath, according to their faith, to serve King Alexander. And it is unsuitable for you to attend on the king now. He has sent a message by me that you are to call on him tomorrow.'

[1] For Amamut (=Imam-Kuli Khan), Persian governor of Genzha, defeated by Özdemiroghlu Osman in 1588, see Commentary 32: Genzha and Areshi.

(188)   On the following day Khurshit rode to the ambassadors and said: 'King Alexander bids you and the monk Zakhkhey with his brethren come to him, and you are to sup with him.' And the ambassadors arrived at King Alexander's court where they were met by General Edishey and the equerries Uman and Abel outside the hall. When they were in the hall King Alexander said to them: 'Go and get Metropolitan Nicholas's blessing.' Metropolitan Nicholas was seated on King Alexander's right; he stood up and gave them his benediction. The monk Zakhkhey immediately said to Metropolitan Nicholas: 'The holiest Job, by the mercy of God patriarch of the reigning city of Moscow and of all great Russia, sent his benediction to you, an icon of the Saviour encased in silver, and a letter of instruction; and at King Alexander's bidding I have given this icon and the letter of instruction to Archbishop Gavril of the monastery of St George. Have this icon and this letter reached you, Metropolitan Nicholas?' And Metropolitan Nicholas said that they had reached him and that he did homage for this great benediction; and he bowed low.

After this, King Alexander bade the ambassadors sit down and said: 'The monk Zakhkhey and his brethren should tell Metropolitan Nicholas the message which the holiest Patriarch Job, who prays to God for the great Sovereign, sent by them to the Metropolitan.'

And the ambassadors said: 'As you, King Alexander, and Metropolitan Nicholas wish. But it is proper for the monk Zakhkhey and his brethren to be alone with Metropolitan Nicholas and the whole consecrated council, for their affairs are spiritual.'

And the King said: 'It is apparent to me that it is proper for them to be alone with Metropolitan Nicholas, and I shall order them to attend on him some other time.' And he let the ambassadors go from the hall to the tent, sending Abbot Athanasius and Khurshit with them.

The ambassadors remained in the tent until King Alexander entered the dining hall, and sat down, and sent for them to come to him. And at table King Alexander said to the monk Zakhkhey: 'You are upright men, great teachers who pray to God for the Sovereign, yet you now live without a church; I can see for myself that it is not proper for you to be without a church, for you are churchmen. And before now I wanted to send you to my great monastery, to a good and prominent place – I have not got another such monastery – so that you should stay in there near a church. You did not go to that monastery, but expressed the wish to remain together with the ambassadors Prince Semen and dyak Torkh. And I decided to follow your wish.'

And the monk Zakhkhey said: 'I am an ordinary monk who prays to God for the great Sovereign, and it was not suitable for me to be without a church; but it is even less proper for (189) my brethren, the priests and the deacons to have no church, for they are churchmen and always offer gifts to God and celebrate mass. We have not offered gifts to God once since we reached your realm, and have not celebrated mass because the priests and the deacons did not dare to celebrate mass without having visited Metropolitan Nicholas and without a spiritual discussion and his blessing. We grieve that we have no church, but we have not gone to the monastery because you had commanded the ambassadors Prince Semen and dyak Torkh to be near you, and we also wanted to be near you together with them, so that the holiest Patriarch Job's affair, on which we have been sent, should more readily receive attention. You postponed this matter until such time as Metropolitan Nicholas would come to you. And he is with you now: what are your orders about our calling on him?'

And the ambassadors also asked King Alexander to order them to attend on Metropolitan Nicholas urgently, so that this matter should not be the cause of further delay.

And King Alexander said: 'Tomorrow is Sunday. And on Monday is the great feast of the Purification. I shall instruct the monk Zakhkhey with his brethren and the priests to call on Metropolitan Nicholas tomorrow; and the Sovereign's priests and deacons should celebrate mass on the holiday. I am constantly concerning myself with your departure so as to be able to let you go back to the great Sovereign soon. Were it possible to get through, I would let you go straight away for my own sake, so that my affairs should receive attention and that the Sovereign should give orders to protect me from Shevkal.'

And the ambassadors said: 'Your affair has been begun by the grace of the great Sovereign. . . . This is known to you; you have been notified of it by your men who have come here. The matter will be concluded. Shevkal will be brought under the Sovereign's hand, and presently will be at peace with you.'

King Alexander said: 'Eat and drink, be full and be merry. Everything belongs to the great Sovereign. If I could only speak your tongue, I too would have known how to honour you, the great Sovereign's ambassadors'.

And Prince Semen and dyak Torkh said: 'By the grace of (190) our great Sovereign, we always have much to drink and eat in your land. And not only is your bounty always plentiful towards us: your *aznaurs*, too, hold us in honour by your grace, and send us provisions'.

The King replied: 'My *aznaurs* also kissed the cross that they will serve the great Sovereign and wish him well in everything. And whosoever does not behave in this way – I shall repudiate him; he who loves me also loves you. What I ask God and the great Sovereign is that the Sovereign's men should move closer to my land and live among my men. The great Sovereign would then hear of my deeds and service.'

Prince Semen and dyak Torkh said: '. . . You should not

suspect or entertain the thought that the great Sovereign could surrender you to anybody . . .'

After the meal King Alexander dismissed the ambassadors. And the equerry Abel accompanied them halfway down the courtyard, and Khurshit as far as the gates; and the attendants Ivan and Lom rode with them as far as their camp.

On the following day, the 2nd of February,[1] the attendants Ivan and Lom came to the ambassadors and told the monk Zakhkhey and his brethren on behalf of King Alexander that they were to ride to Metropolitan Nicholas. And the monk Zakhkhey and his brethren rode off to visit the Metropolitan. On his return Zakhkhey said that they attended on him at the King's court and that they were met by the priest Yakim and by the abbot in front of the hall; when they were inside, the Metropolitan stood up and gave them his blessing and bade them be seated. And Bishop Zakhari of the monastery of Kisik and about ten archimandrites and abbots were in the hall with the Metropolitan, as well as Yason, a nobleman of King Alexander, and some twenty other *aznaurs*. The monk Zakhkhey and his brethren stood up and said to Metropolitan Nicholas: 'King Alexander has bidden the Sovereign's priests to celebrate mass in the churches at Krym and at Tog and here at Zaem; but the priests did not dare officiate without having visited you, Metropolitan Nicholas, and without your counsel and benediction.' And the Metropolitan said: 'I thank you for having held me in honour and for not having officiated (191) without my advice and benediction. And now I give you my blessing and pray you to officiate.' And the monk Zakhkhey and his brethren said: 'We see, Nicholas, that the Christian faith and the service in churches in King Alexander's realm and among your flock are according to the Greek rule. We praise

---

[1] This must be an error for 1 February, since the preceding day, on which King Alexander had entertained the ambassadors, was given as 'the following day' after 30 January, i.e. the 31st.

185

you for this. Yet we entreat your Holiness on one point, and do not be angry with us for asking you: Are your churches consecrated and according to what canons?' And Metropolitan Nicholas together with all the council said: 'Our churches are consecrated.' And the monk Zakhkhey and his brethren said: 'Then why do we see things in your churches which are not in accordance with the traditions of the Holy Apostles and the rules of the Holy Fathers? The altar is not adorned; there is no shirt, or fastening, *antimension* or *endyton* or cross or the Book of the Gospels on the altar – but it is simply covered with a cloth. And the holy vessels on the small altar in which Christ's mystery is accomplished are without *deesis* or cross. Yet no church can be consecrated when any one of these holy articles is missing; and no service, no offering of gifts to God, can take place.[1] Priests and deacons are unable to officiate in a church which has not been consecrated. But if you will order that the church be consecrated and supplied with all the holy articles without which – according to the traditions of the Holy Apostles and the rules of the Holy Fathers – a church cannot be consecrated nor a service held, then, in our love of Christ, we shall consecrate the church and shall supply all these articles and shall celebrate mass.' And Metropolitan Nicholas together with all the council said: 'Our churches have been consecrated according to the Greek rule of mount Athos, and the *antimension* is there, glued into the altar; and there is a cross and the Book of the Gospels in the church;

[1] The vesting of the altar forms an essential part of the consecration service according to the Greek rite (cf. *The Catholic Encyclopaedia*, the article 'Altar (in the Greek Church)'). For an explanation of the vestments and ornaments, see Commentary 24. The 'fastening', to the absence of which Zakhkhey draws attention, must be the rope with which the altar is encircled during the consecration service. This rope symbolizes the ropes with which Christ was bound. The absence of all coverings must have suggested to Zakhkhey that the altar had never been properly consecrated or, having once been consecrated, had been desecrated by despoilers.

and should anything be missing, then supply it and recite a prayer over the altar and bless the water and, having aspersed it with water, celebrate mass. But you cannot consecrate the church a second time.' And the monk and his brethren said: 'There is a prayer for the church and the church is sprinkled with water which has been blessed, but this happens when, through carelessness, an infidel enters the church, or a cur jumps in, or after the church has fallen into the hands of those holding a different faith. But a church cannot be consecrated if even one of these holy articles is missing, and if it is not adorned by all these holy articles together. And you have not got these holy articles on the altar. And how can we regard the church as having been consecrated, and celebrate mass? We can see for ourselves that you have the Book of the Gospels and the cross in your churches, but they are kept lying carelessly on lecterns and benches, and are not on the altar; and it is proper for the Book of the Gospels and the cross to be on the altar. You say that you keep the Greek rule of mount Athos; we, also, have the canons of mount Athos. Shall we compare the two sets of canons and see what they say about the consecration of churches?' And Metropolitan Nicholas together with all the council said: 'Should you want to consecrate a church, King Alexander has got a new stone church built in the village of Tog. Go and consecrate this church according to your customs. But it will not come about for you to consecrate for a second time the church here at Zaem. We have had this church blessed fifty years ago, and you now (192) want to re-consecrate it afresh.' And the monk Zakhkhey and his brethren said: 'In the Russian kingdom the consecration of a church is regarded as a great event by our great Sovereign the Tsar and great Prince Fedor Ivanovich of all Russia, and the consecration of a church is attended by our great Sovereign in person and by his father, the holiest Patriarch Job of the reigning city of Moscow and of all Russia, who prays to God for him; and here it is fit that the consecration of a church be attended by King Alexander himself and by you, Metropolitan Nicholas, with all the council, so that you may see how Christian devotion takes place in the Russian kingdom under our great Sovereign, and be filled with his devotion. You are now sending us off and telling us to consecrate a church in a deserted spot some two versts from the village of Tog. We cannot consecrate a church there.' Metropolitan Nicholas then said with all the council: 'King Alexander has now ridden off to have sport; he will be back on Wednesday, and we shall then report to him and shall inform you of what he says.'

King Alexander returned to Zaem on February 4th, and sent Abbot Athanasius to the ambassadors Prince Semen and dyak Torkh. He told the ambassadors that they should remain at Zaem till Shrove-tide. And the monk Zakhkhey asked Abbot Athanasius: 'Have you reported to King Alexander about our affair?' And Abbot Athanasius said that they had reported the matter to King Alexander who has postponed it until he should come to Krym. And on February 5th King Alexander rode off from Zaem to the village of Tog. On the 24th he sent the attendant Ivan to the ambassadors, bidding them to proceed to the village of Chornour where they had stayed previously. And the ambassadors Prince Semen and dyak Torkh went from Zaem to that village on the same day.

(CXXII)   . . .[1] with precious stones, and small candles are placed in

---

[1] Belokurov suggests that the next paragraphs constitute the sole surviving fragment of the report submitted by Zakhkhey on his return to Moscow. For Kisik, see Commentary 30. The reference is probably to Bodbe, the seat of the Bodbeli, Primate of Kakheti. For the numerous ruins of stone churches and sanctuaries to the east of the Alazani, in the districts of Tsuketi, Eliseni and Zakatali, and as far as the river Gishi within a few miles of the borders of Shirvan, see *MAK*, Vol. VII, pp. 28 ff., Khakhanov, 'Zakatalski okrug'; also, Chubinashvili, *AK*, pp. 30-2. Further on this region see Gan (= von Hahn) 'Puteshestviye v Kakhetiyu i Dagestan (letom 1898 goda)' in *SMK*, Vol. XXXI (1902), pp. 49-96.

front of them. Above the royal gate there is a *deesis* painted on the wall and not on panels, and there is no pulpit. Archbishop Zakhariya officiates there; and there are priests and deacons and all church dignitaries. And here, at Kisik, there are also many stone churches for the laity; their number cannot be remembered.

Archbishopric of Martukop beyond the mountains. Church of the Transfiguration of Christ – built of stone and with a dome. In it there is an icon of our Lord Jesus Christ, which is not man's work, encased in gold, the halo with precious stones; a candle stands in front of it; there is also an icon of the Immaculate Mother of God encased in silver gilt, and there are many other icons encased in silver gilt. An archbishop by the name of Nikolae officiates there. The holy hermit Anthony is buried in the church.[1]

Bishopric of Nekresel.[2] Church of the Assumption of the Mother of God, painted all over in gold and colour. An inset icon of the Immaculate Mother of God, encased in gold with precious stones and a likewise inset[3] icon of the Saviour, encased in silver gilt, and another icon of the Assumption of the Immaculate Mother of God, encased in silver gilt with precious stones, and many other icons; it is impossible to recall their number. A bishop by the name of Iosif officiates in it.

Bishopric of Katsarel.[4] Stone church of the Holy Life-giving Trinity, built of dressed blue stone, painted and gilt inside. There is an inset icon of the Life-giving Trinity in it, encased in gold with precious stones, and many other icons encased in silver gilt. A bishop by the name of Ignatie officiates.

---

[1] For Martukop (= Martqopi), see Commentary 33 (a): Some churches and bishoprics of Kakheti.

[2] For 'Bishopric of Nekresel', i.e. of Nekresi, see Commentary 33 (b).

[3] The name *mestnaya* (plur. *mestnye*) is given to the large icons placed in the main row of the iconostasis and to free-standing icons of the same size and type. See Commentary 24(b).

[4] For Katsarel, see Commentary 33 (c).

Bishopric of Gsarevzhel.[1] Stone-built church of holy Nona, with a dome. In it there is an icon of holy Nona encased in gold with precious stones . . .

[1] For Gsarevzhel, a distorted form of Garedzheli, or Bishop of Garedzha, see Commentary 33 (d).

CHAPTER 6

WORLD AFFAIRS AND THE
FALCONER'S SON

O N the 27th of February King Alexander's treasurer (192)
Garuza[1] and the monk Kiril came to Chornour to
the ambassadors Prince Semen and dyak Torkh
and said: 'King Alexander bids me tell you–"I had been relying
on the great Sovereign . . . to send his army against Prince
Shevkal. But now there is no hope; the Sovereign's army has
not been sent against Shevkal up to now. Yet I want to remain
loyal . . . I intend to let you go back to the Sovereign presently.
King Alexander also bids me tell you – "Prince Alkas . . . has
mended his ways and has sent his son to me. You should (193)
dispatch a man to the Sovereign's commanders on the Terek
with a message to give Alkas's *uʒdens* back to Alkas; and I shall
send my own man along with your man with a similar message.
Send this man of yours with the letter to me straight away
and I will supply him with horses and send him off to the
commanders." King Alexander also bade me, Garuza, go on
to Zaem . . . to prepare the gifts which are to be sent to the
Sovereign and those which are graciously intended for you;
and the King bade me, when I have got them ready, return to
him at Krym quickly so that he can let you go to the Sovereign
without further detaining you.'

[1] King Alexander's treasurer Garuza. 'Treasurer' corresponds to the
Georgian court office of *Sadchurdchilis Mdsignobari* – 'of the treasury
secretary' (see Allen, *HGP*, p. 258). Garuza is a personal not a family
name (= R. Grisha, from Grigori). The Georgian courts seem to have
followed the practice of referring to officials, even of high rank, by their
personal names. This emphasized the dependence of the official on the
monarch, in a filial or even slave-like relationship. For the same practice
at the Muscovite courts, see Chap. 2, p. 105, n. 1 and Commentary 13.

191

(194)   And the ambassadors said: '. . . What are the doubts of your sovereign, King Alexander? He should not even entertain such a thought, for our great Sovereign will not abandon King Alexander to anyone, let alone Shevkal. And why talk much about Shevkal? . . . We have ourselves spoken with King Alexander about Prince Alkas and about his *uzdens* . . . Things will be done as the great Sovereign will lay down in his royal command, and we shall not write about it again.'

Treasurer Garuza and the monk Kiril said: 'King Alexander desires . . . your great Sovereign to give orders for war to be waged on Shevkal quickly, this spring.'

Garuza and the monk Kiril rode off on the same day saying that they would report their message to King Alexander in writing. Garuza said that he was going to Zaem and Kiril said that he was going to his monastery. They said that the ambassadors Prince Semen and dyak Torkh should send to King Alexander with the attendant Ivan the man whom they would dispatch to Terek-town.

And on the 1st of March the ambassadors sent the interpreter Ivan Nikolayev with a message to the royal officials to enquire of the King the date on which they would be given leave to return to the great Sovereign so that they should know when to write to the commanders on the Terek about men and horses and stores to be sent to meet them in Soni-land.

On March 3rd the interpreter Ivan returned and said that he had spoken to the equerry Uman who had reported to King Alexander. The King sent a message to the ambassadors to write to the commanders at Terek-town about Alkas's *uzdens*. He did not know the date on which he would send them off because he was preparing presents for the Sovereign, and he was expecting some from the Kizilbashes where he had sent specially for them.

On the 5th of March the ambassadors sent the interpreter Ivanis Dragichev to King Alexander with instructions to inform his officials that they should be bidden to attend on him for the conclusion of the Sovereign's affairs. They also wished to take leave to set out immediately in order to travel along the river Terek before the spring floods.

Interpreter Ivanis returned on March 7th . . . with a message (195) from the King that he would shortly send messengers to fetch them . . . and that he intended to let them go on the third day in Holy Week. Ivanis also said that he had heard from local people that King Alexander was not letting the ambassadors go because he was waiting for the Sovereign's army to march on Shevkal. He added that the king intended to send with them his own ambassadors, the equerry Uman and Archimandrite Philip to do homage for the Sovereign's gracious bounty.

Prince Semen and dyak Torkh sent the mounted *strelets* Murza Ivanov with a letter for the Sovereign and another addressed to the commanders on the Terek . . . asking for an escort to be sent to Lars a fortnight after the Tuesday following Low Sunday[1] . . .

The attendants Ivan and Lom came to the ambassadors on April 4th and said: 'King Alexander bids you ride to the village of Shilda and remain there until Easter. That village is three versts from Krym.[2] He will bid you come to him at Krym on Easter day.'

---

[1] '*Low Sunday*'=*Radunitsa* in text. Originally a pagan festival of communing with the dead, when the living feasted and made merry at the burial grounds; later the merry-making was explained as rejoicing at the prospect of the Resurrection. Brosset (*EC/BHP*, Vol. II, Nos. 19–20, col. 253, n. 94) derives the word from Russian *radovatsya*, to rejoice. For discussion of these feasts in the early Alanic and Slav world, cf. Vernadsky, *Origins*, pp. 145–6; 'According to the noted Ukrainian philologist Potebnia, the name derives from the same stem as *rod*' (=family, stock) but see also Vasmer, Vol. II, p. 483, *contra*. Brosset, *ibid.*, calculates that in 1590 the feast would fall on 19 April. For practice, in Oseti see Baddeley, *RFC*, numerous refs.; Index, under 'Dead, the'.

[2] *Shilda*: mentioned by Wakhusht as a valley to the west of Didoeti on the Tchelt'is-tsqali affluent of the Alazani (Wak./Brosset, pp. 325, 315). Brosset (*EC/BHP*, Vol. II, Nos. 16–18, col. 246), identifies Shilda

Prince Semen and dyak Torkh set out from the village of Chornour on the same day. They camped that night in the monastery of Theodore, where the monk Kiril lived. They visited the church which is large and built of stone, an old edifice. The following icons are to be found there: opposite the right-hand choir there are two icons of Theodore Tyro, martyr for Christ; and in the same place there is also an image of Theodore Stratilates, martyr for Christ, all of them painted on large panels, encased in silver; and two crosses encased in silver lean against them. Opposite the left-hand choir there is an icon of the Immaculate Mother of God, on gold, of Russian work. Instead of the royal gate there hangs (196) a curtain. The altar in the sanctuary is shrouded in a covering, without any other adornment, and the church vessels are without inscription, as is their custom in the other churches, too.[1]

The monk Zakhkhey and his brethren asked Kiril why things were not arranged in his church in accordance with the canons, as it is laid down in the tradition of the Holy Apostles and in the rules of the Holy Fathers. Yet he, Kiril, was well acquainted with the church canons as applied in their Sovereign's Russian realm and on mount Athos. The monk Kiril replied that he had come to that monastery recently and there had been no time to arrange things. He added that there was one lay priest attached to the church, but he was ill at that time. Kiril, wearing a stole, officiated alone at vespers and at matins and at the Hours, while the Sovereign's priests and deacons stood in

as a village 3 versts from Gremi. Wak/Janashvili, p. 131, n. 421, proposes that Ptolemy's Gelda=Shilda. Shilda must have been more important in the fifteenth century since it was one of the dozen places to which Georgi I of Kakheti named a *mo'uravi* (prefect) (Brosset *HG*, Vol. 11/i, p. 148); see Chubinashvili, *AK*, opposite p. 140 for Severov's sketch of *basilica* of Vartzani near Shilda.

[1] The monastery of St Theodore. It is not mentioned by Wakhusht; nor does Brosset, in describing these events, discuss its location (*EC/BHP* Vol. 11, Nos. 16–18, p. 246). Chubinashvili, *AK*, pp. 193 ff., proposes the basilica of St Theodore at Leliani.

the choir. He did not celebrate mass that Sunday. There are five or six cells in the monastery in addition to Kiril's cell, and they are inhabited by nuns and widows.

The ambassadors arrived at the village of Shilda on the 5th of April. And on the 11th, the Saturday of Lazarus, the attendant Ivan rode up and told the monk Zakhkhey and his brethren that King Alexander bade them come to him at Krym.

Zakhkhey and his brethren rode off to Krym. On their return to the village of Shilda the following day they informed the ambassadors that the attendant Ivan had given them King Alexander's instructions to go to the Monastery of the Archangel, and they rode there.[1] They were met at the gate by Archimandrite Athanasius, who accompanied them to the church of the Archangel, where the church ornaments were in accordance with the canons ... And Archimandrite Athanasius said: 'Whatever shortcomings there were in the church canons have been rectified, so that the Sovereign's priests and deacons can celebrate mass tomorrow, Palm Sunday.' Zakhkhey and his brethren said to the archimandrite: 'We see that the church ornaments are in accordance with the canons. So show us the altar ornaments.' ... The shirt on the altar was placed as a covering not according to the canons, and the fastening was also not in accordance with the canons and there was no *endyton*. The *antimension* was sewn into the cloth according to the canons and was inscribed: 'In the name of our Lord Jesus Christ, the lord Metropolitan Nikodim under the faithful king despot George in the year 6949.'[2] There was only one cross

---

[1] For the Monastery and Church of the Archangel Michael at Gremi, see Commentary 25: 'The town of Krym = Gremi'.

[2] 'The faithful king despot George'. Brosset (*EC/BHP*, Vol. II, Nos. 16–18, col. 246), observes that the year 6949 corresponds to A.D. 1440. In his lengthy note he identifies 'despot George' with Giorgi VIII (son of Alexander, the last king of a united Georgia) who reigned in Kartli, intermittently, 1445–69. He observes that Giorgi had possession of Kakheti

stamped on the Book of the Gospels, and there were no sacred designs on the church vessels. Archimandrite Athanasius said that the church had been built 25 years before; and he, Zakhkhey, and his brethren said that the *antimension* was one hundred and fifty years old according to the inscription. Since the church had been built twenty-five years before, it followed that the *antimension* had been taken from another church; and the altar ornaments and the church vessels were not in accordance with the canons nor was there an *endyton* on the altar.[1] They, the priests and deacons, were unable to celebrate mass. But should King Alexander order that these shortcomings be (197) made good in accordance with the canons, and the church be consecrated, they would rectify the shortcomings and would consecrate the church and would celebrate mass on Maundy Thursday. Should King Alexander not bid the Sovereign's priests consecrate the church and should he, Archimandrite Athanasius, not have a codex of church canons, he should not be ashamed of it, (but) should take from them an abridged copy of the canons on the consecration of churches, and should act according to them. Archimandrite Athanasius said: 'We have not any additional church ornaments on mount Athos; nor do I know anything more than this. You can please yourselves and either celebrate mass or not. But King Alexander will not allow you to consecrate the church, since the church is already consecrated.'

Zakhkhey and his brethren attended vespers at the Monastery of the Archangel on the Saturday of Lazarus, and matins and mass on Palm Sunday. Vespers and mass were sung and mass

from his father, 1442–5, and believes that the difference between the dates 1442 and 1440 on the *antimension* is not important in view of the chaotic contradictions in the surviving chronology of that disturbed period.

For further on Giorgi VIII, see A. Gugushvili, in *Georgica*, Vol. I, Nos. 2–3, 1936, 'The chronological-genealogical table of the Kings of Georgia', pp. 128–30.

[1] For *antimension* and *endyton*, see Commentary 24.

celebrated by Archimandrite Athanasius and by Greek priests and deacons with him. King Alexander listened to church singing at his court church, and did not come to that monastery.

And on Holy Saturday, the 18th of April, the attendants Ivan and Lom told the ambassadors that King Alexander bade them come to him at Krym. The ambassadors arrived at Krym on the same day, and the attendants quartered them where they had stayed before.

On Easter Day the ambassadors attended matins and mass at the Monastery of the Archangel. When they entered the church Archimandrite Athanasius asked that the Sovereign's priests and deacons should sing matins while he would celebrate mass with his own priests. The Sovereign's priests and deacons sang the matins. Archimandrite Athanasius and another archimandrite with him, and Abbot Kiril who had been on an embassy to the Sovereign and two priests and five deacons celebrated mass according to the Greek rite. Greek monks, priests and deacons sang in Greek from the right choir and the Georgian priests and deacons sang from the left choir; and there were five or six persons in each choir. The Sovereign's priests, after inspecting the altar ornaments, told the ambassadors that there was only one addition to what had been there previously, namely the fastening, and even that was not in accordance with the canons. Prince Semen and dyak Torkh said to Archimandrite Athanasius during matins: 'We see that in this church the church ornaments are in accordance with the canons and the singing agrees with that of the Sovereign's priests, and we rejoice at this and praise you . . . [But] we trust that God will also let us witness the rectification of all that is amiss in your church rites . . .'

And Archimandrite Athanasius said: 'I have not been on a (198) visit to your great Sovereign myself; but I have heard from such people from here as have visited him that nowhere under the sun is there another great Christian sovereign such as he,

in whose realm the Christian faith is so firmly established. He is the pillar and hope of all Christian sovereigns. Here King Alexander is also a Christian, and he only lives for God, and expends his treasure for God, on churches and icons – and he relies on us to put the Christian faith right. The Christian faith is old-established here, and the only thing they have lost is the canon. We keep on telling them this, but they do not listen to us. The altar in this church is adorned, and there is an *antimension*, glued into the altar, and fixed among the bricks with
(199) lime when the altar was being built, and the church was consecrated with the *antimension*.' . . .

The ambassadors held counsel on this matter with the monk Zakhkhey and his brethren, the priests and the deacons, who replied that it would be impossible for them to celebrate mass without consecrating the church themselves or being present at its consecration, and that Archimandrite Athanasius was not to be believed.

The attendant Lom came to fetch the ambassadors on the same day, which was Easter Sunday, and said: 'You are to sup with King Alexander now in the tents in the public square. King Alexander is at present riding in the square and he bids you join him.' Prince Semen and dyak Torkh rode to King Alexander. On seeing them the king turned towards them. He had his sons, the princes David and Yuri and some one hundred and fifty – or more – of his *aznaurs* with him. The ambassadors saluted him without dismounting; and King Alexander bade them ride with him. Prince Semen and dyak Torkh rode on King Alexander's right and as they were riding the king said: 'Tomorrow I shall start holding council on how I am to send you off to the great Sovereign.' And the ambassadors pressed him to let them go without delay so that they could get through before the floods. After riding in the square King Alexander moved off towards his court, bidding the ambassadors Prince Semen and dyak Torkh return to their camp and wait for messengers who would come to summon them for the meal.

The attendant Lom came to fetch them presently, saying that they were to proceed to the banquet and bidding the monk Zakhkhey and his brethren also ride along. The ambassadors rode to the tents where King Alexander was awaited. They were met by the equerries Abel and Uman and Chinaley, who told them to go to the tent, and that King Alexander would be there shortly.

The ambassadors entered the tent and sat down; and after that, King Alexander rode into the tent and sat down at his (200) place. Halfway through the banquet he ordered his priests and deacons to sing and said that they were singing a canon in honour of Christ's Resurrection. King Alexander then bade the Sovereign's priests sing, and the priests sang the Easter hymn. During the banquet Prince Yuri and the *aznaurs* got up from the table and drank the health of King Alexander, his father; and King Alexander and his *aznaurs* got up from the table five or six times and drank the health of the ambassadors Prince Semen and dyak Torkh. He said: 'You can see for yourselves how I honour you, his ambassadors, for the sake of the great Sovereign Tsar and great Prince Fedor Ivanovich of all Russia. I myself and my *aznaurs* get up from the table and do homage to you. My entire house belongs to God and to you.' . . .

On the 22nd of April King Alexander went to spend the (201) holiday in the Monastery of St George of Alaverdy; and he returned to Krym on the 27th of April. On the 28th King Alexander went riding with his *aznaurs* in the square outside his palace. And he sent dyak Ters to the ambassadors Prince Semen and dyak Torkh with the message: 'I have been to my village of Elon[1] to have sport and I wanted to stay longer in

[1] Elon=Aloni. Wak./Brosset, p. 321; Wak./Jan., p. 128. Not marked on Wak. Map 4; but indicated as lying between Maghrani on the north

the village of Elon; but my heart could not bear it that I did not see you, the Sovereign's ambassadors, by me. And now, even though I am out riding, I am attending to one thing only – how to send you back to the great Sovereign.'

And the ambassadors said: 'We hear of King Alexander's grace towards us and we do homage on his favours. Regarding our departure, he sent word to us earlier that he would give us leave to go on the third day after Easter. We are now in the second week after Easter; and his royal word cannot be false. King Alexander should now let us have a direct answer. When does he intend to let us go?' ...

(202)   Dyak Ters said: 'We know only four great kings in the entire world under the sun: the first is the great Christian Sovereign, the White Tsar[1] and great Prince Fedor Ivanovich of all Russia; the second is the Turkish king; the third – the Spanish king; the fourth – the Indian king. And there are no other kings greater than they. How could King Alexander our master send you off, the Sovereign's ambassadors, and his own ambassadors in haste to such a great Sovereign as yours, without putting everything right?' ...

The same dyak Ters came to the ambassadors within the

and the Shtoris-tsqali affluent of the Alazani to the south. In *VA*, Vol. I, rapport, p. 81, Brosset gives an attractive description of this upland plain which so delighted the Kakhian kings. 'C'est une prairie, vaste, riche et herbue, destinée par la nature au pâturage de nombreux troupeaux; là se trouvent les villages d'hiver, les haras, les bêtes à cornes et les moutons des Touches (Tush). En été, les hommes gravissent leurs montagnes et vont chercher la fraîcheur, y célébrer leurs fêtes religieuses ...'.

Brosset believed the name Alon or Alwan (as he found it pronounced locally) to equate with Armenian Aghovan, corresponding to classical Albania. It is apparent that the plain of Aloni was favoured by rulers long before the time of the Kakhian kings; for the ecclesiastical council held at Aluen by Vačagan, King of Albania, *c.* 484/5 – 487/8, see Dowsett, *History of the Caucasian Albanians,* Oxford, 1961, pp. 50 and 108, n. 2. For discussion of the name, see Wak./Jan., p. 131, n. 421; Trever, *Ocherki po istorii kultury Kavkazskoy Albanii* (Moskva, 1959), pp. 48-55.

[1] For the origin of the name White Tsar, see Commentary 34.

hour and said on behalf of King Alexander: 'Shevkal has now sent his ambassador to me with the following message: "Before now we had been friends with you, King Alexander, and united under the hand of the Turkish king, and we stood together against all our enemies. But you have now entreated the great Muscovite Sovereign to be taken under his hand; and the Sovereign has extended his grace to you and accepted you under his hand. You sent word to me that you had entreated the Sovereign to raise an army against the Turk's town of Derbent; but I have heard that you are now bringing the Sovereign's army not against Derbent but against me. The Sovereign's men from Tyumen-town are pressing me hard and are depriving me of the river Koysu; and they want to build a fort there. Be now in friendship and unity with me, as in the past. I have heard that you asked Prince Krym-Shevkal, my brother, for his daughter in marriage for your son Prince Yuri. I shall send you my own daughter and Krym-Shevkal's daughter and, after selecting either my daughter or Krym-Shevkal's daughter as a bride for your son Prince Yuri, send the other one to the Kizilbashes as a bride for your other son.[1] Then we shall have one heart with you and we shall stand together against our enemies. I have sent my own ambassadors to Moscow and to the Sovereign's commanders at Astarakhan and at Tyumen-town." Such is the message which Shevkal has sent me by his ambassadors, wishing to deceive me. But the true information which I have is that Shevkal has indeed sent his ambassadors to the great Sovereign and to Astarakhan and Tyumen-town, but not in good faith. He has sent an ambassador in good faith to the Turk. He wrote in his letter to him ... (203) "Show mercy towards me and intervene on my behalf for the sake of the Moslem faith – for you are the hope of all Moslem lands against the Christians. Send a large army this summer against King Alexander, so as to conquer him first and ravage

[1] For discussion of the title 'Krym-Shevkal', see Commentary 35.

his realm or convert him to the Moslem faith, before such time as the Sovereign's army comes against me. And if you do not come to my assistance this summer and do not send your army, but if the Sovereign's army comes against me and King Alexander starts waging war against me from his side – I shall be caught and there will be nowhere for me to escape. And if something evil befalls me or my land, and there is bloodshed or some other outrage and they start converting us to their Christian faith – who but you will have to account to God for our souls? And should they capture my land, how could your Derbent resist, and Shemakha and Shirvan and Genzha and all the towns which you have taken from the Kizilbash and from Alexander's brother-in-law Simon? All these towns will fall to the Muscovite Sovereign; and the Moslems in these towns will be massacred – and you will have to account to God for their souls, too. And when these towns are captured and the Sovereign's army joins up with the Kizilbash Shah and with King Alexander and with Alexander's brother-in-law Simon, you will be unable to resist this army before Constantinople. If this army gets to Constantinople on this side and the Franks and the Spanish king come from the other side, how, then, will you be able to withstand them even in Constantinople? They will seize you and will massacre all the Moslems, and they will convert others to their Christian faith – and our Moslem faith will all be ruined because of you, should you fail to come to our assistance. And God will ask you to account for all these souls." '

And Ters also said: 'King Alexander knows by what route Shevkal has sent his ambassador with this letter; and he has sent his men with orders to lie in wait for him, capture him and bring him in with the letter. Our sovereign does not fear the Turkish king now that the Turk is hard put to it by the Franks and the Spanish king.'

And the ambassadors said: 'Your sovereign, King Alexander,

was in doubts and was losing his faith in our great Sovereign. (204) And have things not now happened as the Sovereign had said they would?' ...

On the following day, the 29th of April, the *aznaur* Suliman, whom King Alexander intended to send as ambassador to the Sovereign, and dyak Ters came to Prince Semen and dyak Torkh.

Ters said on behalf of King Alexander: 'The great Sovereign had sent to me his envoys Rodion Birkin and Petr Pivov, and I sent men of a similar standing to the great Sovereign – Kaplan and his assistants. And now the great Sovereign has extended his grace to me and has sent you, his great ambassadors – you, Prince Semen, a great pasha of a noble family; and in answer to this I am now sending to the great Sovereign a man of similarly noble birth from among my entourage – Prince Suliman.[1] My father Levont favoured his father and loved him like his soul; and I hold him in my favour and love him as my father loved his father; I hold him near to my heart and he is like a son to me. You should let the great Sovereign know that I am sending to him such a faithful man of noble lineage. What he will tell the great Sovereign will be my word, and the Sovereign should have faith in what he says.'

Prince Semen and dyak Torkh replied: 'When we return to the great Sovereign, we shall tell him this.'

And Suliman and dyak Ters said: 'Our sovereign King Alexan- (205) der bade us say to you – "You know the state of my realm and its relations with other countries; and when I have anything on my heart or when news about other states reaches me, I tell it to you so that you may become acquainted with any matters which you may not have known. Merchants come to me from Constantinople and from the Franks, and my merchants travel to Constantinople and to the Franks[2]; and sometimes I send

[1] For the identity of Prince Suliman, see Commentary 36.
[2] For Georgian merchants abroad, see Commentary 37.

203

men to Ghilan and to Kazvin and to Constantinople and to the
Franks, ostensibly for trade, but [in fact] to gather information. And an Armenian of mine, a merchant, has now come to
me. He said that he had been to Rome, to the Pope, and the
Pope ordered him to be seized and brought to him, and he
asked him from what country he came and what sort of man
he was; and he said he was from my realm. He says that the
Pope told him that King Alexander was a Christian king, and
yet had not sent any ambassadors or letters to the Pope; 'and
now go to your King Alexander, and give him my message
that he should send an ambassador to me or should send you
back with a letter'. And the Pope ordered that the chattels
of this Armenian be taken away from him and sealed with his
seal. 'When you return and bring the letter, I shall give your
chattels back to you. I am sending an oral message by you
because I cannot send a letter to King Alexander since it would
not get through on account of the Turks.'[1] And the Pope
bade him come back to Rome by way of the Muscovite
Sovereign's land, since King Alexander had done homage to the
Muscovite Sovereign. The Armenian has brought the news that
the Spanish king has been waging war on the English and the
Pechenskaya lands[2] and has attached both these lands to his

[1] Sixtus V (Felix Peretti, of Dalmatian origin) was Pope, 1585–90. His
interest in Georgia corresponds in time with the missions which he
despatched to the Armenians, the Melkites, the Jacobites and the Chal-
daeans, with the object of bringing their churches into closer communion with Rome; cf. von Hammer, *HEO*, Vol. VII, pp. 196 ff., who
observes that the only practical outcome of this Papal enterprise was the
establishment of the Collegium de Propaganda Fide and the opening of
a printing press for oriental languages in Rome. This press issued *Alpha-
betum Ibericum sive Georgianum*, 8vo, 33 pp., in 1629; and *Syntagmaton
Linguarum Orientalium quae in Georgiae Regionibus Audiuntur*, 4to, 96 pp.,
in 1643.

For a good characterization of Sixtus V, see *BU*, under name: article
by Tabaraud.

[2] '*Angliskuyu zemlyu da Pechenskuyu*': This combination of names
presents difficulties. 'The war on the English land' is clearly a reflection of

kingdom; and together with them and with other lands and with the Franks he sent an expedition by sea against the Turkish king. The ambassador whom I had sent to the Turk in Constantinople and who returned to me during Lent told me that the army of the Spanish king and the Franks had come against the Turk that summer; and they captured or sank some five thousand Turkish galleys.[1] And I now want to send this same Armenian with letters to the Pope of Rome and to the Spanish king and to the Christian Caesar, to tell them who I am and to say that I am under the great Sovereign's hand;

the Spanish Armada in 1588. *Pechenskaya* may refer to Hungary. Since the time of Charles V the Habsburg monarchy in Spain and Austria had frequently been treated as one; and the Turks sometimes referred to the campaign in Hungary as 'the German war of the Spanish King'. *Pechenskaya* is probably Pécs (Fünfkirchen), an important frontier fortress commanding the triangle of territory north-west of the junction of the Drava with the Danube. This fortress was taken in 1587 by the Hungarian Count Zrinyi and two Austrian commanders during a period of armistice between Emperor Rudolph II and Sultan Murat III (cf. Hammer, *HEO*, Vol. VII, pp. 180–2; also Albert Lefaivre, *Les Magyars pendant la domination Ottomane en Hongrie*, Paris, 1902, Vol. I, pp. 195–6). For situation of Pécs see *Atlas de l'Empire Ottoman* (Paris, 1844), by J. J. Hellert, translator and editor of the French edition of von Hammer's great work.

There is a reference to *Petski gorod* in the report of Novosiltsev's embassy to Turkey in 1570: see *Puteshestviya russkikh poslov xvi-xvii vv*, pp. 82, 379.

[1] *Turkish naval defeat before Lent: 1589/90* There was no major Spanish victory over the Turks at that time; in fact, the armistice concluded between Spain and the Ottoman Empire in 1581 was renewed for two years in 1587. Von Hammer (*HEO*, Vol. VII, p. 195, n. 1) cites a Venetian source for a visit of the 'Patriarch of the Georgians' to Constantinople in 1586–7. This may have been Nicolaoz V, half-brother of Alexander of Kakheti (Catholicos, 1584–91, according to the list edited by K. Salia, *BK*, Nos. 41–2, 1963, p. 52). But see Tamarati (*EG*, pp. 365–366): 'Liste des Catholicos dont on sait très peu de chose: Pluralité des Catholicos'. Tamarati gives the date for Nicolaoz V as 1562–97; and during the same period: Evdomios I, 1578; Dorotheos II, 1583–5; Domenti II, 1595–1602.

The tale about the Turkish naval defeat, retailed by Alexander's ambassador, seems to be muddled and *fantaisiste*; it can only refer to the Battle of Lepanto which had taken place nearly two decades earlier (1571).

and I shall send him with my ambassador. You should inform the Sovereign Tsar so that this Armenian may be escorted through his realm on his way to the Roman Pope." '

The ambassadors replied: 'There is no need for us even to transmit this news to our Sovereign, for how could this news not have reached him already? All these Christian kings attacked the Turk at our Sovereign's request; and he intends to oppose the Turk himself together with them, because the Turk rules over Christian realms. Why should your sovereign King Alexander send letters about this to the Roman Pope and to the Spanish king and to the Christian Caesar, and why should he (206) tell them who he is? The great Sovereign has ordered that all these realms be told about King Alexander and that he has extended his grace to him and accepted him under his royal hand. And what more could your sovereign King Alexander wish? Should this Armenian beg of King Alexander to let him go to Rome to the Pope to recover his chattels – it would be improper for us to speak to the great Sovereign about *muzhiks'* chattels. We cannot take this upon ourselves.'

And the ambassador Suliman and dyak Ters said: 'Our sovereign King Alexander begs God that the great Sovereign Tsar and great Prince and all the Christian sovereigns will join together against the Turk and all the Moslems, and that the Christian arm will be raised high above them. Things are moving towards the Moslems' downfall; not much time is left to them to insult Christian peoples: it is written in our books that they will perish very soon. And the Turks themselves are expecting this from hour to hour and they read about it in their books.[1] The Christian arm will first be raised against them

[1] The Russian ambassadors Birkin and Pivov had brought a similar story back on their return from Georgia in 1588. They reported that in Georgia they had met a Lithuanian from Kiev who had escaped from captivity in Turkey and who had told them that 'when he was in Turkish captivity at Bursa he once saw a Turk in the bazaar reading a book who suddenly began to weep and to tell the Turks that this realm at Tsargrad

from Derbent: there will be so many men at Derbent that the gates will be trodden through by their feet as if by the hauling of cannon, and people will start treading on those iron gates which are at present overthrown and lie in the earth.[1] Can these Christian sovereigns, the Spanish king and the Christian Caesar and the Roman Pope and the Franks, come to Derbent, and how far are their realms from Derbent?'

Prince Semen and dyak Torkh replied: 'What God wills, that He will do: it is done by God and not by man's understanding. And, praying for God's mercy, our great Sovereign intends to stand against the Turk. And apart from our Sovereign's patrimony no other sovereign's lands have reached Derbent. The lands about which you are asking us are far away; and they have not even heard about Derbent, let alone come to it. From our Sovereign's patrimony, from Astarakhan, an army in boats with big cannon can reach the wall of Derbent in the third week, sailing down the river Volga and then by sea; and should God grant an orderly sea passage, the army could get there in the second week. And a force of horsemen can also get through. A force from Tyumen-town could get there by sea or overland on the fifth or sixth day.'

And the ambassador Suliman and dyak Ters said: 'Our sovereign King Alexander himself knows that the great Sovereign's patrimony is close to Derbent and that an army

was about to fall and that it would be taken by the Russians within the next couple of years' (Belokurov, *Snosheniya*, pp. 43–4). Prophecies about the imminent downfall of the Ottoman empire, based on interpretations of Leo's oracles, gained wide currency at the end of the sixteenth century; they were re-inforced by speculations in Turkey over the approach of the Moslem millennium (in 1592). It was probably these latter fears which inspired the stories retailed to Birkin and Pivov and to Zvenigorodski. (On this theme see Cyril Mango, 'The Legend of Leo the Wise' in *Recueil des Travaux de l'Institut d'Études Byzantines*, No. 6, Belgrade, 1960, particularly pp. 80 ff.; cf. also art. by L. Lockhart in *Iran*, Vol. VI (1968), p. 30, n. 55.)

[1] For the Iron Gates of Derbent, see Commentary 38.

with artillery can get to Derbent by sea and overland. If the great Sovereign comes against Derbent and King Alexander joins up with the Kizilbash Shah on the river Lozan and attacks on the other side, all the towns which are held by the Turk will be cleared immediately, and none can resist. We know that the men stationed in all the Turk's towns fear the
(207) Sovereign's men greatly, and their thoughts are that should even a few of the Sovereign's men appear, they would abandon the towns and flee. And such of the inhabitants of these towns as are Christian or Armenian all pray to God that the great Sovereign may deliver them from the infidels. And we, Alexander's *aznaurs,* have only one wish – to live to the day when we shall see the Sovereign's men and the men of King Alexander at Tarku; and die afterwards, if it comes to that; and to see Alexander's old age honoured by the great Sovereign, for our King Alexander is old and he wants to see the Sovereign's grace in his lifetime, and he is greatly worried. And seeing him, we fear lest we may not see the Sovereign's mercy.'

Prince Semen and dyak Torkh said: 'Why do you tell us this? We know for ourselves that garrisons hold all towns here only so long as the Sovereign's army has not come. Our great Sovereign Tsar and great Prince is feared not only in these parts; by the mercy of God and his own courage he has put fear into all the lands near his realm, and he has brought many states under his royal hand. How could Tarku withstand the great Sovereign's army? It does not befit you to lose hope and doubt and grieve over this.'

And the ambassador Suliman and dyak Ters said: 'Our sovereign places his hope in no-one except God and the great Sovereign.'

Ambassador Suliman and dyak Ters came to Prince Semen and dyak Torkh on the first of May and said: 'We have told King Alexander that you cannot take the matter of the Armenian upon yourselves; so our sovereign intends to send the Armenian back by the way he has come here. You should find nothing suspicious in our sovereign's wanting to send letters to Christian sovereigns. Our sovereign is gratified that they have joined together and oppose the Moslem faith . . . Apart from the great Sovereign, King Alexander does not desire to place his hope in anybody; he relies on the great Sovereign, upon his head and his eyes and all his heart, for he is a great Christian sovereign, and his Christian faith is like a pillar raised to heaven. And those other monarchs are reported to be Christians; but our sovereign has heard that their faith has become shaken and is not the same as the faith which is established in the Sovereign Tsar's realm. Our sovereign now grieves that Jerusalem with the Holy of Holies and the Lord's tomb, and Constantinople with Divine Sophia and the monasteries and churches, are being trodden under and defiled by the infidel Moslems because of our sins. And he prays to God that He should raise the Christians' arm over the Moslems, so that (208) Christian sovereigns should recover these Christian realms and that Jerusalem with the Holy of Holies and Constantinople with Divine Sophia should belong to the great Sovereign.'[1]

And the ambassadors Prince Semen and dyak Torkh said: 'Our great Sovereign Tsar and great Prince, praying for God's mercy, wants to stand together with all Christian sovereigns against the infidel Hagarenes.[2] And should only God encompass our great Sovereign in His mercy and raise his royal hand against the Moslems, who but our great Sovereign could reign over Jerusalem and Constantinople? He is the great sovereign among Christian sovereigns, and there is none greater than he. And the Christian faith shining in his realm, the Russian kingdom, is the Christian faith which existed in old times under the faithful king Constantine and under the faithful Grand Duke Vladimir, our Sovereign's ancestor. And on hearing that our

[1] For the concept of Moscow as the Third Rome, see Commentary 39.
[2] For Hagarenes, see Chap. I, p. 94, n. 1.

great Sovereign is a seeker after the Christian faith and is merciful, patriarchs and metropolitans, and archbishops and bishops and archimandrites and abbots and many priests and monks come from those lands to him, to his realm. On seeing him, the great Sovereign, they marvel at his zeal for the Christian faith. And even recently, when our great Sovereign sent us to King Alexander, your sovereign, the Patriarch of Constantinople Jeremiah was with our Sovereign in Moscow, with many metropolitans, and archbishops, and bishops, and archimandrites and abbots and priests and monks.[1] Your sovereign's ambassadors, Kaplan and his assistants, saw them, and so what need is there for us even to speak to King Alexander about it? The Patriarch of Constantinople Jeremiah came to our great Sovereign with all his consecrated council because all of them, the four Patriarchs of Alexandria, Jerusalem, Antioch and Constantinople, had resolved in council to ask that the great Sovereign should instal a pope in his Russian realm, in place of the Roman Pope.[2] And all the patriarchs and the metropolitans and the bishops and the priests and all Christians in these countries implore and pray to God that He should bring the Moslem faith into subjection under our great Sovereign's hand. And in the Christian states about which you have spoken to us, there was Christian faith, but it has erred towards heresy and

[1] Jeremiah II Tranos, born at Anchialos on the Black Sea, c. 1530; Bishop of Larissa in 1565. First elected Patriarch on 5 May 1572, he was deposed on 29 November 1579, reinstated on 13 August 1580 and deposed again – and exiled to Rhodes – on 22 February 1584. Released through the intervention of the French ambassador to the Sublime Porte, he arrived at Smolensk on 15 June 1588 on his way to Moscow to seek financial aid to enable him to pursue his fight against his rivals in Constantinople. He was still in Moscow when another turn of the wheel in the politics of the Patriarchate elevated him once again to the Oecumenical throne. He returned to Constantinople early in 1590 and died in September 1595. He was a very learned man, as can be seen from his disputations by correspondence with the Lutheran divines at Tübingen (ref. *Dictionnaire de Théologie Catholique*).

[2] On the idea of a Russian Pope, see Commentary 40.

the Latin rite. As for the Armenian ... the king is free to do what he likes ... There is no reason for us to suspect anything.'

And the ambassador Suliman and dyak Ters said on behalf of King Alexander: 'Stationed in the gorges against the Shevkal and the Didos[1] I have been keeping some Russians who came to me from my brother-in-law Simon to whom they had gone (209) from the Terek of their own free will, as well as some Russian prisoners who fled to me from the Turkish towns and from the Cherkesses and from my brother-in-law Simon. You have brought these men down from their posts, and they now live with you. You should leave these Russians with me until such time as I get the Sovereign's men. I cannot defend myself with them, as they number only about twenty; I only want the rumour to spread that there are Russians stationed in my land. And you should also leave with me the falconer's son and his man Ivashko to look after the falcon.'

Prince Semen and dyak Torkh replied: 'Such prisoners and Cossacks are indeed with us: they came during Advent. They told us that they were on picket duty for your Sovereign, but when winter came they stopped getting victuals. They said that they had petitioned your Sovereign, but he did not issue orders to give them any. Instead, he quartered them among the *aznaurs*. Not wanting to live with the *aznaurs* they came to us; and we sent the interpreter Ivan Nikolayev with them to your Sovereign to enquire whether he needed these prisoners. On his return, the interpreter Ivan told us that he had brought them to the equerry Uman, and Uman reported the matter to your sovereign, who sent word that he did not require them [and that they could go] where they wished. We took them to our camp, and fed and clothed them until now with our own things. But what need is there to talk about it? Nowhere are prisoners detained [for ever], and the Terek Cossacks are likewise prisoners. They came to Simon of their free will but for a short time, and

[1] For the Dido tribe, see Commentary 41.

Simon kept them by force for three and a half years. On hearing that your sovereign is under our Sovereign's royal hand and that the great Sovereign's ambassadors had come here, they came to King Alexander for that reason. And as for your sovereign's men who had been held captive in our Sovereign's land, he ordered that they should all be sought out, and extended his grace to them, gave them provisions and horses, and had them sent to your sovereign with the ambassadors Prince Kaplan and his assistants. The falconer Ivan Sychov has brought his son and his man with him himself: so how can we take them from him and leave them with your sovereign? It is impossible to leave the son for this reason, too, that he has not been in our great Sovereign's service and is not used to looking after birds. We have no-one to whom this could be entrusted.'

On the 2nd of May Suliman and Ters came to the ambassadors Prince Semen and dyak Torkh and said on behalf of King Alexander . . . 'I shall send my Armenian with the letters to the great Sovereign along with my ambassador. And should (210) the Sovereign want to extend his grace to me, let him order my Armenian to be sent on with the letters; but if the Sovereign does not send the Armenian in person, let him send him back to me, and let him forward my letters to the Pope in Rome by his own envoy.[1] You may take with you all the prisoners and the Cossacks – I do not need them . . . But when you are at Tyumen-town send me one hundred *streltsy*; for it is written in the Sovereign's letter to me that the commanders on the Terek have his order to lend me as many men as I may need. But you should leave with me the falconer's son and his man.'

Prince Semen and dyak Torkh said: 'We have already spoken with you about the Armenian . . . As for the King's message about the *streltsy*, we shall convey it to the Sovereign's commanders when we are at Terek-town, and shall send him the

[1] Belokurov's text has been emended from *polonyanik* (captive), clearly out of place in this sentence, to *poslanik* (envoy).

hundred *streltsy*; but your sovereign should send horses to mount them and should order that they be fed here. It is improper for us to leave the falconer's son, for this matter cannot be entrusted to anybody.'

Suliman and Ters went to King Alexander and on their return within the hour said to the ambassadors: 'There were five hundred of the Sovereign's Cossacks here in the past, and they had no horses but marched on foot.'[1]

Prince Semen and dyak Torkh replied: 'A Cossack is free and lives on the land. They are paid by the Sovereign for such time as they serve, and not every year. The Sovereign's *streltsy* cannot be compared to the Cossacks. They are our Sovereign's paid men, and when he orders them to go somewhere for a year, he orders horses with sledges and carts to be issued to carry them and their chattels. The Sovereign's commanders will send these *streltsy* to your king. But how can they do without horses? How would they travel and carry their chattels?'

Suliman and dyak Ters said: 'The Sovereign's *streltsy* should come as far as our sovereign's land of Soni, where horses and provisions will be in readiness.'

And Prince Semen and dyak Torkh said: 'They will need horses to move out of Tyumen-town. Together with you, Suliman, we shall agree with the Sovereign's commanders how many horses your king will have to send. We will send a message to your sovereign king Alexander by the men whom he will send to escort you.'

Suliman and Ters said: 'Our sovereign has ordered us to say (211)

---

[1] The reference is presumably to the several hundred Cossacks in King Levan's pay – either deserters from the Terek or prisoners who had escaped Turkish hands – who were repatriated from Kakheti as part of the agreement between Moscow and the Porte in 1571 which included also an undertaking to raze the Russian forts on the Terek (cf. Tatishvili, *Gruziny v Moskve: istoricheski ocherk*, Tbilisi, 1959, pp. 23, 27, quoting Chubinov, *Kartlis Tskhovreba*, p. 107; also Introduction, Section 4).

to you: "I love you like my soul; and you, Prince Semen, are like a brother to me. Yet it looks as if you were fooling me with words, and as if things will not be done in the way you are telling me; apparently one ought not to have faith even in the Sovereign's word. Nor do I need the falcons. Take the falcon away with you. I do not need anything. Nor shall I send my ambassadors with you." '

Prince Semen and dyak Torkh replied: 'We speak on behalf of our great Sovereign, and our Sovereign's word is never false, let alone in the present matter. It does not befit King Alexander even to say so. Our great Sovereign has graciously presented King Alexander with a falcon from his own royal sport – so let the king enjoy himself with it. Why is he angry with us over this? He bids us do things which are unbecoming to the Sovereign's affairs. The great Sovereign will not refuse him even the falconer himself should King Alexander wish to retain him; he should send a message to our great Sovereign about this by you, his ambassadors.' Prince Semen and dyak Torkh spoke about the falconer because they had heard that the king did not want to retain him.

On the 3rd of May the attendant Ivan came to the ambassadors with King Alexander's message that they should leave with him the prisoners and the Cossacks and the falconer's son and his man. And the ambassadors sent word to the king by the attendant that he should send his ambassador Suliman and dyak Ters to discuss this matter with them.

King Alexander sent Suliman and dyak Ters on the same day to Prince Semen and dyak Torkh who said: 'Your sovereign sent to us the attendant Ivan with the request that we should leave the prisoners and the Cossacks and the falconer's son and his man with the king. We now take the responsibility upon ourselves and shall leave the prisoners and the Cossacks with King Alexander until such time as the Sovereign's commanders send him other men to replace these. Your king should extend his grace to these prisoners and these Cossacks and should order them to be fed; he should not starve them to death. But we are unable to leave the falconer's son. If it is impossible for the falcon to be left without the Sovereign's falconer, the king should keep the falconer Ivan Sychov himself; and he should send a message about this to the great Sovereign by you, Suliman, his ambassador.'

And the ambassador Suliman and dyak Ters said: 'King (212) Alexander wanted to keep the falconer's son by him – but you will not leave him with our sovereign. So you should leave the falconer's man Ivashko.'

Prince Semen and dyak Torkh replied: 'Even the falconer's son is unfit for this important duty. A yokel like the falconer's man will be even more unsuitable for such a royal bird. How can we go back and tell our great Sovereign about such a yokel? And were we to conceal it, the Sovereign might discover it, and we should incur his displeasure . . .'

Suliman and Ters went to the king, and returning within the hour they said ' . . . Our sovereign king Alexander bade us say to you: "I shall not take the prisoners and the Cossacks from you until your departure. I shall think the matter over until then; I shall keep them by me if I find that I need them, and I shall extend my grace to them and have them fed. And if I do not need them, I shall send them off with you. I do not need the falconer's man; the falcon has now settled down, and my men are skilful enough to feed it. And I expect that, soon, the Sovereign will send me falcons and a falconer . . ." '

Suliman and Ters also said: 'Our sovereign King Alexander bade us give you his secret message: "I am sending my ambassador Suliman to the great Sovereign, and I am imparting to him all my heart's thoughts about which he is to entreat the great Sovereign. What my ambassador says will be my heart's message, and what he entreats the Sovereign about will be as if I were entreating him myself. And you, too, should be

(213) acquainted with this thought and supplication of mine. When, if God grants, you and my ambassador come to the Sovereign, you should likewise inform him about it. Before now my father Levont had lived in friendship and unity with Shevkal's father; not only would they not fight each other, but they were united against their enemies. I incurred Shevkal's enmity for the following reason: Shevkal offered me his sister in marriage, but I did not marry into his family – I have married into the family of his cousin, Elim Saltan[1] the Krym-Shevkal. And since then Shevkal has been making furtive raids on my borderland, burning townships and villages, massacring and capturing my people and forcibly converting them to his Moslem faith. This has been going on for many years; and I have been writing it all down in my book – how many of my townships and villages he burnt, and how many people he killed and wounded and took prisoner. Would he so much as stand up to me – but he does not resist me openly and comes like a thief in the night. Sixteen years have passed since my father Levont died; and I have been ruling the kingdom since my father's death. After his death my own nephew Khostrov, my elder brother's son, attempted to seize power, and many *aznaurs* went over to him. I fought him over the realm; and God helped me to defeat him, and I killed him and many *aznaurs* in that battle, and I entered into the possession of my realm. And after that my own brothers Elmurza and Isay fled from me to the Kizilbash and, having collected a large Kizilbash force, they came upon me; and I gave them battle. God helped me again, and I killed many Kizilbashes; and those brothers of mine, Isay and Elmurza, and my third brother who is now Metropolitan, fled from the battle-field to my brother-in-law Simon. These brothers of

---

[1] For 'Elim Saltan the Krym-Shevkal', see Commentary 35. Alexander's reference is to the marriage of his son Giorgi (Yuri) to a daughter of Elim Saltan = the Sultan of Elisu or Eliseni – which the Kakhian King had allowed as a patrimony to Krym-Shevkal.

mine, and my brother-in-law Simon with them, and their *aznaurs*, having gathered a force of Turks and Kizilbashes more than 60,000 strong, came upon me a second time wanting to expel me from my realm. I only had some three hundred *aznaurs*. By God's mercy I again overcame them, and defeated them and captured my brothers Elmurza and the one who is now Metropolitan; and having caught him, I incarcerated Elmurza, and I made the other one, who is now Metropolitan, take the habit; Isay was also caught, and he died in a monastery. I killed nearly the whole of their force; and I lost in that battle three *aznaurs* killed and forty-eight who were taken prisoner. Later on these too came over to me from my brother-in-law Simon. You will not believe what I have been telling you. It was brought about not by me but by God's mercy. I am telling you the truth about what happened; I swear to it upon my soul. For God is free to put a soul into a man and take it away from him. Since then I have been strongly entrenched in my realm.[1] Shevkal continued furtively to raid my borderland by night, without interruption. And I sent my ambassador to him (214) with the following message: 'Before now my father lived in friendship with your father, and why do you now behave in such a way towards my realm and ravage it? Should you want to fight me – come against me in open battle. And should you want to live at peace – we can start living in friendship as our fathers lived.' Shevkal sent his son to me with my ambassador with the message 'I do not want to fight you in any way in the future, and my son is my pledge to you in this; keep him by you. I shall send you my daughter, his sister – and keep her by you too.' Shevkal's son began to live with me. But Shevkal raided my borderland more than of old, and his son was of no help to me. Having thought to myself that his son was of no use to me, I extended my grace to him and let him go to his father, with the message – 'I do not need your sister, either.

[1] For Alexander's account of his own life see Commentary 42.

217

Live with your father. You are of no help to me . . .' And when
Shevkal's son returned to his father and gave him my message,
Shevkal began assembling a force against me. Having assembled
(215) his own men and the Kumyks and various others, 6,000 in all,
he came to the mountains on my border in the summer of
[70]96 [1588]; and he himself remained on high ground with
three thousand men, and he sent three thousand from the
mountains down into my land. And against him I sent only
some three hundred of my *aznaurs*, and they only had one man
each; so my men were some six hundred in all. And . . . my
men inflicted a crushing defeat on Shevkal's men who had come
into my land. Shevkal himself fled with the remainder; and the
heads of those who had been killed were brought to me . . . I
have now instructed my ambassadors to talk to you, the
Sovereign's ambassadors, about two matters. The first one is
as follows: Shevkal furtively raids my borderland, burns townships and villages and kills, wounds and captures my men;
and sometimes God helps me to defeat Shevkal; such things
happened to us here in the past, too, and God judged the dead.
But what I feel worst of all is when they take a Christian alive
and revile him and convert him to their Moslem faith.[1] And
the second matter: Shevkal has written to the Turkish king
asking him to come to his aid for the sake of the Moslem
faith . . . Shevkal is a Moslem, and so he has sought the aid of
a Moslem king; and I, because of my Christian faith, have
sought the aid of the great Sovereign, the Christian Tsar . . .
If the great Sovereign does not extend his grace to me and does
not send his army against Shevkal this summer, and if the
Turk's army comes against my realm beforehand – who will
be answerable to God for the outrage which will be per-
petrated on me and on my realm by the Moslems, for the

[1] In the eighteenth century, both Reineggs and Güldenstädt found
that Georgians who had been kidnapped and converted to Islam were very
numerous in the villages of Daghestan.

blood that will be shed and for the souls? God prevent this – so that both of us may remain pure in our good faith before God . . ." '

And Prince Semen and dyak Torkh replied: '. . . King Alexander should give us leave to return to the Sovereign soon. We shall then be able to inform him of all this and the King's affair will be done.'

CHAPTER 7

ARMOUR AND ARGAMAKS

O N May 4th King Alexander sent the attendant Lom to the ambassadors Prince Semen and dyak Torkh with a message to sup with him in the village of Shilda on the following day.

(216) On the 5th of May Lom came to the ambassadors and said: 'King Alexander has ridden from his court: so you should ride and join him.' And Prince Semen and dyak Torkh rode up to King Alexander who bade them ride with him. While they were riding he said to them 'I shall send you off soon.'

And the ambassadors said: 'We have worried you much about letting us go, and now we do not even dare to trouble you any more. You sent a message to us before now saying that you intended to let us go on the third day in Holy Week, and we sent orders for our men with horses and provisions to meet us in Soni-land by that day. Our men have been waiting for us in Soni-land and they experience great want for they cannot feed themselves there.'

And King Alexander said: 'You are asking me to let you go, but it is necessary for me to send you off to the great Sovereign by a good route. Only four days are left till Sunday, and on Sunday I shall send you off. Now come riding with me and have sport with hawk and hounds. While you in Moscow keep my ambassadors locked up in their house, I give you freedom to go about as you please.'

The ambassadors replied: 'Our great Sovereign did not keep your ambassadors locked up. They were free to ride wherever they wanted, but they had to be accompanied by attendants for their own safety. Since our Sovereign's realm

is vast and there are all sorts of people there from many lands, (217)
your ambassadors could not go about without attendants
lest they be dishonoured by someone, thereby bringing the
Sovereign's displeasure on his officials. You were told that by
an ill-informed man; it does not happen in our Sovereign's
realm that ambassadors and envoys and messengers are kept
locked up.'

While they were attending the Hours in the village of Shilda
King Alexander said to the ambassadors: 'Greeks come to
me and extract largesse from me, but they do not teach local
priests. Local priests are yokels; they do not know anything;
they buy themselves off with bribes and so the Greeks do
not teach them.'

And the ambassadors Prince Semen and dyak Torkh replied: 'It is proper that in such an important matter the priests
should be supervised by the Metropolitan, and the archbishops,
the bishops and the abbots, as is customary in our Sovereign's
Russian realm.'

After the Hours, King Alexander said: 'You have brought
me no diversion. Your sport is too late. The Sovereign
wished to lend me a force against Shevkal, but he has not done
so. And I now intend to plan an army and put on my armour.
For the sake of my enemy – so that he should not laugh – I
intend to disport myself with a children's game and play with
a ball.'

Prince Semen and dyak Torkh said: 'Our Sovereign's army
will be sent against your enemy Shevkal. Do not lose hope in our
great Sovereign; he will defend you from even more formidable
enemies than Shevkal. But what need is there to talk much
about Shevkal? And you are free in your sport.'

King Alexander began playing with a ball, galloping on
argamaks, with his son Prince Yuri and his brother-in-law
Baygram and some twenty of his nephews and his most
prominent *aznaurs*. And they disported themselves, changing

argamaks, for some three hours. After that, the King sent a message to the ambassadors bidding them come to his tent. And he said to them at table: 'I am not a child. I know that it seems to you that I play a children's game. I had some expectations from the great Sovereign – but it is too late to go on hoping. I want to plan my army myself and oppose the enemy. I shall not be downcast: I am disporting myself, and getting myself fit for war. My enemy will not see me in sorrow and will not scoff at me.'[1]

The ambassadors replied: 'The great Sovereign will extend his grace to you and will give you an army against Shevkal; but it is necessary for you, too, to attend to an army, for a realm cannot stand without an army. As regards your own sport – you are free in that.'

After the meal King Alexander gave them leave to return to Krym, and the attendant Ivan rode with them.

On the 8th of May the equerry Uman and Archimandrite Philip brought to the ambassadors Prince Semen and dyak (218) Torkh a pair of vambraces, one each, and a cuirass, all of steel, damascened with gold and precious stones, sapphires and rubies and pearls and turquoises. And they said on behalf of King Alexander: ' "I was to send to the great Sovereign fifty pieces of gold Kizilbash damask and ten carpets, worked with gold and silver thread.[2] But the Sovereign wrote to me in his letter …that I was to send him such fine things as I have in my realm. And, though I could have collected so many lengths of damask and so many carpets, I have thought it better to send to the

---

[1] This game may have been polo, familiar to the Georgians through their many contacts with the Persians, or possibly the account may relate to the traditional Georgian game of *tskhenburti*, or horse-ball, a sort of mounted basket-ball. For an illustration of women taking part in this game in present-day Georgia, see D. M. Lang, *A modern history of Georgia*, London, 1962, pl. 8; for Castelli's near-contemporary drawing of the game, see Allen, *HGP*, opposite p. 357.

[2] See Commentary 43: Kizilbash damask and carpets.

Sovereign such fine things as happen to be in my realm more precious than damask or carpets. I know myself that there is nothing that the great Sovereign does not have in his treasury. I only wish that my gifts should also be numbered among the Sovereign's treasures". And King Alexander also bade us say to you: "You have your customs and I have mine. I shall show you everything that I intend to send to the great Sovereign. Not only that, but I am not hiding from you my wife and my children and all my house and all my thoughts. While you keep my ambassador in Moscow locked up in his house. In future my ambassador should not be kept locked up.' "

The ambassadors replied: 'Our great Sovereign, in extending his grace to your sovereign, wrote to him in his royal letter that if it proves impossible to obtain so many pieces of damask or carpets in his realm, he should send other fine things and good *argamaks* and horses. And we see that these particular things will be useful for the Sovereign's treasury. The man who spoke to your sovereign about [the treatment of] his ambassadors was a rascal: it does not happen in our Sovereign's realm that ambassadors are kept locked up.'

On May 10th King Alexander sent the attendant Ivan to fetch the ambassadors Prince Semen and dyak Torkh and the monk Zakhkhey, bidding them come to his court.

The ambassadors with the monk Zakhkhey rode to King Alexander; and halfway down the courtyard they were met by the equerry Uman. When they entered the tent, King Alexander bade them sit down and said to them: 'The time has now come for me to give you leave to return to the great Sovereign. So start tomorrow, and God speed you on your way. I shall send you my bounty towards vespers tonight. As for the matters about which I sent my officials to you with my instructions – I am now sending the same message to the great Sovereign by you and by my own ambassadors and am putting it in my letter. I am entrusting my ambassadors into your hands and hope that you will safely come to see the great Sovereign's eyes and will present my ambassadors to him. And you know yourselves: when a sovereign is strong and has many mounted and armed men and much treasure, who shall order him to exchange his own free will for vassalage? (219) Has such a thing ever been heard of? I have all this – men and treasure: though my realm is not large it is not short of anything, and I fear no-one in these parts. Yet it was of my own will that I have come under the great Sovereign's royal hand and that I am writing a letter to the Sovereign and am sending it by my ambassadors, as a serf to his master – because he is a great Christian sovereign. He should act as he has written to me in his royal letter patent. And as for the bounty which he sent to me by you, his ambassadors, and the tribute which I am sending to him, I shall write of it also in my letter. Kaplan and his assistants whom I sent before now to the Sovereign proved incompetent in entreating him about my affairs. And I have heard that the Sovereign's envoys Rodion Birkin and Petr Pivov busied themselves with their own affairs, and they did not bring my supplication to the Sovereign's notice, either. For this reason my affairs have not been done. And I have written in my letter that the Sovereign should extend his grace to me and should send me two skilled icon-painters in addition to these icon-painters, and as many of the best falcons as he is gracious enough to give me from among those which he uses for his own sport, and a falconer who would know [how to look after them], and a gunner who would be skilled in firing, and a cannon-smith, likewise skilled. These men are not for me to defend myself with, and I have my own cannon-smiths and gunners; but I am asking for them that the rumour may spread in these parts that the Sovereign's men cast cannon in my realm and that I have the Sovereign's gunners.'

And the ambassadors replied: 'Our Sovereign took you

under his royal hand for the sake of the Christian faith – and it is proper for you, King Alexander, to write so in your letter to him. As for the message which you have given us, we shall convey it all to the great Sovereign. In letting the icon-painters Posnik Dermin and his comrades come to you with us, the great Sovereign gave us the instruction that you should send them back with us. If you need icon-painters, send a supplication with us to the Sovereign about them.'

King Alexander said: 'There is only my head that you do not need – and you speak of icon-painters. Christian faith became established in my realm 1,260 years ago,[1] and during those years many monasteries and churches fell into ruin through the sway of the infidels. I now want to arrange it all in my lifetime as it was in the past. It was for this reason that I sent supplications to the Sovereign about icon-painters – and the Sovereign has extended his grace to me and has sent me icon-painters; but they are too few for my needs. I am sending this message by you and I am asking my own ambassadors to supplicate the Sovereign for additional icon-painters; yet you are depriving me of the Sovereign's bounty – the (220) icon-painters who are already here. Do not talk to me about icon-painters, thereby causing me grief.'[2] King Alexander also said: 'And should God allow you, great monk Zakhkhey, to see the eyes of the holiest Patriarch Job of all Russia, supplicate him on my behalf to mention me in his holy prayers and to be my advocate with the great Sovereign . . .'

Then King Alexander sent all his councillors out of the hall, except for ambassador Suliman and equerry Uman, and

[1] '1260 years ago': This refers, accurately enough, to the date of the traditional conversion of Georgia to Christianity, in the middle of the fourth century A.D.

[2] The influence of Russian icon-painters on the frescoes and icons in some Kakhian churches and monasteries of the sixteenth and seventeenth centuries has been noted in the recent works of Amiranashvili and Chubinashvili (cf. Commentary 23).

said: 'The lands in these parts near my realm were Christian
– Migreli and Tatyany.[1] But because of our sins the Turkish
king conquered them not long ago, and many of the inhabitants adopted the Moslem faith under duress. As soon as
the great Sovereign comes to my assistance, these lands, on
hearing of the Sovereign's grace, will also seek him, the great
Sovereign, and will be converted to the Christian faith; and
there will be great recompense from God for the great Sovereign. You should inform him of all this.'

Prince Semen and dyak Torkh replied: 'We shall convey
all this to the great Sovereign.'

The king sent off the ambassadors Prince Semen and dyak
Torkh and the monk Zakhkhey back to their camp; and on
that day he did not send anybody to them.

On the following day King Alexander sent the equerry
Uman and the dyaks Ivan-bek and Ters with his bounty and
the message 'King Alexander bids you start tomorrow, and
his ambassadors Suliman and Khurshit will meet you on the
road presently.'

(221)   On the 11th of May the attendants Ivan and Lom came to
the ambassadors and said: 'King Alexander is leaving now to

---

[1] 'Migreli and Tatyany': Mingrelia, the coastal plain of western Georgia.
In Georgian, *Sa-m-egr-el-o*. *Sa-* and *-o* represent toponymic prefix and
suffix; hence 'the country of the *M-egr-els*'. The ancient name of the
country was *Egrisi* (cf. Wak./Brosset, p. 337; Wak./Jan., p. 194). For
the alternative, *Sa-egr-o-y*, see A. Gugushvili, *Georgica*, Vol. I, Nos. 2 and
3, p. 55, n. 2. The root *egr* is possibly connected, as first indicated by
Marr, with *gwer*, wolf (see my article in *BK*, Nos. 32–3, 1959, 'Ex Ponto,
III and IV', pp. 6–7, citing Kuftin, Bardavelidze and other recent sources).
The name of the neighbouring province of Guria also derives from the
same root. But for caution on this derivation, see Toumanoff, *SCCH*,
lengthy note 58 at p. 59.

'Tatyany' corresponds to *G. Dadiani*, a territorial title of the rulers of
Mingrelia, probably deriving from the name of an early fief of the family
on the river Dadi. These rulers were also sometimes known under the
style of *Bediani* (in the European form, *Bendian*), from the episcopal
see of Bedia in Abkhazia; thus, Mingrelia sometimes appears as *Sa-
bedian-o*, 'Bediani's country' (cf. Gugushvili, above, p. 130).

have some sport in the village of Elon, and he bids you ride from Krym today after his departure.'

And within the hour King Alexander rode up to the ambassadors' tent with his son Prince Yuri and with a few of his immediate entourage; he left the escort behind, away from the tent. And Prince Semen and dyak Torkh went out of the tent as far as the tent-ropes and did homage to King Alexander for the bounty which he had sent them with the equerry Uman and his comrades.

And the king said: 'God speed you on your road. Go on your journey to the great Sovereign, and my ambassadors will meet you on the way.' And he rode away from the tent, instructing the equerry Uman to take delivery of the prisoners and the Cossacks together with a list of their names.

Prince Semen and dyak Torkh checked these prisoners and Cossacks, twenty-five men in all, against the list, and they gave Uman the list with their names; they appointed Efremka, who had been a Terek Cossack, to be *pyatidesyatnik* over them. The ambassadors set out from Krym on the same day; and the attendants Ivan and Lom rode with them.

And on the 12th Prince Semen and dyak Torkh happened to be passing near the village of Elon where King Alexander was; and they sent the interpreter Ivanis to the king with the request that he should send off his own ambassadors so that they themselves should suffer no delay, and that he should provide an inventory of the tribute which he was sending to the Sovereign.

On his return the interpreter Ivanis said that the king had sent off his ambassadors and that he sent as tribute to the Sovereign by them the pair of vambraces and the cuirass which the equerry Uman had shown to the [Russian] ambassadors, as well as nine lengths of gold damask and a grey *argamak*; and he had enumerated it all in his letter.

The attendants rode along with the ambassadors until the

14th of May, and from the 14th they were accompanied by King Alexander's general Mikhailo Gugono,[1] with some four hundred or more *aznaurs* and retainers of all kinds, until they reached Aristov's land on the 16th of May. According to reports King Alexander sent his general Mikhailo to accompany Prince Semen and dyak Torkh because they had to journey through the land of his brother-in-law Simon. Simon and King Alexander exchange messages but there is still great enmity between them and peace has not been made ...

(222) As from the 17th of May Prince Aristov rode with the ambassadors; and Alexander's ambassadors Suliman and Khurshit met them on the 18th.

On the morning of the 20th of May Prince Aristov came to the ambassadors Prince Semen and dyak Torkh and said that he had just received the news that Alexander's brother-in-law Simon was following them with many men and was not far from them, and that he, Aristov, was going off to defend his land. Aristov rode off straight away, and the ambassadors rode into the mountains without escort.

On the 27th of May, in the mountains, the Kalkan mountaineers attacked the rearguard of the ambassadors' party and captured the *strelets* Naydenek, killing the horse under him; but the ambassadors turned back and defeated these Kalkans and rescued the *strelets* from them.[2]

On the 28th, when the ambassadors came out of the mountains, Prince Alkas rode up to them and said that he had come to meet them and that they should notify the Sovereign of

[1] Gugono: This name does not appear in the Georgian sources but may correspond to the name of Gognia-shvili among the list of 'sons of *aznaurni*' in Kakheti given by Wakhusht (Wak./Brosset, p. 492). The name-root Gog/Guggu is very ancient in Georgia (cf. the form Gugu-shvili in Mingrelia). The late C. F. Lehmann-Haupt was ready to equate it with Asianic *Gyges* and proposed that Magog signified 'Gyges-Land'; cf. his note in *Klio*, Vol. XXVIII, Part 1/2, 1935, p. 199 (following a conversation with the present writer).

[2] For the Kalkan or Karakalkan mountaineers, see Commentary 44.

his service. He also asked that his three *uʒdens*, Yanuk and his comrades, should be released from Tyumen-town. And Prince Alkas rode off on the same day.

The ambassadors Prince Semen and dyak Torkh reached the Sovereign's blockhouse on the Sunzha on the 31st of May; they arrived at Tyumen-town on the 4th of June. The commanders Prince Andrey Khvorostinin and his comrades released Alkas's *uʒdens* Yanuk and Alpsha; but they retained Aslanbek, the third *uʒden*, because Prince Alkas had not come to them at Tyumen-town on the Sovereign's affairs. They sent word to Alkas to come to Tyumen-town himself for the Sovereign's affairs, as the other mountain princes did; they would then release his *uʒden* to him.

The following report, which the ambassadors Prince Semen (122) Zvenigorodski and dyak Torkh Antonov sent from the Sunzha, was received [in Moscow] on the 5th of September [70]99.

To the Sovereign Tsar and great Prince Fedor Ivanovich of all Russia your servants Semenets Zvenigorodski and Torkh Antonov do homage. Sovereign! We, your servants, were allowed by King Alexander to return to you from Krym on the 11th day of May. And together with us King Alexander sent to you, Sovereign, his ambassadors Suliman and Khurshit to do homage on your Majesty's favour and letters patent and to bring tribute. And by these ambassadors of his he sent you, Sovereign, as tribute a breast-plate and two vambraces of steel, damascened with gold and set with spinels and with rubies and with turquoise and with various other stones; and nine pieces of gold damask and a dark-grey *argamak* with a gold caparison and head-band. And to your father, the holiest Patriarch Job of all Russia, who prays God for you, Sovereign, he has sent as presents from himself and his queen each a length of silk worked with gold thread and six pieces of flowered damask without gold thread and two pieces of

striped damask. And Metropolitan Nicholas has sent a bay
(123) *argamak* to Patriarch Job . . . And, Sovereign, we reached
your Majesty's blockhouse on the Sunzha on the 31st of May.
We travelled the same way as when going to Georgia, stamping
down the snow on the mountains and bridging the river Terek
with bridges, having engaged some one hundred men in addition to your Majesty's *streltsy* and to our own poor men,
because the snow had not melted on the mountains and the
Terek was in flood. On the 11th of March we had written to
Tyumen-town to your Majesty's commanders Prince Andrey
Ivanovich Khvorostinin and his assistants to send an escort to
meet us in the mountains on the way to Lars settlement . . . And
on May 16th, as we were on our way back to you, Sovereign,
your commanders sent a letter to us at Aristov's settlement by
Alexander's Cherkess Baygram, asking us to send a messenger
to them on the day on which King Alexander would send us
off so that they could send an escort to us. While we were
on the road we tried to send two *streltsy* to them – Grisha the
priest and Vaska Goryachka; but these two *streltsy* could
not get through the mountains and they returned to us because
their horses had fallen down the mountainside and were killed.
This Cherkess Baygram had come from your commanders
along the Terek before the flood, crossing the plank bridges on
foot; while your Majesty's *streltsy* were unable to get through
even on foot for the flood waters of the Terek had carried
away the planks. We marched through the mountains without
waiting for the escort; we did not dare camp in the mountains
and wait for the escort because of the mountaineers. . .

And, Sovereign, as regards the rectification of the Christian
faith, there was no other council after the one held by Metropolitan Nicholas which was attended by the monk Zakhkhey
and his brethren . . .

And, Sovereign, King Alexander did not allow the icon-
(124) painters, Posnik Dermin and his comrades, to leave with us;

230

they are painting in the church in the village of Tog and in the monastery of St George of Alaverdy – murals and inset icons, a *deesis* and feasts . . .

We have sent back to Astarakhan the mounted *streltsy* from that town who had been with us in Georgia. (126)

This report, and the *argamaks* which King Alexander has sent you and which Metropolitan Nicholas has sent to the holiest Patriarch Job, we are sending on to your Majesty by the *strelets sotnik* Grigori Kumtarinov. We have written to your Majesty's boyar and to the commanders, to Prince Fedor Ivanovich Troyekurov[1] and his assistants and to dyak Menshoy Dyurbenev at Astarakhan asking them to send off the *sotnik* with his report and the *argamaks* to your Majesty without delay. And we, your servants, together with the Georgian ambassadors shall proceed from the Sunzha to Tyumen-town in boats on the first of June.

The Sovereign Tsar and great Prince Fedor Ivanovich of all Russia, having heard the ambassadors' report, commanded that a letter be sent to Kazan, to the commander Dmitri Velyaminov[2] and his assistants, with instructions that Prince Semen and dyak Torkh be sent off from Kazan to Moscow ahead of the Georgian ambassadors.

The Sovereign's ambassadors Prince Semen Zvenigorodski and dyak Torkh Antonov reached Moscow on the 15th of (127) November; and they presented a report to the Sovereign on how they had attended to his affairs in the Iberian land.

---

[1] The Troyekurovs came of ancient stock and several of them were active participants in the events at the turn of the sixteenth century. Fedor Mikhaylovich was sent on an embassy to King Stephen Batory in 1585 and was the Tsar's representative at the Polish Sejm which met to elect Batory's successor. Ivan Fedorovich, perhaps a son of the Fedor Ivanovich of our text, had an adventurous career during and after the Time of Troubles. For this family, see Solovyev, Index.

[2] For the Velyaminov family, see Chap. 10, pp. 416, no. 1 and 421, n. 2.

COMMENTARIES

COMMENTARY I

Monasteries and cathedrals in and around Moscow (ref. Chap. 1, p. 87, n. 3)

As in the west of Europe, the great monasteries were a significant and formative influence in the life of mediaeval Russia. They were at once religious and cultural centres which attracted all classes: the elaborate and pompous visits of the court and the humble pilgrimages of the artisans and peasants. The influence of the monasteries on artistic and literary life was profound; but they were also important land-owners, promoters of industry and handicrafts and entrepreneurs in mining, forestry and fisheries. For many interesting aspects of monastic activities, see Eck, *MAR*, pp. 122 – 84, 388 – 91. The monasteries mentioned in our text were:

(a) *Troitsko-Sergiyevski,* some forty-five miles north of Moscow. Sacred to the Trinity, it was founded by St Sergius of Radonezh in 1337 – 40. Under the special protection of the Grand Dukes and, later, Tsars of Muscovy, the community amassed great wealth. It was a prime centre of learning where books were copied and the best artists in the land, such as Andrey Rublev, worked. The monastery was fortified during the period 1540–50 (line drawing in *BSE*, 1st ed.). See *Ist. Moskvy*, Vol. 1, p. 81, for reproduction of miniature of Rublev painting the frescoes of Troitsko-Sergiyevski Monastery from the sixteenth-century Life of St Sergius. For view of monastery, see Grabar, 1st ed., Vol. II, p. 10. For a near-contemporary engraving, see Olearius/W., Vol. 1, plate between cols. 56 and 57; for a painting of the monastery on a sixteenth-century icon, *OI/PF/xvi-xvii vv,* p. 429.

(b) *The Chudov* – the Monastery of the Miracle – in the Moscow Kremlin, founded in 1365 to commemorate the miraculous cure of Taydulla Hatun, wife of the Tartar Khan Uzbek. She had been suffering from an eye disease (Vernadsky, *MR*, p. 207). (This was the Taitughli or Tai-dula Hatun whose peculiar physical attractions were made known to Ibn Battuta: cf. Gibb, *Ibn Battuta*, Hakluyt Society ed., Vol. ɪɪ, pp. 486–7.)

The Monastery, which was sacred to the Archangel Michael and to St Alexius, was under the direct jurisdiction of the Metropolitans and, later, the Patriarchs of Moscow. During the sixteenth and seventeenth centuries it was a seat of learning where sacred books were translated and corrected. For a view, see Grabar, 1st ed., Vol. ɪɪ, pp. 17, 19. For plans of buildings within the Kremlin, *Ist. Moskvy*, Vol. ɪ, opposite p. 104.

(c) *Prechistenski* – the Cathedral of the Immaculate One in the Moscow Kremlin; its more usual name is the Cathedral of the Dormition of the Virgin (*Uspenski*). After the burning of Moscow by Tokhtamysh in August 1382, the Bolognese architect, Fioraventi, built it on the site of an earlier church founded in 1326–7. Its five cupolas were gilded in the reign of Ivan IV. Some of the oldest and most revered icons were kept in the Uspenski. For views see Grabar, 1st ed., Vol. ɪɪ, pp. 11, 12, 19; and *Ist. Moskvy*, Vol. ɪ, pl. opposite p. 108. For Fioraventi, Eck, *MAR*, p. 357, n. 2.

(d) *Arkhanilski* = Arkhangelski. The original cathedral, built in 1333, was pulled down and reconstructed during the years 1505–9; it is nearly cubical in shape and is crowned by five domes. From the days of Ivan Kalita, it was the burial place of the Grand Dukes and Tsars of Muscovy. Cf. *Ist. Moskvy*, Vol. ɪ, pp. 109 ff. and pl. 38, 39; also Grabar, 1st ed., Vol. ɪɪ, pp. 25, 27.

COMMENTARY 2

Some Russian military and administrative terms (ref. Chap. 1, pp. 88, n. 3, and 89, nn. 4 and 5)

(a) *gorodishche* – an abandoned settlement, usually with ruins of fortifications, cf. Georgian *Nakalakevi* – 'where there was once a town'.

golova, lit. 'head', here, chief, commander. With *golova*, cf. German *Hauptmann*, from which, perhaps, Polish *hetman*, Cossack *ataman*. But see Vasmer, *REW*, Vol. II, p. 31, who indicates alternative derivation of *ataman* from Turko-Tartar *odaman*, 'Altester der Hirten eines Kosakenlagers'.

A *golova* could command from 250 to 500 men and corresponded to a colonel of a regular unit. Under him served *sotniki* commanding 100 (*sto*) and *pyatidesyatniki* commanding 50 (*pyatdesyat*) men. These ranks corresponded roughly to captains and cornets.

ostrog, fort, blockhouse, can also mean gaol, cf. Vasmer, *REW*, Vol. II, p. 287. For the abandoned settlement on the Sunzha (*Sunzhino gorodishche* of Felitsyn's map); and for Terek-town see Introduction, Section 5, 'Terek-town'.

(b) *Streltsy* (sing. *strelets*, an archer, from *strela*, an arrow). The regular troops of the Muscovite state, used for garrison duties and for service in Moscow in peace time when they were paid half a ruble per annum in addition to their keep. This pay was increased to seven rubles per annum during service in the field.

The *streltsy* were organized on a permanent footing by Ivan IV; in his time they numbered about 12,000 men, of whom 5,000 were quartered in Moscow. The force was divided into regiments (*prikaz*), usually 500 strong – commanded by *golovy* who were drawn from the ranks of the landed gentry. *Sotniki* were either landed gentry or boyars' sons. The rankers were recruited from among 'free people'; they served for life and were often themselves the sons of *streltsy*. They lived in special quarters (*slobody*) and enjoyed various fiscal privileges.

Boris Godunov was reported to have had 12,000 *streltsy* in Moscow. Originally archers, they soon became musketeers. During the seventeenth century, this privileged corps tended to become more and more arrogant and mutinous. Like the Janissaries of the Ottoman empire and the Mamluks in Cairo, they showed themselved politically conservative and opposed to technical innovations. The corps was finally dispersed – and many of the *streltsy* tortured and slaughtered – by Peter the Great on his return from western Europe in 1698. (Solovyev, Vols. II and III, *passim*; *BSE*, 1st ed., for bibliographical refs.; Allen, *HGP*, pp. 158 and 163, for reproductions of Castelli's drawings of *streltsy* apparently serving in Georgia during the first quarter of the seventeenth century). In Asafi's miniatures of Russian soldiers opposing Özdemiroghlu Osman Pasha's passage of the Sunzha, in October 1583, the musketeers would seem to be *streltsy* rather than Cossacks, since their headgear resembles that shown in Castelli's drawing (Allen, p. 158); as in the case of Osman's janissaries, they seem to be clad in regulation uniforms.

(c) *kabak*: the etymology is obscure. In Russian the word has the meaning of 'inn'; but see Vasmer, *REW*, Vol. I, p. 494, for Balkar/Karachay '*Ansiedlung, Dorf*'. (Cf. Canadian *quebec* from Algonquin.) According to Brosset *EC/BHP*, Vol. II, pp. 14–15, col. 221, n. 28, *kabak* signifies in Tartar a cup, hence figuratively a plain surrounded by mountains: the word came to signify the residence of a chieftain (inf. Khanykov). See also Genko, p. 691, who emphasizes difficulty in identifying sites of *kabaks* since they were often mobile.

COMMENTARY 3

Religious contacts between Russia and Georgia (ref. Chap. 1, p. 91 nn. 1 and 2)

The reasons which prompted King Alexander of Kakheti – whose country was in frequent contact with the Oecumenical Patriarchate in Constantinople – to seek spiritual guidance from Moscow were political rather than religious; his intention was to win the good grace of the Metropolitan of Moscow who could influence the devout Tsar Fedor.

During the period of the Mongol hegemony in Russia, from the middle of the thirteenth to the end of the fifteenth century, Russia had only intermittent contacts with Constantinople. The uncritical copying and re-copying of sacred books had caused the Russian Church to countenance many unorthodox practices which persisted into the sixteenth century. According to Solovyev, when Ivan IV set up a printing press in Russia he was in part guided by the desire to supply the land with correct church books; even so, some of the early printers had to flee the country because they were accused of heretical views. A return to strict Orthodoxy was not achieved until Patriarch Nikon's great reforms in the seventeenth century.

Job, the first Russian Patriarch, who appears frequently in our texts, was crowned in January 1589 – only three months before the departure of Zvenigorodski's embassy. Of unknown parentage, he was probably brought up by the monks of the Monastery of the Dormition at Staritsa where he later took his vows. Ivan IV noticed him during a visit which he paid to the monastery about 1569 and had him appointed Archimandrite. He became Bishop of Kolomna in 1581, Archbishop of Rostov in 1586 and Metropolitan of Moscow in the same year. In politics he showed himself an active and staunch supporter of Boris Godunov. When Moscow fell to the False Dmitri, Job was deposed (June 1605) and banished to Staritsa where he died on 19 June 1607 (cf. *RBS*, under name).

COMMENTARY 4

The Kizilbashes (ref. Chap. 1, p. 92, n. 1)

Kizilbash was the name given by the Ottoman Turks to the confederation of seven Turkoman tribes who placed the Shaikhs of Ardabil on the throne of Persia and helped Shah Ismail (1487–1524) to found the dynasty of the Safavids. Shah Ismail had given them as headdress the red turban worn by the disciples of his ancestors – hence *kizilbaşlar*, redheads (cf. *EI*, 1st ed., under 'Safawi').

The name is also applied to a religious sect living throughout Anatolia and regarded as Shi'a by the orthodox Turkish Sunnis. This sect is closely connected with the Nusairis of Syria; its adepts call themselves 'Alawi', i.e. followers of Ali, the husband of Fatima, daughter of the Prophet Muhammad. Some of the Anatolian Kizilbashes are Kurds; the others are for the most part Turkomans or Turks and only speak Turkish. (Summarized from Cl. Huart's article in *EI*, 1st ed.; and see also the article by A. Gökpinarli in *IA*; there is also much information on the practices and folklore of the Kizilbashes in an unpublished MS. by Colonel Nazmi Sevgen of Istanbul.) The Kizilbashes are numerous as far west as Amasya and Sivas and the Bulghar-dagh.

Always partisans of the Safavids, the Anatolian Kizilbashes undertook some formidable revolts against the Ottoman sultans during the fifteenth and sixteenth centuries. These revolts were at once mystical and radical in character and derived from obscure undertones in the spiritual and ethnic underworld of the peninsula. (For these 'undertones' see the article by Allen, 'The Trialetian Goblet' in *BK*, Nos. 32–3, 1959, p. 3 and n. 15; for a profound study of the Kizilbashes and other heterodox communities of Asia Minor, see Hasluck, *CIUS*, Vol. 1, Part 2; and V.A. Gordlevski, *IS*, Vol. 1, pp. 241–75; also B. Nikitine, *Les Kurdes: Etude sociologique et historique*, Paris 1956, *passim*; and N.Y. Marr, 'Eshche o slove

chelebi: k voprosu o kulturnom znachenii Kurdskoy narod-
nosti v istorii Peredney Azii', in *ZVO*, Vol. xx, *vyp.* 2–3,
1911, pp. 99–151.)

The name *kizilbash* came to have a pejorative significance
among the enemies of the Safavid dynasty and the Shi'a faith
(cf. 'Roundheads' in seventeenth century England).

'Kizilbash Shah' = Shah of Persia.

COMMENTARY 5

Russian relations with the central Asian khanates (ref. Chap.
I, p. 94, n. 3)

During the period of Mongol hegemony in the thirteenth and
fourteenth centuries, Russian merchants, artisans and mercenaries had penetrated to the cities of central Asia and even
as far as China. At the same time the traders of Bukhara and
Samarkand were attracted by the possibilities of the northern
markets, particularly in furs and walrus ivory. Following the
capture by the Russians of Kazan and Astrakhan and the
establishment of their ascendancy along the Volga during the
latter half of the sixteenth century, the interest of Moscow
in central Asia became political as well as mercantile. As one
of the chief advisers of Ivan IV during his last years, and the
virtual ruler of Russia during the reign of his own brother-in-
law, Tsar Fedor Ivanovich, Boris Godunov showed himself
the sagacious and determined protagonist of a forward policy
along the eastern and south-eastern borders of Russia. And
in the direction of this policy, he benefited from the advice
and encouragement of the numerous English representatives
of the Muscovy Company who were intent on developing
the trade route from the Arctic ports and along the Volga
to Persia, central Asia and India.

Russian diplomatic sensitivity on the subject, and the references in our text to the cities of central Asia are, therefore,
of peculiar interest:

(a) *Bukhara*: Abd Allah ibn Iskander, the greatest prince of the Uzbek house of the Shaybanids, had his capital in Bukhara from 1557 to 1598. During his reign the city was the focus of political power in central Asia. In 1558, four years after the capture of Astrakhan by the Russians, Anthony Jenkinson visited Bukhara bearing letters from Tsar Ivan IV. The Khan showed himself very interested in the Russians who already had a considerable trade there (cf. Hakluyt, *PN*, Vol. II, pp. 471, 473). For Abd Allah's career and campaign in Kazakhstan, see article by V. Bartold in *EI*, 2nd ed.; also Allen, *PTP*, pp. 36–7, and nn. 106–7. The Uzbeks became alarmed at Russian pressures. Threatened also by the recovering power of Persia in Khurasan, Abd Allah was disposed towards the Ottoman Turks who, in 1558, despatched to him a military mission with expert gunners (*topcilar*) from Baku across the Caspian (cf. Togan, *TT*, p. 135 and n. 82; also Allen, *PTP*, p. 36 and nn. 106–8).

(b) *Yurgench* (*Urgench*) – *Khiva* – *I<u>z</u>yur*; The historic state round the basin of the Aral Sea, successively known from the sites of its capitals as Khwarizm (Khorezm), Urgench, Khiva. At the end of the sixteenth century 'this ancient home of civilization had become a brigand state; as a result the caravan road through central Asia lost almost all importance, as may be judged from the report of the only west European to visit Kh^wārizm at the time, the Englishman, Anthony Jenkinson ... Civilisation among the Özbegs in those days was at an incomparably lower level than in Mā warā' al-Nahr' (Bartold, *EI*, 1st ed.; under 'Kh^warizm').

Izyur i.e. Wazir (or Shahr-i-Wazir, city of the *wa<u>z</u>ir*) in Kh^wārizm was visited in 1558 by Jenkinson who correctly foretold that shortage of water in the Amu-darya would soon lead to the abandonment of the region. Jenkinson calls the town Sellysure or Shaysure (Hakluyt, *PN*, Vol. II, pp. 461 ff.; cf. also S. P. Tolstov, *Po sledam*, Chap. XII; Lestrange, *LEC*,

p. 451). The ruins of Wazir are now known as Dev-Kisken.

After the capture of Kazan and Astrakhan and the clearing of the Volga route in the middle of the sixteenth century, the Muscovite tsars assumed much of the prestige and many of the pretensions of the former Khans of the Golden Horde. The central Asian rulers hastened to send embassies to Moscow or, often, merchants would appear representing themselves to be the envoys of their khans. Returning from Bukhara, Jenkinson had in his company, and committed to his charge, 'two ambassadors, the one from the king of Boghar (Bukhara), the other from the king of Balke (Balkh) . . . sent unto the Emperor of Russia'. After leaving Sellysure, he had with him

foure more Ambassadors sent from the King of Urgence, and other soltans, his brethren, unto the Emperor of Russia, with answer of such letters as I brought them . . . The same Ambassadors were also committed to my charge by the sayde Kings and princes: to whome I promised most faithfully, and swore by our law, that they should be well used in Rusland, and suffered to depart from thence againe in safetie, according as the Emperor had written also in his letters: for they somewhat doubted, because there had none gone out of Tartaria into Russia of long time before.

(Hakluyt, *PN*, Vol. ii, p. 475. For visits of Muslim envoys to Moscow in the 1550s, see also Belokurov, *Snosheniya*, pp. li ff.)

COMMENTARY 6

The Russian conquest of Sibir (ref. Chap. i, p. 95, n. 1)

The instructions given to Zvenigorodski should be regarded as an attempt to give a background of legitimacy, dated back nearly a century, to the recent aggression of Ivan IV against the Shaybanid ruler of the Khanate of Sibir.

Ivan III Vasiliyevich (1462–1505) – the great-grandfather of Tsar Fedor Ivanovich, as indicated in the text – assumed the sovereignty of Novgorod in several moves between 1465 and

1488. His success gave him control over the vast hunting and trading grounds extending into the Arctic regions of north-west Siberia. He imposed his authority on the lands of Perm and Yugra (Ugria), which Novgorod had regarded as tributary and which Moscow now claimed as heir to the lands of Novgorod. In 1483 a Russian force was sent against the Voguls who were defeated at the mouth of the river Pelym. The Russians moved down the Irtysh to the Ob and then to the Yugra before returning to their base at Ustyug after a foray which lasted for five months. In 1499, another expedition crossed the Urals and penetrated to the Pechora (cf. Baddeley, *RMC*, pp. lv ff.). As early as 1482, Ivan III was asking the Hungarian Matthias Corvinus to send him master miners stating that 'we have gold and silver but we do not know how to extract it from the mines' (Eck, *MAR*, p. 346). For an early German interest in the mines of the lower Pechora, see Vernadsky, *RDMA*, p. 84; Eck, *ibid.*

Sibir (Siberia) was originally the name of a small Tartar Khanate on the river Tobol, whose ruler, the Taibughid Ediger, offered in 1555 to pay tribute to Moscow with a view to protection against his enemies. Ediger's rival and successor, the Shaybanid Kuchum, followed an anti-Russian policy and attacked the Ostyaks who were tributaries of the Russian tsar. In July 1573, Magmetkul (or Mametkul = Mehmet Kuli), Kuchum's nephew – not his brother, as stated in the instructions given to Zvenigorodski – led a Siberian force to the Chuso-vaya river on a plundering raid. In September 1581, a levy privately raised by the Stroganovs, great merchant princes in the Ural region, and made up of 540 Cossacks and 300 Lithuanians, Germans, Tartars and Russians, under command of the Cossack outlaw Ermak, moved against Sibir. On 26 October, Kuchum's capital fell to the Russians, but Mametkul put up a stout resistance until he was captured in the spring of 1582. He was sent to Moscow where he was treated with great honour and 'given towns and estates'. In the next two years the Russians suffered reverses: Ermak was killed in a river ambush and Kuchum was able to re-occupy his capital for a short time. Several Russian expeditions were sent across the Urals in the 1580s and the town of Tobolsk was founded in 1587. At the time of Zvenigorodski's embassy, Kuchum was still active; he was not finally defeated until 1599 (cf. Solovyev, Vol. II, pp. 316–21, 335–44). The best accounts of Ermak's career in English are in Baddeley, *RMC*, Vol. I, pp. lxix ff.; Howorth, *HM*, Part II, Div. II (= Vol. III), pp. 982–1004, based on Müller's *Sammlung*, Vol. III, Parts 5 and 6, which derives from *Sibirskaya Letopis*, the first MS of which was compiled about sixty years after the events described (cf. Baddeley, *RMC*, Vol, I, p. lxix, n.i; also Allen *PTP*, p. 36 and nn. 106, 107).

After the Russian conquest of the lands east of the Urals vast quantities of furs flowed into the Tsar's treasury. Thus, in 1588, his share of Siberian furs amounted to 466 times forty sable skins and 180 Siberian foxes. Boris Godunov imposed a tribute in kind (*yasak*) on the indigenous inhabitants of Siberia, amounting to ten sables for a married man or five for a bachelor, together with the tenth skin of all other wild animals. The trappers were also expected to send voluntary offerings to the Tsar, a practice which led to much abuse. In 1598, for instance, 3720 sables were sent from Pelym alone (cf. Baddeley, *RMC*, Vol. I, pp. xcvi, xcvii). For a contemporary miniature of the payment of *yasak* in furs in Siberia, see *OI/PF/xv–xvii vv*, p. 699.

COMMENTARY 7

The towns along the Volga route

The Volga, the greatest river in Europe, said to be 3,694 km. in length (*BSE*) has been the natural water route linking the central Russian river system with the Caspian and the Middle Eastern and central Asian lands.[1] After Ivan IV had conquered Kazan (1552) and Astrakhan (1554) there was a rapid development of trade and of military and political activity along the lower course of the river. Only four years after the annexation of Astrakhan Anthony Jenkinson, with the encouragement of Ivan IV, made the journey from Moscow to Astrakhan. He then sailed round the northern coast of the Caspian to the Mangyshlak peninsula on the eastern side and made his perilous way by caravan to Bukhara. Leaving Moscow on 23 April 1558, Jenkinson descended the Moskva to its confluence with the Oka at Kolomna and continued his journey down this river, passing Ryazan, Kasimov and Murom. On the eleventh day he came to Nizhni-Novgorod where he made a halt of eight days to await the arrival of the newly appointed *voyvode* of Astrakhan. This officer had with him five hundred large boats (*strugi*) loaded with troops, munitions and stores, and in his company Jenkinson passed along the parts of the Volga which were still subject to the attacks of dissident Finnic and Tartar tribes. On 29 May, five weeks after leaving Moscow, Jenkinson reached

[1] For the prehistoric and early historic cultures of the Volga region, see A. L. Mongait, *Archaeology in the U.S.S.R.* (Harmondsworth, Middlesex, 1961). Between the lower Volga and the northern Caucasus, the rich economy of the Aorsi, probably of Alanic east Iranian stock, developed in early classical times. In later centuries the region of the Volga 'mesopotamia' saw the rise of the nomadic and mercantile culture of the Khazars and their northern tributaries the Bulghars – who, in the ninth century A.D. were already a link between the lands of the Arab Caliphate and the Viking communities round the Baltic. (Cf. Togan's, Kovalevsky's and Canard's editions and commentaries on the mission of Ibn Fadlan.) According to *BSE*, 1st ed., the origin of the name Volga is unknown. In the Turkish languages it was called Atel, Itel, Idil, Eder. The classical name for the Dnepr, 'Borysthenes' has been connected by Karst, *OM*, p. 436, with Circassian *voarüẑ*, *varüẑ*, Sumptland, Lagune', The *Rha* (Volga) was called *Oarus* by Herodotus, Book IV, p. 123. For proto-Caucasic linguistic elements in the toponymy of the early historic 'Scythic' area, see further article by Allen, 'Ex Ponto', I and II, in *BK*, No. 30–1, 1958.

Kazan, then in course of rebuilding after the savage siege six years earlier. Jenkinson was the first Englishman to visit this city, where he stayed fifteen days, departing only on 13 June. Next day, he passed the mouth of the Kama. On 14 July, he finally reached Astrakhan after a journey of nearly twelve weeks. On his return journey up the Volga, Jenkinson left Astrakhan on 10 June 1559 and reached Kazan six weeks later. The party left Kazan on 7 August, travelling by water as far as Murom, whence they proceeded overland to Moscow where they arrived on 2 September.[1]

The up-stream journey took about the same time as the down-stream journey. At the end of the century, the up-stream journey which has been described by Sherley's companions, Pinçon and Parry, and by Don Juan of Persia who was with them, took even longer – but this was for a larger party. It included English and Persian diplomats and traders and their followers and a strong guard of *streltsy*. They left Astrakhan on 2 October 1599 and reached Nizhni-Novgorod in seven weeks (Parry) or, according to Don Juan, Kazan in two months. Don Juan counts a further six days to Cheboksary and thence by sledge to Nizhni-Novgorod. Here there was a delay of one month while preparations were being made for their reception in Moscow. They then travelled by sledge in relays of three days by Murom and Vladimir to Moscow.[2]

---

[1] The original accounts of Anthony Jenkinson's travels were collated from the volumes of Hakluyt's *Principal navigations* (*PN*) and the MSS. in the Record Office and the British Museum and edited in E. Delmar Morgan's *Early voyages and travels in Russia and Persia* (*EVT*), Hakluyt Society, 1886. Jenkinson died at an advanced age in 1611. He was the ancestor of the earls of Liverpool. The citations in this Commentary are from *EVT*, Vol. 1, Introduction and pp. 41 ff. There is a reproduction of Jenkinson's map of Russia opposite p. cxx. After eighty years, Delmar Morgan's scholarly notes still remain of great value.

[2] In 1599 Ulugh Beg was a member of the embassy which was sent by Shah Abbas I to the courts of Europe. While in Spain he became a Roman

A few decades later conditions were much the same. Travelling with the suite of the ambassador of Holstein, Adam Olearius left Moscow on 16 June 1636. They reached 'Cassimogorod' (the capital of the Tartar khanate of Kasimov) on 7 July and Murom on the 9th. On the 11th they were at Nizhni-Novgorod where they stayed for three weeks awaiting the completion of work on a ship which was being specially constructed for their journey to the Caspian. Here they were lavishly entertained by the Russian and Tartar officials and by numerous Germans, Dutch and Scots resident in the city. The *voyvode* received them in a chamber covered with fine Turkey carpets and embellished with a sideboard heavy with silver plate. Nevertheless troubles were beginning. For their protection against bands of Cossack outlaws below Nizhni, they had to form three armed watches aboard ship. On 2 August they set sail, passing by country still strongly held by Cheremisses and Mordvins; they had frequent trouble running on to sandbanks. On the 13th they reached Swiatski (Svyazhsk) and, after passing several chalk bluffs, anchored off Kazan. Here they encountered a caravan of Persians and Circassians which had left Moscow several days before them. Among the travellers were a Persian merchant who was travelling in the role of ambassador and 'Mussal', ruler of Tarku, who had been to pay his allegiance to Tsar Mikhail Fedorovich. On the 15th they left Kazan and on the 28th reached Samara, not without further alarums on account of running on to sandbanks and warnings of intended Cossack attacks. On 1 September, after having passed several large convoys going up-stream, they were opposite Saratov. Here there was a garrison of *streltsy* to

Catholic and ended his life there, having assumed the name of Don Juan of Persia. There appear to be only four known copies of his original *Relaciones*, published in Valladolid in 1604 – of which one example is in my library. The late Guy Le Strange made a translation which was published in the Broadway Travellers series in 1928. Present citations are from this version, pp. 241 ff.

protect the country and travellers from attacks by the Kalmucks lower down stream. There was a stop at Zariza (Tsaritsyn) which they left on 2 September. (Here they knew that they were in the neighbourhood of Perevolok – the portage where the Volga is separated by only fifty miles from the Don.) On 15 September, they finally reached Astrakhan in fine weather and with a good following wind. The journey down the Volga from Moscow had taken almost exactly three months.[1] The Russian ambassadors seem to have travelled with rather greater speed. Zvenigorodski left Moscow on 23 April 1589 and on 24 June was already writing from Astrakhan. Tatishchev began his journey from Moscow at the beginning of May 1604 and was in Astrakhan by the last week of June. Doubtless officials in the towns en route were on the alert to expedite the Tsar's business.

Passengers travelled in *strugi*, light flat-bottomed river craft with vertical sides. These varied in length between eighteen and sixty feet and could carry up to six tons of cargo. The hold was usually covered; the larger *strugi* sometimes had cabins. They were propelled by oars but when there was a following wind sails were also used (cf Fekhner, *TRG*, pp. 12, 21 and illustration on p. 22). The Duke of Holstein's embassy had had something like a barquentine built at Nizhni-Novgorod – a three-master, 120 feet in length and forty feet in breadth, with ports for oars and only drawing seven feet of water. But although the party finally reached Astrakhan, the 'Frederic' often proved difficult to handle and frequently grounded on

---

[1] Adam Olearius (1600–71), or Oelschlaeger, diplomat and librarian to Frederick Duke of Holstein-Gottorp first published his travels in German in 1647. There was an indifferently printed English edition in 1662. According to Brunet, the best is the folio Hamburg edition of 1696. I have used de Wicquefort's Amsterdam edition of 1727, which is here cited: *Livre Quatrième* covers the journey down the Volga. The second volume of Olearius's work comprises the travels of his comrade, J. A. de Mandelslo, who accompanied the mission to Persia and then continued on to India and the Far East.

sandbanks or was driven by sudden squalls against the banks of the river.[1]

The 'galleys' in which Sir Anthony Sherley and Don Juan of Persia travelled up the Volga from Astrakhan to Moscow in the autumn of 1599 were *strugi* of the larger sort – 'very well built, and each had a crew of a hundred rowers . . . At each stopping place we changed some of our rowers, taking on fresh men to row the galleys. All this was done under command from the soldiers who accompanied us by an order sent from the Duke of Muscovy'.[2] That there were cabins available is clear from the fact that Don Juan complains that Sir Anthony kept a Dominican friar – with whom the knight had a feud which remains obscure – 'prisoner down below decks in a cabin of the galley' (Le Strange, *Don Juan*, pp. 240, 243, 258).

The descriptions by foreigners of the Volga route are much more detailed than the Russians', to whom the journey was commonplace. Olearius's account of the mission of 1636 is the best, with its detailed map of the river below Kazan and the magnificent engravings of the Wicquefort edition of 1727. But the descriptions of Sherleys' companions, William Parry and Abel Pinçon, and of Don Juan, belong to the time o Zvenigorodski and Tatishchev when conditions were less

[1] For illustration see the fine engraving of 'Nisen-Navgorod' in Olearius/W., preceding pp. 393–4 which shows the 'Frederic' and several types of local craft including two cabined *strugi*. Two large *strugi*, armed with cannon, are shewn in a Russian sixteenth-century miniature reproduced in *KRO*, Vol. 1, opposite p. 13. Cf. Plate 5 opp. p. 96.

[2] Ross, *Sherley*, pp. 172–3: 'Since one's course by the river Volga from Astracan to Mosco is upstream, in places where trees and other objects offer no impediment these Caragoli (rowers) haul the boats by means of collars which they wear round their necks and hempen ropes round their waists; and they generally use their oars when they cannot haul the boats by strength of shoulder or when the wind is contrary; for their boats carry a very large sail, and when they sail before the wind they make good way.' For the skill and good nature of the 'Caragoli', see also Olearius, Vol. 1, cols. 385, 399, 400. It is worth mentioning that the recent name for these men was *burlaki*, as in the song 'Ey, ukhnem!'

sophisticated than they were forty years later. The matter-of-fact Parry was not greatly impressed:

From Haster-caune we passed by boat along the mighty river of Volgo, until we came to a town named Negson (Nizhni-Novgorod), which was seven weeks' passage. In which time we saw nothing worthy the noting but three or four wooden castles or block houses to guard that river; which river doth bring marvellous great commodities to the Emperor and to the whole country. Divers Tartars passing from place to place about the river, living in little houses made upon wheels, and are carried to and fro, having abundance of cattle, live so in subjection to the emperor, paying him tribute, etc. One only fair city we saw all that while, called Cassane, wherein we were; from whence we passed to Negson, aforesaid. (Ross, *Sherley*, p. 128).

Pinçon was more enthusiastic:

And although this land between Astracan and Mosco is not inhabited in many parts, nevertheless the way is not so difficult as many people imagine; the river is most delightful by reason of its expanse ... and also because it is bordered almost continuously on both sides by fertile woods; and the said river is so full of fish that one has but to throw in a hook to catch a fish immediately. Every evening they tie up, and everyone lands in order to take a walk; and along the river one finds great heaps of wood, which have been thrown up by the river when in flood, and this wood serves for cooking and for warming oneself, and it is so dry that one needs but to put a light to it for it to flare up. Thus progressing and passing up the river every other day one notices small towns which have beautiful castles, but their only means of resistance against the Tartars are the wooden defences which surround them, such as we noticed in Astracan. Our Baïars (boyars) ... replenished our provisions from place to place, and our boats were unmoored in an instant without noise and without interference on the part of the poor who come to beg (ibid., p. 173).

Don Juan, the Persian, an intelligent observer in a world not very different from his own, gives a long and entertaining description of the journey (Le Strange, *Don Juan*, pp. 241–50) which may be contrasted with the laconic observations of his two English fellow travellers. After interesting remarks on the fisheries and the life of the Nogay Tartars and the practices of the Volga boatmen, he mentions Cherny Yar, Tsaritsyn and Samara. He writes genially of Kazan where 'they provided us with such abundant supplies, that the food we could not eat had to be thrown out of the windows and wasted'.

In this country none are poor, for the victuals are so cheap, that any that are hungry go out to find it in the highways. What they lack is good wine, and they have only one kind of drink, which is made from wheat or barley, and this is so strong that those who drink it are often drunk . . . The climate here is extremely cold, hence all go clothed in marten skins, which are to be had in abundance . They have no succulent fruits, only crab-apples . . . The people of Kazan are a fine race: the men are fair, tall and stout, and the women, as a rule, good-looking. They appear very well dressed in the marten furs of which the robes and hoods that they wear are made (cf. *Don Juan*, p. 244).

At Nizhni-Novgorod Don Juan found provisions very cheap, although clothes-stuffs were dear.

The people . . . are Christians, and subjects of the Duke of Moscovy; but they are of a lascivious habit, and the fame of the place lies in its bath-houses, where the men and the women are wont to bathe in company, promiscuously, with no clothes to cover their nakedness; hence their commerce is exceedingly free, more so indeed than in any other country would be tolerated or possible (ibid., p. 247).

In Vladimir, again, he remarked on the extreme beauty of the women although he found their mode of dress ugly and eccentric. The men were very tall and robust (ibid., p. 249).

On the Moscow–Caspian route, the chief places referred to in the itineraries of Zvenigorodski and Tatishchev were:

(a) *Kasimov* (ref. Chap. 10, p. 415, n. 1): originally Gorodets on the Oka, founded in 1152. In 1452 the town and adjoining lands were granted by Grand Duke Vasili II to Kasim, a fugitive prince from the Golden Horde. 'The foundation of this petty Khanate was no doubt a piece of wise policy on the part of the Grand Prince. He could thus play off his protégé against the Khans of Kazan, whose rising power was becoming a menace to Russia' (Howorth, Vol. II/i, p. 430). Vernadsky describes Gorodets/Kasimov as the main advance post against the encroachments of both the Kazan and Saray hordes. 'While Gorodets was an old Russian town, by the mid-fifteenth century few Russians were left there. The country around was populated mainly by the Meshcherians and the Mordvinians, both tribes of Finnish extraction.' The creation of the Tsardom of Kasimov had significant implications. 'It at once raised Moscow's prestige in the Tartar world and made it psychologically easier for an ever-increasing number of the outside Tartars to enter the Grand Duke's service, both individually and in groups' (Vernadsky, *MR*, pp. 331–2). Kasimov was an early and peculiar example of the Russian genius for creating an Eurasian synthesis out of the Russian Orthodox and Moslem Tartar worlds. For a detailed history, see the three volumes of V. Velyaminov-Zernov, *Issledovaniye o Kasimovskikh Tsaryakh i Tsarevichakh*, chasti IX, X, XI of *TVOIAO*, 1863–6. In 1604 Kasimov was ruled by Uras Muhammad, a Kirgiz Kazak khan; for details see Howorth, Vol. II/i, p. 436 – not by the Siberian Alp Arslan, son of Kuchum, as indicated in Brockhaus and Efron. Kasimov was deprived of its 'appanage' autonomy at the end of the seventeenth century.

(b) *Nizhni-Novgorod* (ref. Chap. 1, p. 98, n. 1): often called Nizhni for short. Founded in 1221, probably on the site of a Mordvinian settlement. Its magnificent site overlooking the confluence of the Oka and the Volga made it a strongpoint against the Mordvins, Bulghars and, later, against the Tartars. It became an important trading centre famous for its fairs. In

1559 Don Juan estimated its population at 8,000 householders (or 36,000 souls) but little credence is to be put on his exaggerated figures for the Volga towns – which, indeed, were often swollen during fair weeks. In 1636, Olearius (cols. 393–4) describes the town as not so large as Veliki Novgorod (which was then in decline). Many Germans and Hollanders lived there, and some Scots. It had a Protestant church which could accommodate five hundred worshippers. In 1621–2 the town had 1,300 houses with a permanent population of about 5,000 but Olearius described the suburbs as incomparably larger than the town itself: see his fine engraving in Olearius/W., Vol. 1, between pp. 391 and 393. For a brief description in English see Tikhomirov, *TAR*, pp. 442–3; cf. also Vernadsky, *RDMA*, *passim*.

(c) *Svyaẓhski* (Svyazhsk or Sviyazhsk) (ref. Chap. 9, p. 405, n. 2): 'Swyasko' on Jenkinson's map of 1562; 'Swiatsk' on Olearius's map of the course of the Volga. Built in 1551 by Ivan IV in the territory of the Khanate of Kazan, it served as an advance base in the final campaigns against the Khans. It was once a prosperous place but declined in the eighteenth century when most of the inhabitants moved into Kazan. Indicative of its former importance as a garrison town is the fact that 417 *streltsy* and 20 gunners were stationed there in 1565–8; at that time the town had 254 shops and a population of 300 Russian families. (Cf. *OI/PF/xv–xvii vv*, pp. 60, 669–73; notably pp. 670–1 for two miniatures reproduced from the Litsevoy Chronicle, showing construction of the town in 1551, and local tribes declaring allegiance. The miniatures show the town on the left bank of the Volga, as indicated on Olearius's map, and not on the right bank as given on Jenkinson's map and *EVT*, Vol. 1, p. 48, n. 1).

(d) *Kaẓan* (ref. Chap. 1, p. 98, n. 1): the capital of a Tartar Khanate set up about 1436 after the break-up of the Golden Horde; it finally fell to the Russians on 2 October 1552.

The conquered town retained its former appearance and its military importance under Russian rule for a long time. The town had ten gates and a citadel separated from the other quarters of the town by a ditch; the old wooden wall was replaced by one of stone in 1555. The town was then about 600 cubits (= a mile) in length and 500 cubits (= 1,500 yards) in breadth (cf. article by Barthold in *EI*, 1st ed.; and a longer account based on Turkish manuscript sources by R. R. Arat in *IA* – with map of Khanate). Jenkinson and other English merchants were frequenting Kazan from the 1550s onwards (Hakluyt, *PN*. Vols. II and III *passim*). In the seventeenth century, Kazan had a population of some 20,000. In the winter of 1715–16 John Bell of Antermony enjoyed a long halt there, enlivened by the society of Swedish officers who were living there in relative comfort six years after the battle of Poltava (Bell, *Travels* Vol. I, pp. 24–5). The importance of Kazan lay in its command of the caravan routes from central Asia converging towards 'the mesopotamia' formed by the valleys of the Kama, the middle Volga and the Oka. For views of Kazan, see Olearius, Vol. I, half folio plate at cols. 411–12; and Witsen, plate opposite p. 621; for a contemporary miniature of the entry of Ivan IV into Kazan see *OI/PF/xv–xvii vv.*, p. 365.

(e) The Portage (*R.* Perevolok) (ref. Chap. I, p. 98, n. 1): as the name implies, it was a site on the portage route, about forty miles long, linking the Volga with the easterly bulge of the Don. Along this route, in 1569, a Turkish expeditionary force directed against Astrakhan had started work with a view to building a canal – or at least a timbered track for the haulage of galleys – from the Don to the Volga (see Inalcik, pp. 52 ff; also Allen, *PTP*, pp. 27–8 and n. 67). On 1 July 1716, John Bell of Antermony passing by Kamoshinka, on the right bank of the Volga some distance above Tsaritsyn, encountered 'Captain Perry, an Englishman, with many workmen ... employed in cutting a canal between the Volga and the Don, which would have opened a passage to the Euxine Sea; but the ground being very hard, and rising in some places considerably above the level (*sic*), the enterprize was laid aside, though the distance was not above fifty verst' (Bell, *Travels*, Vol. I, pp. 34–5).[1]

(f) *Uvek* (ref. Chap. 1, p. 98, n. 1): 'Oueak' of Christopher Burroughs, *EVT*, Vol. II, p. 443, who says that it was called Sodom by the Russians for the evil reputation of its former inhabitants. 'Ouvesescaia' on Olearius' map. It lay on the right bank of the Volga some nine versts south of Saratov. Prosperous in the days of the Golden Horde, the place was ruined during the campaigns between Tokhtamysh and Tamerlane. It was a 'Carawool' (*karaul*) or fortified settlement of the Russians along the lower course of the Volga. For the further five 'Carawools' between Tsaritsyn and Astrakhan, see Burroughs, *EVT*, p. 444.

(g) *Astrakhan*: (R. sixteenth–century Astarakhan; *T.* Astirhan; Contarini, 1487, Citricano; Ibn Battuta, mid-fourteenth century, Hajj Tarkhan) (ref. Chap. 2, p. 107, n. 1).[2]

---

[1] Bell's anecdote about Perry is a variance with the article in *DNB* under 'Perry, John (1670–1737)' which states that Perry left Russia in 1712 owing to failure to recover arrears of salary from Peter the Great. He was working in London in 1715 and, in 1716, published *The State of Russia under the present Czar*. In 1710 Perry had been surveying the Don and, later, was planning a canal to link St Petersburg with the Volga. Bell's book came out in 1762, half a century later. He was then an old man living in Scotland and working from notes and journals of his early life. He may well have got his dates and encounters mixed; but he is a modest matter-of-fact writer, and there must be some basis for his story. As Bell only arrived in Russia in the autumn of 1714 he can hardly have met Perry there; on the other hand his account of the Englishman in charge of a labour force at Kamoshinka is quite circumstantial. Bell did not return to Britain until 1746, when Perry had been dead nine years, so it is not likely that he ever met Perry.

[2] For the origin of the form Hajji Tarkhan, see Gibb, *Ibn Battuta*, Vol. II, p. 496, n. 302. It is possible that the name is connected with the title of the commander of the Alayin (Alan or As) troops of the Khazar Khakhans, *Rās-torkhān*, *Ās-tarkhān*; for these forms see Minorsky, *HSD*,

Under Uzbek Khan, in the fourth decade of the fourteenth
century, Ibn Battuta found Astrakhan 'one of the finest of
cities, with great bazaars, built on the river Itil, which is one of
the great rivers of the world' (Gibb, *Ibn Battuta*, pp. 496–7).
After the breakup of the Golden Horde in the middle of the
fifteenth century, a Tartar dynasty of Nogay princes had ruled
in Astrakhan. Their khanate extended as far as the middle Volga
and the Orenburg steppe and, in the south-west, to the Kuma
river. Contarini, the Venetian envoy to Persia, got barbarous
treatment there and was only ransomed from slavery by the
intervention of the ambassador of Ivan III. By contrast with
Ibn Battuta, a century earlier, Contarini found Astrakhan a
poor place with a few brick houses surrounded by a brick wall.
It had, however, a substantial trade with Muscovy – which
seems to have passed over the steppe by caravan rather than
by boat along the river route (Contarini, *TVP*, pp. 151 ff.).

Old Astrakhan was on the right bank of the Volga, 75 miles
upstream from the Caspian (Contarini). After the conquest,
the Russians built a new town seven miles lower down, on the
left bank and commanding the main channels in the estuary.
Jenkinson, who was there in 1558, described it as 'an Island
upon a hillside, having a castle within the same' but it was, in
fact, rather a peninsula protected by channels running into the
main stream of the Volga (cf. plans and panorama of eighteenth-
century Astrakhan in Gmelin, Vol. II). Jenkinson noted that
the castle was

walled about with earth and timber, neither fair nor strong . . . The
towne is also walled about with earth; the buildings and houses
(except it be the captain's lodging, and certain other gentlemens')
most base and simple. The Island is most destitute and barren of
wood and pasture, and the ground will beare no corne; the aiere

p. 147, n. 1, also Artamonov, *Istoriya Khazar*, pp. 244, 246 *et passim*;
and for critical and learned notes, Dunlop, *The history of the Jewish
Khazars*, p. 180, nn. 43, 44.

is there much infected, by reason (as I suppose) of much fish, and specially Sturgion, by which only the inhabitants live, having great scarsitie of flesh and bread. They hang up their fish in their streets and houses to dry for their provision, which causeth much abundance of flies to increase there, as the like was never seen in any land, to their great plague.

Jenkinson speaks poorly of local trade and states that the region was full of multitudes of famine-stricken Nogays, many of whom were being sold into servitude (Hakluyt, *PN*, pp. 454 ff.).

Vernadsky has observed that 'from a geopolitical point of view, Ivan IV's dash down the Volga to Astrakhan was an important move since it cut the steppe zone into two sectors, each of which could be taken care of separately' (*MR*, p. 390). During the three decades which followed the Russian capture of Astrakhan, the policy of the Ottoman sultans and the Crimean Khan was directed to re-establishing the belt of Turkish states along the Volga and checking Russian expansion south round the shores of the Caspian. This was the explanation of the Don-Volga canal project and the Turkish-Crimean drive against Astrakhan in 1569, when Banister and Duckett of the Muscovy Company were held up there for some weeks (*EVT*, Vol. II, p. 424). The hold of the Moscow authorities on the Volga estuary remained doubtful for two decades, and convoys down the river were subject to attack by the Nogays or wild bands of Cossack outlaws. Nevertheless the position became more stable; in 1582 the Russians built a stone wall round the town; and in 1589, the year of Zvenigorodski's visit, the construction of a fortress was finished. The majority in the new city were Russians, but there grew up large Armenian and Tartar suburbs; many Persian and Indian merchants settled there, a few Georgians – and even Japanese (cf. Abel Pinçon in Ross, *Sherley*, p. 171). See articles by B. Spuler in *EI*, 2nd ed. and R. Rahmeti Arat in *IA*; also Z. V. Togan, *TT*, *passim*; for fine engravings of Astrakhan in seventeenth and

255

eighteenth centuries, Olearius/W., Vol. 1, between cols. 451 and 453, and Le Brun, Vol. 1, between pp. 92 and 93.

COMMENTARY 8

Shah Abbas and his Georgian connections (ref. Chap. 1, p. 95, n. 2; also Chap. 11, p. 442, n. 4)

'The new Kizilbash Shah', Abbas I, was sixteen years old when he was proclaimed in 1587.[1] He was a younger son of Shah Sultan Muhammad Khudabanda, who was said to have been the eldest son, but who was not the immediate successor of Shah Tahmasp I. As in the case of several of the Ottoman sultans, the maternity of both Muhammad Khudabanda and of Abbas remains obscure and rests on contradictory indications.

Shah Tahmasp had died on 14 May 1576 at the age of sixty-four, after a reign of fifty-three and a half years. Eleven of his sons are enumerated in the *Ahsanu't-Tawarikh* – of whom nine at least were alive at the time of his death.[2] The eldest, Muhammad Khudabanda, was about forty-five years of age but he was passed over for the succession because he suffered from partial

---

[1] R. M. Savory in *EI*, 2nd ed., gives the date of his birth as 21 January 1571. Cl. Huart, in *EI*, 1st ed., gives the erroneous date 1557 which is repeated in *IA*.

[2] Cited by E. G. Browne, *A literary history of Persia*, Vol. IV, p. 98. There is a condensed English edition of *A–T* by C. N. Seddon, published as Vol. LXIX of Gaekwad's Oriental Series, Baroda, 1934.

Hasan-i-Rumlu, the author of *A–T*, and a contemporary of Shah Tahmasp, gives a curious pen-portrait of that monarch:

In his youth his heart was inclined to writing and drawing. And later he would ride Egyptian asses, on which he put golden saddles, and coats of gold embroidery, so that 'Buqu'l-'ishq wrote that writers and painters, and Qazwinis, and asses, flourished without trouble. In middle age he would work in his office from morn till eve, and all work he did himself. Without his orders his officers could not pay a farthing to any man. And he would pare his nails one day, and spend the whole of another day in the baths. He thought all things unclean, and often would spit out what he was eating. And at banquets he would eat nothing. When he drank, he drank to excess. He would dissolve nearly five hundred tumans' worth of opium in water. Later he abandoned all luxuries; and, for twenty years, he did not ride . . . In his person he was tall with a long face, long arms, sallow complexion, and a white beard.

(Cited from Seddon's translation, pp. 208–9).

blindness (probably trachoma). According to H. L. Rabino di Borgomale, *Mazandaran and Astarabad*, p. 143, Muhammad Khudabanda's mother was a member of the family of the Marashi Sayyids of Mazandaran. On the other hand, Wakhusht states no less than three times that the mother of Khudabanda was the daughter of Otar Shalikashvili, a notable of Samtskhe (Brosset, *HG*, Vol. ii/i, p. 217 and n. 2; ibid., p. 35; and 'Suite des Annales', ibid., p. 361). Shalikashvili's daughter was the last favourite of Shah Tahmasp and she retained great influence at Kazvin even after his death; but she was only taken into his harim in 1548, and could hardly have been the mother of the middle-aged Khudabanda.[1]

Two younger brothers of Khudabanda were in competition for the succession after the death of Shah Tahmasp. The senior, Ismail, was about forty-three and had been imprisoned for years by his father in the castle of Qahqaha, to the north-east of Tabriz. He was preferred by the Afshar and some others of the powerful Kizilbash Khans of Azerbaijan and was known to

---

[1] *Muhammad Khuda-banda*. The last name is the equivalent of the Arabic Abd-Allah, servant of God. His character is described by Riza Kuli Khan in his Supplement to the *Rawdatu's-Safa*: 'He had some knowledge of all the current sciences, and was incomparable in understanding and judgment, virtue and discernment, bounty and generosity, and expression and eloquence ... In consequence of his weak eyesight he seldom gave public audience, and, while he tarried in the women's apartments, the Sayyida (his wife) gave effect to his commands, and, in order more effectively to control affairs, herself sealed the documents ... In short he was a king with the qualities of a religious mendicant (*dervish*), or a religious mendicant endowed with regal pomp' (cited from Browne, Vol. iv, pp. 102–3). His contemporary, Don Juan of Persia, comments that 'it was common knowledge that all matters of state and government were foreign and distasteful to him' (Le Strange's translation, p. 129).

Asafi, who was brought as a prisoner in chains before Khudabanda, was questioned and, at the last moment, reprieved from execution. But they took his sabre from him and gave it to Shah-oghlu – the young Abbas. This was in 1581 when the prince must have been ten years old. In Asafi's MS. a miniature, f. 153r., shows the Shah seated cross-legged in a small pavilion, with the young prince on a chair on his right.

favour a reversion to the Sunni creed (Le Strange, *Don Juan of Persia*, p. 132). This fact, and Don Juan's somewhat confused references (pp. 130 ff.) to his relations with his half-sister, the energetic and intriguing Pari-Khan-Khanum and her uncle 'Shamkhal Khan' (described by Don Juan as 'a Georgian noble')[1] seems to indicate that Ismail was the candidate of the 'Cherkess' or Daghestani faction in Kazvin.

The second claimant, Haydar Mirza, was only eighteen years of age (cf. *VP*, 'Narrative of Vincentio d'Alessandri', p. 214). He was, therefore, of a more likely age to have been the son of Tahmasp's last favourite, the Shalikashvili princess. The existence of Haydar is ignored by Wakhusht who, however, emphasizes the continuing influence of the Georgian dowager in Kazvin during the subsequent reign of Khudabanda. Von Hammer, following the Turkish historian Ali, indicates that Haydar was protected by two Georgian uncles, Ali and Sal (Zaal) (cf. also *A–T*, Vol. II, p. 202). Haydar had another brother, Bahram, and two half-brothers, Mustafa and Imam-Kuli, sons of Tahmasp by 'a Georgian slave' (von Hammer-Vol. VII, pp. 72–4).[2]

Whether or not the Shalikashvili princess was the actual mother of Haydar or of his two half-brothers, it would seem that he was the candidate against Ismail of the Georgian faction in the harim.

In the event, the youthful Haydar was proclaimed Shah in Kazvin.[3] But he lost heart and took refuge in the harim where he was stabbed to death by 'Shamkhal Khan with a number of those nobles who were partisans of Ismail'.[4] Ismail was released

---

[1] For Shamkhal Sultan Charkas, see Seddon, *A–T*, Vol. II, pp. 202 ff.

[2] Don Juan, says that Mustafa's mother was 'a Christian princess from Georgia'. This description probably applies to Otar Shalikashvili's daughter.

[3] Apart from the Georgian faction, he had the support of the powerful *oymak* of the Ustajlu Turkomans.

[4] *Don Juan*, p. 131; and cf. Seddon, *A–T*, Vol II, pp. 292–3. Shamkhal

from Qahqaha and proclaimed Shah in the principal mosque of Kazvin only nine days after the death of Tahmasp (Browne, Vol. IV, p. 98). He promptly put to death his numerous brothers, including Mustafa and Imam-Kuli, the young sons of Tahmasp by a Georgian mother (*Don Juan*, pp. 130–1). Of his brothers, the purblind Khudabanda alone escaped, and the latter's son Abbas Mirza, then only six years of age, was spared by 'a most wonderful chance' – until the sudden and sordid death of Ismail put an end to the slaughter of potential pretenders.

In default of other sons of Shah Tahmasp, Muhammad Khudabanda was now proclaimed Shah; his eldest son, Hamza Mirza, a young man of character and military skill became virtually regent, until his assassination by his own barber in 1587.[1]

The four sons of Khudabanda were all by the same mother – a lady of the Marashi Sayyids of Mazandaran – 'who seems to have resembled her sister-in-law Pari-Khan-Khanum in her masterful character as well as in her tragic fate, for she, together with her aged mother and many of her kinsfolk and countrymen, was murdered by some of the Qizil-bash nobles who objected to her autocratic methods and dominating influence over her irresolute and peace-loving husband, being of opinion that "No luck remains in that household where the hen crows like a cock" ' (Browne, Vol. IV, p. 102). The young Abbas's mistrust of the Kizilbash chieftains of the great Turkoman tribes and the favour which he showed in later life for the Caspian provinces, doubtless stemmed from the Mazandarani environment of his mother and grandmother. But the influence of the Georgian faction in the royal harim seems to have been

Khan was allied with the chieftains of the Afshar and Rumlu Turkomans and some of the Kurdish nobles.

[1] For a miniature of the young and handsome Hamza Mirza, receiving the surrender of Adil Khan Giray, in Shirvan in November 1587, see Asafi, f. 76r. For details of his assassination see *Don Juan*, pp. 203 ff.

equally pervasive. We know that soon after the death of Shah Ismail, in November 1577, Shah Tahmasp's Shalikashvili dowager procured the release of King Simon of Kartli, in prison in Shiraz, and sent him into Georgia to raise forces against the Turks (Allen, *HGP*, p. 156). It may be suspected that she had a hand, too, in the execution of the partisans of Shah Ismail, of the 'Cherkess faction': Pari-Khan-Khanum, whose head was displayed on a lance in Kazvin, 'all bloody and dishevelled', and Shamkhal Sultan Charkas – a vengeance for the slaughter of Haydar Mirza and the two princes, Mustafa and Imam-Kuli.[1] In 1579, a Georgian wife was found for Hamza Mirza – a daughter of Alexander II of Kakheti by Tinatin, daughter of Bardzim Amilakhori (cf. Brosset, *HG*, Vol. ii/i, Genealogical Trees, p. 634; also idem, *EC/BHP*, Vol. ii, Nos. 14–15, col. 269, n. 131).

An intelligent youth, Shah Abbas realized that he owed his life and his throne to the support of the Mazandarani and Georgian factions at the court in Kazvin. He resented the arrogance of the great Kizilbash chieftains, mistrusted their politics and disliked their tribal conservatism. In his youth he had suffered the same dangers and humiliations which had haunted the boyhood of Ivan IV, and he developed rather the same split personality: brilliant, vigorous and enterprising; but calculating and cynical. He could be witty and friendly but sometimes savagely cruel.[2] Like Peter the Great, he showed

[1] Cf. *Don Juan*, pp. 131, 135; and Browne, Vol. iv, pp. 98–9, 101. Also Seddon, *A–T*, Vol. ii, p. 295, n. 9. The second of Shah Tahmasp's daughters, Pari-khan-khanum was born in camp on the bank of a river, in the year 1548.

[2] Abel Pinçon has left the following description of Shah Abbas of the years 1598–9: 'He is about thirty years of age, small in stature but handsome and well-proportioned, his beard and hair are black. His complexion is rather dark like that of the Spaniards usually is: he has a strong and active mind and an extremely agile body, the result of training, and far more so than one might expect. He is very gracious to strangers, specially to Christians . . . But this prince of Persia treats in another way his own

great favour to foreigners, merchants, military adventurers such as the Sherleys, and even Roman Catholic missionaries. Like Peter, again, he had no scruple in deporting whole populations from one quarter of his dominions to another: Armenians were moved in great numbers to his new capital at Isfahan; and tens of thousands of peasants from Kakheti were transferred to the interior of Persia, notably to the Caspian provinces.[1]

In order to protect himself against the pressures of the Kizilbash amirs, the young Shah armed and trained as regular musketeers the Tats – his kinsmen, pure Persians from the Caspian provinces. At the same time he formed a regular cavalry corps of Georgians, sometimes forcibly and sometimes voluntarily converted to Islam and paid direct from the royal treasury. These were known as *ghulams* – personal slaves of the Shah who were trained in special schools on the lines of the contemporary Ottoman *devshirme*. Eventually men drawn from this corps filled 20% of the higher administrative posts. One of them, Allahverdi Khan, originally protected by Shah Tahmasp, was entrusted with the reorganization of the army

subjects, behaving towards them inhumanely and cruelly, cutting off their heads for the slightest offence, having them stoned, quartered, flayed alive and given alive to the dogs, or to the forty Anthropophagi and man-eaters that he always has by him.' George Manwaring observed that 'the King's disposition is noted by his apparel which he wears that day; for that day which he weareth black, he is commonly melancholy and civil; if he wear white or green, yellow or any other light colour, he is commonly merry; but when he weareth red, then all the court is afraid of him, for he will be sure to kill somebody that day: I have oft-times noted it' (cited from Ross, *Sherley*, pp. 158 ff., and 221). Father John Thaddeus, in 1624, says that the Shah wore red on festival days (*Chronicle of the Carmelites in Persia*, Vol. I, p. 285; see ibid., opp. p. 285 for the reproduction of a miniature in the British Museum by the Indian painter Bishndas, done in 1613 showing Abbas in a red *kaftan*, sewn with gold thread, and red boots, wearing a sabre in silver scabbard – very similar to one in my possession bearing the inscription 'I am from the armoury of Shah Abbas').

[1] After the Shah's Kakhetian campaigns of 1615–16, no less than 130,000 peasants were marched away into Persia.

on plans prepared by the English adventurer, Robert Sherley.

A new corps of 12,000 musketeers (*tufanji*), for the most part mounted, was recruited locally from the peasantry; the strength of the *ghulams* was raised to 10,000 by further recruitment from the Georgian converts; 3,000 more were selected as *mulaẓiman* or personal bodyguard; and a corps of artillery, comprising 12,000 men and 500 guns, was also recruited from the *ghulams*, cannon being cast under the supervision of Sherley. Abbas thus had a standing army of 37,000 men (Savory, *EI*, 2nd ed.).

At the time of Zvenigorodski's embassy, the Persian army and state was still in process of reorganization.

In the view of V. Minorsky 'the infiltration of Caucasians into Persia is a highly important phenomenon which profoundly modified the social basis of the ruling classes ... As time went on Persia became brimful of Caucasian elements'.[1] The personal preference of Shah Abbas for Georgian advisers and Georgian mercenaries was one aspect of the strong interest in Caucasian politics which marked his reign. His determination to dominate the politics of Kartli and Kakheti – traditional fields of Persian influence – was reinforced by his justifiable mistrust of Ottoman and Russian ambitions in the two kingdoms. The political dangers which he foresaw explain his brutal treatment of the young Kartlian King Luarsab II – strangled in prison near Shiraz in 1622 following an attempted Russian intervention on his behalf; the torture and execution of Queen Ketevan, mother of Taymuraz I of Kakheti, and the mutilation of her two grandsons, who were living ,in Shiraz as hostages (1624). Yet both Shah Abbas and his grandson and successor, Shah Safi, had Georgian wives and Georgian influences at the Persian court remained potent down through the seventeenth and eighteenth centuries. (Very comparable

---

[1] Minorsky, *TM*, pp. 18–19. Della Valle, writing about 1616, thought that they might even attempt to take over power in Persia in the event of the death of Abbas, *Voyage*, French ed., pp. 146 ff.

was the influence of Slavs in the Seraglio of the Ottoman sultans – notably during the ascendancy of Hürrem Sultan, the Russian wife of Sulaiman and mother of Selim II.)

Among the most eminent of the servants of Shah Tahmasp and of his grandson, Abbas, were Allahverdi Khan (Loverdi Khan of Tatishchev's text, Chap. 11, p. 442, n. 4) and his son Imam-Kuli Khan. Allahverdi Khan, with Tahmasp-Kuli Khan – both 'Georgian renegades to Islam' (cf. Ross, *Anthony Sherley*, pp. 19, 125) were among those in the entourage of Shah Abbas who, in 1599, supported the proposal of Sir Anthony Sherley that he should undertake an embassy to the courts of Europe on behalf of the Shah. Allahverdi was an able soldier and 'at the head of 12,000 Georgian troops, all of them renegades' had conquered Luristan for Shah Abbas (*Don Juan*, p. 217). Tahmasp-Kuli Khan was apparently Hanis, son of Melik Maren of Somkheti – a house of Armeno-Georgian stock (cf. Brosset, *HG*, Vol. ii/i, p. 423 and n. 1 – from whom descended the later Loris-Melikovs, meliks of Lori). Arakel of Tabriz, a contemporary Armenian historian, states that Tahmasp-Kuli belonged to a group of Georgians who were strongly anti-Turkish and pro-Persian: this would explain both his and Allahverdi's support for Sherley's project for a coalition against the Ottoman empire. In the spring of 1604, Tahmasp-Kuli was sent by Shah Abbas to Kartli to bring King Giorgi X to attend the siege of Erevan (Brosset, *HG*, Vol. ii/i. p. 463, citing Iskander Munshi).[1]

Writing in 1619 the well-informed gossip, Pietro della Valle (*Voyage*, French ed., 1745, Vol. iv, pp. 66–7), states that Allahverdi was a Christian of Armenian origin but from the country of the Georgians – perhaps, like Tahmasp-Kuli, from the mixed Armeno-Georgian border region of Somkheti. The fact that

---

[1] Cf. Pinçon printed in Ross, *Sherley*, p. 158: 'Stammas Culibeg, without whom the King could not live a single day'.

as a youth he had been sold as a slave for thirty sequins and had worked as an artisan indicates that he was not, like Tahmasp-Kuli, of noble origin. Having attracted the notice of Shah Tahmasp, he had become a royal *Kuli* and rose to the position of governor of Shiraz and, later, under Shah Abbas, 'Captain-General'. 'En éfet, il ne se trouvoit personne dans la Perse qui lui fût comparable, ni en valeur, ni en prudence; ni, ce qui est de plus important, qui fût plus heureux que lui dans tous les combats, et dans les guerres qu'il entreprenoit.'

The son of Allahverdi, Imam-Kuli Khan, 'Qui a pour mère une Dame Géorgienne et de qui toutes les femmes sont Géorgiennes' succeeded his father as governor of Shiraz. To him was entrusted the guardianship of Queen Ketevan of Kakheti and her two grandsons, sons of Taymuraz I, when they arrived in Shiraz as hostages in 1615 (ibid., pp. 68–9).

Friendly to the English and hostile to the Portuguese in the Gulf, Imam-Kuli, like many renegades, from time to time showed his hostility to Christians. Nevertheless in 1629 he allowed the widow of Sir Robert Sherley, the Circassian Teresa,[1] to leave the country after her persecution by Khusrau-mirza, governor of Kazvin, another Georgian renegade, natural son of David IX, who later became King of Kartli under the name of Rostom I (*Chronicle of the Carmelites in Persia*, Vol. 1, pp. 291–3). Imam-Kuli was virtually regent of Persia, during the early years of the reign of Abbas's grandson, Shah Safi, but became suspect of overweening ambitions and was beheaded with three of his sons in 1633 (ibid., pp. 312–13).

For further details of Imam-Kuli Khan and of his brother, Da'ud Khan, see the brilliant and penetrating study by

[1] There is a portrait of Teresa, Lady Sherley, by Sir Anthony Van Dyck, in the possession of Lord Egremont, reproduced in *Illustrated London News*, 4 June 1955.

Z. Avalishvili, 'T'eimuraz I and his poem "The Martyrdom of Queen K'et'evan"' in *Georgica*, Nos. 4 and 5, pp. 17–42. Avalishvili has established that the family name ·of Allahverdi Khan and his two sons was Undiladze and he reproduces a drawing of David Undiladze (Da'ud Khan), done by Castelli 'probably about 1633'.

When, in 1624, Shah Abbas, infuriated by the alliance which Taymuraz had sought with the Turks, ordered the forcible conversion to Islam of Queen Ketevan, Imam-Kuli sought to persuade her to conform and, later, to delay the cruel vengeance of the Shah; but finally as the Khanlar-Khan of Shiraz he became the authority for her torture and death (see further Chap. 9, p. 401, n. 2). The final ruin of the Undiladze family was encompassed by Imam-Kuli's rival for Shah Safi's favour, Khusrau-mirza; the occasion was a revolt in Georgia concerted between Taymuraz I and Da'ud Khan, then Begler-Beg of Genzha.

COMMENTARY 9

Derbent and Baku (ref. Chap. 1, p. 96 n. 1)

Derbent was a very ancient site which barred the north-south route along the foreshore of the Caspian. Successively held and fortified by the Sasanians, the Arab Caliphs and the Mongol Ilkhans of Persia, it had acquired by the end of the fifteenth century a Turkish rather than a Persian character. On the main trade route, both by land and sea, from the Volga estuary to the southern shores of the Caspian, Derbent was, with Tarku, the centre of attraction for the tribes of Daghestan and the inhabitants spoke 'Circassian and Turkish'. During the sixteenth century Derbent was under Safavid control and the local sultan was subject to the Khan of Shirvan. In 1578, during the Ottoman invasion of the Safavid dominion in eastern Caucasia, the town was taken by Özdemiroghlu Osman Pasha and remained in Ottoman hands until 1606 when it was restored to Shah Abbas. The celebrated walls of Derbent formed a parallelo-gram between the mountains and the Caspian shore; according to Katib Chelebi in his *Cihan-Numa* (seventeenth century), they were 10,500 ells long and 550 broad; protected by seventy towers they were as high as those of Istanbul (cf. Barthold in *EI*, 1st ed.).

Originally a dependency of the Shirvanshahs, Baku, at the end of the sixteenth century, was rising in importance at the expense of Derbent (cf. Asafi's glowing description, f. 119 v.). The town fell to Osman Pasha and, like Derbent, remained in Ottoman hands until 1606. Christopher Burrough and other agents of the Company of English Merchants were in Baku and Derbent in 1580, and were well received by the Ottoman officials (*EVT*, Vol. II, pp. 450 ff.). The best near-contempo-rary description of Derbent and Baku is by the Turkish traveller Evliya Çelebi (mid-seventeenth century: see von Hammer's English version, 1834, Vol. II, pp. 162 ff.). For views of Derbent between seventeenth and early twentieth century, see Kosubski, *IGD*. The sixteenth-century Turkish version of *Derbend-Name* based on an earlier work, was edited by Mirza Kazem-Beg in English, SPB, 1851; a revision with valuable commentary by V. Minorsky is in *HSD*; see also his brilliant reconstruction of the mediaeval topography of Derbent, pp. 85–91.

COMMENTARY 10

Furs, fish teeth and cuirasses (ref. Chap. 1, p. 98, n. 2)

Furs. According to M. V. Fekhner, *TRG*, p. 61, the price of furs (per pelt) on the Moscow market in the sixteenth century ranged as follows: Sable – 10 altyns/7.5 rubles; black fox – 8–10 rubles; marten – 6 altyns 4 dengi/11 altyns; arctic fox – 5 altyns; ermine – 1 altyn; squirrel – $\frac{1}{2}$ denga. It is thus clear that there were wide variations in price, according to quality and supply. Sables were usually sold in 'forties', except for the best pelts which were priced in pairs or singly. (1 altyn = 3 kopeks or 0·03 ruble; 2 dengi = 1 kopek.) Spasski, *RMS*, pp. 54–8, states that the value of the Russian ruble in relation to bullion remained unchanged between 1534 and 1610: 3 rubles worth of coin weighing 1 grivenka (approx. 200 grams) of silver; the standard coin of the realm was the kopek, a silver piece weighing about 0·68 grams. But Alexander Eck, *MAR*, p. 361, affirms that the purchasing power of the ruble dropped considerably during the second half of the sixteenth century; the real value of silver money declined by three times after 1550 although the weight remained the same. The depreciation began in Western Europe – because of the import of vast quantities of bullion from America to Spain. The repercussion in Russia demonstrates that the commercial links between Muscovy and Western Europe were already rather close. However, the contemporary crisis in agriculture in Russia, which raised the price of wheat, contributed also to the decline in the value of money.

Eck, *MAR*, p. 361, note, gives the comparative value of the ruble in European currencies at the end of the sixteenth century; the English valued it at 16s. 8d., or 1¼ rubles to the guinea. For derivation of several Russian monetary terms, see Brosset, *EC/BHP*, Vol. II, Nos. 14–15, pp. 222, n. 29. Baddeley, *RMC*, II, opposite p. 194, gives a reproduction from a copy of the rare print by Michael Peterle of Prague, representing ambassadors from Tsar Ivan IV to Emperor Maximilian II, in 1576, carrying their letters of credence and the royal gift, chiefly sables, which were presented in 'forties' and 'pairs' (ibid., Vol. I, p. cclxvi).

Fish teeth were probably walrus tusks. Walrus were hunted since Palaeolithic times in Arctic waters. Their curved tusks may still be found among the Eskimos of the Bering Strait, long and sharp as swords. In the Middle Ages they were valued both as material for carving and for their magical properties. In 1675 Spathary, the Russian envoy to the Chinese court, had to send to Yakutsk fort for walrus tusks which 'are in great esteme with the Bogdikhan, if only they are of large size; and those supplied to me in Moscow were particularly small' (Baddeley, *RMC*, Vol. ii, p. 308). These big tusks came from the Okhotsk ('hunting') Sea where 'the Russians trade in walrus ivory' (ibid, p. 239). The tusks brought by Zvenigorodski to Kakheti can have come from Vaygach in the Kara Sea or from the Gulf of Ob.

A cuirass (R. pansyr, pantsyr, cf. *Ger.* Panzer) and helmet (R. Shlem cf. *Ger.* Helm): Fine specimens of sixteenth-century Russian armour, and of Persian (notably from Azerbaijan) and Turkish pieces received as gifts, are preserved in the Moscow Kremlin (see numerous plates in *GOPMK*). Armour and weapons figure often in the lists of gifts sent by the Tsars to the rulers of Persia, the Crimea, the central Asian khanates and the Nogay Horde. Their free sale in the open market was banned and foreigners visiting Russia had to procure a special permit from the Crown before they could buy and export weapons; even then quantities were strictly limited. Diplomatic documents of the period contain only one reference to permission being granted to Persian merchants to export 120 cuirasses, the usual quantities being 10–50, Fekhner, *TRG*, p. 68. On the whole the export of Russian armour and weapons to the east was of political rather than economic significance. Z. V. Togan (*TT*, pp. 117–18) attributes the failure of the rulers in central Asia to modernize their armed forces to the difficulty in procuring firearms either through Russia or Persia. During the same period the Russians were receiving arms and technicians from England (despite Polish protests) and the Persians from England and Portugal. The English, on the other hand, became seriously short of gunpowder during the wars with Spain and were dependent on precarious supplies of saltpetre from Morocco (Bovill, *GTM*, pp. 136, 185; Bovill, *BA*, Index under 'saltpetre' for various refs.).

COMMENTARY II

Murat Giray (ref. Chap. 1, p. 103, n. 1)

Murat Giray (Kireyev) was a son of Mehmet II Giray, Khan of the Crimea, 1577–88, to whom he was *nur-al-din* (second heir apparent). He married a daughter of the Shevkal (see above, text, p. 156). Together with his brothers, Saadet and Safa, Murat fled from the Crimea after their defeat at the hands of their uncle Islam who had killed Mehmet and usurped the throne. Murat entered the Tsar's service and was allowed to settle in Astrakhan. In negotiations with the Austrian envoys, the Russians stated that Murat had helped to secure the allegiance of the Nogay and Tartar hordes between the Don and the Volga and beyond the Volga. It was claimed that he was preparing to march on the Crimea at the head of 200,000 Tartars and 30,000 Russians to expel the Sultan's man Islam and to become Khan with the Tsar's blessing. In fact Murat failed the Russians while his pretensions and his way of living irritated them. In 1591 he died at Astrakhan – of poison administered on the orders of either the Tsar or Islam Khan. (For Crimean affairs see the article 'Giray' by Barthold in *EI*, 1st ed.; and fuller treatment by Halil Inalcik in *IA*; also *idem*, 'The origin of the Ottoman-Russian rivalry' in *BTTK*, *Sayi* 46. The long article 'Kirim' by Mirza Bala in *IA* should also be consulted; and Howorth, *HM*, Vol. II, pp. 2, 515, 521, 525, 527.)

See also von Hammer-Purgstall, *GCK*, pp. 58 ff. for the creation by Mehmet Giray, Murat's father, of the title *nur-al-din*, as 'zweiten Nachfolger' to the *kalga* or heir to the throne.

For a sarcastic couplet on the sons of Mehmet Giray, see I. H. Danişmend, *IOTK*, *Cilt* III, p. 78).

COMMENTARY 12

The princely families of Kabarda (ref. Chap. 1, p. 88, n. 2, and Chap. 2, p. 108, n. 4 and p. 115, n. 1)

The Kabardans appeared in the valley of the Kuban towards the end of the fifteenth century. They came from the Crimea where elements of Circassian toponymy recall their former presence: the plain of Kobarte in the upper valley of the river Belbek; Cherkess-tus; Cherkess-kermen (Pallas, *TSP*, Vol. 1, p. 392). They established a fortified base at Shantgir on a peninsula formed by the southern bank of the main channel of the Kuban and the two streams Nef and Pfif – the remains of which were to be seen in the time of Pallas (ibid., Vol. 1, pp. 388–9). From there they moved along the valley of the Kuban and established an ascendancy over the mixed population inhabiting the upper valleys of the Kuban and its feeder, the Teberda, and they spread eastward up the left bank feeders of the Terek. All this country came to be known as Great Kabarda. To the east of the Terek, as far as the Sunzha, was Little Kabarda. In the north, in the triangle formed by the upper streams of the Kuma, in Besh-tau (Pyatigorsk) – 'the five mountains' – they found superb grazing grounds for horse-breeding and a strategic centre which commanded the approaches along the Kuban to Taman and the Azov Sea; across the Nogay steppe to the Caspian and Astrakhan; to the lower Terek and Daghestan; and to the upper Terek and the passes into Georgia. (See Introduction, p. 24.)

The language of the Kabardans was a dialect of Circassian which, owing to their social ascendancy in northern Caucasia, became the fashionable pattern of a speech which had no written literature. In their relationship to the rest of the population,

Pallas has compared them to the Livonian Knights (Vol. 1, p. 391). They certainly differed from the mixed population of Circassians (Adighe), Alans (As), Bulghars (Balkars) and Tartars whom they mastered in the Kuban steppes and the northern foothills of the Caucasus. Pallas (Vol. 1, p. 409) states that 'their Princes and Usdens speak a peculiar dialect, which is kept secret from the common people, and used chiefly in their predatory expeditions'. Reineggs/W., Vol. 1, p. 275, has preserved a few words of this 'secret or court language which is called *Sikoswschir*'.

Pallas also contrasts the Kabardans with the earlier Cherkess population of the left bank of the Kuban whom they either enserfed or drove up into the higher valleys of the Caucasus. These Abassins or Abaza, calling themselves *Apsu'a* (pl. *Apsne*), display a peculiar national character: their narrow faces, their laterally compressed heads, and their prominent noses, are as characteristic as 'the dark brown hair which is almost general among them' (Vol. 1, p. 90). The Kabardans, especially the upper classes, were 'of tall stature, thin form and Herculean structure'. Some bore traces that their mothers were of Nogay descent. A stout build, certainly in later life, was admired.[1] In the nineteenth century, Hahn remarks on the black hair and dark eyes of the Kabardans and adds that fair-haired children are seldom seen. He often saw reddish beards with black hair. (In the eighteenth century, according to Reineggs, the Kabardans wore their heads and beards shaven; they only suffered the moustaches to grow long and paid particular attention to

[1] Cf. characterization of individuals in Genealogical Lists of the Kabardan princes edited by Belokurov, *Snosheniya*, pp. 1–8; and plates in Pallas, *TSP*, Vol. 1, nos. 19 and 20. Also Ibn Iyas's eulogy of the Circasian Mamluk Sultan Kansuh el-Ghori: 'tall, bulky, big-bellied, fair-complexioned, round-faced, sleek-eyed and loud-voiced, with a circular beard scarcely showing any white hair in it' – cited from Lt.-Col. Salmon's translation, *An account of the Ottoman conquest of Egypt*, Oriental Translation Fund, New Series, No. xxv, 1921, p. 58.

them.) Hahn found the women often very beautiful 'with fine features and fiery dark eyes'.[1]

According to Pallas, the Kabardans believed themselves to be descended from the Arab armies sent to the Caucasus by the Caliphs in the early centuries after the Hijra; others traced descent from the Mamluks of Egypt. Claims to Arab ancestry were not uncommon among Caucasian (e.g. the Sharvashidzes of Abkhazeti) and Kurdish princes; such ancestry gave a certain *chic* to a ruling family – at least nominally Moslem. But a connection with the Mamluks is less unlikely and is, indeed, apparent. The progenitor of the different branches of the Kabardan princes was said to have been a certain Inal (in Arabic, Aynal). Shora Bekmurza Nogmov, the first historian of the Circassians in the mid-nineteenth century, indicates the death of Inal about the year 1427.[2] Temryuk (*C.* Kemirgoko), Prince of Great Kabarda, the contemporary and father-in-law of Tsar Ivan IV, was descended from him in the fifth generation (Belokurov, *Snosheniya*, Genealogical Lists, pp. 1–8). The biographer of the Russian Chancellor Prince Aleksey Mikhaylovich Cherkasski (1680–1742), a grandson of the Kabardan Prince Yakov Kudenetovich, son of Kudenet Kanbulatovich, a nephew of Temryuk, identifies his subject's ancestor Inal as 'former sultan of Egypt'. The Mamluk sultan Inal (Aynal) was living 1379–1460 and died in Cairo at the age of eighty-one after a reign of seven years; his son, Ahmad, was only sultan for four months and later lived in retirement in Alexandria.[3]

Sultan Inal was certainly a Circassian and flourished at the beginning of the period of Circassian ascendancy in the Mamluk corps in Cairo. The name Inal seems to have been of Turkish

[1] Hahn C. (= Gan), *Kaukasische Reise und Studien*, Leipzig, 1896, p. 17.
[2] Nogmov, *Istoriya Adykheyskago naroda*, Tiflis, 1861, pp. 71–2.
[3] Article by N. Soberheim, 'Inal' in *EI*, 1st ed.; also cf. Sir William Muir, *The Mameluke or slave dynasty of Egypt*, 1896, pp. 163, ff.

derivation and originally an honorific.[1] It was not uncommon among the Mamluks in Egypt in the fifteenth and sixteenth centuries. There was, for instance, an Inal the squint-eyed, Deputy for Safad. Names indicating tribal origin, such as Kurt, Allan, Cherkess, were also frequent. Among the near contemporaries of Sultan Inal were two Jani Beks, recruited perhaps from the small Zhane (Jani) tribe who, in the late fifteenth century were neighbours of the Kabardans on the lower Kuban and, in the mid-sixteenth century, their rivals for the favours of the Russian tsars.[2] The Circassians had risen at the expense of the Kipchak Turks; and Sultan Barkuk (1336–1399), himself a Circassian born in the Crimea, had brought about the final ascendancy of his race in Cairo by the systematic purchase of increasing numbers of Circassian slaves for training in the Mamluk corps and by drastically cutting purchases from other nations.[3]

[1] A. N. Genko in 'Iz kulturnogo proshlogo Ingushey', *ZKV*, Vol. v, 1930, pp. 690–1, n. 7, has observed that the name *Inal* is of Turkish origin but its derivation remains obscure. He cites Radloff, *Uigurische Sprachdenkmaler*, Leningrad, 1928, pp. 28, 221, and dictionary, for 'the name of a grade (*dolzhnost*), title, also used as a proper name'. At a much earlier date the name or title was current among the Oghuz, cf. Canard, 'La relation du voyage d'Ibn Fôdlan chez les Bulgares de la Volga' *Extrait des Ann. de l'Institut d'Etudes Orientales, Fac. des Lettres de l'Univ. d'Alger*, n.d. but after 1956, pp. 65, n. 93; 83, n. 125; 77, n. 138; where there is the combination *yinal tekin* (for *tekin*, see below, p. 279, n. 1) with the sense *wali-'l-'ahd*; and p. 79 where it is doubled with *tarkhan* in the sense of '*chefs militaires*'.

[2] Janbulat was the name of a family, Druze in religion and Kurdish in origin. It can mean 'soul of steel' in Turkish, but the Mamluk Janbulat al-Nasiri, governor first of Aleppo and then of Damascus in 1497–9, sultan of Egypt for six months under the name of al-Malik al-Ashraf al-Nasiri, seems to have had no connection with this family; cf. article by P. Rondot under 'Djānbūlat' in *EI*, 2nd ed. Since one of the most eminent families in Kabarda in the eighteenth century were the Jambulats, a Circassian connection may be detected here.

[3] See article by Sobernheim under 'Barkuk' in *EI*, 1st ed; also David Ayalon, 'The Circassians in the Mamluk Kingdom', in *Journal of the American Oriental Society* (*JAOS*), Vol. 69, No. 3, pp. 135–47, stating

After the capture of Constantinople in 1453, the Ottoman sultans seem to have been determined to break the long connection which had existed between the Golden Horde and the Circassians with the Mamluk kingdom in Egypt. Ibn Iyas complained that Ibn Othman (Selim I) displayed open hostility to Sultan Kansuh el-Ghori 'by preventing both the merchants and slave-dealers from bringing Memlooks into Egypt, or furs or sables, squirrels and foxes', adding 'we have no more woollen cloths; oh, the years we have waited for wool – but no merchant brings any' (Salmon, p. 65). Selim, himself, showed violent animus against the Circassian régime in Egypt: 'if you do not obey us, then I will enter Egypt, and kill all the Circassians there, ripping open those with child and destroying the unborn' (ibid., p. 92.) When the Ottomans entered Cairo in May 1517 there was a general slaughter of the Circassian Mamluks which seems to have been supported by the Arab, Moroccan and Greek elements (ibid., 110 ff.). But the Circassian Mamluks continued their resistance in upper Egypt and a compromise eventually emerged which resulted in a symbiosis of Ottoman and Mamluk interests.[1]

that: 'One of the most characteristic features of the Circassian period is the practice of the sultans and amirs to bring over their relatives from their country of origin in numbers unprecedented in the earlier period ... Indeed it would be no exaggeration to call the second half of the Circassian period the period of rule by brothers-in-law and relatives. It is, for instance, related that Aynal (Inal) sat securely on the throne because all the amirs were his brothers-in-law,' citing Ibn Iyas, Vol. II, p. 264. For further details, see Ayalon, 'The Wafidiya in the Mamluk Kingdom' in *Islamic Culture*, Vol. xxv, Hyderabad, 1961, Part I, pp. 89–104.

[1] As P. M. Holt has rightly pointed out, the Circassian Mamluk, Özdemir Pasha, became the chief agent of Ottoman expansion along the Red Sea littoral during the reign of Selim's successor, Sulaiman, when the newly acquired provinces were administered as dependencies of the Cairo Beylicate: cf. article by Holt, 'The Beylicate in Ottoman Egypt', in *BSOAS*, xxiv/2, pp. 214 ff., particularly p. 317, n. 2; and for other refs., Allen, *PTP*, p. 46, n. 31. (According to Asafi, MS. f. 186 r., Osman, the equally distinguished son of Özdemir, when campaigning against the Russians on the Terek in 1583, was greeted by his (Kabardan) cousins).

Sultan Inal cannot be identified with the Inal who was the ancestor in the fifth generation of Temryuk and the founder of Kabardan power in the western Caucasus, since he never returned to Caucasia; but it is possible that kinsmen of his may have appeared in the Crimea after the deposition of his son Ahmad in 1461. Following the accession of the Greek Mamluk Khushkadam as sultan, Janim Bek, a powerful supporter of the late Sultan Inal, fled to the Ak-Koyunlu Turkomans. He was soon murdered, while the guest of the Ak-Koyunlu Sultan Uzun Hasan, who was concerned to remain on good terms with the new Mamluk ruler in Egypt: cf. the article 'Khushkadam' by N. Sobernheim in *EI*, 1st ed. But it is not unlikely that some of the kin and followers of Janim Bek survived.

Uzun Hasan had as wife Despoina Catherine, niece of David Comnenos, the last Greek emperor of Trebizond. David, in turn, was married to Maria, sister of Isaac Gabrades, the Greek ruler of the principality of Gothia in the Crimea.[1] The capital of the Gothian princes was at Mankup, called also Doros or Theodore (Vasiliev, *passim*), on the northern decline of the great coastal range of the Tauric Chersonese: here, in the Middle Ages, lived a very mixed population. 'In the course of time', wrote a thirteenth-century Byzantine historian, 'the people dwelling in the inland parts, I mean the Alans, Zikhi (Adighe), Goths, Russians, and other neighbouring peoples, mixed with them (the Nogay Tartars); they adopted their customs, assumed their tongue and clothes, and became their allies' (Vasiliev, p. 172, citing Pachymeres). A little later, the Arab historian, Abu'l Fida, describing the great castle of Kerker (now Chufut-kale=Jews' castle), says that the

---

[1] The princely family was of Trapezuntine origin: cf. A. A. Vasiliev, *The Goths in the Crimea*, Cambridge, Mass., 1936, pp. 153 ff. The name Gabrades might have been of Laz-Mingrelian origin.

inhabitants 'belong to the race called Ass' (Vasiliev, p. 166).[1] A near contemporary of Abu'l Fida, Theodore Bishop of the Alans (c. 1240), reports that the Alans were 'neither wanted nor voluntary (settlers); they served the city of Cherson (now Sevastopol) as a sort of wall and fortified enclosure'. They lived under very primitive conditions, 'scattered in the mountains, deserted places and caves, having neither cattle folds nor huts' (ibid., p. 167). The Gothic *Climata* and Cherson were both in the mid-thirteenth-century vassal possessions of Trebizond ... 'One thing is certain, that the Alans also occupied some portion of the territory of Gothia' (ibid., p. 168). Referring to the forms Dory-Doros-Doras, alternative names for Mankup, Vasiliev makes comparisons with Osetian *dor*, stone, and *duar*, gate (ibid., p. 57).

Shora Bekmurza Nogmov, in his interesting but confused account of early Circassian history, gathers a number of traditions which seem to have some basis in fact but which lack all chronological order. For instance, he gives in some detail the campaign in 1516 of 'Sultan Isgak' (Selim I of Turkey, whose name is confused apparently with that of the contemporary Sultan of Karaman – Ishak) against the Mamluks in Syria and Egypt and the death of the last Circassian sultan, 'Tumanai' (Nogmov, pp. 65 ff.). 'Khan Larun' in Nogmov's story is, perhaps, Tumanbay's predecessor, Sultan Kansuh el-Ghori.[2] As his name implies el-Ghori belonged to *al-Ghur*, the division of Mamluks recruited from Afghanistan.[3] This could explain Nogmov's reference to his 'Babylonian origin'. But Muir, p. 187, describes Kansuh as a Circassian and adds that *Kansuh*

---

[1] The name Kerker, like other toponyms in this region, noted by Pallas and Dubois de Montpéreux, is probably of Circassian origin: cf. classical *Kerketes*.

[2] For phonetic change in *Larun*: cf. *al-Larisa*=Arsiya (=Alania) (Minorsky, *HSD*, p. 147).

[3] Article under name by Sobernheim in *EI*, 1st ed.

(*Arab.* Kansowiah, *C.* Kansavuk), was a popular name at the time (ibid., p. 182).

Kansuh, following his purchase as a slave, turned out to be a brother of Sultan Kaitbey's wife Assilbai (ibid., p. 185). Kaitbey (*regnabat* 1468–95) was a Circassian; as a boy he had been purchased by Barsbey (*EI*, 1st ed.) and manumitted by Jakmak, both Circassian sultans in Cairo. Kansuh el-Ghori certainly moved from his youth in the highest circles of the Circassian clansmen in Cairo; indeed, it looks as though he may have been a Circassian attached to the Ghorid (Afghan) contingent, perhaps as a liaison or training officer. 'Tumanai', indicated by Nogmov as the successor of 'Khan Larun', and his comrade 'Arab Khan' are described by Nogmov as 'the closest kinsmen' of 'Larun' (Nogmov, p. 65). 'Tumanai' was killed by 'Sultan Isgak'. 'Arab Khan' took refuge with 'the Greek Emperor' who 'allowed him to settle with his followers on the river Kobarte, in Taurida, intending by this favour to set up a new bulwark for his empire by establishing on his frontier people known for their strength and outstanding valour' (Nogmov, p. 67).

It would seem that accounts of the crises of the deaths of the Circassian sultan Inal in 1460 and of 'Larun' (Kansuh el-Ghori) and 'Tumanai' (Tumanbay) in 1516 have been amalgamated and at the same time confused in Circassian tradition. 'Arab Khan' can have been a close kinsman of Sultan Inal, and, along with the historical personality, Janim Bek, he can have taken refuge with Uzun Hasan. Among the Circassians in the Crimea he may have been called 'Arab Khan', the Arab lord, from his Egyptian background.[1] Uzun Hasan, the several rulers of the Seljuk 'successor' states surviving in Anatolia, the Comnenian emperor of Trebizond, the prince of Gothia and

[1] Cf. *Urus-bey* = the Russian lord; *Abaza Pasha* = the Abaz Pasha; and *Misier-Munekhin* = 'Egyptian' (Misri) Munekhin (Vernadsky, *RDMA*, p. 90).

the Genoese in the Crimea, were all greatly concerned with the prospects of Ottoman aggression round the shores of the Black Sea following the conquest of Constantinople by Sultan Mehmet II in 1453. In the year after the death of Sultan Inal, Trebizond fell to an Ottoman army, 1461. Mankup, the Gothian capital in the Crimea, on the northern slopes of the Chatyr-dagh, in the region of the Kabarda (Kobarte) valley, survived until its capture by Ottoman troops under Gedik Ahmet Pasha in 1475. It is known that in the intervening years the Gothian princes and the Genoese in Caffa were seeking support and mercenaries wherever they could find them. Stephen the Great of Moldavia sent to Prince Isaac of Gothia 300 Sicilian soldiers, provided by the Hungarian king Mathias Corvinus, under a Hungarian noble (Vasiliev, pp. 206 ff.). It would seem that Mamluk fugitives from Egypt, passing through the lands of the Ak-Koyunlu and Trebizond, distinguished and experienced military men, would have been a welcome addition to the strength of the Mankup rulers – capable of training and leading the As and Cherkess elements who already formed part of the mixed population of Gothia.

After the fall of Mankup in 1475, the victors did not penetrate the countryside beyond the capital. With the fall of the Gothian principality and of the Genoese towns along the coast, the southern Crimea must have been in a state of anarchy. The migration of the surviving Mamluk leaders and their followers, with the local Cherkess and As levies, across the strait of Kerch would have been a natural move.[1]

Five generations (Nogmov, p. 67) intervene between 'Arab Khan' and a second Inal who appears as a historical personality in a war with the Georgians in the year 1532 or 1533. Dubois de Montpéreux, Vol. 1, p. 68, calls him Inal Teghenn. With this title 'Teghenn' may be compared 'Techiur', the style attributed

---

[1] Gärber (1728) states that Arabs and Turks called the Kabardans 'mountain Mamluks'. See Kosven, *IGED*, p. 67.

to the ruler of Mankup by the Kurdish historian Sa'd ed-din.[1] Georgian sources refer to 'the execrable Tsandia-Inal-Daphita'.[2] This form may perhaps be interpreted as Inal of Shantgir, *defterdar*. During the preceding two decades the Ottomans had been pursuing an aggressive policy against the Georgians in Samtskhe and Imereti while the Cherkesses had been raiding Guria and Mingrelia. At the same time the Ottomans were seriously interested in the Azov region and concerned themselves in the tribal politics of Circassia. It is possible that Inal may have received from them the honorific of *defterdar* (normally the title of a high official) – as later the Princes of Kabarda were named *vali* by the Turks.

If this (second) Tsandia-Inal-Daphita is identical with the Inal who is the common ancestor of the princely lines given in Belokurov's Lists, it must be admitted that four generations separate the famous victor over the Georgians who died in 1533, and whose tomb near the river Bzib was still known in the nineteenth century (Nogmov, p. 71) from Temryuk (*c.* 1550–70) who was the contemporary of Tsar Ivan IV. Therefore, we find nine generations, according to the genealogical indications of Nogmov and the Lists of Belokurov, within the course of a century. If 'Arab Khan' was the original link with the octogenarian Sultan Inal (d. 1460), it is likely that he was an elderly man when he reached the Crimea. His son, Abdan Khan, led the migration out of the Crimea about 1475. Abdan's son Kesa (the first of the line to bear a Cherkess name) is said by Nogmov, p. 67, to have been born during the sea journey to the Circassian coast (ibid., p. 67). Kesa was responsible for establishing the authority of the Kabardan immigrants

[1] See Vasiliev (p. 256 and n. 3), who interprets it as 'Tekur = Tekfur', ruler, prince. But cf. also Minorsky (*HA*, p. 288, n. 1) for *tekin*, a title given to the younger sons or other relatives of a khakhan among the Turks; and Atalay, *DLT*, under 'tegin' with same interpretation; and p. 273, n. 1 above.

[2] Brosset, *Chronique Géorgienne*, pp. 7–9.

over the Adighe (Cherkess) tribes already living between the Kuban and the Black Sea coast. Kesa was followed by a son, Ado, and a grandson, Khurophatlae,[1] neither of whom ruled long. The latter was the father of the historical Inal. One of Inal's sons was Unarmesa (Nogmov, p. 71); he is clearly the Inarmaz of Belokurov's genealogical lists and the grandfather of Temryuk. An interval of only thirty years between even a mature Temryuk and his great-grandfather Inal is scarcely acceptable and it is apparent that there is some confusion in the lists which may have arisen from a desire to fit the chiefs of various lines into a common pattern of descent from the second Inal, when in fact they may have had only a more dubious descent from the remoter Abdan Khan and the legendary Sultan Inal.[2]

Remarking on the genealogical fragments given by Pallas, Reineggs, Potocki and Klaproth, Dubois de Montpéreux (Vol. 1, p. 92, n. 2) observed that 'ces ... généalogies ne s'accordent point du tout. Que faire?' It seems that here is another case of 'the Companions of the Conqueror'. But there remains evidence for a migration of the Kabardans from the Crimea in the latter part of the fifteenth century; and the tradition of Mamluk descent may well derive from a connection with Mamluk elements coming from Egypt. These gave the Kabardans the concept of a military fraternity and some of the training techniques which enabled them to offer the stiff resistance recorded of the defenders of Mankup in 1475 and later to impose their hegemony over the tribes of north-western Caucasia.

Halil Inalcik has observed that, until the end of the first

[1] This name, otherwise unknown in Circassian history, has a suspicious resemblance to the Byzantine title *kuropalat* – which may have survived until the last quarter of the fifteenth century in Trebizond or Gothia.

[2] In this connection, Nogmov makes Beslen, the eponymous hero of the Beslenei Cherkesses, a son of the second Inal, although he does not figure in the Lists edited by Belokurov.

quarter of the sixteenth century, the Ottoman Porte looked on Moscow as an element in the balance of power in the north and considered Moscow as its natural ally in the politics against Lithuania-Poland (Inalcik, *O-RR*, pp. 54 ff.). In the middle decades of the century, however, circumstances changed and it became clear that a conflict was impending between the Ottoman and Muscovite states for hegemony over the vast territories into which the former empire of the Golden Horde had broken up (Kazan, Astrakhan, the Nogay steppe and the Crimea). The Circassian lands were important to the contending powers and the disparate tribes were attracted alternately to the Ottoman Sultan, the Khans of the Crimea and the Muscovite Tsar. As early as 1538, Cherkess troops (probably Kabardans, Smirnov, *Politika*, p. 24) took part in the civil wars of the Khans of Astrakhan; and in 1552 the last Khan Yagmurci was reinstated with the help of the Cherkesses (cf. Inalcik, p. 59, n. 48). In November of the same year the first Cherkess envoys visited Moscow. They spoke on behalf of the Beslenei tribe who were living in the strategically important region of 'the five mountains' (Besh-tau, Pyatigorsk). In 1553 the Russian envoy Shchepetev visited Besh-tau and returned to Moscow with Sibok Atsimgok of the Beslenei and other princes from the Zhane (Jani) Cherkesses of the lower Kuban (Namitok, *CR*, Vol. II, p. 21). (In earlier years Kansavuk (= Kansuh) Bey of the Zhane had accepted the *tuğ* and banner of the Sultan – Inalcik, p. 59.) In 1556 'the Pyatigorsk Cherkasses' took part in the Russian campaign against the Crimean Khan and captured the towns of Anapa and Temryuk on the Taman peninsula.

'Seeing the success of the Beslen and Zhane princes in Moscow, the Kabardan princes decided to follow suit', and in July 1557 sent an embassy to the Tsar, headed by Prince Kanklych Kanuko. Kanuko spoke on behalf of his cousin Temryuk. 'In this race for the friendship of the Muscovite

Tsar the winners were the Kabardan princes', and the marriage in 1561 of Ivan IV to Kuchenei (baptized as Maria), daughter of Temryuk, finally consolidated Russo-Kabardan relations. 'Henceforth the Tsar became interested in his father-in-law's situation alone and developed his relations with Kabarda on the basis of kinship' (Namitok, p. 22).

Such a turn of events could not help but influence the behaviour of the Beslen and Zhane princes, as the undisguised rivals of the Kabardan princes ... The relations between the Beslen and the Zhane princes and the Tsar became so bad that Sibok's sons (baptized as Alexei and Gavril) left the Tsar and went to the Lithuanian king. Sibok's brother had already been there with the intention of getting as far as the Crimea, which by that time was already allied with the Cherkess princes against Temryuk. (Namitok, ibid).

Enmity between the rival groups became acute in 1563 and 1566. Kasim Pasha *Sikki sani defterdari*, that is Defterdar of the Zhane Adighe (Cherkesses) was *sanjakbey* of Kefe (Caffa) and the inspirer and commander of the great Ottoman expedition against Astrakhan in 1569. One of the side results of this campaign proved fatal to the interests of Temryuk (cf. Allen, *PTP*, pp. 26 ff. and n. 65).

As the eldest son of Idar, whose father Inarmaz was the senior of the three grandsons of Inal (according to the genealogical lists) Temryuk was the most distinguished of the Kabardan princes. The marriage of his daughter to the Tsar brought him enhanced prestige and his kin access to all the favours of the Moscow court. But he was not lucky in the outcome. The Tsaritsa Maria died without issue in 1569. Temryuk himself was heavily defeated by the Crimean Khan and the Nogays in 1570 (*Ist. Kabardy*, p. 43). A year or two later he died. His sons Domanuk and Mamstryuk, who appear in the correspondence of Zvenigorodski, were later killed by their cousin, Kazy Mirza. A third son, Saltanuk, ennobled in Moscow as

Knyaz Mikhail Temryukovich Cherkasski (see *RBS* under name), for some years a favourite of the Tsar, was executed in 1571 (see Chap. 2, p. 108, n. 4). After the death of Temryuk, power in Kabarda passed to his brother Kanbulat.

The line of the Kabardan princes was continued in the numerous houses of Cherkasski, whose biographies occupy no less than forty-nine columns in the Russian Biographical Dictionary. A handsome race of bold and able men, they managed to survive and succeed in the turbulent politics of Russia over a period of more than two centuries, rising to high distinction in the service of the army and the state and making, often, brilliant marriages. Kanbulat's son, Boris Kanbulatovich (Khoroshay murza) was *voyvode* and *boyar* at the end of the sixteenth century and married the sister of Fedor Romanov; his son Ivan was first cousin to the first Romanov Tsar Mikhail. For the next half century both Tsar Mikhail and his successor Aleksey Mikhaylovich treated their Kabardan kin with confidence and favour. A grandson of Kanbulat, Yakov Kudenetovich was a particular favourite of Tsar Mikhail and later became a leading personality in the circle of the young Tsar Aleksey. His son, Mikhail Yakovliyevich, was *voyvode* of Tobolsk (a profitable if arduous post) in the last years of the seventeenth century. He married a Kurakina and was the father of Aleksey Mikhailovich Cherkasski, a distinguished figure in Petrine Russia and the first Chancellor of Empress Elizabeth Petrovna.

The direct line of Temryuk was continued through Mamstryuk (see Chap. 2, p. 108, n. 4) in Prince Dmitri Mamstryukovich. Although he was said to be illiterate, he was a particular favourite of Aleksey Mikhailovich and was best man at both his weddings.

From the line of Minbulat, uncle of Temryuk, through Mundaraki, came Kordanuk (Kazy Murza), the killer of Temryuk's two sons, Mamstryuk and Domanuk. Kazy's son

Vasili Kordanukovich, was already in the Russian service in 1582 and he fought with distinction against the Swedes. In later life, he seems to have been much engaged in Baltic affairs. In August 1599, he was present in Moscow at the state dinner for Crown Prince Gustav of Sweden; and in September 1602 he was attached to the suite of the Danish Prince John during his stay in Moscow. His support of the False Dmitri seems to have brought an end to his career.

The line of Zhelegot, another brother of Temryuk, remained active in the politics of northern Caucasia throughout the seventeenth century. Zhelegot's son, Kanklych, had a son Suncheley who was settled in Little Kabarda between the Terek and the Sunzha – hence his name 'Suncheley', 'of the Sunzha'. Suncheley had no less than seven sons of whom the third, Alkas, may be identical with the Alkas in the reports of the Zvenogorodski mission. In the crisis of 1603 Suncheley went to Moscow accompanied by some of his younger sons. Of these Mutsal had a son, Kaspulat Mutsalovich, who, during the later decades of the seventeenth century, took an important part in the administration of the northern Caucasus. Suncheley's youngest son, Suncheley (Prince Grigori Suncheleyevich), was serving in Russia in 1645. He married Praskovya Odoyevskaya, a grand-daughter of his patron, Prince Fedor Sheremetev. In 1655 he became first 'Voyevode of the Mountain Cherkasses and Astrakhan Tartars' (cf. p. 572). His son Daniel married the sister of Field-Marshall Boris Sheremetev and his daughter Elena became the wife of Prince Yuri Trubetskoy.

The Solokh who appears in the Zvenigorodski reports was descended in the fourth generation from Yankhot or Yankhont, a great-uncle of Temryuk. In the last decade of the sixteenth century he came to the fore among the Kabardan princes through the force of his personality but he failed to impose himself as Prince of Kabarda in 1597. Nevertheless in the middle of the eighteenth century, when the brilliant Cherkasskys were long since Russianized, princely power in Kabarda lay with the descendants of Yankhot's line – the Antokzhyukos (Atazhukins), Yanbulats (Iambulats) and Misosts.

COMMENTARY 13

The term kholopy (ref. Chap. 2, p. 105, n. 1)

'*Kholopy tvoi Ondreyets s tovarishchi*': It was customary for Russians, when addressing the Tsar, to use the pejorative diminutive of their Christian name without the addition of the patronymic. Kotoshikhin, p. 127, reports that boyars, senior officials and ambassadors, in their letters to the Tsar, described themselves as his 'bondsmen' (*kholopy*) and did not mention their own ranks and titles. Townspeople and peasants signed themselves 'your slaves and orphans'. The latter formula, with the writer's Christian name only, was also used by women of all ranks; but a woman who, in her letter to the Tsar, had occasion to refer to her father or husband, did so by his full name and title.

For etymology of *kholop* and its forms and meanings in various Slavonic languages see Vasmer, *REW*, Vol. III, p. 357. In the view of the writer, the word may derive from a pre-IE linguistic stratum; cf. Circassian *thlep(ke)*, 'Rasse, Volkstamme' (Karst, *OM*, p. 403). *Tleps* or *Lepch* was the god of fire of the Circassians (Namitok, *OC*, p. 27), comparable and, perhaps, etymologically identical with Hephaistos, the smiths' god of the Pelasgo-Greek world. The form *Lepch* may also be compared with Leipoxais, the eldest of the three eponymous hero brothers of the Pontic Scyths (Herodotus Book IV, 5, 6). The word *kholop* may also be remotely connected with the Khalybes of the Greek geographers. These people, according to one tradition were migrants from Scythia into Anatolia. In this connection see article by X. de Planhol, 'Geographica

Pontica, I–II' in *JA*, tome CCLI, 1963, fasc. 3–4, pp. 304–5 and nn. 101–7. Further for pre-IE (? proto-Circassian) elements in South Russia, see Allen, 'Ex Ponto V' in *BK*, No. 34/35, p. 86 and n. 19.

COMMENTARY 14

Shikh murza of the Okok and 'the little mountain lands' (ref. Chap. 2, p. 106, n. 1 and p .117, n. 4)

Shikh murza (properly *P.* Shaikh mirza) of the Okok and his nephew Batay (*R.* Baitev) had attached themselves to the Kakhian mission which reached Moscow in the autumn of 1587 and had returned with the embassy of Rodion Birkin and Petr Pivov which arrived on the Terek in the following spring (cf. Introduction, Section 10). In Birkin's report the Okok are grouped with 'the little mountain lands' (*gorskiye zemlitsy*), together with Kumuki, Minkizy, Indili and Shibuti (cf. Belokurov, *Snosheniya*, p. 33). From Birkin's itinerary, it is clear that these 'little mountain lands' lay between Sunzha fort and the *kabak* of the Kabardan prince Alkas in the region of the northern approach to the Daryal pass. The name covered the foothills between the Terek flats and the higher mountains of Avaria. It was a rich, well watered, 'black earth' country (cf. *SSTO*, Vol. I, (1878), p. 32).

The *Okok* may be identified with the Akko sub-tribe of the Ingush Chechens (Steder, *Tagebuch*, p. 44, *Agi*: and cf. *Ist. Kab.*, p. 46). Shikh murza was an influential man in his day and a good friend of the Russians, as witness the rich gifts brought for him by Zvenigorodski (cf. also, Belokurov, *Snosheniya*, pp. 63, 64, 558). He claimed to be able to put five hundred men into the field. His *kabak* may be located on the Gekhi affluent of the Sunzha (cf. Genko, p. 684). From this district a passage across the main chain might be made up the difficult valley of the Argun (cf Baddeley, *RFC*, Vol. I, pp. 107,

164 and Map II, where the author indicates the villages of Upper and Lower Kii on the northern flank of the Basti-lam watershed of the Tchanti Argun). Steder, who stayed on the Fortanga among the Karabulaks in 1781, noted a settlement of *Akkinyurtsi* on the Sunzha, (*Tagebuch*, p. 27). Genko, p. 686, derives the name from Ingush *aǧǧij*, Chechen *äqqoij*, and observes that Ingush *aexkiyurt* means precisely 'the village of the ravine'. With this may be compared the ancient Georgian name for the Caucasus east of the Daryal gorge, *Dʒurʒuk-eti*, which, in the view of Genko, has still, in Ossetic, the sense of 'land of ravines'.

The Okok had their *sloboda* ('quarter' of free men) only ½ verst from Terek-town. Nevertheless, in 1721, the 'free Okok' surviving in Terki, under their chief Batyr murza, only amounted to sixteen men. They had been reduced by the attacks of the Kumukhs and hostile Chechens and, in 1691, they had been ravaged by the plague (cf. Butkov, *MNIK*, Vol. I, pp. 15, 77, 525). Together with the Michkizi, they are mentioned in the Book of the Great Map (cf. *IZ*, No. 23 (1947), p. 298, n. 20). Güldenstädt records an Okok quarter in Kizlar at the end of the eighteenth century. Here they seem to have become submerged with Kumukhs and Nogays and were living apart from the Cherkess retainers of Prince Bekovich Cherkasski. For many details of Okok tribal affairs at the beginning of the seventeenth century see Belokurov, *Snosheniya*, pp. 524–6, 553–61.

The *Minkiʒy, Michkiʒi*, may be identified with the canton of Michik (cf. Felitsyn's Map 2, 64N, 43E). According to Bronevski (Vol. II, p. 153), *Buturul Myʒkigs* ('the Myzkig people') is the Andi name for the Ingush; while the Tartars and Cherkesses apply the name to all Chechens; (cf. also Minorsky, 'Caucasica III' in *BSOAS*, Vol. XIV/2 (1952), p. 235). For the comparatively recent origin of the names 'Chechen' and 'Ingush' – both adopted by the Russians from place-names – see the article by Allen, 'The Volga-Terek Route in Russo-Caucasian Relations' in *BK*, No. 43/44 (1963), p. 165, n. 26.

Indili in the Russian reports may be Enderi.

COMMENTARY 15

Metsk, Batsk (ref. Chap. 2, p. 111, n. 1)

'Dont la position est absolument inconnue' Brosset (*EC/BHP*/II, Nos. 14–15, col. 236). Some of the topographical indications of this passage are obscure but it would seem that the Georgians were proposing a route up the valley of the Argun, leading by tracks over the main chain of Caucasus into the upper valleys of the Aragvi and the Alazani. This route would cross the territory of the Akko Chechens (Shikh murza's *Okok*) who were friendly to the Russians and had a *sloboda* at Terek-town (see Introduction, Section 5 and Commentary 14). The villages of Upper and Lower Kii (Akki) lie on an affluent of the Tchanti (White) Argun, the westerly feeder of the Argun (Baddeley, *RFC*, Vol. II, index under 'Kii' and Map V, and for description of Argun route as far as the Tchanti Argun, ibid., Vol. I, pp. 90 ff.). West of the Tchanti Argun a track crosses the Basti-lam (*lam*=mountain, ridge, in Ingush), the boundary between Chechnia and Georgia (ibid., Vol. I, p. 114) to Shatil (1,524 m.) west of the great peak of Tebulos-mta (4,494 m.); then by the Anatori Pass to Khamkheti and paths leading to the upper valleys of the Aragvi and the Alazani. From Shatil, Baddeley states, a ride to Tiflis 'in summer or early autumn' would always be feasible. Compare Radde's 'Marschroute', 1876, in *Die Chews'uren und ihr Land*, as far as Djarego on the Tchanti Argun. West of this river *Meesti* ridge or plateau is marked on Güldenstädt's map; it seems to correspond to *Miskin-doukh* of Baddeley's Map V. Bronevski (Vol. II, p. 166) refers to an

Ingush commune of *Meesti*, and also to the *Aka* and *Betsi* communes of the upper Kombulei. These indications explain the *Metsk mountain range* of Zvenigorodski. *Amaley* is the river Kombulei (Reineggs/W., Vol. I, p. 311; Bronevski, Vol. II, pp. 91, 152, 160), whose upper valley runs parallel with the Sunzha, the Assa and the Argun, and finally enters the Terek a few miles above Tartarup. *Burnash* remains obscure.

Reineggs/W. (Vol. II, p. 39), described the *Basti* as a sub-tribe of the Kists, then settled on the left bank of the middle Sunzha. They were neighbours of the Alti (cf. Baddeley, *RFC*, Vol. I, p. 79, for the commune of Aldee, famous as the base of Sheikh Mansur in 1785). These *Basti* may have been a fragment of an older Batsi agglomeration along the Sunzha. The Batsi (Georgian plur. *Batsebi*) were held to be Kists (Baddeley, *RFC*, Vol. I, p. 90) who are related to the Chechens (Reineggs/W., Vol. I, p. 41). (Bronevski, Vol. II, p. 158, finds that the Kist language has some resemblance to Tush, and he believes therefore that the (Georgian) Tushes must be of Kist origin; it would seem here that he is in fact refer-ring to the Batsi whose dialect has been much influenced by Georgian: see Desheriev.) In 1575 the communes of the Batsi in the Tchanti-Argun district sought the protection of King Levan of Kakheti against the Avar *nutsal*; they were allowed to pasture their flocks in the highlands of upper Kakheti, south of the main ridge of Caucasus and south-east of the great peak of Tebulos-mta and the Kadowanis Pass (3,048 m.), where they mixed with the Tushes. During the last century they moved as far south as Akhmeti and Alvan on the Alazani (cf. Desheriev, *Batsbiyski yaჳyk*, and Radde, *Chews'uren*, pp. 330 ff., and map). For the suggestion that the Batsebi represent a surviving fragment of the classical Bessoi, see Karst, *OM*, p. 504; also Allen, 'Ex Ponto, I and II' in *BK*, No. 30/31 (1958), p. 51.

COMMENTARY 16

Relations between the Circassians and the Crimean khans (ref. Chap. 2, p. 117, n. 1)

On the intimate relations between the Cherkesses and the Crimean khans, see the article by Halil Inalcik in *EI*, 2nd ed., under 'Çerkes'. After the occupation by the Ottomans of points on the Circassian coast 'the tribes in the hinterland continued to be dependent on the Crimean Khans, who as under the Golden Horde, sent their sons to be brought up among the Circassians (under the *atalik* or fosterage system). Along with the marriages of the Crimean princes with the Circassian noblewomen this secured the attachment of the Çerkes; they gave the Khans a yearly tribute consisting of slaves as well as auxiliary forces'. Aytek Namitok observes that the children of the Crimean khans were usually sent to the Beslenei Cherkesses (of Besh-tau) for their education and only returned when they were grown up and had become thoroughly 'Cherkessianised'. 'In addition the khans and their sons used mostly to marry Beslen women' (*Caucasian Review*, No. 2, p. 20).

For the *atalik* system, see the article 'ata' by M. F. Köprülü in *IA* (the cross-reference from *atalik* in *EI*, 2nd ed., is misleading); also Nogmov, pp. 33 ff. For comparable system of fosterage in the Scottish Highlands, still practised in the seventeenth century, see Skene, *Celtic Scotland*, Vol. III, pp. 321 ff.; for Ireland, ibid., pp. 190 ff.

COMMENTARY 17

The personality of Solokh of Little Kabarda (ref. Chap. 2, p. 122, n. 1)

Solokh (or Sholokh) was a cousin and rival of the sons of Temryuk and Kanbulat (cf. Commentary 12). Chapolov and Kudenek, sons of Kanbulat, had accused him of intrigue with the Crimean Khan (cf. p. 115 above). Mamstryuk, son of Temryuk, declared him to be anti-Russian, while Solokh himself sought cover through Murat Giray who was protected by the Russians (cf. Commentary 11). Solokh frankly voiced the difficulties of his position to the Russians; at the same time his critic Mamstryuk could not avoid entertaining the Turkish envoy who had just left Solokh's settlement (pp. 117 and 119 above).

A natural desire to ride all horses at once was characteristic of the north Caucasian chieftains and arose from the political and social circumstances in which they found themselves involved. Comparable dilemmas taxed the ingenuity of the Scottish and Irish chieftains who had to play between the Scottish Stewarts and the English Tudors, and French and Spanish interventionists, in the fifteenth and sixteenth centuries. The breakup of the Lordship of the Isles at the end of the fifteenth century may be compared with the disintegration of the Kabardan principality after the death of Temryuk; in the sixteenth century the circumstances of the breakup of the O'Neill rule in Ulster and of the Desmond patrimony in Munster presented similar phenomena. In fact, the very complex and antique clan systems could not sustain the pressures of developing bureaucratic states nor even of feudal monarchies.

COMMENTARY 18

The itinerary of the ambassadors from Sunzha-fort to Daryal (ref. Chap. 2, p. 126, nn. 2 and 3, p. 129, n. 1, p. 130, n. 1, p. 131, n. 1)

The itinerary of the ambassadors – particularly after leaving Sunzha-fort at the junction of the Sunzha and the Terek until their arrival at the settlement of Soni at the southern exit of the Daryal gorge – presents topographical problems. From the text, their itinerary in the early autumn of 1589 may be summarized as follows:

24 June	Zvenigorodski in Astrakhan.
6 Aug.	Arrives at Terek-town (Terki).
23 Aug.	Leaves Terek-town.
4 Sept.	(Cherkesses reach Sunzha and camp 2 versts from the fort.)
8 Sept.	Zvenigorodski camps on Sunzha. (Avar and Black Princes arrive on Sunzha.)
9 Sept.	Cherkess notables visit camp of Zvenigorodski.
12 Sept.	Visits of Alkas and Solokh to Zvenigorodski.
14 Sept.	Zvenigorodski leaves Sunzha and camps at 'Hot Well on Osman's Road'. (See n. (a) below.)
17 Sept.	Zvenigorodski leaves Hot Well and camps at 'lower bend' of Sunzha, probably near the site of modern Grozny. (See n. (b) below.)
18 Sept.	Zvenigorodski camps at Kholopenski site ('which had been the town of Temireksak'). (See n. (c) below.)
19 Sept.	Camped on R. Sunzha (? 'where it forms a bend'). (See n. (d) below.)
20 Sept.	Camped by Bystraya stream. (See n. (e) below.)
21 Sept.	Camped on Terek to left (east) of Alkas's old settlement. (See n. (f) below.)
22 Sept.	Having twice crossed the Terek, Zvenigorodski camped in the Black Mountains. (See n. (g) below.)
23 Sept.	Remained camped in Black Mountains and sent back *streltsy* to Terki.
24 Sept.	Marched from Black Mountains and 'camped beneath Mount Shat'. (See n. (h) below.)
25 Sept.	Continued encamped. (They were about one verst 'beyond Saltan murza's settlement at Lars on the River Terek' – i.e. south of Lars.) (See n. (i) below.)
26 Sept.	The ambassadors rode along the Terek gorge and camped below Cherebash's settlement. (See n. (j) below.)
27 Sept.	Cherebash's settlement – the frontier post of Aristov Sonski. (Nugsar Eristav of the Aragvi.) (See n. (k) below.)

6. 'The Rus attack the Ottomans as they cross' (the Terek).
From the *Sheja'atname* of Asafi, MS. TY 6043, fol. 186r. of Istanbul University Library.

The following notes help to clarify the details of this itinerary:

(a) *14 Sept. u Goryachego Kolodezya na Osmanovskom shlyakhu*: according to the Book of the Great Map, pp. 63–6, there are a number of hot wells in this region: 'Twenty versts below the Kurpa (an affluent of the Terek) a hot spring flows into the Terek from the right. Forty versts below this spring, another hot spring flows into the Terek. The river Sunzha flows into the Terek below the hot spring.' This last would appear to be the spot where Zvenigorodski had his camp on the left bank of the Sunzha, covering the ford on 'Osman's road' which led from the Kumukh lands towards Kabarda. It may be identified on Felitsyn's Map of North-Eastern Caucasia under the hybrid name of *Tepli* (*R.*, hot) *Kuchu* (for *T.*, *Kuyu*, well). The reference to Osman's road is to the route followed by Özdemiroghlu Osman Pasha from Derbent to the Crimea in October 1583. Cossacks and *streltsy* opposed his crossing of the Sunzha behind wooden stockades, or possibly wagons drawn up in square formation (*T.*, *tabun*). Heavy fighting went on until on the fifth day the Russians withdrew to their base at Sunzhenski-ostrog – the 'second Terki' at the junction of the Sunzha with the Terek (cf. Introduction, Section 5). There is an eye-witness account of this battle in Asafi, *Sheja'atname*, MS. TY 6043 of Istanbul University Library (for a summary of which I am indebted to Dr. V. L. Ménage). See ff. 182–8, with two miniatures at 186r and 188v: 'The Rus attack the Ottomans as they cross' (reproduced as pl. 6) and 'Asafi's brother wounded – the Rus in their stockade'. Osman Pasha marched thence to the river Terk (Terek) where he was met by 'the *begs* of Kabartay', including kinsmen Arslan and Ghazi (presumably the Kazy of Zvenigorodski's narrative: cf. *Ist. Kab.*, p. 45), who built a bridge over the river for his troops. Osman's further march was to Kashka (Kash-tau: see Baddeley, *RFC*, Maps III and VI and Vol. II, p. 179) and along the Kuban to Kerch – a formidable undertaking in the late autumn weather. The Ottoman perils through snow and ice are graphically depicted in Asafi's MS., fol. 196 r, (reproduced as Plate 1).

(b) *17 Sept.* 'From the Hot Well to the Sunzha at its lower bend'. It is difficult to pinpoint this and the two following halts on 18 and 19 September. The halt at the 'lower bend' of the Sunzha was probably near the site of modern Grozny; cf. Reineggs/W., Vol. 1, p. 53, for a 'boiling hot spring ten versts from the river Siun-tse . . . where the forests of the Tchetchens have decreased'.

(c) *18 Sept.* 'The Kholopenski settlement which had been the town of Temireksak'. The latter name is from *Timur aksak* (*T.*, Timur the Lame). This site cannot be identified on earlier maps, nor is it indicated by Bronevski nor Felitsyn. A big battle between Tamerlane and Tokhtamysh Khan of the Golden Horde took place round Tartarup on the Terek during the last week of April 1395 (cf. Howorth, *HM*, Vol. ii/i, pp. 251 ff., based on Sherifuddin; also Baddeley, *RFC*, Vol. ii, p. 228). As late as the eighteenth century, several sites between the Terek and the Kuma were associated with the name of Tamerlane (cf. Herber (Gärber), cited in Kosven/Khashayev, pp. 67, 78). The Kholopenski settlement may be located along the Sunzha somewhere between Zakan-yurt and Kazakh-kichu, cf. Baddeley's map, 'Murid Invasion of Kabarda', in *RCC*, opposite p. 426. (Incidentally, Howorth's *Jullad* or *Kulat* may be identified as Verkhni-Zhulat on Felitsyn's Map. It lies just north of Tartarup.)

(d) *19 Sept. na reke na Sunshe v rovnoy luke:* 'a meadow where the river Sunzha forms a bend'. Probably Nazran, a settlement of Shikh murza's Okok Chechens. For a picturesque description of Nazran and the small Nazran affluent of the Sunzha, see *Tagebuch*, pp. 25–6. The author noted the ruins of a Kabardan settlement there; also, further, Genko, pp. 691–2 and n. 2.

(e) *20 Sept.* 'The Bystraya stream', literally *R.* swift or rapid. Not identifiable on modern maps but mentioned in *The Book of the Great Map*, p. 64, as east of the river Belaya ('white'), which latter appears to be the Urs-don. Probably the Kombulei – which does not, in fact, fall to the Sunzha, but flows north-west to join the Terek just below its junction with the Urs-don (cf. Baddeley, *RFC*, Map III). Urs = 'white' in Osetian.

(f) *21 Sept.* 'On the river Terek to the left side of Alkas's old settlement': for Alkas see Chap. 2, p. 120, n. 1; also Commentary 12, p. 284; and Genko, p. 702 with n. 2. It is difficult to identify the site of the *kabak* of Alkas. Writing at the end of the eighteenth century, Steder (*Tagebuch*, p. 3) says: 'I followed (from Mozdok) the well-known way to Georgia which leads past the Akhlov and Mudarov *kabaks*.' Pallas (*TSP*, Vol. 1, p. 395) refers to 'Princes descended from Kanuka and divided into families of Tausultan and Gilakhstan. The former resides in the eastern part of Tartarup; but the villages of the latter known by the names of Akhlov and Mudarov *kabaks* are situate near the horizontal mountains over which the road leads to Georgia'. Solokh Tausultanov (cf. Belokurov, *Snosheniya*, p. xxxix, n. 45, citing Nogmov, p. 93), the Solokh of our text, was the ancestor of the Tausultanovs flourishing in Pallas's time. Reineggs/W., Vol. 1, p. 292, states that *Aghlo Kabak* corresponds to Little Kabarda. On Bronevski's map, *Aghlovi kabaki* are shown as south-west of Mozdok, ten versts north-east of Tavsultanovi and twenty versts north-east of Tartarup. Baddeley's map in *RCC*, opposite p. 426, marks Akhlova on the river Kourpa (for river *Kurpa* see n. (a) above) about twenty versts north-east of Tartarup. From all this it seems clear that Zvenigorodski's party made their halt of 21 September on the Tausultan lands which Pallas describes as 'the eastern part of Tartarup'. This district, together with the Akhlov and Mudarov lands constituted 'Little

Kabarda' – between the great bend of the Terek and the valley of the Sunzha.

(g) *22/23 Sept.* 'Having twice crossed the Terek they camped in the Black Mountains': In the wider sense of the name the Black Mountains are the more southerly of the two ridges which flank the main spine of the Caucasus on the north. The Black Mountains, which take their name from the dark schistose rocks flanking the central granites are contrasted with the 'Mottled' (*Pestrye*), also 'Red' or 'White', Mountains of Jurassic limestones which run roughly parallel with them. 'Between these lines of "Black" and "White" is a narrow trough or succession of transverse valleys – divided from each other by *cols* or passes – the hollows ranging from 3,000 to 5,000 feet above sea-level, the passes from 5,000 to 8,000 feet. Along all these, from the Assa, at least, to west of Kazbek . . . runs a still narrower belt of Palaeozoic schists, giving increased fertility. It is these valleys, for the most part, that the mountains tribes inhabit' (cf. Baddeley, *RFC*, Vol. I, pp. 26, 56, 74, 116; *SSTO*, pp. 22 ff.).

Zvenigorodski spent two nights (22 and 23 Sept.) in the Black Mountains and on 24 September reached the neighbourhood of Lars. With his large party and escort, it is doubtful whether he would have covered more than 30 versts in one day. His camp for 22/23 September must therefore have been located somewhere in the foothills south of Vladikavkaz, between the Ghizel-don and the Terek.

(h) *24/25 Sept.* 'They camped beneath Mount Shat about one verst beyond Saltan murza's settlement at Lars on the river Terek.' Mount Shat is not identifiable on the older maps; but Baddeley (*RFC*, Vol. I, p. 139) refers to driving *tur* (Caucasian wild goat) between the Kavri-don and Lars from *Sat* – which point equates with Tchas of his Map I, transcribed from the Russian 5-Verst Map. This name corresponds to *Chach* (=*Shash*) of Freshfield's map 'Peaks, Passes and

Glaciers of the Central Caucasus' in his *Exploration*, Vol. I. The name applied to Chach-kokh, the north-westerly peak of Mount Kazbek (*G.* Mqinvari), 5,047 m. The poet Lermontov wrote a dialogue between the twin peaks of Shat and Kazbek (*Sochineniya*, Vol. II (1954 ed.), pp. 193–6).

(i) Saltan murza's settlement at Lars: Lars was the well-known post at the head of the Daryal gorge, indicated on Bronevski's map of 1813. At the beginning of the nineteenth century Lars was in the hands of the Dudarov family who gave trouble to the Russians, acting, it was believed, at the instigation of the Kabardan princes (cf. Genko, p. 748 and n. 2, citing Butkov). They were removed from this important bottleneck and compensated with lands west of the Georgian Military Road (Baddeley, *RFC*, Vol. I, p. 137 and n. 1). The Dudarovs derived their origin from the village of Kii in the wild country of the upper Argun and were thus of Akki (Okok) stock. For the Dudarovs, see again Baddeley, *RFC*, Vol. I, 194–5. It is not clear whether Saltan Murza was an ancestor of the Dudarovs or whether his line was displaced by them.

At Lars Saltan Murza told Zvenigorodski that 'the Sovereign's envoys have hitherto gone from my settlement to Mount Shat, because they happened to be travelling in the summer when there was no snow on the mountains. They took three and a half days by that route to get to Soni-land . . . But now you cannot cross that mountain because great snows live in these mountains in the autumn'.

This passage indicates that in summer when the Terek would be in flood, travellers used the roundabout route: Khiakh Pass – Saniba – Dargavs – to the upper Fiag-don at Zvighiz and thence by the Khiliak Pass to Resi and the upper valley of the Terek to Kobi which would bring them out just south of the seat of the eristav of the Aragvi at Sioni. Cf. Baddeley, *RFC*, Vol. I, Maps I and III, pp. 31 ff., and p. 166: 'Supplementary Note on the Khiliak or Kolota Route', citing

Tagebuch, p. 89: 'In summer it is for the most part free of snow, or, at most, the snow hardly covers it.' Also Wak./ Brosset, Map III and pp. 442–3: 'From Kwara (Kora on Baddeley's Map I) is a track which crosses the Khokhotis-mta and leads to Nara and Zrogo' – and thence by the Zakka Pass to the source of the Terek (Wak., T'ruso). And Reineggs/W., Vol. I, 312: 'A narrow vale extends from Schimmit (Baddeley, *RFC*, Vol. I, Map I = *Tchmee* + G. *mta*) to the southern side of the principal chain of the Caucasus, which separates the eastern from the western; and probably has been produced by the old bed of the Terek' (= route by Resi).

(j) *26–7 Sept*. 'Along the defile between the mountains, up the river Terek': The reference is to the famous Daryal gorge which penetrates the central ridge of Caucasus, following the bed of the river Terek. For a good description in English of the Daryal gorge and an ascent of Mount Kazbek, see Fresh-field, *Exploration*, Vol. I, Chap. 4; Sella's fine photograph of Kazbek and the bed of the Terek, opposite p. 87. Freshfield says that the modern name Kazbek was derived from that of a local chieftain – Kazi Bek; the Georgian name *Mqinvari* he interprets as 'The Ice Mountain'. For distances between Lars and Kobi, ibid., Vol. II, p. 236; cf. also Baddeley, *RFC*, Vol. I, Map I: from (Old) Lars, Saltan Murza's settlement, to Daryal Fort (and the ruins of Tamar's Castle) at the southern head of the gorge is about six versts. See fur-ther Commentary 19: The Daryal Gorge: its history and topography.

(k) *Cherebashov kabak:* 'Cherebash's settlement'. The word *Cherebash* is not a personal name but a rank – literally head or captain of troops. In Turkey a *çeribaşi* was an officer of *sipahis*, cavalry recruited from the provincial feudal holdings (*ziamets*). They ranked below the *Alay-beyis*, who were elected war-leaders by the feudatories in each province (*sancak*). In peace time the *çeribaşis* performed the duties of police (cf. H. A. R. Gibb and Harold Bowen, *Islamic society and the West*, Vol. 1, pp. 51 ff.). In our context Cherebash would be the commander of the frontier post – the name borrowed from the Turks by the Georgians as was not infrequent in military terminology. The term sometimes occurs in the text of Evliya Chelebi (cf. the Russian translation with notes and commentary by A. D. Zheltyakov, *Evliya Chelebi: Kniga puteshestviya*, Vol. 1, p. 294).

A certain Cherbysh, in Ingush-Chechen tradition, is the hero of a legend in which he ambushes a party of Kabardans on their way to raid Georgia – after destroying bridges behind and in front of them. He was a native of Gumlet (Gveleti according to a pencilled note by the late J. F. Baddeley), a few versts to the south of Kazbek. He was rewarded by the 'Georgian' king Giorgi (? Giorgi X of Kartli, d. 1605) with the grant of lands between Gveleti and Kazbek (cf. *Etnograficheskoye Oboʐreniye*, 1901, No. I, article by V. F. Miller, 'Stranichka iz severo-kavkazskago bogatyrskago eposa', p. 63). The story has some resemblance to the Köroghlu cycle of tales where, in Anatolia, the hero is a highwayman and ballad-singer while, among the Uzbeks, he is a frontier officer serving a great lord or khan (cf. Allen, *PTP*, n. 21 and p. 50). It is clear from our text that Cherebash's settlement was the first Georgian post covering the exit from the Daryal Gorge.

COMMENTARY 19

The Daryal Gorge: its history and topography (ref. Chap. 2, p. 131, n. 1)

On 25 September 1901, Baddeley stayed at the post-station at Kazbek, marked as Dariel Fort on the right bank of the Terek on his Map I. 'Just above the fort, on the left bank, looking down upon road and river, were the ruins of Tamára's Castle, so called, which in its day must have commanded

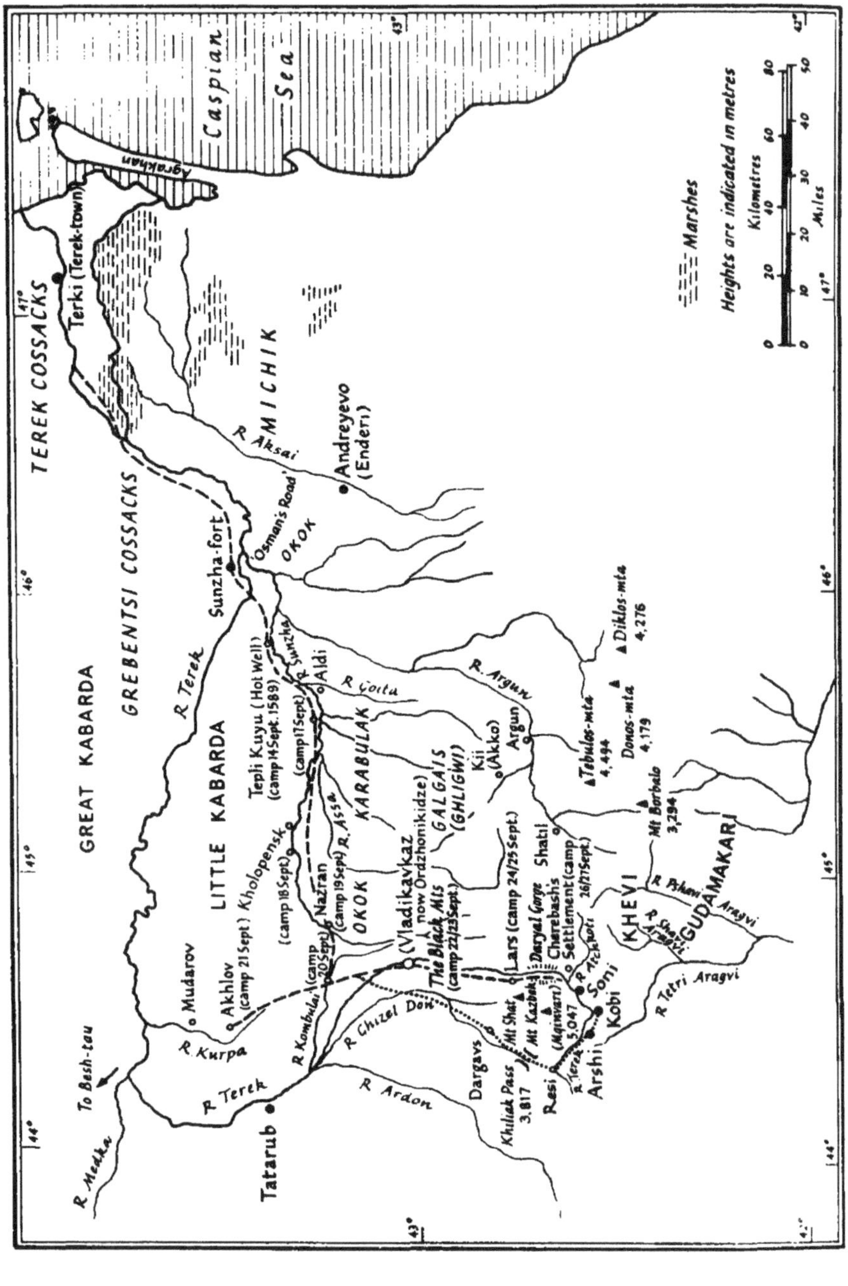

Map 5. Sketch map of the Central Caucasus illustrating Commentaries 15, 18, 19, and 20.

impregnably the southern entrance of the defile. This latter has commonly been identified with the 'Gates', to which Classical, Byzantine and Eastern authors applied at one time or another such epithets as Caucasian, Iberian, Alan, Sarmatian, Dariel, and even Caspian . . . Queen Tamára, of course, had possession here, and may well have built or rebuilt the castle' (Baddeley, *RFC*, Vol. I, pp. 190–1). Reineggs described the castle at the end of the eighteenth century: 'We still see, besides its much injured walls, a handsome aqueduct, hewn out of the hardest rocks, to introduce a sufficient quantity of water into the fortress. But as the collection of water from the mountains was probably not always adequate, the builders smoothed this difficulty by a covered passage, arched with bricks, that was carried at the back of the rocks down to the banks of the Terek, which flows close by the fortress, at the depth of 680 feet' (Reineggs/W., Vol. I, p. 252).[1]

In the tenth century A.D., when the Georgian kingdom was still weakened by the Arab hold on Tiflis, the exit from the Daryal gorge was in the hands of the Alans who, sometimes, in alliance with the Georgians, operated both through the Daryal and over some of the more difficult passes into Daghestan. According to Ibn-Rusta (*c*. A.D. 902–12): 'Travelling to the left (to the west) of the kingdom of the Sarir (Avaria) you journey among mountains and meadows for three days and arrive in the kingdom of al-Lān (Alān) . . . Then you travel for ten days among rivers and trees before reaching the castle called "The Gate of the Alans". It stands on the top of a mountain and under the mountain runs a road. The castle is surrounded by high mountains and its walls are guarded every day by 1,000 men from among its

---

[1] I have observed similar engineering at the ancient castle of Tortom in the ravine of the Tortomis-tsqali, a castle which suffered destruction by a column sent by Tamerlane in 1403 (cf. Allen, *HGP*, p. 125).

inhabitants posted by day and by night' (cited from Minorsky, *HSD*, p. 169).

Genko cites from the work known as *The Conversion of Georgia* that soon after the fall of the Iberian Kingdom 'the Persians grew strong and seized the province of Erov (?Hereti) and Armenia, but especially they made themselves masters of Georgia and built themselves the Osetian Gates (*karni ovsetisani*) namely one set of great gates in Osetia itself (at Daryal), two sets of gates in Dvalia (Dvaleti – covering the passes west of the Daryal leading south to the valleys of the Ksani and the Lyakhvi), and one set of gates in Durdzuketi-Parachvan. They established local mountain people as a frontier guard (*gumartad* from Iran. *gumard*) and then appointed one man in the *Tsanar* ravine' (for Tsanar see Commentary 20; and Genko, pp. 711–12 and footnotes). Genko believes that the gates in Durdzuketi may be the so-called Assa Gates (ibid., p. 712, n. 3, where, in 1781, Steder observed ruined walls and a tower, *Tagebuch*, pp. 33–4, which Baddeley, *RFC*, Vol. I, Map II, identifies as 'Split Rock', north-east of the village of Barkin). The most extensive section of the so-called Caucasian Wall – which was in fact a series of fortifications covering different passages over the main chain – was at Derbent (Darband) the headquarters of the command for the north-west frontier of the Sasanian dominions; for details and plan see the learned observations of Minorsky (*HSD*, pp. 86 ff.; particularly p. 87, n. 2). 'Negotiations between the Romans and the Persians about the fortifying of the passes, for which purpose the former were willing to pay subventions to the latter, are known already under Theodosius I (379–95)'.

Janashvili, in his edition of Wakhusht (p. 77, n. 297), follows Brosset (Wakhusht, index, p. 506), in indicating the possible derivation of Daryal from *darg-alant'-kari* – 'the long gate (or passage) of the Alans'. For *darg*, *Os.* long, cf. neighbouring Dargavs on Baddeley's *RFC*, Vol. I, Map I. Brosset prefers to leave the matter undecided between this and the traditional interpretation: *Dar* (*P.* gate) – *i-Alan* (of the Alans). But Janashvili has an ingenious alternative. He recalls the following passage of Pliny (*Natural History*, Book VI, Chap. 12): 'On leaving these [i.e. the *Diduri*=Didos and *Sodi*=? Tsounta] one comes to the Caucasian Gates . . . an enormous work of Nature, who has here suddenly rent the mountains asunder. Here gates have been placed, with iron-covered beams, under the centre of which flows a river emitting a horrible odour; and on this side of it on a rock stands the fortress called Cumania, erected for the purpose of barring the passage of innumerable tribes. At this spot therefore the world is divided by gates into two portions; it is just opposite (i.e. on the same line of latitude as) the Hibernian town of Hermastus (i.e. Armazis-tsikhe, overlooking Mtskheta from the east). Beyond the Gates of the Caucasus (i.e. going west) among the Gurdinian Mountains are the Valli (*G. Dval* or *Tual*) and the Suani (*G. Svanni*), races never yet quelled, who nevertheless work gold mines. After these, right on to the Black Sea, are a large number of tribes of Heniochi and then of Achaei. Such is the present state of one of the most famous regions in the world'.

Janashvili compares Pliny's 'iron-covered beams' with Georgian *dire* (Mingrelian, *dvire*, Svanian *dvir*), a squared beam, a long rough-hewn log; hence *G. diruli, dereli*, a place fortified with logs ('stockade'). Moreover *Kumani* (Cumania) is a Georgian name and means a narrow compressed place, from *kuma*, to compress, shut. Compare, here, John Garstang and O. Gurney, *The geography of the Hittite Empire*, p. 38, where the name of the fortress of *Kumaha* in Hayasa is said to equate 'fairly easily' with Kemakh at the head of the great gorge of the western Euphrates; also *Kummanni* which Garstang/Gurney identify with classical Comana of Cataonia (*T.* Shahr); see also article by Allen in *BK*, No. 34-5, 1960,

'Ex Ponto V: Heniochi-Aea-Hayasa', *passim*. Recent excavations at Mtskheta have revealed the sophisticated architectural techniques of the Iberians of the Classical period and there is little reason to doubt that Pliny's Cumania as an Iberian fortress preceded the Sasanian and Bagratid fortifications on the same site overlooking the Terek (cf. *Mt͟zkheta*, Vol. I, Chap. 6 *passim*).

The direct route from Daryal to Mtskheta and Tiflis went up the valley of the Terek (the *khevi*, G. valley, of Wakhusht) past Sioni and Kobi and crossed the *col*, named *Krestovaya* (Cross Pass) by the Russians when they built a road at the beginning of the nineteenth century. This route debouched southward to the village of Mleti at the head of the valley of the Black Aragvi. (For Mleti, not mentioned in the older sources, see Baddeley, *RFC*, Vol I, Map III). It is the way described by Wakhusht (Brosset ed., p. 225; Janashvili, p. 75) who, from the south, directs the traveller from the country west of Khada in Mtiuleti across the *col* (Wakhusht's *qeli*, G. pass) to the ravine of the small Shtasqvali feeder of the Terek. The track over the *col* is described by Wakhusht as 'not high' (Janashvili *nevysok*, Brosset *basse*) and without woods: 'in winter the depth of the snow prevents passage on horseback – but in summer there is plenty of flowering pasture' (? clover). The *col* seems to equate with the name Kumlis-Zighe ('castle of Kumli or Kumuli' of Reineggs/W., Vol I, pp. 391, 393): 'To the north-east we see the habitations of the Ghefsur (Khevsurs); to the south-west the numerous Tiuletian (Mtiuletian) vales covered with houses: and to the north the dwellings of the Ossi, with the accumulated craggy points of Caucasus'. Reineggs/W., Vol. II, p. 393, continues: 'Seven versts north of Kumulis-Zighe rises the Terek. It winds through narrow valleys to the eastward, but as soon as it reaches the *Patknis-klde* (G. lime rocks) receives the rapid Tetris-tskali ("white water") and directs its course due north'. The Tetri

7. Astrakhan, c. 1634. From Olearius/W., Vol. I, pp. 452/3.

8. The church of Tsno (by courtesy of Prof. Irakli Tsitsishvili).

stream seems to correspond to the Shtasqvali of Wakhusht's text. It is notable that Wakhusht makes no reference to Kobi: his landmark after the infall of the Shtasqvali is Arshis-tsikhe – 'a citadel not built by the hand of man, on a high cliff, surrounded by rocks, inaccessible, on the slope of Mqinvari (Mount Kazbek)'. But Kobi is marked on Italian maps of the fifteenth century (see Introduction, Section 3). And Wakhusht (Brosset ed., p. 227) mentions Gergeti – which Reineggs/W. (Vol. 1, p. 394) clearly identifies as belonging to the community of Kobi: 'An Ossic-heathen tribe, called Gobi, lives at the junction of the Tetri-tskali with the Terek. They have extended their numerous miserable villages as far as Thiulet to the south; and to the north, as far as Stepan-Zminda (Holy Stephen), a considerable village on both banks of the Terek. It is inhabited only by Ossic Christians, who hold the same faith with the Georgians. An old stone church, called Gergete, on a high hill beyond the Terek, belongs to the village.'

Reineggs/W. (Vol. 1, pp. 252–4) gives very interesting details of the system of organized porterage and tolls (or 'hold-ups') along the Daryal route – which doubtless existed long before the Russian ambassadors came along with their formidable escorts. 'There are certainly other roads, to come from Russia over Caucasus to Georgia; but this through the *Porta Caucasica*, along the Terek, as neck-breaking as it is, is always reckoned the most convenient; because the porters who are accustomed to carry the goods of the merchant or of the traveller over the mountains, live in the neighbourhood, and are to be had in sufficient numbers.

'Whoever wishes to travel from Georgia to Russia, must deposit his packages or bales at the last Georgian village, Stepan-Zminda; and have them carried by the Ossi over the mountains as far as Schimmitt (Tchmee of Baddeley, *RFC*, Vol. 1, Map I), a distance of thirty versts. A bale must not weigh more than 200 to 240 lbs.;[1] and generally three men are appointed to each, partly to carry alternately, and partly to assist and support the bearer, if he should happen to make a false step over those dangerous rocks. The expense of porterage for each bale must be paid with six shirts; or, what is the same thing, with six coarse pieces of linen, nine ells long, which are worth about four rubles. When the merchant or traveller is arrived at Schimmitt, he must pay the Takaur (Tagauri) tribes assembled there other six pieces of linen as bridge-toll; and, not to expose himself to any danger, must besides satisfy all remaining demands . . . But even then the traveller is not at the end of his troubles, for some versts below Schimmitt, the road is guarded by a small watch-tower, with two lurking Ossi, where, high steep rocks to the left, and a deep precipice on the right, scarcely allow a narrow footpath. Here also two pieces of linen must be deposited, and then everyone may continue his journey in peace, if other nations, the Kisti (Ingush) etc., do not attack him.'

Wakhusht (Brosset ed., pp. 229; Janashvili, p. 77) gives the difficult lateral by-passes east of the Terek. 'Below Gveleti, a valley (*G. khevi*) falls to the Aragvi (=here, Terek) running from the south-east, from Gudamakari and Dzurdzuketi and going north-west. The valley is uninhabited (see unnamed stream on Wak./Brosset, Map 3). By this valley a difficult and perilous road crosses into Dzurdzuketi and Kisteti (cf. Baddeley, *RFC*, Vol. 1, Map II, Kistinka river and pass); another road crosses into Gudamakari (the Djouti river and pass at 10,269 ft. of Baddeley's Map II; Atchkhotis-tsqali of Wak./Brosset, Map 4).

Wakhusht gives an attractive description of the region which merits quotation: 'The valley (*khevi*) is fertile in corn,

[1] A pack of 1 cwt. was considered a good load for a trekker in the Yukon fifty years ago; 200 lbs. evenly balanced for a mule in the Sudan Defence Force, 1941.

barley, linseed and oats. From Shtasqvali to Gveleti there are no other fruits but mountain berries, barberries (*G. kotsakhuri*), (wild) currants, myrtle, mountain strawberries ... In the forests are a mass of many-petalled red roses and quantities of other mountain flowers. There are as many beasts as the land can hold: sheep without fat tails; great numbers of mountain goats (*R. tur*, *G. mdjikhvi*), and chamois (*G. artchvi*). Birds abound: the mountain turkey (*G. shurtkhi*), the grey partridge (*G. glon*) and in summer countless quail. There are said to be deposits of gold and silver. The climate is healthy; the men are warlike, strong, brave, of good carriage, like those of Mtiuleti, but excelling them in all qualities. They follow the Georgian faith – without understanding it.' (Utilizing renderings of Brosset and Janashvili, with Janashvili's translation of Georgian names for animals, birds and plants left untranslated by Brosset.)

The first passage by an organized military force – four regiments with cannon – was made in 1769 by General ¸Todleben, a German adventurer in the Russian service who had captured Berlin in 1760. The passage was unopposed and Todleben was met by the Georgian King Irakli II at Kobi. 'He had nothing but the beds of those two rivers (Terek and Aragvi) for road and to have got his artillery over them was an astonishing feat' (Baddeley, *RFC*, Vol. I, p. 31, citing the Marquis Paulucci, *Akty*, Vol. 5). For Baddeley's cautious views on the practicability of the Daryal Gorge and the Krestovaya *col* as an invasion route before the road was built, see ibid., Vol. I, p. 191 and Vol. II, p. 241.

COMMENTARY 20

(a) *'The great settlement of Soni and the monastery of the Immaculate Mother of God'* (ref. Chap. 3, p. 133, n. 1)

There is an ancient settlement of Sioni on the upper Terek (Baddeley, *RFC*, Map I), described by Dubois (Vol. IV,

p. 64) in picturesque terms. In continuing south, the ambassadors would have taken the direction of Kartli via Kobi. Brosset, *EC/BHP*, Vol. II, Nos 14–15, col. 237, n. 67, seems to accept this direction in suggesting that Qovlat-tsminda (='the Immaculate Mother of God' marked on Wak./Brosset, Map 3) was 'le fameux couvent de Throuso' on the upper Terek (here erroneously called 'Aragvi' by Wakhusht). There is, however, another Qovlat-tsminda marked on Wak./ Brosset, Map 3, situated some three versts to the south-east of Sioni. This lies on the eastern side of the Atchkhotis-tsqali (='river of Atchkhoti'), a right bank affluent of the upper Terek. Along the Atchkhoti ran the route which led to Gudamakari and the upper valley of the Black Aragvi (cf. Wak./Brosset, p. 227; Wak. Janashvili, pp. 76–7).

In his preceding note (ibid., p. 66), Brosset, citing Güldenstädt, has already observed that the country of the Khevsurs encloses two cantons, Soni and Mekevani, and includes, among dependent villages, Tsno, 'sans doute le Tsno de la carte de Klaproth'. Beyond Sioni, at four versts from Kazbek, Dubois de Montpéreux (Vol. IV, p. 64) visited the church of Tsno, built of stone and mortar and vaulted. He believed that 'cette église isolée peut aussi dépendre d'Atchkhoti que de Sno ou Tsno'. It would seem to be identical with the second Qovlat-tsminda marked on Wak./Brosset, Map 3, as overlooking the river Atchkhoti. For view of church see Dubois, Atlas, 2 Ser., pl. 6; and for plan, 3 Ser., pl. 4, fig. 15. Also Plate 8, opposite p. 305.

The route by the Atchkhoti would enable the ambassadors to avoid the borderland of King Simon I of Kartli, with whom Alexander of Kakheti was on bad terms and who proved anxious to intercept them on their return journey; see text, p. 228.

(Gvritishvili (*ISO*, pp. 53–4) accepts the conclusion that Sioni was the seat of Aristov Sonski – the Eristavi of Sioni when *Khevi* ('the Valley') existed as an autonomous political unit (cf. below (b).) He observes that Sioni was situated on the right bank of the Terek in the present Kazbek *rayon*, where there are many remains of ancient buildings, defensive towers, the walls of a fortress and monumental structures. On the walls of some churches are fragments of ancient Georgian inscriptions. The favourable situation of the settlement indicates that just here must have been the seat of the ruler of 'the Valley'. It was the centre of routes converging from Daryal, from Truso (the upper valley of the Terek, south-west by west of Kazbek) and from Tsno on the way from Khevsureti. Across the Terek to the south-east was the powerful castle of Arshi (Archa on Wak./Brosset, Map 3) which could afford a refuge, in times of stress, to the people of the district.

(b) *'Aristop (Aristov) prince of Soni' (Aristop sonski)*: note on the Eristavs of the Ksani and the Aragvi (ref. Chap. 3, p. 133, n. 2)

Here the Russian envoys refer to a title and territory which is unknown in this form in the Georgian sources. Aristop or Aristov is clearly the Georgian administrative title *eristavi* (which later became transformed into the family name of the Eristovs). *Eristavi* is a compound formed from *eris* (gen. of *eri*, people, later, army) and *tavi*, head, hence 'head of the army'; it corresponds to the Greek word *strategos* in which sense it is used by mediaeval Georgian translators, cf. Allen, *HGP*, pp. 237 ff. Prince Aristov appears, therefore, as the commandant or governor of Soni-land.

Eristavoba was originally a personal office like an earldom or county in Anglo-Norman England; although in view of the antiquity of these Georgian institutions and their mixed tribal and feudal background, it may, perhaps be compared more aptly to the Scottish *mor-tuath* (cf. W. F. Skene, *Celtic Scotland*, Vol. III, pp. 215–16). It was only in the process of time that *eristavoba* became *sagwareulo* or hereditary; and the *eristav-n-i* ranked as *tavad-n-i* – peers enjoying extensive lordships (*sa-tavad-o*). The greatest of these *tavadni* also held the rank of *didebuli* which corresponds literally to magnate or grandee.

According to *Dzegli Eristavta* ('The Monument of the Eristavis (of the Ksani)'), the duties of an eristavi included 'the administration of churches, service of the King and government of the province'. In the crises of the Georgian monarchy the administrative officials who had gradually become territorial magnates naturally pretended to extend their power and possessions at the expense of the central authority. During the fifteenth century, when the ancient Georgian kingdom disintegrated into seven independent territorial units, more – and smaller – eristavates came into being. In Kakheti, during the sixteenth century, the centralizing policies of Av Giorgi, Levan and Alexander, checked this tendency; but in Kartli the eristavates of the Ksani and the Aragvi became more or less autonomous of the kings in Tiflis. The same process was seen in the neighbouring kingdom of Imereti in the growth of the eristavate of Radcha. This was natural since the rich mountain valleys on the southern slopes of Mount Caucasus were less accessible to invaders (although both Tamerlane at the end of the fourteenth, and the troops of Shah Abbas in the first quarter of the seventeenth century, penetrated them): cf. Introduction, Section 9.

Of the northern lordships, that of the Ksani (*Ksnis-eristavoba*) was the most important and its rulers increased their power between the sixteenth and eighteenth centuries. Its boundaries extended from the main ridge of the Caucasus in the north to the left bank of the Kura in the south, and from the river Lyakhvi in the west to the mountains of Alevi and Gremi in the east – which formed the watershed between the valleys of the Ksani and the Aragvi. South of the Kura were the domains of the Baratashvili or Baratiani clan (*Sa-baratian-o*) and between the Kura and the Aragvi the fief of the Mukhranian princes (*Sa-mukhranbaton-o*), a cadet branch of the

Kartlian royal house. Sometimes these lordships supported the crown against the Eristavni. Along the middle Kura, west of Mtzkheta, were, again, the domains of the Amilakhoris (spelt also Amilakhvari, from Persian *mirakhor*) – hereditary Grand Equerries of the Kartlian Kings – a clan who were an important factor in the balance of feudal politics and who often inclined towards the Eristavni of the Ksani to whom they were bound by generations of marriage ties.

The ruling family of the Ksani, the Bibiluri, claimed to trace their descent from the Kings of Oseti (Alania) of the time of Justinian in the sixth century. The eristavate of the Aragvi was rather less important and the families that had ruled there were more obscure. According to D. Gvritishvili, p. 49, an eristavi of the Aragvi, Mihai Shaburidze, is first mentioned in a document of 1380. This family was still flourishing in 1474 when another document refers to the *eristavt' eristavi* Vamek Shaburidze who, amongst other sons, had one named Nugsar, a name which recurs in the later Sidamoni family. Platon Iosseliani (*Opisaniye goroda Dusheti*, p. 35), traced the descent of the Shaburidzes from the Persian Sasanid dynasty of the third century A.D. Shapur is a Sasanian royal name, and the hypothesis cannot be excluded in view of the very ancient descent of the Bagrations, Artsrunis, Malhazunis, Khorkhuniantzs, Gamrakelis and other Caucasian royal or feudal families. Other names appear in the eristavate – Tek Turmanidze and Charmeuli – but these may have been branches of the Shaburidze stock, taking their names, as in the first case, from a younger son or, in the second, from a personal estate. Gvritishvili, p. 51, believes that the country watered by the three streams of the Aragvi may have constituted more than one eristavate and that a reference to the eristavate 'of the lower part' (Bazaleti – with a capital at Dusheti or Ananuri) implies an eristavate 'of the upper part' (in Mtiuleti, Gudamakari and the Khevi).

Some time after 1558, an obscure *aznauri* had, on the order of King Simon I, taken the castle of Vanati where the commandant was in rebellion. Vanati was in the district of Ziri on the left bank of the Little Lyakhvi, in the domain of Savakhtango, a part of the eristavate of the Ksani. The *aznauri* belonged to the Sidamoni family – one of the several noble Os clans who had penetrated and settled on lands south of the main chain of the Caucasus after the final destruction of the Alanic kingdom by the Mongols in the second quarter of the thirteenth century. This Sidamoni was rewarded by King Simon with Vanati and some other lands. In 1569 the king was taken prisoner by the Persians, and Kartli placed under the rule of his unpopular brother David (Da'ud Khan). There followed many conflicts between the partisans of the two royal brothers – including an attack by the Eristavi of the Ksani and the Amilakhoris on Simon's queen in her retreat at Kavtis-khevi. With the aid of the Eristavi of the Ksani, the new lord of Vanati attacked and killed Tek Turmanidze and Charmeuli and overran Bazaleti along the western bank of the Aragvi. After the Sidamoni's death a nephew, Nugsar, became his successor and forced Mtiuleti also into submission (cf. Brosset, *HG*, Vol. II/i, p. 48). In Wakhusht's *History of Kartli* the account of the Sidamoni's conquest of Vanati and, later, of Bazaleti and Mtiuleti, is interpolated into the story of the alliance between Nugsar and 'the great *Mo'uravi*', Giorgi Saakadze, about the year 1610. Nugsar was only a boy at the time of his uncle's death; and he was still a youth when he got control from his illegitimate cousins (cf. Brosset, *HG*, Vol. II/i, p. 48; and ibid., Genealogical Tables: Eristavis of Ksani and the Aragvi, pp. 630–2, who dates his accession to the eristavate at 1578). This was the year in which Lala Mustafa Pasha invaded Georgia; and Simon I was released from prison in Shiraz to defend Kartli against the Turks. During the winter Simon took vengeance on the Eristavi of the Ksani and the Amilakhoris – friends of the young Nugsar. In 1580 Simon defeated Alexander of Kakheti at Chotori. But Nugsar, who, from Belokurov's account, was a dependant of Alexander, seems to have escaped Simon's attentions. Simon in the following years was fighting the Turks and prosecuting campaigns in Samtskhe and Imereti with the object of restoring the unity of the old Georgian kingdom. In 1586 he became reconciled with Alexander of Kakheti through the intervention of their sons – both Giorgis, and first cousins bound by 'a mutual affection' (cf. Brosset, ibid., p. 40). In 1589, it would seem, therefore, that Nugsar, still a young man probably under thirty, was in peaceful possession of Soni-land (*Sonskaya ʒemlya*) which represented certainly the northern part of the eristavate of the Aragvi. In 1602, during the brief usurpation of David, son of Alexander II of Kakheti, Nugsar fell foul of this arrogant prince, and in the following year he seems to have already transferred his allegiance to Giorgi X of Kartli who promised him a daughter in marriage to his eldest son Baadur. Nugsar was now master of all the country between the three Aragvi streams – since in 1610 he received his son-in-law, Giorgi Saakadze, in Dusheti. He last appears in the annals in 1611 – after which date his sons, Baadur (Bahadur) and Zurab, played a leading role in the anarchic politics of Georgia during the invasions of Shah Abbas. In 1619, supported by the Persians and by Simon II, their puppet king in Tiflis, Zurab drove his elder brother Baadur out of Bazaleti, 'began to make raids against the inhabitants of Mtiuleti and the Khevi, subjugated these countries and became extremely powerful' (Brosset, ibid., p. 52). Wakhusht observes that 'in effect, Mtiuleti and the Khevi belonged to the King (of Kartli), and until then had not depended on the Eristavis, but the Mtiulni only rendered slight obedience'. Zurab had married in the same year Darejan, a daughter of Taymuraz I of Kakheti. During the reign of Simon II (1619–29), when Zurab Sidamoni and Giorgi

Saakadze set themselves at the head of a national resistance to Shah Abbas, there was much fighting in Bazaleti and Mtiuleti (Brosset, ibid., pp. 53, ff.). In one campaign, from Dusheti, the Persians crossed Mtiuleti and, penetrating the Khevi, reached Arshi, the castle overlooking the Terek at the southern approach to the Daryal gorge, whence they returned down the valley of the Ksani where they were ambushed by the levies of 'the great Mo'uravi'. These operations form the background to the legends about the campaigns of Shah Abbas in the central Caucasus (cf. Baddeley, *RFC*, Vol. I, pp. 156–9). Zurab met his death in 1629; his younger brother and successor as eristavi, was killed in Dusheti in 1635 on the orders of the Kartlian King Rostom. From all this it will be seen that the Eristavate of the Aragvi was a unit of varying extent and allegiance during the half century between 1578 and 1635; and that the name *Sonskaya zemlya* was applied by the Russians and Kabardans to the north-eastern part – the upper valley of the Terek, called by the Georgians *Khevi* – 'the valley' *par excellence*. For this region the name Sonti is still preserved in the Russian Atlas of 1745.

(c) '*Soni-land*' (= *Sonskaya zemlya*): note on the ethnology of the eristavate of the Aragvi (ref. Chap. 3, p. 133, n. 2)

The name Soni as applied to the region and people south and east of the Daryal gorge has always puzzled historians (cf. Lurye and Miller in *Puteshestviya russkikh poslov*, 1954, pp. 207, 420, n. 9, where in the context the reference is to Svaneti). In 1845, Brosset discussed the name in *EC/BHP*, Vol. II, Nos. 14/15, cols. 223–4 and n. 30, and remarked that the Georgian pronunciation of *Swanni, Swanethi*, is Soni, Sonethi – conforming with the Russian transcription Soni. Four years later, in his *HG*, Vol. I/ii, p. 44 and n. 3, he records the tradition that the second (legendary) king Saurmag (237–162 B.C.), because of the over-population of the mountains of north-eastern Caucasus (Durdzuketi), removed half the people and settled them 'in Mtiuleti from Didoeti as far as Egrisi (Mingrelia), this is to say Svaneti'. Wakhusht (ibid., n. 4), has the variant 'Didoeti *and* Svaneti'. Brosset observes that 'anyhow it is remarkable that the country of the Kists and Khevsurs and the Khevi of the Georgians bears the name of Soni in the journals of the Russian embassies which traversed it from the end of the sixteenth century'. He concludes that 'perhaps at an ancient epoch the name Svaneti was common to all that part of the inhabited valleys of the Caucasus indicated in our text'.

Baddeley (*RFC*, Vol. II, p. 14), recalls that Gärber (1728 – a German in the Russian service) divided the inhabitants of *Tavlistan* (= Os. *Tau*-li-stan = Daghestan) 'amidst four high mountains bordering on Georgia' into *Sonti* and *Tavlintsi*. Baddeley observes: 'to the former belonged the community of Tsounta-Akhvakh, which up to 1873, when Komaroff wrote his account of the population of Daghestan, was still according to him one of the rudest in all that country. "Even now they prefer raw meat to cooked." Tradition says that they allowed no strangers to pass through their country and that they devoured enemies slain in battle. Why these people should differ so greatly from their neighbours on all sides does not appear. But they speak their own dialect, and, possibly, may derive from some wild and unknown ancestry, though, as the Deedos, a better-known tribe, were also called Tsounta, meaning "Eagles" an Avar version of their own name for themselves, "Tsesi", it may be that Gärber referred to them.' In passing, it may be noted that the name *Akhvakh* seems to denote a survival of the ancient Aghvan'k – the classical Albanians whose independent kingdom came to an end in the seventh century A.D. (cf. Dowsett, *The history of the Caucasian Albanians*; also Trever, *Ocherki po istorii i kulture Kavka*ʒ*skoy Albanii*).

The Didos have been connected with the *Diduri* of Pliny

and Ptolemy by Janashvili in his edition of Wakhusht, p. 131, n. 421; affirmed most recently by Trever, p. 48. According to Wakhusht (Brosset ed., p. 325), they had migrated at a remote epoch from *Sa-rkin-eti*, literally, 'the country of iron', a troglodytic settlement to the west of Mtskheta (ibid., 213). As the Georgian root *rkin* implies, the settlement may originally have been the site of iron-mining; and the name *Did-ur-i*, cited by the classical authors, is really a Georgian form 'great', 'big' which can have been derived from Tsikhe-didi or Skhal-didi or Did-Gor – all toponyms in the neighbourhood of Sarkineti (cf. Wak./Brosset, p. 195). The Tsounta/Akhvakh of Baddeley seem to correspond rather closely with the Sodi/Albani of the classical period. The association of the eagle – an obvious totem of mountaineers – sarcastically altered by their neighbours and enemies, the Os/Alans, to a kite (*maeqqael*) has been discussed by Genko (p. 707 ff.). (In this context, it is of interest to recall that Marco Polo, in writing of 'Georgiana and the Kings thereof' records that 'in old times all the kings were born with the figure of an eagle upon the right shoulder', cf. Sir Henry Yule, *The Book of Ser Marco Polo*, 1929 ed., Vol. I, p. 50 *bis*.)

Neighbours of the Didos to the north-west were the *Sodi* of Pliny, VI, 10, whom Trever (p. 202, n. 3) equates with the *Tsavdi*. There is a reference to the Tsavdi in the fifth century A.D. when they are bracketed with the *Lipni* or *Lbini* (Trever, p. 202), who are none other than the Lupeni of the classical authors (Trever, p. 48), a people perhaps to be identified with a wolf totem (cf. Commentary 41 for the cult of a black dog without spots surviving among the Didos).

The name *Tsavdi* corresponds to the Tsova of Wakhusht (Brosset ed. p. 327). It is possible to pinpoint the Tsavdi/Sodi from Wakhusht's account of Tusheti at the beginning of the eighteenth century (see Brosset's ed., pp. 327–9 and map 4 – 'Kakheth'). Tusheti is placed north of Mount Lopeti and the Lopotis-tsqali, clearly toponymic fossils of the old Lupeni, i.e. Lop-eti=the country of the Lup-en-i). The district lies on the flanks of the main chain where it forms the watershed of the Argun flowing north to the Terek and the Andi-koysu flowing north-east to the Sulak and into the Caspian. Tusheti is divided into two valleys running from north-west to south-east. It has its own river (Tchanti-Argun on Baddeley's, *RFC*, Map II where the place-name "Shoundee" still survives) which goes to join the *Sona* (here Argun) which crosses Tchatchan (Chechnia) and at Baraghan falls into the Terg (Terek). Tsova is beyond the Caucasus (i.e. south of the main ridge) in the direction of Pankisi; below Tsova is Gometsari, and lower down Tchagma; from this last place the route leads to the valleys of Torga (cf. Commentary 28: The Village of Tog) and Lopoti: there are situated the principal villages of Tusheti but there are thirty-seven others. Of the remnants of the 'Tsoff' at the beginning of the twentieth century Baddeley, *RFC*, Vol. I, p. 90, observes that ',amongst the Tousheens there is a whole community, known formerly by the name of Tsoff . . . which speaks a dialect of the Kist (Ingush) language and is, presumably, of Kist origin, though cut off from them as far back as history goes'.

Another group of these Sodi/Tsavdi/Tsova maintained their individuality into mediaeval times in the district of Sagaredzho, along the middle reaches of the Iori, since Janashvili, in his edition of Wakhusht (p. 104, n. 351), cites *Kartlis-Tskhovreba*, Vol. I, p. 239, for *Sudzheti* as an alternative name for Sagaredzho, naming the inhabitants *Sudzhi* or *Sodzhi* — forms which closely correspond to the classical Sodi.

Genko, p. 698, recalls that Tsiskarov, in his 'Notes on Tusheti' published in 1849 in the Tiflis journal *Kavkaz*, gives 'Vabua' as a second and ancient name of the original homeland of the Tsov who were then inhabiting the enclave among the Tush. He comments that 'there can be no doubt that the ancient Tsov name for Tsovata, Vabua, is identical with the tribal appelation of the Veppintsy (contemporary form *fäppij*) who were grouped around their ancient centre Erzi *aul* (Arzee on Baddeley's *RFC*, Map II) – on the river Arm-khi (Kistinka) which enters the Terek some versts below Old Lars'. According to the same author (p. 707), *erẓiy* (*ärẓij*) is the Ingush word for 'eagle' – 'in all probability an old Iranian loan-word'. This may be compared with the totemic implications of 'Tsounta' and 'Tsesi', see p. 315 above. In the present writer's view, the Veppintsy (*fäppij*) can be a remnant of the classical Bessi of Macedonia and the Psessoi of the Cimmerian Bosporus, a widespread ethnic group of very ancient origins: for refs. see *BK*, Nos. 30–1, article by Allen, 'Ex Ponto I: Heni-Veneti and Os-Alans', *passim*. To the same remote background belong the Soni / Sodi / Sonti / Tsavdi, who can be identified with the varying forms of the name Heni in classical sources.

In the 'Conversion of Georgia', a record compiled in the tenth century and relating to events of the sixth century, the Daryal gorge is named the 'Tsanar ravine' (cf. Genko, p. 711). The identity of Tsanar (in Georgian *Ts'anar* with ejaculative *ts'*) with Ptolemy's *Zanarioi* has been accepted by Minorsky (*HA*, pp. 400 ff.). Zan-ari-oi, in fact represents the root *ẓan* > *son* with the duplication of the Svanian plural in -*ar* and the Greek plural in -*oi*. 'In the ninth to tenth century A.D. the Tsanar are often identified with the Kakhs. Finally, the Georgian-speaking peoples entirely absorbed the Tsanar... As regards the nucleus of the Tsanar tribe, N. Y. Marr (*Iẓ. RAN*, 1916, pp. 1397–8), hinted at its common origin with the present day Chechen. Such is also the opinion of A. N. Genko, the undisputed authority on that part of the Caucasus' (Minorsky, ibid., and Genko, 711).

The region occupied by Ptolemy's Zanarioi and by the mediaeval Tsanar corresponds to the country round the Caucasian Gates where Pliny places the Suani and 'the numerous tribes of Heniochi'. *Heni-och-i* is, in fact, another example of a duplicated plural, with Armenian *kh'* and Latin *-i* added to the original Caucasic *heni*. Again, *He-n-i*, with the enclosed Georgian plural form *-n-*, recovers an original singular *He-i*: cf. Armenian, *Hai*, plural *Hai'k*. This name-form, representing perhaps a breath articulation, occurs in many languages and can signify 'man' or 'self'. In *VDI*, 1950, Vol. 4, p. 31, Melikishvili gives the Hurrian word for 'brother' as *šeni*, with variants found in personal names, *-šina, ẕana*. This seems to correspond closely with the concept of *heni* as a collective name for men, brothers, *combroges* in the Celtic sense. *Soni* is a variant of forms widespread through the Ponto-Mediterranean world – where often the Georgian locative termination *-eti* is retained, as in *Chan-eti* (*G.* name for Lazistan), *Eneti, Heneti, Veneti* (here see Strabo, Loeb ed., index). In Caucasia the variations may be noted in *Svan-n-i*, the Svans, Strabo's *Soanes*, inhabiting *Svan-eti*; in the name of the Armenian principality of Siunik; and, possibly, *Honi* (Arm. *Hon'k*) which has often been taken to signify 'Huns' (see Trever, p. 193 and n. 4; and further Allen, *BK*, No. 33, 1959, pp. 10–11, particularly notes 55 and 56).

To conclude, *Sonskaya ẕemlya* should not be confused with Svaneti, the region round the upper Ingur, more than a hundred miles to the west of Daryal, which is also named *Sonskaya ẕemlya* or *Soni* in the reports of F. Elchin's mission to Mingrelia in 1650 (*Put. Russ. Poslov*, pp. 207, 225, 420). In our text, it is the country south of the Daryal and round the sources of the Aragvi; the land of the mediaeval Tsanar and of 'the numerous tribes of the Heniochi' of the classical writers.

COMMENTARY 21

The rivers of Kakheti: the Aragvi, the Iora (Iori) and the Alazani (ref. Chap. 3, p. 134, n. 1; p. 136, n. 2)

(a) *The river Aragvi* (ref. p. 134, n. 1). Flowing west to east and then north–south, the river formed the boundary between the kingdoms of Kartli and Kakheti at the turn of the sixteenth century. The Aragvi joins the Kura (*G.* Mtkwari) to the east of Mtskheta which stands on a peninsula between the two rivers. 'It takes its name "Black Aragvi" from its nature – flowing fast and carrying all before it and appearing black from its depth. It is a river without use. No fish are taken from it, except salmon at certain times of the year (Wak. Brosset, p. 215). Below Ananuri the Black (*shavi*) Aragvi receives the smaller White (*tetri*) Aragvi coming out of Khevsureti from the north-east (ibid, p. 297). For a good description of the country through which the Aragvi flows, see Dubois, Vol. IV, p. 242.

The White Aragvi is sometimes called Khevsuretis-Aragvi, Aragvi of Khevsureti, by contrast with its left-bank feeder, Pshav Aragvi, Aragvi of the Pshav (tribe). The last has its source on the south-west flank of Botanis-mta, a westerly shoulder of Mount Borbalo (3,294 m.). On the northern flank of Botanis-mta the Argun, an affluent of the Terek, has its easterly feeders.

The two other principal rivers of Kakheti, the Iori and the Alazani, find their sources from the southern outliers of Mount Borbalo and flow in a general direction east-south-east to unite before entering the Kura. The sources of the Aragvi, the Iori and the Alazani, are distant from each other not more than fifty miles as the crow flies. These features are indicated well enough on Wak./Brosset Map 6, compiled as early as the 1720s (see Allen, *IM*, Vol. XIII, pp. 157 ff.); and on Delisle's *Carte Générale* of 1766. For a good account of the topography of the region, see Radde *Chew'suren*, pp. 3 ff. and 171 ff., and *Übersichts Karte* at end of volume.

9. The citadel of Gremi (by courtesy of Prof. Irakli Tsitsishvii).

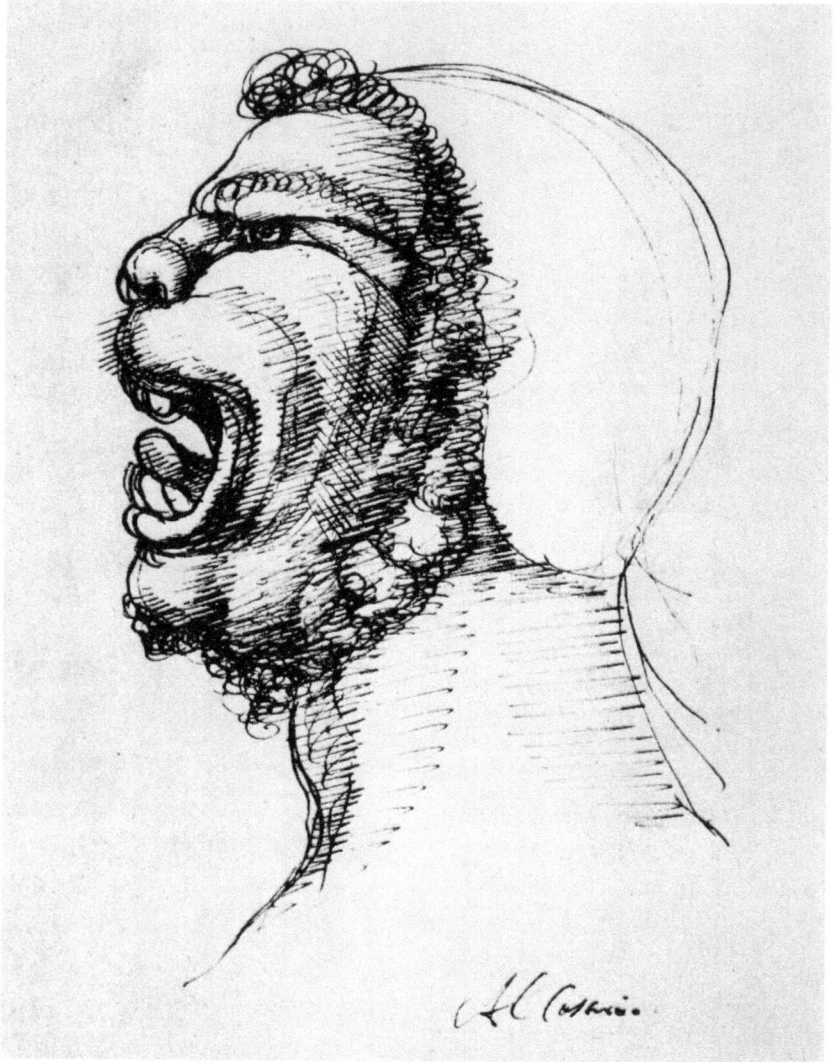

10. A Caucasian mountaineer. After Castelli.

The Aragvi is the Aragon of Strabo (Book XI, 3, ii); for discussion see also Cellarius, Vol. II, p. 311. The first Russian Atlas, published by the Academy of Sciences of St Petersburg in 1745, omits the Aragvi, and is, in fact, inadequate for all the eastern Caucasus. It is clearly delineated on Wakhusht's maps, prepared c. 1724 (cf. Wak./Brosset, Maps 3, 4, 6) and in J. N. Delisle's *Carte Générale*, 1766. The latter had access to Wakhusht's maps – which remained in MS. until Brosset published them three quarters of a century later.

(b) '*Loẓan*' (ref. p. 136, n. 2)=Alazani river. 'The great rivers of this country are the Alazani and the Little Alazani or Iori (*G. Ioris-tsqali*) which take their name from (the plain of) Aloni' (Wak./Brosset, p. 289). The valleys of these two rivers, each some hundred miles in length, form the oblong body of Kakheti – between the course of the Kura, virtual boundary with Kartli, and the mountains of Daghestan. Along the upper and middle reaches of the two rivers 'the climate is excellent, winter is mild, and the heat of summer not extreme ... The country is very fertile in all sorts of grains, in vines and in fruits; full of animals, game, birds and fish ... You find there silk, cotton and rice; the date-palm and chestnut' (Wak./Brosset, pp. 287 ff.).

In the lower reaches the two streams unite below the site of Khoranta before entering the Kura. This region was in ancient times called Hereti – from which the name of the important trading centre of Areshi, mentioned in our texts, apparently derives (cf. Commentary 32: Genzha and Areshi). Commanding the approaches to Kakheti and into Kartli along the middle course of the Kura, it was always a region of strategic importance. (On the small Kanak (or Kinik) tributary of the Alazani, above Khoranta, there was heavy fighting between the Ottomans and the Persians in 1578: cf. Asafi MS., f. 22v, for passage of the river Kinik by Özdemiroghlu Osman). Round the lower reaches of the two rivers and extending along the middle course of the Kura, the country was flat – *Kambechovani*, the plain of buffaloes, Cambysene of the classical writers. 'It is warm in winter, grassy, with little snow; it has game and birds and the air is of a pleasant temperature; but in summer it is hot, un-healthy and unbearable' (Wak./Brosset, p. 289).

For classical references to the river Alazani, see Cellarius, Vol. II, p. 316; and Trever, pp. 102 ff. For an attractive descrip-tion of the country-side and its antiquities see Brosset, *VA*, *1er rapport, Tiflis-Thélaw*, pp. 80 ff. For the more remote connotations and cult-significance of the root *hal*, see Allen, *BK*, Nos. 32–3, article 'Ex Ponto', nn. 15 and 43 and ibid. Nos. 34–5, p. 85; also cf. E. Cavaignac, *JA*, Vol. CCXI/vii/3, pp. 297–301, article 'Alashia-Elise'.

According to Wakhusht 'the banks of the Iori river, both of them, are very fruitful, for water channels have been dug, the fields are irrigated and all kinds of grain grow there. Small groves follow the Iori and reeds and bulrushes, and much game and birds, and especially pheasants, until it falls into the Alazani'. In his edition of Wakhusht, Janashia (p. 102, n. 346) connects the name Iora/Iori with Georgian *Ivris-kheoba*= 'the valley of Ivri' – from the old name Iberia.

COMMENTARY 22

The horses called 'argamaks' (ref. Chap. 3, p. 138, n. 2)

'A fine Asiatic horse' (Sreznevski, *MSDY*), the name first cited in a Russian source in 1483: 'Give me a fast (tempestuous) *argamak*.' According to Vasmer, *s.v.*, the word for 'this best race of central Asian horse' is derived from Chagatay *argamak*, Uigur *argumak*, Old Turkish *argumak*, Mongol *argamag*. See also Dahl *s.v.* Herberstein (*NR*, Hakluyt ed., Vol. II, p. 135), refers to 'beautiful horses of that race which we call Turkish, but which they call *argumak*'. Jenkinson (*EVT*, Vol. I, p. 89), states that the Persians 'bring thither (to Muscovy) Argomaks'.

The editors (ibid., n. 1), describe the *argamak* as 'a Turkoman horse crossed with Arab stock'. It was habitual to send them as presents to Russian Tsars and Chinese emperors; in this connection see text, p. 227. In the fourteenth century, the Mongols exported thousands of horses each year from the north Caucasian steppe for sale in India. 'The people of India do not buy them for (their qualities in) running or racing, because they themselves wear coats of mail in battle and they cover their horses with armour, and what they prize in these horses is strength and length of pace.' Racing stock was imported from the Yemen, Oman and Fars (Gibb, *Ibn Battuta*, Vol. ii, p. 479). Pallas (*TSP*, Vol. i, pl. 20), depicts a Circassian prince in chain mail mounted on a high-stepping *argamak*, the right flank branded with the particular mark (or *tamga*) of the clan that bred him. (Güldenstädt, Vol. ii, p. 21, states that the Kabardans always branded on the left flank.) Pallas writes: 'The Circassians endeavour to breed not only beautiful, but at the same time strong and durable animals, which are capable of undergoing hunger and fatigue, and also excell in swiftness ... Almost every family of distinction, whether Princes or Nobles, boasts of possessing a peculiar race of horses ... The most celebrated race of Circassian horses has received the name of *Shalokh*, and is in the exclusive possession of the Tausultan family (of Little Kabarda – descendants of the Solokh of our narrative) ... The horses of *Tramkt* and *Lof*, among the Abassines (Abaza), and those of *Misaost* (Mosost) in the Great Kabarda, are also highly valued, as well as the Persian race termed *Tshepalau*.' (See Pallas's pl. 21 for *tamgas* of the different breeds.)

See also Güldenstädt (Vol. ii, p. 21), for an account of 3,000 mares and their foals, with a few stallions, belonging to twelve princes of Great Kabarda, which all came to drink water of the salt lake Tambi, near Besh-Tau. This herd apparently belonged to the Beslenei princes; but Baddeley (*RFC*, Vol. ii, p. 225), identifies the breed of Tram or Tramkt with the lake Tambi. Baddeley adds 'the large liquid eyes, the chief bodily character-istic of the genuine Shaulokhs, through which their mild yet indomitable spirit shone, were unmistakable; besides which, according to Pallas, they had another more definite peculiarity in that the hoof was quite full and without frog'.

The high value placed on these blood horses in the mediaeval Caucasus is indicated by the fact that David Soslan, the swash-buckling Alan husband of Queen Tamar (1189–1212), gave a village and a castle for the bay charger of the Prince of Khachen – 'a famous animal' (Allen, *HGP*, p. 333, citing Brosset, *HG*, Vol. I, p. 441).

COMMENTARY 23

St George of Alaverdi (ref. Chap. 3, p. 139, n. 1)

There is good account in Amiranashvili (pp. 158–62 and *passim, risunki*, pp. 39 and 40 for plan and elevation). He places it, with Oshki, Khakhuli, the cathedral of Kutaissi, Sveti-Tskhoveli, Kumurdo and Nikortsminda, among the finest examples of the mature period of mediaeval Georgian architec-ture. Built in the first half of the eleventh century, it was later damaged by earthquake, and reconstructed at the end of the fifteenth century. Partly destroyed by the troops of Shah Abbas in 1615, it was restored in the eighteenth century by Irakli II. This was the structure which Brosset described in 1850, *VA, 1er rapport*, pp. 64 ff.: 'L'enceinte du monastère est, comme celle de Mtzkhétha, carrée, avec des tours; à l'intérieur sont adossés à la muraille, le couvent proprement dit, les maisons d'habitation des serviteurs, les magazins, la cave . . . L'église de S. Georges d'Alawerd m'a paru plus haute et presque aussi vaste que celle de Mtzkhétha. Elle est construite en croix, avec coupole conique, et toute blanchie par dehors, ce qui la fait détacher de loin sur le fonds de verdure dont elle est entourée.'

Güldenstädt (Vol. I, p. 241), visited Alaverdi in the suite of Irakli II, on 18 March 1772. For brief description, with details of icons, cf. Bakradze, *Akty*, Vol. v, pp. 994–5. According to Wakhusht, the monastery takes its name from *Alon-gwerdi*, 'the flank of Mount Alon' (for Aloni, see above, p. 199). The Alaverdeli, or Bishop of Alaverdi, was the premier bishop of Kakheti, and his see covered all mountain Kakheti; cf. Wak./ Brosset, p. 321, Wak./Jan., p. 127, n. 1, and Bakradze, *Akty*, Vol. v, pp. 994–5.

An account of the remnants of frescoes, and the icons and MSS remaining in the monastery in the 1890s was published by A. S. Khakhanov (Khakhanashvili) in *MAK*, Vol. vii (1898), pp. 8 ff., with a good view of the cathedral, *ris.* 3; fullest and most recent account, with plans and views by G. N. Chubinashvili, is in *AK*, Vol. i, pp. 369–405 and *passim*.

For Iskander Munshi's description of the Alaverdeli's crown and treasures, found by the Persians in the castle of Tharaghai (Torga) in 1615, see Brosset, *HG*, Vol. ii/i, p. 477.

COMMENTARY 24

The sacred decorations of a Georgian church (ref. Chap. 3, p. 141, n. 1, Chap. 5, p. 186, n. 1)

(a) *Note on the Altar*. According to the rites of the Eastern Church the altar, which should be at least partly of wood, must have several coverings spread over it. The first is of white linen and is next to the altar itself; it is called the 'shirt' (*R. srachitsa, Gr. katasarka*). Golubinski thinks that the original purpose served by the 'shirt' was to protect the richer covering placed on top of it; it was not necessarily present in the days before Simeon of Salonica. The outer covering, or *endyton*, was often made of rich brocade or embroidery. A folded piece of cloth or wrap, called the *heileton*, should lie on top of the *endyton*. These altar vestments symbolize Christ's death and resurrection.

The *antimension* should be kept on the altar, folded in the *heileton*. It consists of a strip of fine linen or silk, usually ten inches wide and about thirteen or fourteen inches long, ornamented with the instruments of the Passion, or with the representation of Christ in the Sepulchre; relics of saints are sewn into it. Originally, the *antimension* was a portable altar which missionaries or travelling priests could use, but gradually it came to be used for all altars in the Greek church.

The following articles should be kept on the altar: the Book of the Gospels, a cross, the vessels in which communion bread is kept and containers – often shaped like models of churches, for keeping the Sacraments. (Golubinski, pp. 167–74; *The Catholic Encyclopaedia*, articles 'Antimensium' and 'Altar (in the Greek Church'); Brockhaus and Efron.)

(b) The icon called *deesis* (*R. deisus*), in its simplest form, showed Christ with the Virgin and John the Baptist in prayer on either side; the figures of other saints were sometimes added. The *deesis* was the principal, and sometimes the only, icon in the *iconostasis*. It was placed above the central, or royal, gate into the altar precinct. The main tier of icons consisted of images of Jesus Christ and of the Virgin and Child immediately to the right and left of the royal gates, respectively, and of icons of important saints including the patron saint of the church; these large icons were known in Russia as *mestnye* (lit. 'local'), a term the interpretation of which gives Golubinski a lot of trouble, particularly since it was applied not only to the large icons in the lower tier of the *iconostasis* but also to free-standing icons of the same size. In Russian churches the icons representing the principal festivals of Christ and the Virgin were placed in the second tier of the *iconostasis* (in their description – see p. 140 – the ambassadors draw attention to the fact that the Georgians had placed the icons of the festivals in the row below their customary place in Russian churches). (c) *Korsun* is the Russian form of Kherson (Cherson – the later name of Chersonesus Taurica – the site of which is just south of Sevastopol). The name is applied to all sorts of objects, because of foreign, mostly Genoese, trade in the fourteenth and fifteenth centuries, both from the east and the west, passing through Kerch and Kherson. The icons which bear in Russian tradition the name of *Korsun* are all of them distinguished by a scale of dark chocolate or brown upon a buff ground and these Korsun icons which came to Russia from Chersonesus Taurica, Caffa and Trebizond were copies of Greco-Oriental models (ref. Minns/Kondakov, pp. 15, 77–8).

COMMENTARY 25

The town of Krym = Gremi (ref. Chap. 3, p. 137, n. 1. and see Plate 9, facing p. 320.)

Gremi lay on the stream of the same name which flows south-west from the slopes of the Caucasus into the Alazani. The remains of this once important place are about 18 versts east-north-east of the modern town of Telavi. Strategically Gremi was well situated for the defence of Kakheti since it commanded the approaches over the flanking ridge of Didoeti, forming the watershed from which flow, in a general north-easterly direction, the several *koysus* feeding the Sulak, the principal river of the country of the Avars and Kumukhs – frequent raiders of Kakheti during the period of the Russian embassies.

According to Wakhusht Gremi became a town only in 1466, after the division of the united Georgian kingdom, when the kings of Kakheti made their residence there. In the sixteenth century the church and houses were still intact; but after the invasion of Shah Abbas, at the beginning of the seventeenth century, Gremi declined to the status of a simple burgh (Wak./Brosset, p. 317; Wak./Jan., p. 123). In March 1772 Güldenstädt (Vol. I, p. 241), visited Gremi with King Irakli II and wrote that five churches still remained, some with Georgian and some with Armenian inscriptions. Khakhanov, in his excellent description (*MAK*, Vol. VI, pp. 4, ff.) refers to Gremi as *nakalakevi*, 'where there was once a town'; he states that it had existed from the first centuries of Christianity and, according to tradition had covered an area of two versts, doubtless straggling along both banks of the river, as in the case of old Kutaissi. There were Georgian, Armenian and Jewish quarters with extensive cemeteries. To the west, on the slope of the mountain, some two hundred yards to the west of the Armenian cemetery, rose a three-storied castle with a walled enclosure which protected the church of the Archangel Michael (cf. Amiranashvili, pl. 171), where King Levan was buried. No less than ten churches were grouped around this area. A little to the north was the palace of King Levan, later destroyed by Shah Abbas.

Abbas's biographer, Iskander Munshi, describes *Ghirem* (Gremi) as 'an agreeable and charming place, where there is a magnificent church' (Brosset, *HG*, Vol. II/i, pp. 476–7). Janashvili (p. 123, n. 406) cites from the Georgian work *Archiliani*, composed in 1681, an account of the celebrations at Gremi in 1605, on the occasion of the return of the young King Taymuraz I from Persia and his marriage.

For a recent description of Gremi, see Amiranashvili, pp. 268–270, where, on the remains of the frescoes, he notes the influence of Russian restorers at the beginning of the seventeenth century; for further refs., not available to me, see Amiranashvili's n. 1 at p. 270. Also Chubinashvili, *AK*, Vol. I, pp. 440 ff.

The name root g(k)-r-m recurs in Gremis-khevi in the valley of the Aragvi; it may be compared with Gimri in Daghestan; Gümrü in Armenia (=Aleksandropol=Leninakan); Kemir-goi, the name of a branch of the Kabardans; and Kirim (=Crimea). These names are all, perhaps, fossils of a Cimmerian (Gimir) toponymic stratum in the east Pontic area.

COMMENTARY 26

On royal falcons and falconry in Russia and Georgia (ref. Chap. 3, p. 144, n. 2)

(It has not been found possible to use strict hawking parlance to translate Russian sixteenth-century terms in the text.)

A noted sportsman in his day, King Alexander of Kakheti proved more interested in the gerfalcons than in the other sacred or luxury gifts which had been sent to him by Tsar Fedor Ivanovich. It is of interest, therefore, to examine in detail the description of these noble birds and to establish their significance in the scale of royal gifts. It would seem that the finest gerfalcons were regarded as the equals of the splendid *argamak* horses which it was the custom of the Georgian kings to send as gifts to the Muscovite court.

In our text the word *krechet* signifies gerfalcon as distinct from *sokol*, hawk (cf. Dahl; also Vasmer, *REW*, *s.v.*, who cites Ukrainian *krechet* as meaning 'weisse Edelfalke', and prefers to reject borrowing from Mongol *hýrcŭt*).

Sokol has numerous forms in Slav languages, see Vasmer, *REW*, Vol. II, p. 688, who does not accept derivation from Arabic *sakr* – from which comes *saker* (through the Portuguese *sacre*), a name for a kind of falcon common throughout Mediterranean Europe and the Levant. It would seem therefore that the rendering of *krechet krasny* as 'a female saker' in the list of Russian falconry terms in *Bibliotheca accipitraria* (Hastings, 1891, pp. 191–2) is unacceptable.

In *De arte venandi*, the Emperor Frederick II of Hohenstaufen (*c.* 1238) treats in detail of the gerfalcon and its coloration:

Out of respect for their size, strength, audacity and swiftness, the gerfalcons shall be given first place in our treatise . . . Gerfalcons are fledged in or near the most distant parts of the seventh climatic zone, not infrequently on high cliffs, often in crannies, caves and holes on mountain sides, either near to or distant from the seacoast;

the farther the birthplace from the ocean the more beautiful and noble they are. Some of them are brooded on the high cliffs of the Hyperborean territory, particularly on a certain island lying between Norway and Greenland (*Gallandia*); called in Teutonic speech Iceland (*Yslandia*) . . . These falcons are the best birds for hunting . . . They generally build their nests and sojourn in the seventh climatic zone, but never in the sixth, fifth, or fourth zones . . . The feathers of gerfalcons are some of them grey, some of them white, while others are whitish – particularly on the breast. Others again, show a mixture of white and grey which many call hemp-coloured. The white tints on the breast are the most brilliant; those on the back during the first year are partly reddish, partly rust-coloured. After moulting, the red feathers assume a black shade, the whole of the plumage becomes more marked, and the mandibles and claws of the white gerfalcon, more than those of other birds of the genus, have a decided iridescence. Grey gerfalcons display, before moulting, feathers of a variety of color; some of them are dark or blackish, others rust-coloured. These latter are of two types: they may have spots all over the back and tail, or they may be entirely free of such markings. Some are decidedly speckled, some less so. Very dark specimens may turn reddish, dark and grey after the moult; if they are not of the spotted variety the coloration may turn to bright grey and red; if bespeckled, hemp-coloured. Bright grey birds after their moult become either whiter or greyer.

(Cited from *The art of falconry* . . . *of Frederick II*, translated and edited by C. A. Wood and F. M. Fyfe, Oxford, 1943/55,

Vol. III, p. 121.)

Following these indications, it would seem as though the *krechet krasny* which survived the journey from Moscow to Kakheti was a red or rufous gerfalcon in its first year. The *podkrasny*, which died, may have been a dark specimen which turned reddish after moulting, while the *kroplenoy* was of the speckled variety. The distinctive colours described by Prince Semen are met with elsewhere in Russian texts: for instance – *i prisylat k nam Velikomu Gosudaryu krechaty i cheligi krechety samye lutchiye, krasnye i podkrasnye i tsvetnye* = 'and send to us, the Great Lord, gerfalcons and fledglings of the very best gerfalcons, red and reddish and speckled'. (*STsSRY*, Vol. IV, col. 900, under *chelig*.)

Dresser (*Birds of Europe*, London, 1871–81, Vol. VI, p. 16, with fine coloured plates) describes the gerfalcons as brown rather than red but states that they are subject to considerable variations in shade and colour. 'The range of the so-called "Norwegian" or true gerfalcon, in contradistinction to the Iceland or Greenland species, is somewhat extensive as it inhabits Northern Scandinavia and North Russia, and thence is found right across Northern Asia into Arctic America.'

A near contemporary of the falconer Sychov, Pierre Belon du Mans (*Histoire de la nature des oiseaux* (Paris, 1555), pp. 94–6, with a fine woodcut) describes the gerfalcon as 'one and a half times as big as the falcon', and of a proud and daring nature. 'We would not see him if he were not brought from foreign lands, and they say that he comes from the part of Russia where he makes his eyre, and that he frequents neither Italy nor France, and that he is a bird of passage in High and Low Germany.'

From all this it would seem that the gerfalcons known to Frederick II in the thirteenth century may well have been brought from Norway or from Iceland, even from Greenland where the Norwegians kept in touch with their colonies by ship convoys from Bergen; but the gerfalcons of the Russian Tsars in the sixteenth century were natives of Russia.

In an account of the regimen of the Tsar's mews of the year 1668, with notes in the hand of Tsar Alexey Mikhailovich who was devoted to the sport of falconry, it is clear that his birds came mostly from Kholmogory, the depot for the White Sea peninsulas, from the Pechora, and Siberia. His favourite bird was the speckled Siberian gerfalcon Gamayun. The Tsar favoured particularly grey gerfalcons (the taste of Emperor

Frederick), but he kept in his mews also *yastreby* (goshawks – *Astur palumbarius*) and *kobetsy* (*Falco apivorus*, according to Dahl). It is of interest to note that falconers (*sokolniki*) of the royal mews, reported as drunken, quarrelsome, intriguing or merely stupid, were liable to be transported in chains to the Lena – which was a region where falcons were sought. (For details see *DRV*, *i*χ*d. vtoroye, chast* III (Moskva, 1788), 430 ff., '*Kniga glagolemaya uryadnik: novoye ulo*χ*heniye i china sokolnich'ya puti*', particularly 456 ff.) Three centuries before the time of Tsar Alexey Mikhailovich, falcons were already being brought from the far north-east, for we read that in the year 1329 Grand Duke Ivan Danilovich of all Russia bestowed a gift on eight falconers from the Pechora (M. I. Sreznevski, *Materialy dlya slovarya drevnerusskogo ya*χ*yka*, Vol. III, p. 459, under *sokolnik*).

In the early eighteenth century John Bell of Antermony, writing of Zabak-Zar (Cheboksary) on the middle Volga, alluded to this region as a main source of supply for the Middle East:

In this country are caught the best and largest faulcons in the world, much esteemed for their strength and beauty; particularly by the Turks and Persians who purchase them very dear. The Russians take few young hawks from the nest, preferring the old ones, which they man very dextrously to fly at swan, goose, crane or heron. The Tartars fly them at antelope and hares. I have seen them take a wild-duck out of the water, when nothing of her could be perceived but the bill, which was obliged to put up for air. Some of them are as white as a dove. The manner of catching them is very simple. They erect a tall pole upon a hill, free from wood, on a bank of the river, near which is placed a day-net (= clap-net); under the net some small birds are fastened by a cord, which the hawk-catcher pulls to make them flutter, on the appearance of the hawk, who observing his prey first perches on the pole, and when he stoops to seize the birds, the person, who is concealed by the bushes, draws the net and covers him (Bell, *Travels*, Vol. I, p. 18).

On long journeys falcons were transported in large padded boxes, but despite all the precautions taken, the birds often failed to reach their destinations alive; thus the birds which Andrey Zvenigorodski was carrying to Shah Abbas in 1594 died during the crossing of the Caspian, while two others sent in 1597 with the ill-fated Tyufyakin mission succumbed to the heat of Ghilan. The standard instructions to ambassadors were to feed a falcon on two pigeons or one hen a day, and to get as much ice as was required for the bird (cf. *TVOIAO*, Vol. xx (1890), N. K. Veselovski, '*Pamyatniki diplomaticheskikh i torgovykh snosheniy Moskovskoy Rusi s Persiyey, I, Tsarstvovaniye Fedora Ioannovicha*, pp. 246 ff., 430 ff.). In these documents a falconer is styled *krechetnik* and not *sokolnik*.

The Caucasus and notably the coasts of the Caspian were famed for falcons. For the tenth century, Mas'udi has a dissertation on the falcons of the Caspian:

In this sea are islands opposite the coast of Jorjan (Gurgan), where a sort of white falcons are caught. These falcons are soon made tame; and one has little to fear that they will associate (with the wild birds); but they are rather weak, for the sportsmen who catch them in those islands feed them with fish; and if any other food is given to them they become reduced in strength. Men who distinguish themselves by their knowledge of falconry, and of the different sorts of rapacious birds which have been employed for the same purpose, among them Persians, Turks, Byzantines, Hindus and Arabs, say that falcons of a white colour are quickest and handsomest; that they have the best shape and chest; and that they are soonest tamed, and the strongest of all falcons to rise in the air; that they have the longest breath, and fly furthest, for they are light and spirited, and they have a hotter temper than any other species of falcons. The difference of colour depends upon the difference of climate. Hence they are of pure white in Armenia, and in the country of the Khazar, in Jorjan, and in the neighbouring countries of the Turks, on account of the great fall of snow in these climates.

(Mas'udi= *Maçoudi, Les Prairies d'Or, texte et traduction par*

333

C. Barbier de Meynard, 8 vols., Paris 1883, citation from Vol. I, p. 423, anglicized by Allen, *HGP*, p. 328.)

According to Dr. Radde, the Caucasian goshawk (*Astur Palumbarius*, Russian *yastreb*, Georgian *kori*, Persian/Tartar *tarlan*) when old was particularly light-coloured, sometimes completely white, and sold at a very high price in Daghestan; but a young specimen was called *kizil-kush*=red bird. Radde records that Feizulla Bey of Akhaltsikhe had told him that white goshawks were very rare in western Georgia and Radde himself would not admit of the existence in the Caucasus of the light-coloured, or completely white 'noble' falcons of the northern countries. He believed it to be a white variety of the goshawk (*utyatnik* or 'duck-hawk') already described by Pallas (*Zoographia*, p. 369) or a very light *Falco Sacer* (*R. galoban*). Radde only once saw one *Falco Sacer* among the Tartars of the Caspian lowlands; in a few hours he killed fifteen or twenty partridges (*R. kuropatka*) and Caucasian snow partridges (*Tetrogallus Caucasicus*, *R. turach*), small bustards (*Otis tetrax*, *R. strepet*) and pheasants. These white falcons of which he heard stories were very costly. One belonged to a bey in Elizavetopol and was priced at sixty gold rubles. Nearly the same prices were paid by Kalmucks to the east of the middle course of the Volga where, according to Bogdanov (*Zveri i ptitsy Povolzhya*, p. 44), they bartered them against horses. (Dr Gustav Radde, *Ornitologicheskaya fauna Kavkaza* (*Ornis Caucasica*), with plates, Tiflis, 1885, pp. 81–3.)

In his brief account of 'Georgiana and the kings thereof', Marco Polo says that the country produces the best goshawks in the world which are called Avighi. Sir Henry Yule cites Jerome Cardan as noting that 'the best and biggest goshawks came from Armenia' – a name which, as Yule observes – often included Georgia and the Caucasus. He adds that 'Major St John tells me that the Terlan or goshawk, much used in Persia, is still generally brought from Caucasus'. Yule proposes that 'the name of the bird is perhaps the same as *Afji Falco montanus*, the hen-harrier' (Yule, Vol. I, p. 50 (twice) and n. 5). *Avighi* is near enough to Turkish *avji*, 'hunter', and can indeed have the sense of harrier; in a thirteenth century Georgian context it was probably a loan-word from the Seljuks with whom the Georgian nobility were in frequent contact.

In the Georgian epic poems of the turn of the twelfth century, allusions to falconry are frequent; although poetic licence seems to take precedence over zoological precision. (For *Vepkhis Tqaosani*, I cite the English version of Miss Marjory Wardrop, *The man in the panther's skin*, Oriental Translations Fund, New Series, Vol. XXI, London, 1912; for *Visramiani*, Sir Oliver Wardrop's English version, *OTF*, New Ser., XXIII, 1914; for *Amiran-Darejaniani*, R. H. Stevenson's English reading, Oxford, 1958.

Vepkhis Tqaosani, p. 703, *kori*: 'The king mounted. How can the pomp of those times be told now? By reason of the beating of the copper drums no word was heard by the ears. The hawks darkened the sun; hither and thither coursed the hounds; the fields were dyed purple with the blood shed by them.'

Ibid., pp. 459/62, *shavardeni* as a synonym for *kori*: 'I apparelled myself, I went into the hall of audience; a pack of harriers (*avaza*=hunting panther) met me, all the space around the hall was full of falcons . . . We hunted over the plain, mountain-foot and hill; there was a multitude of hounds, falcons and hawks. We returned early without having gone a stage from the long road.'

Visramiani, p. 277: 'He had slain so much game that mountain and plain could not find room for them: a needle even could not fall on the earth because of the hunting panthers and dogs; the air was full of hawks (*kori*), kites (*gavazi*) and falcons (*shavardeni*).'

Amiran-Darejaniani, p. 1 and n. 5: *k'ori t'et'ri da mçqazari*:

which the writer translates as 'white falcons and hawks', with the note that 'falcon' is used merely to avoid repetition: 'it would appear that *mçqaẓari* denotes a particular species of hawk, but it is impossible to determine which'. (Prof. Lang citing D. Chubinov, *Gruẓino-russki slovar*, SPB, 1887, col. 932, writes that *mçqaẓari* means 'fair', 'snow-white'.)

These descriptions reflect the scenes in Persian miniatures, and, again, Marco Polo's near-contemporary account of the hunting expeditions of Kubilay Khan (1260–94); 'He starts off on the 1st day of March, and travels southward towards the Ocean Sea, a journey of two days. He takes with him full 10,000 falconers, and some 500 gerfalcons besides peregrines, sakers and other hawks in great numbers; and goshawks also to fly at the waterfowl . . . And as he goes there is many a fine sight to be seen, and plenty of the very best entertainment in hawking; in fact there is no sport in the world to equal it' (Yule, *Marco Polo*, Vol. I, p. 404).

The more modest hunts of the Georgian kings were, in their way, lavish and ceremonial. According to Wakhusht (Brosset's ed., pp. 19–20) the Chief of the Falconers (*Baẓiert' Ukhutẓesi*) ranked after the Grand Equerry (*Amirakhori*). This latter office derives from the Persian *mirakhor-bashi* – 'master of the marshals' (*mirakhoran*=grooms of the stables) (Minorsky, *TAM*, pp. 52–3, 120–1). (The post became hereditary and the name is borne by the distinguished Georgian family of Amilakhvari; one of the name was killed in command of a battalion of the Foreign Legion at the Battle of Bir-Hakeim in 1942.) The Chief of the Falconers was responsible for the management of the royal falcons (*baẓni*, pl.) and falconers (*baẓierni*, pl.), the hounds and kennel-men, and of the keepers of the woods and plains of the royal hunting demesnes. Alexander II of Kakheti is the hero of the only anecdote of hawking which occurs in the Georgian annals. Wakhusht records that 'having learnt from his falconers that they had seen strange birds in the plain of Aloni, he went off in haste and found that they were peacocks. He wanted to take them alive, but not a single falcon would take any notice of them; there was only a red falcon which took as many as there were; they were brought to Gremi where they called incessantly, which made Kakheti seem like the fabulous land of the Qapuzuna, where the sheep go to'. (*Histoire de Kakheth*, in Brosset *HG*, Vol. II/i, pp. 154–5; the Qapuzuna, says Brosset, are monkeys, and the reference is to a passage in the Book of Kalila and Dimna.)

It is permissible to surmize that 'the red falcon' may have been the *krechet krasnoy* which had survived the journey from Moscow to Gremi and which the falconer Ivan Sychov had assured the king, could take swans (*lovit lebedi*). The capture of swans would demand the strength and courage of gerfalcons (Frederick's *falcones absolute gentiles*) as in the Tale of Igor (for citation, cf. Sreznevski, Vol. III, p. 459, under *sokolnik*; or in the great hunts of Kubilay Khan.

Additional Note: The Georgian Kori (falcon) and the Egyptian god Hor.

The Egyptian Hor was a solar god identified by the Greeks with Apollo. He was represented by a falcon or a falcon-headed being. 'Under the name Hor – which in Egyptian sounds like a word meaning "sky"–the Egyptians referred to the falcon which they saw soaring high above their heads, and many thought of the sky as a divine falcon whose two eyes were the sun and the moon. The worshippers of this bird must have been numerous and powerful; for it was carried as a totem on prehistoric standards and from the earliest times was considered the pre-eminent divine being. The hieroglyph which represents the idea of "god" was a falcon on its perch' (*Larousse Encyclopedia of Mythology*, London, 1959, pp. 18 ff., with several illustrations of Horus as the falcon-headed god).

Again, Janashvili, in his edition of Wakhusht (p. 203, n. 564) alludes to the correspondence of the Mingrelian river-name Sebeka, an affluent of the Rioni, with that of the ancient Egyptian crocodile-god Sobek, a marine deity (cf. Karst, *MA-C*, p. 337).

These semantic coincidences make it tempting to recall the statement of Herodotus (Book II, *Euterpe*, 104): 'It is obvious that the Colchians are an Egyptian race. Before I heard any mention of the matter from others, I had remarked it myself.' He attributes the tradition to the belief that the Colchians were descended from the army of the legendary Sesostris. For the identity and conquests of 'Sesostris' and for the exaggerated concepts of 'world empires' among the ancients, see A. W. Lawrence's interpretation of Herodotus, Book II, p. 103, n. 1. Commenting on Herodotus's statement about the Colchians, Lawrence adds (Book II, p. 104, n. 1): 'The suggestion that they were of similar stock to the Egyptians is comparatively plausible because of archaeological indications that Egypt received immigrants from the Caspian area at the end of the Old Kingdom; Egyptian culture subsequently had some slight influence in the Caucasus (Avdieff, *Ancient Egypt*, 1933, p. 29).'

In an article 'The Caucasian counterpart of an old Egyptian racing chariot' in *Georgica*, Nos. 4 and 5, 1937, L. Muskhelishvili drew attention to a paper by Prof. Schäfer, in which the latter discussed a racing chariot excavated in Egypt and came to the conclusion that 'the present Russian Transcaucasia can probably be established as the source of the coach-building wood (chiefly birch and ash), or that of the ready-made vehicles'. Muskhelishvili compared the design and structure of this chariot (now in the Egyptian museum in Florence) with the engraving of a vehicle with two horses and a driver on a bronze girdle unearthed by J. de Morgan at Akhtala in Lelvar, *Mission scientifique au Caucase*, Vol. 1, 1889, pp. 140–2. He accepted Schäfer's view that the two-sheeled chariot was introduced into Egypt only in the seventeenth century B.C., and preferred the conclusion that the Akhtala chariot was the more primitive and archaic.

The connections between Egypt and Colchis – both spiritual and cultural – remain tenuous but the emphatic views of Herodotus may receive further confirmation from future research. In the opinion of Karst (*MA-C*, p. 85), 'Hori parait avoir été une divinité préarménienne, dont les vestiges se sont conservés sous la figure du héros mythique Chor (Hor) . . . Il sera toutefois permis de présupposer un ancien génie du soleil'. In another context (p. 100) Karst contends that the Urarto-Alarodian *Menuas* (=later Armenian *Manavaʒ*) is a doublet of *Humanu-baʒ* which may be compared with Finno-Ugro-Mordvin *Çim-paʒ*, god of the sky and the sun – in which the element *baʒ*, *paʒ*, signifies 'sun'. According to Chubinov, as indicated above (p. 336), *baʒi* was the alternative Perso-Georgian name for *Kori*= *Falco gentilis*.

COMMENTARY 27

King Simon I of Kartli (ref. Chap. 4, p. 158, n. 1)

Kheli Swimoni – 'Mad Simon' was the most remarkable personality among the Georgian royalties of the latter half of the sixteenth century. Born 1537; succeeded his father as King of Kartli, 1558; married Nestan-Darejan, daughter of Levan of Kakheti, and grand-daughter of Shevkal Kara Musal, 1559. Outlawed and taken prisoner by the Persians, 1569; replaced by his brother, Daviti (David or Da'ud Khan). Simon remained many years a prisoner in Alamut and Shiraz where he became a Moslem under the name of Mahmud Khan. Here he developed his addiction to opium to which Alexander refers. (For the prevalence of opium smoking in Shiraz in the nineteenth century, see E. G. Browne, *A year amongst the Persians, passim*, where the author himself took to the fashion.) In 1578 Simon was released through the influence of the

Shalikashvili dowager of Shah Tahmasp and was sent back to Kartli to organize resistance against the Turkish invasion of Caucasia. He had many military successes against the Turks and aimed, eventually, at the re-unification of all the lands of the old Georgian Kingdom. In 1589, contrary to the denigration of Alexander, his fortunes were on the up-grade. In 1600 Simon was taken prisoner by the Turks, and died in the Seven Towers, probably in 1611. From 1600 to 1605 the Kartlian throne was occupied by his son Giorgi X. For characterization and further details, see Allen, *HGP*, pp. 140 ff. and 155–60. For a curious story of Simon's ill-treatment of a French clock-maker whom he took with him to Japan, see E. Denison Ross, *Anthony Sherley: his Persian adventure*, pp. 158–9. 'Japan' is probably a misreading for 'Ispahan'. For a miniature showing the King charging with lance, see Asafi, f. 109r – 'the men of Erzurum attacked by Simūn' (reproduced as frontispiece to Vol. II).

COMMENTARY 28

The village of Tog or Torga (ref. Chap. 4, p. 159, n. 1)

There are two places named *Tog* or *Torga* marked on Wakhusht's map of Kakheti (Wak./Brosset, Map 4): (1) Torga on the Matsis-tsqali, described as a summer residence of the kings (Wak./Brosset, p. 313); (2) Torga on the Shtoris-tsqali, lying some miles to the north-east of Alaverdi. This latter place, Wakhusht describes as a stronghold which in his time had been abandoned (Wak./Brosset, p. 319). Brosset (*EC/BHP*, Vol. II, Nos. 14–15, col. 243, n. 76) prefers the 'résidence royale' on the Matsis-tsqali. In his edition of Wakhusht, Janashvili (p. 123, n. 406) quotes the *Archiliani* that the wedding of Taymuraz I, in 1605, took place in the fortress of Torga, and this would again imply the royal residence on the Matsi. For its capture by the Persians in 1615, see Brosset, *HG*, Vol. II/i, p. 477. For Torga, and its murals, see Polievktov,

ND, pp. 15–17; Chubinashvili, *AK*, pp. 394, n. 5, 461, n. 1.

According to Janashvili (ibid., p. 120, n. 398) Toga or Torga was a hero whose praise was sung among the Khevsurs and Pshavs even as late as the nineteenth century. In the time of Queen Tamar Torgadzes were among the leading families of Kakheti, and the name *Torgi* in Kakheti means 'something strong'. For this name *Torgi*, cf. also the mythical giant – ancestor of the Armenians and Georgians – Targamos or Torgom = Togarma of *Genesis*, x. 2. Brosset, *HG*, Vol. 1/i, p. 16, n. 1; also Karst, *M A-C*, pp. 64 ff. for 'le géant mythique Torkh' and further bibliographical references.

COMMENTARY 29

The organization of the Kakhian army (ref. Chap. 4, p. 159, n. 2)

Under the united Georgian Kingdom the royal army was marshalled in four 'banners' (*G. droshani*) or divisions assembled on a regional basis (Wak./Brosset, p. 35). The tradition and the pattern were retained in the smaller successor kingdoms of Imereti, Kartli and Kakheti. The Kakhian 'banners' were (i) Martqopi, headquarters for *Garet* ('outer') Kakheti, ancient Kukheti – the country between the river Iora and the Kartlian border; in battle this 'banner' fought on the left flank; (ii) Bodbe, headquarters for Kisiqi 'banner', covering south-east Kakheti between the Alazani and the Iora and forming the advance-guard in battle; (iii) Nekresi, headquarters for *Shignit* ('inner') Kakheti (also called Gaghma-Mkhari: i.e. 'on that side of' (= beyond) the Alazani); in battle this 'banner' formed the right flank (Wak./Brosset, pp. 305, 309–11, 315). The fourth 'banner' would appear to have been the King's household troops, holding the centre in battle.

On the occasion of the review reported by Zvenigorodski (see p. 161 above) the household troops were under command of Prince Yuri; the Bodbe or Kisiqi banner – of Prince David; and the Nekresi banner – of Edisher. The Martqopi banner is not named (cf. Brosset, *EC/BHP*, Vol. II, Nos. 16–18, col. 242, n. 75). A fifth 'banner' to which no reference is made by Wakhusht may have been formed from the mountain clans; Tushes, Pshavs and Khevsurs. The five hundred 'janissaries' to which reference is made, would seem to have been paid and trained musketeers on the model which Shah Abbas was organizing during the same years (see Commentary 8).

COMMENTARY 30

The banner of Kisik (G. Kisiqi) (ref. Chap. 4, p. 161, n. 5, Chap. 5, p. 188, n. 1)

Kisik=G. Kisiqi: For this 'banner' see Commentary 29 (ii) above. Kisiqi formed the triangle of territory between the lower streams of the Alazani and the Iori before they unite to enter the Kura. By Wakhusht it was identified with Kambechovani, 'the plain of buffaloes', classical Cambysene (cf. Wak./Brosset, p. 311 and Map 4; also Allen, *HGP*, p. 64; for classical references, Cellarius, II, pp. 313, 342). Strategically, the Kisiqi 'banner' covered the approaches from the predominantly Moslem regions of Sheki and Shirvan; ethnically the whole of this borderland was very mixed. Since the disappearance of the ancient kingdom of Albania (Aghovanq), Georgian and Armenian elements had been in contact and, often, conflict there. Fine hunting country, it had never recovered from the devastations of the Mongols in the thirteenth century; and Turkoman tribes were accustomed to nomadize there. The Kakhian administration was centred towards the north at Bodbe in the mountainous district of Tzivi. There is a fine cupola church at Bodbe, where St Nino is said to have been buried, and its prestige gave to the bishop (Bodbeli) primacy among his Kakhian peers. According to Wakhusht the Kisiqni had a reputation for roughness, but were robust, daring and war-like and close-knit among themselves. For the ancient church of Bodbe, said to have been first built by King Mirian in the fifth century, and many times restored – see Bakradze, *Akty*, Vol. v, p. 1008; Amiranashvili, *IGI*, p. 99 and Chubinashvili, *AK*, Vol. i, pp. 83–6. For photograph of church, Tamarati, *EG*, p. 96. For thefts of precious objects by Russian ecclesiastical officials during the 1860s, ibid., p. 386. For derivation of the name *Kisiqi*, which seems to belong to a primitive linguistic substratum in the Pontic area – cf. Cyzicus in Mysia – see Brosset's lengthy n. i (Wak./Brosset, pp. 310–11).

COMMENTARY 31

The town of Zaem, Zagem, Zegan, Zakam (ref. Chap. 4. p. 170, n. 1)

There has been some controversy about the exact location of Zaem. In the form Zakam, it is frequently mentioned by the seventeenth century Persian historian, Iskander Munshi, cited by Brosset (*HG*, Vol. ii/i, pp. 480, 481); as *Zagain* it occurs in the work of his contemporary, Pietro della Valle (*Voyage*, Vol. v, p. 156, Vol. viii, p. 317 and *passim*); while King Archil, in his life of King Taymuraz I, has references to the place (*Archiliani*, paras. 179, 273, 716).

Writing in 1844, in his commentary on the Zvenigorodski mission, Brosset identifies Zaem with Zegani – a village in the neighbourhood of Welis-tsikhe, very near to the river Alazani, to the south of Telav (Brosset, *EC/BHP*, Vol. iii, Nos. 5–7, col. 90 and n. 103). He seems, however, to have overlooked the details in the Book of the Great Map, which are fairly specific: 'From the source the course of the Laban (Alazani) is thirty versts long to where on it there stands the town of Krym (Gremi); and downstream from Krym the river Laban flows for a hundred and ten versts between (?) the mountains. The town of Zaem stands on the river Laban and there is a stream flowing into the river from the mountains near the town. Forty versts below the town of Zaem the river Laban flows into the Kur' (Spasski's ed., p. 60). Wak./Brosset, Map 4, shows a village of Bazari to the south-east of the river Fifineti, a left-bank affluent of the Alazani. While Bazari is not shown as standing on the Alazani, Wakhusht marks it as some forty versts to the north of the junction of the Alazani with the Kura.

In March 1639, the Volkonski mission accompanied King Taymuraz I from Gremi to Zagem. The journey occupied five days. On arrival the mission was lodged in the *gostinny-dvor*, 'the guest-court', or characteristic square *caravansaray* with interior court of Oriental towns. About them the Russians saw the ruins of stone-built shops – surviving doubtless from the devastating campaigns of Shah Abbas. Volkonski wrote later that it was four good days riding from Gremi to Bazar-Zagen (Brosset, *EC/BHP*, Vol. iii, Nos. 5–7, col. 90 and n. 3; also col. 93 and n. 107). Here two points seem to be established: the four or five days riding confirms the estimate of the Book of the Great Map that a hundred and ten versts separated Gremi from Zaem; and the pair Bazar-Zagen seems to identify Zagen/Zaem with Wakhusht's Bazari.

The earliest reference to *Zaghem* (Zaem) seems to be that of the Englishman Jeffrey Duckett who went from Shemakha to *Arash* (= G. Areshi) – perhaps derived from the ancient name *Hereti* which covered the whole district, and not to be identified with Genzha (Ganja) as proposed by Delmar Morgan (*EVT*, Vol. ii, p. 432, n. 2) – to collect the goods of Thomas Banister and four other Englishmen who had died or been killed there during July 1571. He wrote: 'Within three days journey of Arash is a country named Grousine, whose inhabitants are Christians, and are thought to be they which are otherwise called Georgians. There is also much silk to bee solde. The chiefe towne of that country is called Zegham, from which is carried yeerely into Persia an incredible quantitie of Hasell nuts, all of one sort and goodnesse, and as good and shaled as our Filberds; of these are carried yeerely the quantitie of 4,000 camels laden' (ibid., p. 432).

The Book of the Great Map (Spasski's ed., p. 60) lists the belt of trading towns along the right bank of the Kura: Achekala, Shyunkyur (Shamkhor), Kgenzha (Genzha, *T.* Gence) and Birde (ancient Barda'a). Ten versts below Barda'a, at Karabaş (? Pirazan = Barzan), there was portage across the Kura to Shemakha, the great centre of the silk trade where roads forked to Baku and to Derbent and the north. Opposite Genzha, following up the valley of the Alazani, and with an eastward fork along the valley of the Gishi, were the districts of Eliseni (Elisu) and Sheki, with a mixed population of Georgians, Lesghians and Azerbaijanis, whose allegiances varied with the circumstances of the day. The Kakhian kings, from time to time, exerted a strong influence in Areshi and Sheki south and east of the Gishi river. But their principal base remained at Zaem (Zagem) on the border of Tsuketi and Eliseni. Although the Kakhian kings were at Zaem, sometimes in the months of winter or spring, Duckett is probably wrong in describing 'Zegham' as the chief town of the country; nor is Amiranashvili, p. 261, correct in describing it as 'the capital' (*stolitsa*). Recently, G. N. Chubinashvili (*AK*, Vol. 1, text, p. 459 and *passim*) has identified the ruins of Zagem at Eski Bazar (*T.* 'Old Bazar'), formerly marked on the 4-Verst Map (and on Wakhusht's Map 4) as 'Bazar', scattered over level ground in the middle of thick forest.

COMMENTARY 32

Genzha and Areshi (ref. Chap. 5, p. 181, n. 1)

Genzha (= *T.* Gence, *Arm.* Gantzakh, later *R.* Elizavetopol, now *Sov.* Leninakan) succeeded Barda'a as the principal city of Aran and became the capital of the local Shaddadid dynasty in the tenth century. On the main route from Tiflis to Ardabil, Kazvin and Rayy, it was important in trade and war. For general history see Bartold, *EI*, 1st ed., and the longer article by Mirza Bala in *IA* under 'Gence' with useful bibliographical notes. For earlier mediaeval period, see the recent study by Minorsky in *HSD, passim*.

During the Turko–Persian wars of 1578–92, the Persian governor Imam Kuli Khan (not Mahmoud as conjectured by Brosset, *EC/BHP*, Vol. II, Nos. 15–18, col. 251, n. 89), the Amamut of our text, was defeated by the Turks in 1583 and, again, in 1588. (For the defeat of Imam Kuli Khan, who had the support of Georgian troops under Alexander's general Yoram, by Osman Pasha on the Samur in May 1583, see Asafi's miniature, f. 179r.) In that latter year the town fell to the Georgian, Ferhat Pasha. The Turks modernized the fortifications of Genzha and made it the centre of a new vilayet (Mirza Bala in *IA*; cf. also von Hammer, *HEO*, Vol. VII, pp. 85, 150). The place was retaken by Shah Abbas in 1606, after a siege of six months, when he built a new town one *farsakh* ('the distance covered in an hour by a horse walking') 'higher up' (i.e. to the south-west – Bartold).

Genzha (Ganja) is frequently confused by Delmar Morgan (*EVT*, index) with Arash (= G. *Areshi*), which had its own importance and was the road junction between Genzha and Shemakha.

Evliya Chelebi, who visited Aran and Shirvan in 1647, gives the best near-contemporary account of the two places and clearly distinguishes them. 'Gence' (Genzha) is

a large town, but the Shah destroyed its castle; it is now an elegant town of six thousand houses with gardens and vineyards, a *khan*, a bath, and *imaret*, situated in a large plain. Its gardens are watered by the Kúrek, which joins the Kúr; the *Kiblah* side of the town is a mountainous track, and the foot of the mountains is cultivated in gardens and vineyards; the silk of Gence is famous. On the plain round Gence are seven districts of infidel villages, where cotton, silk and rice are cultivated; here are rich Moghs (= Magians, ancient Persians, worshippers of fire) and beautiful youth of both sexes; the horseshoes of Gence are not less famous than the silk. The town is governed by a Khan, who commands three thousand men.

Of Areshi, Evliya writes that the town was captured in 1577 (rather 1578) by Lala Mustafa Pasha, and he goes on to give an account of how a Persian relieving force, including detachments of Koks, Dolaks and Georgians, was dispersed. (For Gök Dolaks, see Chap. 10, p. 418, n. 1.)

The Turkish general, having convinced himself of the importance of the town of Aras, situated between Gence and Shirvan, collected masons and workmen, and enclosed the town with a wall, including the garden of Shah Khibán, which was outside the town; three gates led through this wall of clay the circumference of which is 9,600 paces. It was finished in forty days . . . From its situation at the foot of a mountain, the town resembles that of Brusa, surrounded with gardens of fruit and flowers, vineyards and rosebuds. It consists of ten thousand houses with terraces and forty mosques ... The Turkomans and Komuks of Dághestán, pronounce the name of this town Arash ... Forty quarters may now be reckoned, and as many mosques, sixteen baths, eight hundred shops, and seven coffee-houses. The youth are gazelle-eyed, with faces shining like the sun, because their women are Georgians, Dadians (Mingrelians), Achikbash (= bare heads = Imeretians) and Shushad (another Turkish colloquial name for Georgian: see Evliya/Hammer, Vol. II, pp. 173, 177, − derived perhaps from Shavsheti, as proposed in a letter from Prof. Minorsky.) Around it are seven great districts each of which reckons one hundred populous *kents* (*Arm.* village), the most populous is that of Levend Khan near Aras (Evliya/Hammer, Vol. II, pp. 154–5).

The reference to Levend Khan identifies King Levan I of Kakheti (1520–74); it is interesting evidence of the south-eastward extension of the Kakhian border into traditionally Muslim Shirvan during his relatively prosperous reign. Again,

347

Evliya, *ibid.*, p. 156, attributes the building of the castle of Sheki to 'Alexander Prince of the Shusháds' and states that 'though situated on the frontier of Dághistán it is reckoned to belong to Georgia, the more so as its builder was a Georgian'.

(The late Professor Minorsky wrote, 7 September 1963:

(i) Bash-achuq is hardly 'shaven heads' but only 'uncovered'; in western Georgia people wear *bashliqs* – often hanging behind their necks and twisted round the head in bad weather. In my time Russian golden coins on which the Emperor was represented bareheaded were called *bash-achiq*.

(ii) Shushad is apparently Shavshetia (in Georgian Shavshet'i), the mountains of which form the frontier between Georgian SSR and Turkey (south of Batum). One has to note that Evliya describes independently the regions adjacent to the Black Sea, and then his trip from Erevan to Aresh, Sheki, Derbent and Tiflis. He very probably inserted into his general description of Georgia the talks first heard in Shavsheti; after which he invented the general term 'Shavshadistan'. Possibly the memories of the ancient so-called 'Abkhazian' dynasty of Georgia contributed to his exaggerations.

(iii) The district of Aresh lay between (south of) Sheki and the Kura on the lower course of the river Turiyan. Agdash can be found at the east end of the present day (?) arm of Almogachihr, which I saw from the air in 1960. Aresh (not Aras, etc.) is a well-known district (*uyezd*) in Russian administrative terminology. Its head (*nachalnik*) lived in Agdash, I believe.)

For an account of Areshi as 'a great trading centre' in 1578, see Asafi, MS. fol. 22 v.

COMMENTARY 33

Some churches and bishoprics of Kakheti (ref. Chap. 5, p. 189, nn. 1, 2 and 4, p. 190, n. 1)

(a) *Martukop=Martqopi*. 'Beyond the mountains' – that is beyond the Kukhetis-mta, forming the watershed between the Iori and the Kura. Only some thirty versts from Tiflis, it was the headquarters of the 'banner' covering the Kartlian border (cf. Commentary 29). 'Situated in a magnificent valley, watered by a river of the same name' (Brosset, *VA, 1er rapport*, p. 51), the land was rich and thickly populated down to the invasion of Shah Abbas in 1615. In the mid-nineteenth century, Bakradze remarked ruins extending over an area of four versts (*Akty*, Vol. v, pp. 1052–3). The cupola church of *Ghutaeba* (The Transfiguration of our text) stood higher up the valley of the Martqopis-tsqali – 'a great building surrounded by walls and towers like a citadel' (Wak./Brosset, p. 303; and cf. Wak./Jan., pp. 114–15 and n. 373). It was reputed to have been founded in the sixth century A.D. by St Anthony, one of the thirteen Syrian (Monophysite) Fathers who took refuge in Georgia and who, in spite of the later adherence of the Georgian Church to the tenets of the Council of Chalcedon, became cult figures in many parts of Georgia (cf. Lang, *LL*, p. 81). Of the Ghutaeba Brosset (*VA*, p. 54) remarked that nothing remained but the wall. Amiranashvili, p. 196, cites the late K. S. Kekelidze for the view that these 'Syrian' fathers were, for the most part, Georgian monks, who fled from Syria to avoid the persecution of Monophysites. The ascetic movement which they sponsored was, in effect, pan-Christian. Cf. the movement of the Culdees (= Célé De, companions of God) in Ireland – which was possibly initiated by Armenian and Coptic priests and masons (the latter always an itinerant body of men) as early as the sixth century (see Allen, *PS*, p. 85, n. 134, citing sources). It is even possible that the Culdee *Ui Suanaigh* round Rathan (where Mlle Henry noted remarkable Armenian architectural influence) were Siunians (of Siunik) in origin.

Bakradze (*Akty*, Vol. v, p. 1053) states that in 1615 Shah Abbas deported from Martqopi and surrounding districts fifty thousand people whom he settled in Mazandaran, Khurasan and other parts of Persia. The new villages in

Persia were named after the villages which they had left in Kakheti; and the descendants of the deportees continued to speak Georgian and to retain their customs, even after conversion to Islam. Icons of St Anthony were common among them. Bakradze recalls that in 1872 a certain Atama Onilashvili, in company with an Englishman, visited Martqopi and said that he came from a village of Martqopi in Persia, about six days ride from Isfahan. In 1959 I was informed by Prince Zourab Matchabelli, for many years resident in Tehran, that some of these Georgian-speaking communities still survive. (For further details, see article by P. Oberling, 'Georgians and Circassians in Iran', in *Studia Caucasica*, The Hague, 1963, pp. 127–43.)

(b) *Bishopric of Nekresel*: i.e. of Nekresi, on the right bank of the Qwarelis-tsqali, north-east of Gremi; the Bishop was known as *Nekreseli*. At the beginning of the eighteenth century Wakhusht wrote that 'there is no longer a town; however, a general has his "banner" there and it is the headquarters for the troops of Gaghma-Mkhari and Eliseni' (Wak./Brosset, p. 315; and cf. Wak./Jan., p. 122, n. 403, where the name is given as Nekresi or Nelk'ari. One of the oldest continuously inhabited sites in Kakheti, said by Wakhusht to have been founded by the fourth king of Iberia, Farnadjom (112–93 B.C.), it was a centre of pagan cults and, later, of Magism. Amiranashvili (p. 98, citing Chubinashvili) affirms that the remains of the oldest church date from the fourth century A.D. – which confirms the tradition that the Church of the Mother of God was founded by Tirdat, the fourth Christian King of Iberia (A.D. 379–405) (cf. Bakradze, *Akty*, Vol. v, p. 1064). The first bishop was Avivos or Abibos (? Habib), one of the thirteen Syrian Fathers who came to Georgia in the sixth century. He tried to convert the Didos and other mountaineers and was stoned to death by order of a Magian governor (Bakradze, ibid.).

In 1762 Irakli II, with the intention, perhaps, of reviving the tradition of the neighbouring mediaeval university of Iqalto, founded a college of Nekresi, and wrote to Bishop Dositheus to occupy himself 'diligently with the work'. The last bishop was Ambrosius (d. 1813), a learned man celebrated for his large volume of sermons (Wak./Jan., p. 122, n. 403). For a brief account of the church and 'the unexplored ruins of the town of Nekresi' (1892), see *MAK*, Vol. VII, Khakhanov, p. 4. Also for recent detailed account see Chubinashvili, *AK*, Vol. I, pp. 37–45, 173–6, 321–5 and *passim*.

(c) *Katsarel*: the name form implies the *Katsareli* or Bishop of Katsareti. Not mentioned under this name by the earlier authorities, but Khakhanov (*MAK*, Vol. VI, pp. 38–9) describes the *Katsareti Sameba* (Trinity) monastery in the village of Katsareti, on the banks of the Iori, six or seven versts from the commune of Khashmi. This corresponds to the monastery of Sameba in the district of Sagaredjo in the foothills of the Gombori ridge of the Kukhetis-mta (Wak./Brosset, p. 293, Map 4). Wakhusht states that there was a fortress and a monastery and a great cupola church, the seat of a bishop who governed all the high country as far as Ertso. The little Sameba stream which fell from the north into the Iori was the limit between Kakheti and ancient Hereti; Khakhanov believed that the area of Katsareti originally covered over three versts. In 1634 Taymuraz I allotted the lands and peasants to the princely families of Andronikashvili and Cholokashvili – who seem to have had an hereditary lien on the bishopric and the abbacy. Khakhanov wrote that the architecture of the Trinity Church showed signs of European influences – which he attributed to Genoese craftsmen working in Georgia at the turn of the fifteenth century. Cf. also Chubinashvili, *AK*, Vol. I, pp. 55–65 for recent description with numerous figures in text.

(d) *Gsarevʒhel*: this distorted form = the *Garedʒheli* or

Bishop of Garedzha. One of the group of monasteries and hermitages founded by the thirteen Syrian Fathers who inspired the ascetic movement in Georgia during the sixth century A.D. (see (i) above). The monastery of St David of Garedzha was on the eastern slope of the ridge of the same name, looking westward over the plain of Karaia which stretched as far as the Kura. Karaia was a favourite winter grazing of the nomad Turkomans who in summer moved their herds up to the heights of Garedzhis-mta. (This same ridge formed the border between the kingdoms of Kartli and Kakheti.) Said to have been of Mesopotamian (possibly Assyrian) origin, St David was, in spirit, a precursor of St Francis of Assisi in his love of animals and care for them; indeed, his sanctity may perhaps be linked with the survival locally of animistic cults, particularly of the deer which was widespread in Caucasia, notably among the Alans. For the curious account of St David's unsuccessful intervention with the Deity in favour of a dragon with which he had converse and which was terrified of thunderbolts, see Lang, *LL*, pp. 85–6. Here again, we may suspect the survival of the tradition of the Caucaso-Armenian thunder-god in sixth century Kakheti.

According to Wakhusht, 'on a height of Garedzhis-mta are monasteries with cells, as well as refectories and rooms, cut out of the rock, warm in winter and fresh in summer' (Wak./Brosset, pp. 181, 289; Wak./Jan., p. 54). (For Vardzia, Uplis-tsikhe, and other rock-towns in Georgia, see H. F. B. Lynch, *Armenia: Travels and studies*, vol. 1, *passim*; Allen, *HGP*, *passim*, and, for greater detail, I. I. Pantyukhov, *O peshchernykh i podzemnykh zhilishchakh na Kavkaze*, Tiflis, 1896. A good example of a monastic cave-town, dating from the early centuries of Christianity is near Ürgüp in Anatolia.)

For 'holy Nona' of our text, Zakhkhey has doubtless confused the more celebrated St Nino with St Dodo, who was a disciple and constant companion of St David, and had his retreat nearby (Wak./Brosset, p. 293, cf. also Tamarati, *EG*, pp. 218–19). In the opinion of Amiranashvili (pp. 178 ff.) 'the most characteristic frescoes of the tenth century are in the church of St Dodo at Garedzha'. Here there is a remarkably beautiful Christ Enthroned (Amiranashvili, pl. 59) and at the church at Udabno, a representation of St David and his dragon struck by a thunderbolt (pl. 60).

For a more detailed account of Garedzha, see *MAK*, Vol. vii, pp. 39 ff., by Khakhanov who states that in the time of Shah Abbas the number of monks dwelling in the Garedzha 'wilderness' amounted to six thousand. See also Chubinashvili, *AK*, *passim*.

COMMENTARY 34

The origin of the name 'White Tsar' (ref. Chap. 6, p. 200, n. 1)

For several explanations of the origin of the name 'White Tsar', see Brockhaus and Efron (Vol. v, pp. 246, 249). George Vernadsky has re-examined the problem in his *Mongols and Russia*; for detailed discussion, see pp. 139–40, 388–9. In his view, Juchi's *ulus*, conventionally known among historians as the Golden Horde, was originally designated the White Horde. Thus Tinibeg, a mid-fourteenth century Khan of Kipchak is described in a Persian source as ruler of the White Horde; and the German traveller, Johan Schiltberger, in the early fifteenth century, wrote of White Tartary. The convention of describing western hordes as 'white' goes back to the Chinese practice of assigning colours to the different points of the compass. For an earlier period cf. the name 'White Huns'. The Russian Autocrat, as successor to the empire of Juchi's *ulus*, called himself the White Tsar. As late as the eighteenth century he was still the White Khan (*tsagan khan*) to the Kalmucks and Buryats.

Russian pretensions to the succession to the Khans of the

White (Golden) Horde was an important psychological factor
in asserting their authority over princes and tribes who had
formerly been subject to the House of Juchi. These pretensions
in the east may be compared with their claim, in the west, to the
heritage of the Byzantine Emperors among the Orthodox
Christian population. (Cf. Commentary 39, below.)

COMMENTARY 35

The title 'Krym-Shevkal' (ref. Chap. 6, p. 201, n. 1)

Krym-Shevkal: This personality and title remain somewhat
ambiguous in the texts of the Posolski Prikaz. (Cf. Brosset,
EC/BHP, Vol. II, Nos. 16–18, col. 250, n. 87.) In our text
(p. 201), and again in May 1590, through his envoy in Moscow,
Alexander explained that his quarrel with the Shevkal had
arisen because his son Giorgi had been married into the
family of the Krym-Shevkal Elisam Sultan (cf. above, Chap. 4,
p. 161, n. 2). (Elisam was Elisu, Georgian Eliseni, the region of
south-east Kakheti, to the north of the Alazani which had been
partly peopled by intrusive Lesghian elements; see also Chap.
11, p. 447, n. 2.) During the embassy of Pleshcheyev to Kakheti
in 1592, there is reference to a proposal to conquer the country
of Kumukh – 'of which half belongs to Krym-Shevkal, friend
of Alexander' (Brosset, ibid., col. 258). In 1593 a combined
operation against Tarku, with a view to displacing the Shevkal
and installing Krym Shevkal, 'the ally of the King of Georgia'
and the father-in-law of Prince Giorgi, was under negotiation
(Brosset, ibid., col. 259). In a letter dated 15 January 1963, the
late Mr Haidar Bammate, a descendant of the Shevkal's house,
stated that 'la succession dans la dynastie des Chamchal se
faisait de père en fils et l'héritier présomptif portait le titre de
Krim-Shamkhal'. Alexander described Krym-Shevkal as the
cousin of the reigning Shevkal (p. 216 above). The Shevkal in
his turn referred to Krym-Shevkal as 'my brother' (p. 201
above). But in Turkish, the language of intercourse between

Kumukhs and Kakhians, *kardeş* can mean either 'brother' or 'cousin'. Since 'Krym-Shevkal' was the title of the heir-presumptive to the Shevkalate (as affirmed by Haidar Bammate) it would seem that our Krym-Shevkal was either an elder brother of the reigning Shevkal or the son of an elder brother of 'the old Shevkal'. In either case Krym-Shevkal would have had a good claim to the Shevkalate.

For further on the Shevkal line, see Vol. II, p. 593. Genealogical Notes, 8: 'The Shamkhals (Shevkals) of Tarku'.

It is possible that the cognomen 'Krym' may derive from the town of Ghimri on the Ghazi-Kumukh-Koysu, although it has been suggested that the word is a distortion of the Turkish *yarim* = half, thus 'half-Shevkal'.

COMMENTARY 36

Prince Suliman (ref. Chap. 6, p. 203, n. 1)

Prince Suliman: Brosset (*EC*/*BHP*, Vol. II, Nos. 19–21, col. 290, n. 1), identifies him as Suliman Boulalin, son of Baindour: 'Le nom de Souliman et celui de sa famille, si une telle famille exista dans la Cakheth, qui serait en géorgien Boulaladze, me paraissait indiquer un musulman.' Suliman was head of the Georgian mission to Moscow in 1590 when he is referred to as 'a man of great family, one of the King's confidants, whose father, a long time ago, had been in the good graces of King Levan' (ibid., col. 255; cf. also col. 271); and again as 'son of Baindour'. The name of the father is, perhaps, the key to Suliman's identity and origin. From the Turkoman clan of Bayindir, who nomadized over the great uplands round the sources of the river Kura, sprang the dynasty of the Ak-Koyunlu. It is a reasonable guess that 'Baindour' or Bayundur/Bayindir (cf. Minorsky under 'Ak-Koyunlu' in *EI*, 2nd ed.), was a refugee from the royal line of the Ak-Koyunlu, which was finally liquidated by the Safavids in 1502/3. He could have been a contemporary of Levan of Kakheti (1520–74) and, perhaps, earlier, took service with Levan's father, *Av* Giorgi ('bad George'), 1511–13, who is remembered for his massacre of the great nobles and his attempt to set up a political structure based on prefects (*mo'uravni*) removable at will; he favoured minor officials and, doubtless, foreigners without local connections. In the complex relationships of the sixteenth century, it would not be extraordinary for a Moslem refugee to hold a high position at the Kakhian Court. (The same was true of Muscovy where political refugees from the Golden Horde took service under the Tsars and families of Tartar origin attained the highest standing, e.g. Glinskis, Godunovs, Naryshkins.) Among families of the higher nobility in Kakheti (*tavadni*), we find Andronikashvilis (who claimed descent from Andronicus II Comnenus); Rusis-shvilis and Cherkezis-shvilis (doubtless of Rus and Cherkess origin); and among *aznaurni* – T'urkistanis-shvilis (surely of Turkistani origin), (cf. Wak./Brosset, p. 488, cols. 2 ff., for list of the noble families of Kakheti).

The name Boulalin has the Russian termination -*in*. The root *Bulal* may perhaps be connected with Turkish *bülent*, high, lofty, exalted. Suliman's name can therefore be reconstructed as Bülent Sulaiman Bayindirli or Bayindiroghlu= Bülent Sulaiman of the Bayindir, or son of Bayindir.

COMMENTARY 37

Georgian merchants abroad (ref. Chap. 6, p. 203, n. 2)

'My merchants travel to Constantinople and to the Franks.' In Byzantine times Georgians were to be found in Constantinople and throughout the empire as monks and soldiers; later, under the Ottomans, as slaves and fighting men, they often rose to high rank. Georgian merchants were organized in guilds and there are frequent references to them in the mediaeval epic, *The man in the panther's skin*; but they do not seem to have been very active abroad, although they are mentioned in Astrakhan and Moscow in the sixteenth century and, doubtless, frequented the Persian markets. The commercial relations of the Georgian kingdoms with foreign countries were mainly sustained by the old-established colonies of Georgian Jews (numerous in Kakheti) and by the Armenians who formed a substantial part of the population of Tiflis and other Georgian towns. From the context, it would seem that Alexander had in mind his Armenian merchants who would have been in regular contact with their compatriots settled in large communities, not only in Constantinople and the Persian cities, but as far afield as Venice and Vienna, and in Transylvania and Poland. In Shemakha, in 1562, Anthony Jenkinson was in touch with an Armenian agent of the 'King of Georgia' (although it is not clear whether this was Simon I of Kartli or Levan of Kakheti); subsequently he sent Edward Clarke to Areshi, with the object of securing freedom of trade in Georgia. Clarke had conversations with 'certaine merchants Armenians', but nothing came of the affair (*EVT*, pp. 150–1). In Tabriz, in 1568, Laurence Chapman chanced to meet 'with the gouernours merchant of Grozyne, who was not a little desirous to bargen with me for a hundred pieces of karsies (kersey – a coarse woollen cloth) for his master called Leuontie, and offering me so good bands (bonds) for the payment of the money, or silke, to the merchants contentment, upon the delivery of them as in any place within all this country is to be had; and offering me besides his owne letter in the behalfe of his master, that no customs should be demanded for the same, and the obtaining also at his maisters hand as large a priuilege for the worshipfull to trauel into all parts of his dominion, as the Shaugh (Shah) had given them' (*EVT*, Vol. II, pp. 408–10). Here, again, the business with Leuonte (Levan of Kakheti) proved a disappointment to Chapman, but it is interesting to note the details of the mercantile network to which the Kakhian negotiators referred in their talk with Zvenigorodski. For Georgian merchants in Terki and Astrakhan, at the period, see Brosset, *EC/BHP*, Vol. ii, Nos. 19–20, p. 298, n. 26; and in Lvov, Zheltyakov, *Evliya Chelebi, vyp.* i, pp. 18, 76, where reference is made to Laz, Persian, Hungarian, Jewish, Armenian and Frank merchants occupied with the trade between the Black Sea ports and Danzig. Also for Georgian trade and the merchant guilds see Meskhia, *Goroda i gorodskoy stroy feodalnoy Gruzii, xvii–xviii vv.* (Tbilisi, 1959), *passim*; and Z. Chichinadze, *Sakartvelos vatchroba . . . Indoetchi* (Georgian trade with India) (Tiflis, 1905).

COMMENTARY 38

The Iron Gates of Derbent (ref. Chap. 6, p. 207, n. 1)

The Iron gates of Derbent: Famous in Caucasian lore, they gave the name, often used, *T. Demir-Kapi* to the city. Minorsky has made a brilliant study of the history and topography of Derbent in *HSD*, in which, p. 46, he cites an Arab source that 'in the same year (A.H. 382/992) amir Maymun had the gate of Damascus and that of Palestine made of pure iron'. Brosset (*HG*, Vol. i/i, p. 386, n. 1), discussed the tradition that David the Restorer, King of Georgia, 1089–1125, after a successful campaign in Daghestan, 1124, removed the iron gates to Gelati in Imereti. He finds, however, that there is no evidence for David's victories as far as Derbent; and accepts the suggestion of Fraehn that the iron gate at Gelati, with an inscription in Arabic indicating that it was made in 1063, was carried away from Genzha, following the earthquake of 1139, when the city was pillaged by the troops of Dmitri I of Georgia (1125–1154). The earthquake at Genzha might indeed explain the tradition that the iron gates of Derbent were 'overthrown and lie in the earth'.

For Brosset's views see further 'O zheleznykh vorotakh

khranyashchikhsya v gelatskom monastyre v Imeretii' in *Kavkaz* (1847), pp. 163–7.

Moscow as the Third Rome (ref. Chap. 6, p. 209, n. 1)

By the end of the sixteenth century the view that Moscow had succeeded Constantinople as the centre of Orthodoxy, thus becoming 'the Third Rome', and that the Tsars were the rightful heirs of the Byzantine Emperors, was widely held in Russia (cf. N. F. Kapterev, *Kharakter otnosheniy Rossii k Pravoslavnomu Vostoku v* XVI *i* XVII *stol.*, 2nd ed., Sergiyev Posad, 1914, pp. 349 ff. For a more recent discussion, see Vernadsky, *RDMA*, pp. 169–70). The theory of Moscow as the Third Rome was first formulated by Abbot Filofei in his letter to Vasili III in 1510. In Vernadsky's view 'Filofei's theory has been grossly misunderstood'. It has been interpreted in the sense of Moscow's desire to dominate the world, whereas Filofei wrote in an eschatological connotation. As the first two Romes had been destroyed, Moscow remained the sanctuary of Orthodox Christianity, and the Grand Duke of Moscow was the only remaining Orthodox Christian ruler in the world. It fell to him to guard the last abode of the Orthodox Christian Church and to make Russia a truly Christian power. Our text indicates that by the final quarter of the century, the theory of the Third Rome had already attained political and, indeed, wide imperial significance, in the mind of an Orthodox Christian prince like Alexander of Kakheti. For a modern Russian interpretation, omitted from Vernadsky's bibliographical note, see Dmitri Obolensky, 'Russia's Byzantine heritage' in *OSP*, Vol. I, 1950, pp. 36–61. Again, B. H. Sumner (*OSP*, Vol. II, 1951, 'Russia and Europe', p. 7), who considers that Muscovy was 'a state imbued with powerful national feelings, but little influenced in politics or diplomacy by the messianic mirage of

"Moscow the Third Rome", monkish offspring of the Council of Florence and the Ottoman conquest of Constantinople'. See also, C. Toumanoff: 'Moscow the Third Rome: Genesis and Significance of a politico-religious idea' in *CHR*, Vol. 40 (1955).

COMMENTARY 40

On the idea of a Russian Pope (ref. Chap. 6, p. 210, n. 2)

There is a close parallel between Zvenigorodski's reference to a Russian 'Pope' and the instructions given to the Tsar's ambassadors to Lithuania, Saltykov and Tatishchev: 'If you are asked about the installation of a Patriarch you will say "Joachim, Patriarch of Antioch, who came from the Greek country to visit the great Sovereign, told Boris Fedorovich Godunov, the Sovereign's brother-in-law, that it had been laid down at the seven Councils in olden days that in Rome there should be a Pope of the Greek rite, and that in the Greek realm there should be four Patriarchs. The Popes of Rome abandoned the Greek faith after Pope Eugene had arbitrarily convened the eighth Council. Had there been any devout Christian kings in the Greek realm before now, the Patriarchs would have installed a Pope in the Greek realm. These four Patriarchs have now consulted the Oecumenical Council of the Greek lands with a view to setting up the Oecumenical Patriarch of Constantinople in the Roman Pope's place, and elevating a fourth Patriarch in Muscovy." ' (Solovyev, Vol. ii, col. 658.)

The idea of having the Metropolitan of Moscow elevated to the rank of Patriarch had long been dear to the hearts of the Tsars, for political as well as for religious reasons. It was made known to Joachim, the Patriarch of Antioch, when he visited Moscow in 1586. The following year a Greek named Nicholas brought news that the Patriarchs of Constantinople and Antioch would call a council which would also be attended by the Patriarchs of Jerusalem and Alexandria.

When Jeremiah arrived in Moscow in 1588 (see Chap. 6, p. 210, n. 1 above) he was not the incumbent of the Oecumenical throne, and it remains a moot point whether or not he had the power to instal Metropolitan Job as Russia's first Patriarch. Whatever his right in that respect, he clearly over-stepped the mark in promising that the new Patriarch would rank third in seniority. While the Council held in Constantinople in May 1590 endorsed Job's elevation, it assigned to him the fifth place, after the Patriarchs of Constantinople, Alexandria, Antioch and Jerusalem, in that order. The Tsar expressed his displeasure at this turn of events, but the Patriarchs reaffirmed their decision at the Council held in February, 1593.

COMMENTARY 41

The Dido tribe (ref. Chap. 6, p. 211, n. 1)

Didos; One of the wildest – and most interesting – tribes in the Caucasus. In 1927 they still numbered about 6,000 (cf. I. I. Zarubin, *Spisok narodnostey SSSR*, p. 18). They occupy the country to the east of the Lopoti affluent of the Alazani, settled in two upland valleys in the mountains which form the watershed between the Alazani and the feeders of the Andi-koysu. The Kodor Pass (2392 m. on Déchy's map, Blatt 2, 'Östlicher Kaukasus') was approached by the gorges to which Alexander's men referred.

For origin of the name, see above, Commentary 20, pp. 315–316. Baddeley (*RFC*, Vol. II, p. 14), records *Tsounta* 'meaning "Eagles"', an Avar translation of their own name for themselves, "Tsesi". For a lengthy description of their character and strange customs, see Wak./Brosset, pp. 325–7; also Wak./Jan., pp. 129–131, n. 420. To them was attributed the worship of the invisible devil and of a black dog 'without spots' (see Janashvili, 'Izvestiya Gruzinskikh letopisey o ... Didoeti, etc.,' in *SMK*, Vol. XVI/i, 1899, p. 95; and cf. Allen *BK*, Nos. 32–3,

1959, 'Ex Ponto', IV, 'Dogs' heads and wolves' heads'). Wak./Jan p. 131, n. 420, notes that Ptolemy places the *Touskhoi* and *Didouroi* (Tushes and Didos) between the Caucasian and Keraunian ranges (cf. Ptolemy, cap. VIII and Second Map of Asia). Janashvili identifies the latter as Georgian Kornis-mta. Trever, p. 48, cites Pliny for the *Diduri* and *Sodi* and identifies the *Diduri* with the *Didoi* of Armenian, and the *Dido-el-ni* of Georgian writers. *Sodi* can, perhaps, be compared with Avar *Tsounta* (see Baddeley above, and Commentary 20, pp. 315 ff).

For Arab references to the Didos, see Minorsky, *HSD*, p. 107, n. 4, *Al-Dūdāniya* or *al-Diduwāniya*: in the eleventh century they were employed as mercenaries by the ruler of Shirvan (ibid., p. 121). Mas'udi writes of the pagan *Dūdāniya* who have not submitted to any king: 'There are curious reports concerning their nuptial and social customs.' This part of Daghestan (*Lakʒ*), he says, 'has valleys, gorges and defiles in which live tribes not knowing one another, in view of the arduous nature of the mountains rising to the sky, their inaccessibility, their abundance in woods and thickets, their torrents rushing in cascades from above and the enormous rocks and boulders' (ref. Minorsky, ibid., p. 145).

COMMENTARY 42

King Alexander's account of his own life (ref. Chap. 6, p. 217, n. 1)

Alexander's somewhat specious account of his own life adds some facts which are not revealed in the Georgian sources published by Brosset (cf. *HG*, Vol. II/i, pp. 334–9). Born in 1527, he was (probably) the second son of Levan by Tinatin, daughter of Mamia I Gurieli, whom Levan repudiated in 1529 – to marry a daughter of the Shevkal (Shamkhal) Kara Musal, grandfather of the Shevkal Andi of our text. In old age Levan favoured the succession by a son of his second marriage.

It was doubtless for this reason that Alexander killed his father – as stated in the apologia of his own son and killer, Constantine (see text below, p. 464). He seems also to have killed an elder brother (a son of Tinatin): this would explain his reference to the revolt of his nephew Khostrov (Khosro). His half-brothers of the Shevkal line then rallied against him. Wakhusht mentions Eli Mirza, Wakhtang and a second Khosro (Brosset, *HG*, Vol. ii/i, pp. 153–4). Alexander adds another half-brother, Nicolaoz, the Metropolitan of our text; and a full brother Isay (Yese). They had the formidable support of the Shevkal and of Lesghian auxiliaries. On the other hand, Alexander was aided by David (Da'ud Khan) of Kartli (brother and supplanter of Simon I who was married to a sister of the princes of the Shevkal line and was at that time a prisoner in Shiraz) (cf. Commentary 27). Alexander had further support from his own father-in-law, Bardzim Amilakhori, a powerful *tavadi* in northern Kartli and of the Eristav of the Ksani (*Ksnis-eristavi*). The rival armies met at Torga: for identification see Commentary 28. Alexander was the victor and, according to Wakhusht, three of the four brothers of the Shevkal line were later eliminated. Only Nicolaoz survived (cf. Wakhusht, above). Wakhusht gives no date for the battle but it must have taken place about 1576.

In October 1587 Simon was released from Shiraz and, with Persian support, returned to Kartli to fight the Turkish invaders. He soon took vengeance on Alexander's supporters in northern Kartli, Bardzim Amilakhori and the Eristavi of the Ksani; but, with few troops, Simon was defeated at Dighwami, 1580 (Brosset, *HG*, Vol. ii/i, p. 37). This action clearly corresponds to the victory to which Alexander makes such an inflated reference. Simon shortly rallied, and defeated Alexander at Jotori, just south of Martqopi. Subsequently, in 1587, relations between Simon and Alexander improved, 'leurs fils étant cousins-germains et ayant une affection réciproque' (Brosset,

HG, Vol. ii/i, p. 40, rendering Wakhusht's *Histoire et actions des Rois de Karthli*).

For the casual attitude to parricide and fratricide among the Georgian nobility, see Gvritishvili, pp. 149–55. For the prevalence of these practices among Os families in the valleys west of Daryal at the end of the eighteenth century, see Baddeley, *RFC*, Vol. i, p. 173, citing Steder, *Tagebuch*, p. 68: 'A son shot his old father in my presence for having verbally insulted him.' For parricide in Daghestan as late as 1873, see Baddeley, ibid., Vol. ii, p. 238.

Baddeley, ibid., Vol. i, p. 174, comments: 'It was Kovalevsky who pointed out that the customary law of the family communities of the Caucasus gave the key to many at first sight strange characteristics of ancient criminal legislation. In particular the absence of all mention of punishment for parricide, whether in the oldest codes of Greece or of Russia, was due not to the hope that such a crime could not occur ... but to the fact that there was no such thing as crime within the family. Crime implied an outside criminal against whom, to satisfy the dead, vengeance could and must be taken. But vengeance within the family was to the Ossetines unthinkable. It would have been vengeance against oneself, with which the family, dead or living, was completely identified', citing Maxim Kovalevsky, *Sovremennye obychai i drevni ʒakon*, etc., 2 vols., Moscow, 1886, Vol. ii, pp. 122–5. (Summarized by Delmar Morgan in *JRAS*, 1888, Vol. 20.)

A miniature in the Asafi MS. (f. 19v) shows 'Levendoghlu' conferring with 'Lala Mustafa Pasha' – which may be dated to the autumn of 1578. This is reproduced as Fig. 13. Levendoghlu refers to Alexander, then about fifty. Levend is a Persian word used in Turkish meaning rapscallion, so Levendoghlu is possibly a pun on the proper patronymic for Alexander, Levanoghlu. The pair are seated on stools placed on a fine Isfahan carpet in front of a luxurious tent. In the foreground are two of Alexander's favoured hawks. The King and his counsellors are dressed in the Persian manner – later criticized by Wakhusht. The corpulent, white-bearded Lala Mustafa, who had just made the arduous march across Anatolia and through Georgia, was seventy-six.

COMMENTARY 43

Kizilbash damask and carpets (ref. Chap. 7, p. 222, n. 2)

'Fifty pieces of gold Kizilbash damask and ten carpets, worked with gold and silver thread.' For gifts of *kaftans* see Chap. 1, p. 98, n. 4; for 'Kizilbash damask', see Chap. 4, p. 155, n. 1. See also A. U. Pope, *A survey of Persian art*, Vol. III, Text Chap. 10, Sect. 52 (B), 'A Russian Document on Persian Textiles', by Phyllis Ackerman who states that during the eighteenth century over sixty different kinds of textiles were imported into Russia from Persia through Astrakhan, according to the Custom House accounts. Many of these were of the cheapest varieties (p. 2173). The word *zari* was the common Persian term for metal-thread-enriched silks. For examples of satins and silks enriched with metal thread, contemporary with Alexander of Kakheti, see ibid., Vol. VI, pl. 1013 ff.; for carpets, pl. 1165 ff.

Following the tradition of many Moslem rulers of working daily with their hands and being expert in at least one handi-craft, Shah Tahmasp I is himself reputed to have woven carpets in Tabriz. (A small Tabrizi dated 1542 is in my collection.) Chardin (*Voyages*, Langlès ed., 1811, Vol. VII, pp. 330 ff.), and Tavernier (*Les six voyages*, Paris, 1681, pp. 361 ff.) give valuable accounts of the Persian weaving industry for the latter half of the seventeenth century. Tadeusz Mánkowski (*History of Persian art*, Vol. III, p. 2431), cites the Polish Jesuit Krusinski, who lived in Persia from 1704 to 1729, for Shah Abbas's creative interest in the industry. According to the Shah's orders, each place was to weave in its own manner.

Evidently the Shah intended to preserve the specific characteristics of the artistic weaving of each locality. Krusinski states
that during the siege of Isfahan by the Afghans in 1722, when
the weavers were stricken by famine, the special technique of
inter-weaving silk tissues with a silver thread . . . was completely lost.

In the spring of the year 1601, the Polish King Sigismund III
Vasa sent the Armenian merchant Sefer Muratovicz from
Warsaw to Persia to procure the weaving of several carpets
bearing the royal coat of arms. Muratovicz travelled through
Moldavia and Turkey and, after a difficult passage of the Black
Sea, reached Trebizond on 31 May 1601. 'From there I went to
Erzurum . . . and Kars, and thence I travelled through the
Christian lands of Prince Alexander of Georgia to the towns of
Grym (Gremi) . . . Erivan . . . Nakhichevan . . . There I crossed
the large river Araxes near Julfa, in which place there are
15,000 Armenian houses or families' – whence he proceeded
through Tabriz and Kazvin to Kashan. Some of the rugs purchased on this expedition have been identified as part of the
dowry of Princess Anna Katarina Constanza of Poland on her
marriage, in 1642, to Philip William, Elector Palatine of the
Rhine. Five were exhibited in the Munich Exhibition of 1910
(cf. F. Sarre and F. R. Martin, *Meisterwerke Muhammedanischer
Kunst*, Vol. I, pp. 55, 60, 61, 62).

For examples accessible to the English reader, see *Victoria
and Albert Museum, Brief guide to Persian woven fabrics*, with
several plates of Persian textiles dating back to the sixteenth
and early seventeenth centuries. It is probable that the carpets
at Hardwick, showing the Cavendish arms, were ordered in
Persia at the turn of the sixteenth century – perhaps through
one of the Sherley brothers.

COMMENTARY 44

The Kalkan or Karakalkan mountaineers (ref. Chap. 7, p. 228, n. 2)

Kalkan or Karakalkan: from Turkish *kalkan*, a shield or buckler; Genko (p. 703, n. 1) remarks that 'the appellation, "black-shielded' would splendidly suit the inhabitants of the Truso gorge, Osetians by nationality, whose carrying of a shield is particularly noted by travellers'. Reineggs/W. (Vol. I, p. 370) placed the Karakalkan (which he interprets as 'Black Settlers') north-east of Akhalgori, i.e. in Mtiuleti 'where every habitable part of the mountain is covered with their houses'. The author rather naively explains that 'they are so-called because they never wash their faces'. Brosset (*HG*, Vol. I, *Add. et Ec.*, p. 388, n. 3) summarizing Sheref-eddin, states that in the autumn of 1393, Tamerlane penetrated the country of certain Georgians called Karakalkanlik who were fortified in castles situated in steep mountains. Brosset identifies them with the Pshavs, Khevsurs and Gudamakaris – who lie to the east of the Daryal gorge and along the route which the embassy would have been following. Baddeley (*RFC*, Vol. II, p. 263) aptly translates the name as 'Black Bucklers'. In fact the Khevsurs and their neighbours carried a small leather target or hand-shield (for illustration see Allen, *HGP*, opposite p. 203, reproduced from *MAK*, Vol. x). (This target is very like, in shape and studding decoration, to the targets of the Gaels of Ireland and the Scottish Highlands (cf. Joyce, *Social history of ancient Ireland*, Vol. I, pp. 124 ff., and Figs. 61, 62). These targets were made of yew.)

In June 1625 Giorgi Saakadze, 'the great *Mo'uravi*', and Zurab, Eristav of the Aragvi, captured a Georgian notable in the Persian service, Abdul Jafar Beg (*G.*, Andouqaphar) (Brosset, *HG*, Vol. II/i, pp. 493 ff., also, p. 493, n. 2, citing Iskander Munshi) – who was a member of the Amilakhori family with his wife, a grand-daughter of Shah Abbas (ibid., pp. 56–57, citing Wakhusht) and imprisoned the couple in the fortress of Arshi – which commands the easterly exit from the Truso Gorge and overlooks the southern entry to the Daryal Gorge (Wak./Brosset, Map 3 and pp. 226–7). Arshi thus guarded the valley of the Terek at its junction with the Atchkhotis-tsqali along which led the track from Sioni into Kakheti. This fortress lay in *Qara-kuli-Khan*, according to Iskander Munshi – which Brosset identifies as Karakalkan. It would therefore seem clear that the name Karakalkan could be applied either to the Os of the Truso Gorge, as proposed by Genko, or to the Pshavs, Khevsurs and Gudamakaris, as indicated by Brosset. Indeed, the word *Karakalkan* may have derived from a defensive accoutrement characteristic of the armament of all these neighbouring tribes. It seems a term comparable to *Bash-achik*, bare heads, or *Kizil-bash*, red heads. For further discussion and detailed references see Genko (pp. 702 ff., and particularly p. 702, n. 1) who finds that 'whatever may ultimately have been the actual content of the term *Kalkan*, the contemporary Ingush name for the owners of the Kazbek settlement on the Georgian Military Road, *gealxie*, is probably cognate with it'.

According to Dubois de Montpéreux (Vol. IV, p. 248) the name Karakalkan-Kala was applied to Ananuri during the period of Persian domination.

Principal trade routes
Marshes
Pass
Heights are indicated in metres

Kilometres
0 20 40 60 80
Miles
0 10 20 30 40 50

C a s p i a n   S e a

Khanate of Kuba
Kuba
Derbent (Bab-al-Abwab) (Demir-Kapu)
S. TABASSARAN
Land and sea routes to Astrakhan from Derbent
Khanate of Sheki
R. Samur
Kasum Kend
Khanate of E. Kumukh
Kiurin
Akti
Khanate of W. Kumukh
(L E K E T)

S H I R V A N

Khanate of Kara-Kaituk
Utsmi of Kara-Kaituk
Ulemish o
Boynak
Koyden
Dergeli
Ukhli
R. Manas
Khili
Emir-Khan-Shura
Shamkhal of Tarku
Tarku

Terki (Terek-town)
TEREK COSSACKS
Lake Tuzluk
Aghakhan
R. Oseh
R. Salah
Erpeli
Kazanich o
Jenghutay
R. Osen
KUMUKHS
MICHIK
KUMUKHS

NOGAY TARTARS
KABARDA
LITTLE KABARDA
GREBENTSI COSSACKS
Sunzha
"Oman's Road"
Andreyevo (Enderi)
OKOK (AKKO)
R. Sunzha
R. Argun
KARABULAK
INGUSH
OKOK
Kholopensk
Meestio
Shatoj o
Shatil
GALGAIS (GHLIGHWI)
Argun
R. Assa
Nazran
KISTI
Lars
Daryal Gorge
Kobi
Mleti
Pasanauri
Ananuri
Dusheti o
Mukhrani
R. Terek
R. Kombulei
R. Sunzha
R. Tchanti-Argun
R. Tchanti-Argun
Tebulos-mta 4,494
Donos mta 4,179
Mt Berbalo 4,276
A N D I S
Diklos-mta 4,276
Adalae 4,151
DIDOETI
R. Andi Koisu
R. Kodor Koisu
R. Avar Koisu
A V A R S
D A G H E S T A N
Julti-dagh 4,131
R. Kazi Kumukh Koisu
Akusha
Antsukh
Tsakur
Jaro
SAIN GILO
Belakani o
Dshauri o
Buyutan o
Zegem (Bazar) o
TSUKETI
R. Eljlseti
TSUKETI
ELISENI (ELISU)
R. Alazani
Kornabuji
Nubha o
Areshi o
R. Gishi
Khoranta
Kornabuji o

R. Mkhvari (Kura)
HERETI
KISIQI
Bodbe •
GARET KAKHETI (KUKHETI)
GAGHMA MKHARI
SHIGNIT KAKHETI
ALONI
Nekresi o
Gremi o
Shilda o
Qwareli o
Telavi o
Alaverdi o
Bodcharma o
Pankisi
TUSHETI
PSHAVETI
R. Pshavi Aragvi
HEVSURETI
TIANETI
Torgo o
Tianeti o
Akhmeti o
Ipalto o
Zidazadeni o
Mtzkheta
KANDO
BAZALETI
ERTSO
Vanati o
Gori o
Mejuda o
R. Ksani
MTIULETI
SHIDA KARTLI
Beri-tzikhe
Mt Shat
Mt Kazbek (Mqinvari) 5,047
Gudauri
Soni
Kavtis-khevi
R. Liakhvi
KVEMO KARTLI
Tiflis (Tbilisi)
LILO
MARTQOPI
Ujarma o
Rustavi o
KARAIA
Garezhda o
SOMANI-KHEV
KAZAKH
SHAMSHADILO
R. Mtkvari (Kura)
R. Iori
R. Alazani
R. Debeda
TASHIRI
SOMKHETI
Akhtala o
Kulp o
Tetri-tzikhe o
BAIDAR
Garisi o
Dmanisi o
R. Algeti
R. Ktzia
R. Mashavera
R. Debeda
R. Berduji (Borchalo)
Kiz Kala
Tetri-tzikhe
To Samtzikhe
C H E C H E N S
KARABULAK
Tebulos-mta

To Besh-tau
Tatarub o
Mudarov o
Akhlov o
OSSETI
DIGOR
DVALETI
R. Ardon
R. Kuma
R. Terek
Shemta (Shua-mta)
Combursi-Mta
Baurtzikhe
Gombori o

Key map of Eastern Caucasia to illustrate the Embassies.